P9-BAT-550

Frommer's®

New York City with Kids

11th Edition

by Alexis Lipsitz Flippin

Here's what the critics say about Frommer's:

"Amazingly easy to use. Very portable, very complete."
—**BOOKLIST**

"Detailed, accurate, and easy-to-read information for all price ranges."
—**GLAMOUR MAGAZINE**

"Invaluable in planning your family's pit stops."
—**SAN DIEGO FAMILY**

"Frommer's Guides have a way of giving you a real feel for a place."
—**KNIGHT RIDDER NEWSPAPERS**

WILEY
Wiley Publishing, Inc.

ABOUT THE AUTHOR

Alexis Lipsitz Flippin is a freelance writer and editor who lives in Manhattan's Greenwich Village with her husband, daughter, and springer spaniel. She is a former Senior Editor at Frommer's and the author of *Frommer's New York Day by Day* and *Frommer's Portable Turks & Caicos.*

Published by:

WILEY PUBLISHING, INC.

111 River St.
Hoboken, NJ 07030-5774

ISBN: 978-0-470-38219-6

Editor: Marc Nadeau
Production Editor: Lindsay Conner
Cartographer: Liz Puhl
Photo Editor: Richard Fox
Production by Wiley Indianapolis Composition Services

Front cover photo: New York City skyline, young girl pointing at skyscraper

For information on our other products and services or to obtain technical support, please contact our Customer Care Department within the U.S. at 800/762-2974, outside the U.S. at 317/572-3993 or fax 317/572-4002.

Wiley also publishes its books in a variety of electronic formats. Some content that appears in print may not be available in electronic formats.

Manufactured in the United States of America

5   4   3   2   1

CONTENTS

4 GETTING TO KNOW NEW YORK CITY 50

5 FAMILY-FRIENDLY ACCOMMODATIONS 63

6 FAMILY-FRIENDLY DINING 94

7 EXPLORING NEW YORK CITY WITH YOUR KIDS 144

8 NEIGHBORHOOD STROLLS   192

9 FOR THE ACTIVE FAMILY   202

10 SHOPPING WITH YOUR KIDS   231

11 ENTERTAINMENT FOR THE WHOLE FAMILY   263

12 SIDE TRIPS FROM NEW YORK CITY   284

APPENDIX: FAST FACTS, USEFUL TOLL-FREE NUMBERS & WEBSITES   291

INDEX   300

LIST OF MAPS

ACKNOWLEDGEMENTS

First of all, I'd like to thank Holly Hughes, who shepherded this book through 10 editions with unparalleled reportorial skill and a keen eye for detail; she made my job that much easier. This book is dedicated to my husband, Royce, for his infinite patience and love, and my daughter, Maisie, for her overall wonderfulness. —*Alexis Lipsitz Flippin*

AN INVITATION TO THE READER

In researching this book, we discovered many wonderful places—hotels, restaurants, shops, and more. We're sure you'll find others. Please tell us about them, so we can share the information with your fellow travelers in upcoming editions. If you were disappointed with a recommendation, we'd love to know that, too. Please write to:

Frommer's New York City with Kids, 11th Edition
Wiley Publishing, Inc. • 111 River St. • Hoboken, NJ 07030-5774

AN ADDITIONAL NOTE

Please be advised that travel information is subject to change at any time—and this is especially true of prices. We therefore suggest that you write or call ahead for confirmation when making your travel plans. The authors, editors, and publisher cannot be held responsible for the experiences of readers while traveling. Your safety is important to us, however, so we encourage you to stay alert and be aware of your surroundings. Keep a close eye on cameras, purses, and wallets, all favorite targets of thieves and pickpockets.

Other Great Guides for Your Trip:

Frommer's New York City
Frommer's Portable New York City
Frommer's New York City Day by Day
Pauline Frommer's New York City
Frommer's Memorable Walks in New York
New York City For Dummies

FROMMER'S STAR RATINGS, ICONS & ABBREVIATIONS

Every hotel, restaurant, and attraction listing in this guide has been ranked for quality, value, service, amenities, and special features using a star-rating system. In country, state, and regional guides, we also rate towns and regions to help you narrow down your choices and budget your time accordingly. Hotels and restaurants are rated on a scale of zero (recommended) to three stars (exceptional). Attractions, shopping, nightlife, towns, and regions are rated according to the following scale: zero stars (recommended), one star (highly recommended), two stars (very highly recommended), and three stars (must-see).

In addition to the star-rating system, we also use seven feature icons that point you to the great deals, in-the-know advice, and unique experiences that separate travelers from tourists. Throughout the book, look for:

(Finds)	Special finds—those places only insiders know about
(Fun Facts)	Fun facts—details that make travelers more informed and their trips more fun
(Kids)	Best bets for kids and advice for the whole family
(Moments)	Special moments—those experiences that memories are made of
(Overrated)	Places or experiences not worth your time or money
(Tips)	Insider tips—great ways to save time and money
(Value)	Great values—where to get the best deals

The following abbreviations are used for credit cards:

AE	American Express	DISC	Discover	V	Visa
DC	Diners Club	MC	MasterCard		

FROMMERS.COM

Now that you have the guidebook to a great trip, visit our website at www.frommers.com for additional travel information on more than 4,000 destinations. We update features regularly to give you instant access to the most current trip-planning information available. At Frommers.com, you'll find scoops on the best airfares, lodging rates, and car rental bargains. You can even book your travel online through our travel booking partners. Other popular features include:

- Online updates of our most popular guidebooks
- Vacation sweepstakes and contest giveaways
- Newsletters highlighting the hottest travel trends
- Podcasts, interactive maps, and up-to-the-minute events listings
- Opinionated blog entries by Arthur Frommer himself
- Online travel message boards with featured travel discussions

What's New in New York City

New Yorkers may be feeling the pinch of a sputtering U.S. economy, but the international visitors flooding our shores are spending money like drunken sailors. The city is a giant bargain basement for those whose currencies are holding strong against a weak dollar. In fact, New York City in 2008 jumped to the top spot in the nation in tourism spending, and international markets accounted for 54% of total visitor spending. International visitors stay longer and spend more, and the city that they see today is at the top of its game, with low crime rates, dynamic activity in all boroughs, new and newly renovated attractions, and a vibrant, world-class restaurant scene. And things are only going to get busier: Mayor Michael Bloomberg announced that the city was on track to see 50 million visitors a year by 2012.

WHAT TO SEE & DO Two major tourist attractions have opened after 2-year renovations. The **Liberty Science Center** (© 201/200-1000; www.lsc.org) right across the river in Jersey City, New Jersey, has expanded to twice its former size. The **Intrepid Sea-Air-Space Museum** (© 212/245-0072; www.intrepidmuseum.org), on the Hudson River in west Midtown, should be back in its dock at Pier 86 by the time you read this, newly refurbished and ready for tours.

The **Sports Museum of America** (28 Broadway; © 212/747-0900) opened in downtown Manhattan, the only museum dedicated to all sports under one roof.

In 2008, both the **New York Yankees** and the **New York Mets** held sentimental last seasons in their old ballparks. New-and-improved baseball stadiums, adjacent to each team's current ballparks, are scheduled to be ready for the 2009 season. The Mets' new stadium will be called **Citi Field.** And what will become of the legendary 85-year-old House that Ruth built? Most of it will be razed to make room for parkland.

To learn all about New York City's best sightseeing attractions for families, see chapter 7.

DINING Ye of sweet tooth, listen up: The **gelato wars** have heated up with the emergence of several new premium brands in the city. **Grom** (233 Bleecker St., at Carmine St.; © 212/206-1738; www.grom.it/eng), rich, handmade gelato created by two gentlemen in Turin, Italy, opened its first U.S. store downtown in 2008. Joining it nearby is another heralded purveyor of boutique ice cream, **L'Arte del Gelato** (75 Seventh Ave. S., btwn Bleecker St. and W. 4th St.; © 212/924-0803; www.lartedelgelato.com), where gelato is made fresh daily. The newest kid in town, **Capogiro** (www.capogirogelato.com), is sold in the summer on the skating-rink steps at Rockefeller Center. They join the established premium brands **Il Laboratorio del Gelato** (95 Orchard St., btwn Broome and Delancey sts.; © 212/343-9922; www.laboratoriodelgelato.com) and **Ciao Bella** (285 Mott Street, near Houston St.; © 212/431-3591; www.ciaobellagelato.com).

The much-loved **Florent,** the 24-hour restaurant in the Meatpacking District, friend to both late-night revelers and neighborhood families, closed its doors in 2008. It was one of our favorite places to go for breakfast, with crayons to draw with and big tasty pancakes. Au revoir, Florent!

See chapter 6 for full reviews of kid-friendly New York eateries.

IN THE PARKS Two downtown parks should be close to completing major renovations by the time you read this. **Washington Square Park,** with its tradition of bohemian spirit and political rabble-rousing, has been transformed by a redesign/renovation that moved the famous fountain so it more neatly aligned with the equally famous Washington Square Arch. A serious grooming has tamed its famously rakish appearance; we'll see how long it lasts before the barkers and troubadours slip back in. Over in **Union Square Park,** another famous public bastion of political discourse, the north side of the park is getting a much-needed refurbishment, with newly renovated playgrounds, a bigger space for the Union Square Greenmarket, and the restoration of the park's vintage pavilion. Architect David Rockwell's **Imaginarium Playground,** a nontraditional play space of "loose parts," will open in the South Street Seaport's Burling Slip in 2009. Check out more recreational options in chapter 9.

SHOPPING Lilly Pulitzer's new flag-ship store (1020 Madison Ave., at 79th St.; (C) 212/744-4620; www.lillypulitzer. com) opened on a tony Madison Avenue block in 2008. The store has a selection of girls' clothes in sizes 3 months to 14.

For more information on this and other stores, see chapter 10.

ACCOMMODATIONS The century-old landmark **Plaza Hotel** ((C) 212/759-3000) at 57th Street and Fifth Avenue has reopened after a major $400-million renovation. It's now a multiuse complex, with condos, a boutique hotel, restaurants, and bars. Oh, yes, and the winsome portrait of **Eloise,** the famous and fictional little girl who lived in the Plaza, has been ceremoniously replaced on the wall near the hotel's legendary Palm Court.

The Mark (25 E. 77th St., btwn Madison and Fifth aves.; (C) 212/772-1600) reopened in late 2008 upon completion of an exciting top-to-bottom redesign by France's most celebrated interior designer, Jacques Grange. The Mark will be a combination hotel/co-op with a smaller number of hotel rooms.

See chapter 5 for complete details on a wide range of family-friendly lodgings.

How to Feel Like a New York City Family

It goes without saying that New York is a city of unparalleled cultural richness, boasting world-class museums, performing-arts troupes, and restaurants. But what *isn't* so widely known is how much of New York is accessible to families. Before we had our daughter, my husband and I dined out in restaurants whenever we felt like it, went to movie theaters in the afternoon, and spent hours leisurely strolling through art galleries and museums. As grown-ups, we found that there was no shortage of fun things for us do to. After Maisie came along, in my quest to become a typically overinformed New York parent, I did some digging. What on earth do I *do* with this poor child? I felt it was my duty as a concerned citizen to make the city more hospitable to children. But hold up there—what's this? Who knew that New York City had some 1,000 playgrounds, and that Central Park alone has 21 magical playgrounds, where kids can scamper on fanciful stone bridges, porpoise sprinklers, and 45-foot-long curved slides? Or that regular story-time hours for kids are held all over the city, including in the beautiful MoMA sculpture garden? Or that the original Winnie-the-Pooh bear resides in the New York Public Library—and you can see it for free? It seems that while I was gallivanting around Manhattan untethered by children, a number of forward-thinking pioneers were busily making the city a better place for its kids. Hooray!

We've discovered that the public parks are a wonder, and a godsend for families whose habitat is the concrete urban jungle. We've learned that the city's museums have unparalleled collections and thrillingly innovative programs for children. We've found that the zoos are some of the finest and most forward-thinking in the country. And we've found ourselves, as parents, falling in love with the city all over again. It's like mining a vein of pure gold in your own backyard.

Still, even with the parks, the museums, the boat rides, and the seasonal spectacles, sometimes the most memorable New York moments are the serendipitous ones you encounter as you stroll about the city. You can see the most amazing things just by turning a corner. We've stumbled upon ballet aerialists swinging from the New York Stock Exchange. We've seen dragon dances on Chinatown streets. We've listened to Brazilian drummers doing impromptu concerts on the street. Some new company is always handing out free energy drinks or chewing gum (one day we got a free kitchen baggie sealer). Movie sets pop up all over the city, and you never know when you'll stumble upon a major production with megawatt stars hanging out in hair rollers and eating a bag of chips (Stars: They're just like us!). Why, just last Sunday, while pushing our daughter in a stroller, we encountered a gentleman with two parrots on his shoulders, one of whom was named Gazpacho. And to my daughter's delight, Gazpacho clambered onto my hand and gave me a tweak with his beak. Who can beat that?

ON YOUR MARK, GET SET, GO!

This is a big place to tackle in just a few short days. The pulse and tempo of New York City can be discombobulating at first if you're not used to it—my North Carolina nephew actually got dizzy from his first encounter with the noise and commotion—but once you attune yourself, you'll find it a tremendously exciting place, especially for youngsters. It's easy to spot a native New York City kid: They tend to stride down the sidewalk with an unerring radar for other people, bikes, and cars. But I've also seen many kids who've only been here a few days shed their skittishness and start to walk with that same savvy, confident stride, smoothly maneuvering their way around the city. Kids are sponges, remember? They learn fast, and the city's got a lot to teach them.

This guidebook is filled with all the wonderful things you and your family can do in the city. So let's dispense with some of the negatives right from the get-go. First of all: **Yes, there's crime in New York.** But the good news is that crime rates have fallen dramatically in the past 10 years. So dramatically, in fact, that when a mugging occurs in my neighborhood, it's a shock. Still, the city is not the place to drop your guard. Stay alert, and follow the tips in "Safety," in chapter 3.

Second: **Yes, it's deliriously easy to spend money here.** Whenever I visit the suburbs or go down to my native state of North Carolina, I'm always convinced I'm being vastly undercharged at grocery and convenience stores. Why on earth do businesses charge such high prices in New York City? *Because they can.* You are a captive shopper on this island, and there's so much to do and see, who has time to schlep to a discount store in another borough just to save a few bucks?

But there *are* ways to cut costs with your family in tow. (Back in the day, we used to crash art openings in SoHo for the free hors d'oeuvres and wine, but, oh, never mind. . . .) Grocery stores are costly enough in the Big Apple, but Korean delis, the convenience stores of the city, *really* inflate prices. Four soft drinks will cost you six bucks—seven if you throw in a small bag of chips. If your hotel has a **kitchenette,** stock up on drinks and snacks at a local chain supermarket. Also take advantage of **complimentary breakfasts** or—even better—hotels that have a **"Kids Eat Free" policy.** Hit the city's **greenmarkets** for fast, healthy, inexpensive snacks like delicious apples, breads, fruit, cheeses—you'll be supporting local farmers in the process. Check out **www.cenyc.org/greenmarket** to find out what's in season and if there's a greenmarket near you. **Eat ethnic**—good, cheap Chinese restaurants can be found everywhere in the city, and Ninth Avenue between 57th and 34th streets is just one great ethnic eatery after another, from Brazilian to Thai to Peruvian. It's a tourist trap, but Little Italy will fill your kids up with their three-course prix-fixe lunches, and decent pizza places are on every corner of the city. And don't forget **transportation costs.** Buy unlimited-ride MetroCard passes if you plan to crisscross the city by bus or subway. Or walk: It's the cheapest and best way to get the flavor of the city by far.

Third: **Street people remain a reality of life in 21st-century New York.** In your travels, you and your kids will likely spot vagrants sleeping in doorways or pawing through corner trash bins. People may ask you for money, and it's certainly your prerogative to offer them some change. But it's also fine to smile and simply say "Sorry," and move along. While these encounters may be uncomfortable at times, that's just the flip side of one of this city's great pluses: Everybody, from the Wall Street banker to the greengrocer to the starving actor waiting tables, shares the streets. It's all part of the fabric of this crazy-quilt, melting-pot, gumbo stew we call New York City.

1 FROMMER'S FAVORITE NEW YORK CITY FAMILY EXPERIENCES

- **Spending the Christmas Holidays in New York:** Crusty old New York turns unabashedly giddy with celebration during the holidays. At Christmas, you really feel the heart of the Big City. In December, Rockefeller Plaza is an especially thrilling holiday sight, with the city's biggest Christmas tree (a real doozy) twinkling with lights. The tiny Rockefeller Center ice rink is lively with the clash of blades and the tinny blare of piped-in music. Two spectacular holiday shows run the length of the season: The New York Botanical Garden's **Holiday Train Show** and **Radio City Music Hall's Christmas Spectacular.** *The Nutcracker* ballet is produced in two different venues. See chapter 11.

- **Taking a Boat Ride Around Manhattan:** When you're out on the sparkling waters of New York Harbor, with the salt air in your hair and the sea gulls gliding overhead, you'll thrill to the Manhattan skyline in all its glory. It's a fantastic way to see the town. See "Getting Around," in chapter 4.

- **Visiting Chinatown:** The kids I know from out of town always head down here for good food, cheap toys, and excellent street theater. Come during the Chinese New Year for thrilling dragon dances in the street. The neighborhood always feels exotic to me, too. See chapters 6 & 8.

- **Spending a Sunday Afternoon at the American Museum of Natural History:** Weekends are definitely family time at this magnificent big museum on the Upper West Side, but the more, the merrier—these dim, cool, high-ceilinged halls never seem too crowded. Head for the musty old back corners where there are old-fashioned dioramas

or stop by the Natural Science Center in the early afternoons for hands-on puttering with plants and live animals (for ages 4 and older). See p. 152.

- **Talking to the Animals in the New York Zoos:** The Central Park Zoo is perfect for toddlers: It's small and compact but still spacious enough to feel like a real nature outing. Check out the feeding schedule as you walk in the front entrance—the Sea Lion Pool is the centerpiece of this tidily landscaped little gem of a zoo. Don't expect fancy tricks, but there'll be enough barking and diving and splashing to satisfy everybody. Just yards away is the charming Tisch Zoo, where little ones can feed baby llamas, sheep, and goats as the traffic above on Fifth Avenue whizzes by. In the world-class Bronx Zoo, forward-thinking zoo officials have created enclosures as close to animals' natural habitats as possible, where visitors ride a monorail above free-roaming tigers, elephants, and rhinos. See p. 157, 158, and 182.

- **Riding a Bike Through the Canyons of Wall Street on Sunday:** The suits have the weekend off, and the streets are quiet and pretty empty. Rent a bike, and cruise the narrow corridors with the muscular skyscrapers of the 1920s looming above. It's a thrill. See chapter 8.

- **Playing in Central Park:** It's über kiddie land in every way, with a breathtaking array of playgrounds, pools, and attractions to keep children busy and happy for hours, days, weeks. Point toddlers to the Carousel and the Swedish Marionette Theater; and send the older kids to the state-of-the-art playgrounds, ball fields, and pools. See chapter 9.

- **Root, Root, Rooting for the Home Team:** On a sunny summer afternoon, there are few pleasures more fully satisfying than heading to the Bronx to see the Bronx Bombers play in the new Yankee Stadium, or to Flushing, Queens, to catch the Mets in their the new ballpark, Citi Field. In either case, nobody minds if your kids make noise, you can leave early if they get tired, and there's plenty of food available—especially the overpriced hot dogs that are so much a part of the experience. In the winter, head to Madison Square Garden to watch the Knicks (basketball) or the Rangers (hockey) play—and, if you can snag tickets, take a bus to the New Jersey Meadowlands to watch a football game starring the 2008 Super Bowl champs, the New York Giants, or the New York Jets, with new quarterback Brett Favre. See "Spectator Sports" in chapter 11.

2 THE BEST HOTEL BETS

- **Most Family-Friendly:** The **Doubletree Guest Suites,** 1568 Broadway (© **800/222-8733** or 212/719-1600; p. 79), provides not only standard two-room accommodations sleeping four or six, but also kitchenettes, baby equipment, childproof rooms, and a super toddler playroom. The Upper East Side's **The Loews Regency,** 540 Park Ave. (© **212/759-4100;** p. 77), offers kids all sorts of amenities, including their own concierge; and **Le Parker Meridien,** 118 W. 57th St. (© **800/543-4300** or 212/245-5000; p. 79), has special welcoming packets for young guests; concierges at both of these hotels are full of great tips for kids visiting NYC.

- **Best Suite Deals:** The **Doubletree Guest Suites,** 1568 Broadway (© **800/222-8733** or 212/719-1600; p. 79), is a sensible family option, sleeping the whole crew in one unit for a relatively easy price. The **Embassy Suites Hotel,** 102 North End Ave. (© **800/EMBASSY** or 212/945-0100; p. 90), offers some very favorable rates on weekends for its roomy, sleek suites.

- **Most Peace & Quiet:** It's all relative in New York, of course, but the **Excelsior,** 45 W. 81st St. (© **800/368-4575** or 212/362-9200; p. 70), is buffered by Central Park and the park surrounding the Museum of Natural History, and the **Gracie Inn,** 502 E. 81st St. (© **212/628-1700;** p. 78), is tucked away on an Upper East Side street near the East River. Even in Midtown you can find residential quiet at the **Millennium U.N. Plaza,** 1 United Nations Plaza (© **866/866-8086** or 212/758-1234; p. 86), and the **Holiday Inn Midtown 57th Street,** 440 W. 57th St. (© **888/HOLIDAY** or 212/581-8100; p. 82).

- **Best Views:** Two downtown hotels feature dynamite New York Harbor views starring Lady Liberty and Ellis Island: The **Ritz-Carlton New York,** 2 West St. (© **800/241-3333** or 212/344-0800; p. 89), wins hands down for its glorious open westward views from a majority of guest rooms, but there are several rooms with great harbor views also at the **Marriott New York Downtown,** 85 West St. (© **800/228-9290** or 212/385-4900; p. 91).

- **When Price Is No Object:** My vote goes to **The Carlyle,** 35 E. 76th St. (© **800/227-5737** or 212/744-1600; p. 75), for its dignified East Side calm; its well-nigh-perfect service; and the spaciousness of its designer-decorated rooms, which really deserve to be called apartments. Spring for a suite with a Central Park view and a grand piano. The **Four Seasons,** 57 E. 57th St. (© **800/819-5053** or 212/758-5700; p. 83), has a stylish Midtown address, sleek if somewhat small rooms (but then, you can afford a suite, right?), fabulous service, and a surprisingly kid-friendly gourmet restaurant.

- **When Price Is Your Main Object:** You can't go wrong with the **Travel Inn,** 515 W. 42nd St. (© **800/869-4630** or 212/695-7171; p. 83), which delivers roomy, clean, fairly quiet motel rooms, plus a huge pool and free parking, for around $150 to $200 a night.

- **Best Lobby:** You've gotta love the classic Art Deco lobby of the **Waldorf= Astoria,** 301 Park Ave. (© **800/WAL-DORF,** 800/HILTONS, or 212/355-3000; p. 85), with its marble-faced pillars, deep carpeting, ornamental plasterwork, the magnificent Park Avenue entry chandelier, and that amazing clock near the front desk.

- **Best Pool:** The pool at the **Millennium U.N. Plaza Hotel,** 44th Street and First

Avenue (© **866/866-8086** or 212/758-1234; p. 86), has it all: views, cleanliness, handsome tilework, and not much of a crowd.

- **Tops for Toddlers:** When all is said and done, the **Hotel Wales,** 1295 Madison Ave. (© **212/876-6000;** p. 77), wins for its Carnegie Hill location, friendly staff, breakfast buffet, residential calm, and Puss-in-Boots theme. The **Double-tree Guest Suites,** 1568 Broadway (© **800/222-8733** or 212/719-1600; p. 79), scores big here, too, for its suite convenience and toddler playroom.

- **Tops for Teens:** Budding bohemians may want to be in Greenwich Village at the **Washington Square Hotel,** 103 Waverly Place (© **800/222-0418** or 212/777-9515; p. 89), while trendsetters will gravitate to the way-cool decor and hipster cachet of **The Paramount,** 235 W. 46th St. (© **866/760-3174** or 212/764-5500; p. 81), or the art-jazzed vibe of the **Gershwin Hotel,** 7 E. 27th St. (© **212/545-8000;** p. 88).

3 THE BEST DINING BETS

- **Best Place to Eat Outside:** It's a seasonal occupation, of course, but when the city starts to thaw after a long, chilly winter, everyone heads outside—and you should, too. We love the **Boat Basin Café,** W. 79th St., at the Hudson River (© **212/496-5542;** p. 112), for the spectacular Hudson River views, the vaulted limestone setting, and the wonderful smell of burgers sizzling on an outdoor grill.

- **Best Genuine Time Warp:** The city's vintage venues are a dying breed these days, but you can always count on the **Lexington Candy Shop,** 1226 Lexington Ave. (© **212/288-0057;** p. 116), for good old-fashioned vibes. It's a living relic from 1925, with wooden

booths, chrome-rimmed stools, and a classic New York egg cream.

- **Best Store Dining: American Girl Café,** 609 Fifth Ave. (© **877/247-5223;** p. 118), will thrill your American Girl aficionado as much as it impresses her parents. The food is actually good, and there are special doll seats where girls can prop their American Girl dolls while they eat.

- **Best Dinner Entertainment:** Even seen-it-all city kids get a kick out of the table show at **Benihana,** 47 W. 56th St. (© **212/581-0930;** p. 118), the trail-blazing Japanese steakhouse where flying knives and dexterous teppanyaki chefs became a showbiz standard. But it's the little ones whose eyes will light up at the spectacle.

- **Best Tea Party:** Afternoon tea couldn't be cozier than at the whimsical **Alice's Tea Cup,** at 102 W. 73rd St. (© **212/ 799-3006**) or 156 E. 64th St. (© **212/ 486-9200**).

- **Best Healthy Comfort Food:** You may not think that a place that specializes in healthy, organic, sustainable foods would draw kids by the barrelful—but when a place like **The City Bakery** (3 W. 18th St.; © **212/366-1414;** p. 128) includes unbeatable versions of fried chicken, mac 'n' cheese, French toast, and quesadilla, why wouldn't they come? A spinning chocolate wheel, fresh hot chocolate (with homemade marshmallows), and the city's best chocolate chip cookies don't hurt either.

- **Best Breakfast:** TriBeCa's **Bubby's,** 120 Hudson St. (© **212/219-0666;** p. 143), welcomes kids for breakfast until 4pm daily; the weekend brunches are especially popular.

- **Best Pancakes:** Okay, so my daughter has rarely met a pancake she doesn't like, but the big, thick numbers at **The Smith** (55 Third Ave.; © **212/420- 9800;** p. 133) leave her speechless; they also come with a cinnamon-dusted banana-and-walnut topping.

- **Best Family-Friendly Restaurant for Grown-ups:** For further proof that this truly is the golden age of children in NYC, witness as more and more city restaurants develop kid-friendly menus and attitudes. My current favorite is **Odeon** (145 W. Broadway; © **212/233- 0507;** p. 142), which has transcended its übertrendy 1970s past to become a great neighborhood *boîte,* with solid food for the whole family and no cutesy kids' menu.

- **Best Food Court:** The Grand Central Dining Concourse is much better than it needs to be—why, I'd even go out of my way to eat there at lunch. It's got Two Boots Pizza, Brothers Barbecue, Manhattan Chili, Junior's, Zocalo, and Hale and Hearty Soups, among others (oh, and you can stop at the little window outside Grand Central Oyster Bar for some great clam chowder). But my favorite food court—and the perfect place for a sit-down family lunch—is **Chelsea Market** (75 Ninth Ave.; p. 130). It's a very cool place, set in an old biscuit factory whose hardworking industrial parts have been transformed: a waterfall here, castlelike torches there. The food is great, from the Cleaver Company's delicious sustainable fare to Buon Italia's pastas, frittatas, and pizzas to Fat Witch's rich brownies.

- **Best Theme Restaurant:** If you must dine in a theme restaurant (and I know that sometimes you have no choice in the matter), head to **Ellen's Stardust Diner,** 1650 Broadway (© **212/956- 5151;** p. 122), where the waitstaff belt out their favorites to a karaoke machine in this Times Square cafe's weekend dinner shows.

- **Good Neighbor Award:** To **Keith McNally,** whose painstakingly re-created French bistros and Italian trattoria have become warm, comfortable neighborhood favorites among both the cognoscenti and families alike. Neat trick, that. You and your children will be treated well at **Pastis, Morandi,** and **Schiller's Liquor Bar.**

- **Best Venue for a Children's Party:** You can have a party in any number of restaurants these days, but few restaurants are as capable at handling splendid kids' celebrations as **Sarabeth's Central Park South** (40 Central Park South; © **212/ 826-5959;** p. 124). And few places will leave the grown-ups happier.

- **Best Dim Sum:** When it comes to the Chinatown lunchtime tradition of dining on small servings of dumplings, skewers, rolls, and other delectables right at your table, you can't go wrong with **Ping's** (22 Mott St.; ✆ 212/602-9988; p. 141) or **Golden Unicorn** (18 E. Broadway; ✆ 212/941-0951; p. 141). For true spectacle, head to **Jing Fong,** at 18 Elizabeth St. (✆ 212/964-5256; p. 142), whose giant Hong Kong–style banquet hall is pure Vegas.

- **Best Pizza:** The nod goes to **John's Pizza;** the original Greenwich Village location, at 278 Bleecker St. (✆ 212/243-1680; p. 132), is still the best, but the branches at 408 E. 64th St. (✆ 212/935-2895; p. 117) and 260 W. 44th St. (✆ 212/391-7560; p. 127) serve up thin-crust brick-oven pies that are pretty darn close to perfection.

- **Best Family-Style Italian:** If you can't get to Arthur Avenue in the Bronx, then head to **Carmine's** (200 W. 44th St., ✆ 212/221-3800; or 2450 Broadway, ✆ 212/362-2200; p. 120 and 109) for great big platters of Southern Italian–style pasta, salads, and more. The food is remarkably good and the ambience properly clamorous (and amazingly satisfying) for a place this big. It's quite an efficient assembly line.

- **Best Desserts:** Yes, it's often packed and probably overexposed, but the hot-fudge sundaes and whimsical decor at **Serendipity 3** (225 E. 60th St.; ✆ 212/838-3531) make children very, very happy.

New York City in Depth

When one thinks of New York City, I'm not sure children are necessarily the first thing that pops into mind. The New York of lore and noir is a sexy, smoky Jazz Age city of grown-up folks doing grown-up things, the men in crisp fedoras moving smoothly into the blue-black night, the women singing torch songs of love and loss. But this city of grown-ups has also raised millions of children over the years. For a century, kids have been riding the hand-carved horses on the Central Park Carousel. For 200 years they've played along the banks of the Hudson and East rivers. And the first immigrant to pass through Ellis Island was red-haired Annie Moore, who arrived in New York harbor on her 15th birthday. New York has been home for children in good times—as evidenced in Berenice Abbott's wonderful 1930s photographs of children playing in the streets, opening fire hydrants, and being kids—and in hard. Children were once a big part of the labor force in New York, and many grew up within the impermeable walls of city slums. When I moved here, in the 1980s, crack dealers and users—many of whom could only be described as children—hung out in doorways and storefronts, projecting a defensively menacing air.

So it may be reasonable to say that I don't think children have ever had it so good as they do in the New York of the early 21st century. In fact, this may be the **golden age of the family in New York City.** These days, being a child in New York is often a wonderful and privileged existence. Not only is crime at record lows (the FBI has rated New York as the safest big city in the United States), but streets are cleaner than they ever were and parks more accessible. According to the Citizens' Committee for Children of New York, which measures and tracks the well-being of New York City's children, greater numbers of children are enrolled in child-care, preschool, and out-of-school time; more children have health insurance—91% of all NYC kids were insured in 2005!—and academic achievement is improving across all race and ethnic groups and age ranges.

In my own neighborhood, I see the progress in small but telling details. I see city parks bursting with flower beds that remain untouched over the summer. Newspapers dropped on door stoops are there until the owners retrieve them. Small children chase fireflies on July nights in once-forbidding city parks. Yes, this is still a city of slums and gangs and children in wretched situations. But big progress has been made, and the progress is palpable. Which is to say: This is one family-friendly city, with more and more restaurants, hotels, museums, and retail shops going out of their way to cater to children and parents alike. Welcome to the Big Apple.

1 NEW YORK CITY TODAY

There's no question that New York is in the midst of a renaissance. This rebirth helped bring in an estimated 46 million tourists in 2007; even more are projected in the next few years. And many are deciding to stay longer: In fact, it's predicted that New York City will add one million more residents by 2030.

At the same time, these are uneasy times in America. The economy is sputtering, corporations are making big cutbacks, and people are losing their homes. A new administration is taking over the White House after 8 years of Bush rule. But in New York, things appear to be, well, not so bad—in many ways, even thriving. The real estate market is holding steady, international visitors are spending money hand over fist, and sleek new condos are rising in every corner of the city. People are also raising children in the city in record numbers, reflecting a long-view commitment to the urban life, circa 21st-century New York. The city's schools, both public and private, are bursting at the seams, and new schools are in the works in every sector of the city.

For visitors, the city has never been more welcoming—and since statistics show that families compose the largest group of travelers to New York City, that means that children are getting the royal treatment as well. It's a grand time to be a child in New York, whether they're here on a permanent basis or unofficial New Yorkers for a few glorious days.

2 LOOKING BACK AT NEW YORK CITY

COLONIAL DAYS (1524–1776)

The area that became New York City was the home to many Native Americans before Giovanni da Verrazano arrived in 1524. And it wasn't until 1609, when Henry Hudson, while searching for the Northwest Passage, claimed it for the Dutch East India Company, that New York was recognized as a potential, profitable settlement in the New World.

Hudson (the river that separates Manhattan from the mainland is named after him) said of New York, "It is as beautiful a land as one can hope to tread upon." The treading didn't really start until years later, but by 1625, Dutch settlers established a fur trade with the locals and called their colony New Amsterdam. A year later, Peter Minuit of the Dutch West India Company made that famous deal for the island. He bought New Amsterdam from the Lenape Tribe for what has widely been reported as $24.

New Amsterdam became a British colony in the 1670s, and during the Revolutionary War it was occupied by British troops. England controlled New York until 1783, when it withdrew from the city 2 years *after* the end of the American Revolution.

Two years after that, New York was named the first capital of the United States. The first Congress was held at Federal Hall on Wall Street in 1789, and George Washington was inaugurated president. But New York's tenure as the capital didn't last long. A year later, the government headed south to Philadelphia for a decade, and eventually, to the newly created District of Columbia.

A MELTING POT CITY

By 1825, New York City's population swelled to 250,000 and rose again to a half-million by midcentury. The city was a hotbed of Union recruitment during the Civil War; in the 1863 draft riots, Irish immigrants violently protested the draft and lynched 11 African Americans.

With industry booming, the late 19th century was termed the "Gilded Age." New York City was an example of this label in action; millionaires built mansions on Fifth Avenue, while rows of tenements teeming with families (made up of the cheap, mostly immigrant laborers who were employed by the industrial barons) filled the city's districts. In 1880, the city's population boomed to 1.1 million.

More European immigrants poured into the city between 1900 and 1930,

New York City Timeline

1524   Sailing under the French flag, Italian Giovanni da Verrazano is the first European to enter what's now New York Harbor.

1609   Henry Hudson sails up the Hudson River, exploring for the Dutch East India Company.

1626   The Dutch settle in Nieuw Amsterdam and make it a fur-trading post; Peter Minuit, governor of Nieuw Amsterdam, buys Manhattan Island from the Algonquin Indians for trinkets worth 60 florins (about $24).

1664   English invaders take Nieuw Amsterdam from the Dutch (wooden-legged Peter Stuyvesant is the Dutch governor).

1673   The Dutch take back Manhattan.

1674   Under the Treaty of Westminster, the Dutch finally give Nieuw Amsterdam to the English, who rename it New York after James, duke of York.

1776   American colonists topple the statue of King George on Bowling Green on July 9, but by year's end New York becomes a British stronghold for the rest of the American Revolution.

1783   Victorious Gen. George Washington bids farewell to his troops at Fraunces Tavern in Lower Manhattan.

1789   Washington is inaugurated as the first president at Federal Hall in New York City, the first capital of the new United States.

1790   Philadelphia deposes New York City as the nation's capital.

1792   The first U.S. stock exchange is founded in New York City, making it the country's financial capital.

1820   New York City is the nation's largest city, with a population of 124,000.

1853   The World's Fair is held in New York's Bryant Park.

1858–73   Central Park is laid out by Frederick Law Olmsted and Calvert Vaux.

1883   The Brooklyn Bridge is completed, linking Manhattan and Brooklyn.

1885–86   The Statue of Liberty is erected in New York Harbor.

1892   Ellis Island opens; begins processing more than a million immigrants yearly.

1904   The first subway departs from City Hall.

arriving at Ellis Island and then fanning out into such neighborhoods as the Lower East Side, Greenwich Village, Little Italy, and Harlem. With the city population in 1930 at seven million and a Depression raging, New York turned to a feisty mayor named Fiorello La Guardia for help. With the assistance of civic planner Robert Moses, who masterminded a huge public works program, the city was remade.

Moses did some things well, but his highway, bridge, tunnel, and housing projects ran through (and sometimes destroyed) many vibrant neighborhoods.

POST–WORLD WAR II & TODAY

While most of the country prospered after World War II, New York, with those Moses-built highways and a newly forming car

1911 The Triangle Shirtwaist factory fire downtown kills 148 garment workers, among them children as young as 12 and 13. The fire led to legislation protecting worker safety and eventually to the banning of children from the labor force.

1920 Babe Ruth joins the New York Yankees.

1923 Yankee Stadium opens.

1929 The stock market crashes on October 29, sending not only Wall Street but also the entire nation into an economic tailspin that results in the Great Depression.

1931 The Empire State Building opens and is the tallest building in the world.

1939 The New York World's Fair opens in Flushing Meadows, Queens.

1947 The Brooklyn Dodgers sign Jackie Robinson, the first African American to play in the Major Leagues.

1957 Elvis Presley performs live in New York on the *Ed Sullivan Show.*

1969 The Gay Rights movement begins with the Stonewall Rebellion in Greenwich Village.

1990 David Dinkins becomes the first African-American mayor of New York City.

2000 The New York Yankees beat the New York Mets in the first Subway Series in 44 years. New York's population exceeds eight million.

2001 Terrorists use hijacked planes to crash into the Twin Towers of the World Trade Center, bringing the towers down and killing more than 3,000 people.

2003 Smoking is banned in all restaurants and bars.

2005 Throughout February, tourists from around the world stroll through Christo & Jeanne-Claude's *The Gates,* a joyous art installation that fills Central Park with strategically placed saffron-colored flags.

2006 Construction begins on the controversial Freedom Tower, to be built at the site of the World Trade Center.

2008 The last season for old Yankee Stadium; the new stadium opens in 2009.

culture, endured an exodus to the suburbs. By 1958, the Dodgers had left Brooklyn and the Giants had left the Polo Grounds in upper Manhattan. This economic slide climaxed in the late 1970s with the city's declaration of bankruptcy.

As Wall Street rallied during the Reagan years of the 1980s, New York's fortunes also improved. In the 1990s, with Rudolph Giuliani—whom they haven't named anything after yet—as the mayor, and then followed by the current mayor, Michael Bloomberg, the city rode a wave of prosperity that left it safer, cleaner, and more populated. The flip side of this boom was that Manhattan became more homogenized. Witness the Disney-fication of Times Square—the ultimate symbol of New York's homogenization—and the growing gap between the rich and poor.

Everything changed on September 11, 2001, when terrorists flew planes into the Twin Towers of the World Trade Center. But New York's grit and verve showed itself once more, as the city immediately began to rebound emotionally from that terrible tragedy. The financial aftermaths of the attacks were also short-lived, and the city has experienced an unprecedented building boom in the first decade of the 21st century.

3 NEW YORK CITY'S ARCHITECTURE

New York City contains a wealth of architectural styles, from modest row houses to ornate churches to soaring skyscrapers. Constructed over 300 years, these buildings represent the changing tastes of the city's residents from Colonial times to the present. A brief look at the city's most popular styles provides a unique perspective on the city's past, present, and future.

GEORGIAN (1700–76)

This style reflects Renaissance ideas made popular in England, and later in the United States, through the publication of books on 16th-century Italian architects. In the United States, the style was seen as an appropriate expression of the relative prosperity and security of the colonies. It was a sharp contrast to the unadorned Colonial style that preceded it.

St. Paul's Chapel, on Broadway between Vesey and Fulton streets (1764–66, Thomas McBean), the only pre-Revolutionary building remaining in Manhattan, is an almost perfect example of the Georgian style, with a pediment, colossal columns, Palladian window, quoins, and balustrade above the roofline (see illustration). Although it's a 20th-century reconstruction of a formal English house built here in 1719, **Fraunces Tavern,** 54 Pearl St., is another fine example of the style.

Pediment

Palladian Window   Quoins

St. Paul's Chapel

FEDERAL (1780–1820)

Federal was the first truly American architectural style. Federal was popular with successful merchants throughout the cities and towns of the eastern seaboard. Its connection to the prosperous empires of Rome and Greece was seen as an appropriate reference for the young United States.

In New York, the Federal style was popular for row houses built after the 1811 creation of the city's grid pattern of avenues and streets.

In the **West Village,** near and along Bedford Street between Christopher and Morton streets, are more original Federal-style houses than anywhere else in Manhattan. House nos. 4 through 10 (1825–34) on Grove Street, just off Bedford, present one of the most authentic groups of late Federal–style houses in America.

GREEK REVIVAL (1820–60)

The Greek Revolution in the 1820s, in which Greece won its independence from the Turks, recalled to American intellectuals the democracy of ancient Greece and its elegant architecture, created around 400 B.C. At the same time, the War of 1812 diminished American affection for the British influence, including the still-dominant Federal style. The style was so popular it came to be known as the National Style, and was used for numerous state capitols, as well as the U.S. Capitol in Washington, D.C.

Federal Hall National Memorial

Perhaps the city's finest Greek Revival building is **Federal Hall National Memorial** (1834–42), at 26 Wall St., where George Washington took his presidential oath in 1789 (see illustration). It has a Greek temple front, with Doric columns and a simple pediment, resting on a high base, called a plinth, with a steep flight of steps.

GOTHIC REVIVAL (1830–60)

The term *Gothic Revival* refers to a literary and aesthetic movement of the 1830s and 1840s that occurred in England and later in the United States. The revival style was used for everything from timber cottages to stone castles and churches. Some structures had only one or two Gothic features, most commonly a steeply pitched roof or pointed arches, whereas other buildings, usually churches, were accurate copies of English Gothic structures.

Trinity Church, at Broadway and Wall Street (Richard Upjohn, 1846), is one of the most celebrated, authentic Gothic Revival structures in the United States. Here you see all the features of a Gothic church: a steeple, battlements, pointed arches, Gothic tracery, stained-glass windows, flying buttresses (an external bracing system for supporting a roof or vault), and medieval sculptures. This was the tallest building in the area until the late 1860s.

ITALIANATE (1840–80)

The architecture of Italy served as the inspiration for this building style. Its adaptability made it immensely popular in the 1850s. In New York, the style was used for urban row houses and commercial buildings. The development of cast iron at this time permitted the mass production of decorative features that few could have afforded in carved stone. This led to the creation of cast-iron districts in nearly every American city, including New York.

New York's **SoHo–Cast Iron Historic District** has 26 blocks jammed with cast-iron facades, many in the Italianate manner. The single richest section is **Greene Street** between Houston and Canal streets. Stroll along here and take in building after building of sculptural facades.

EARLY SKYSCRAPER (1880–1920)

The invention of the skyscraper can be traced directly to the use of cast iron in the 1840s, as seen in New York's SoHo. Experimentation with cast and wrought iron eventually allowed buildings to rise higher. (Previously, buildings were restricted by the height supportable by their load-bearing walls.) Important technical innovations—involving safety elevators, electricity, fireproofing, foundations, plumbing, and telecommunications—combined with advances in skeletal construction to create a new building type, the skyscraper. These buildings were spacious, cost-effective, efficient, and quickly erected—in short, the perfect architectural solution for America's growing downtowns.

Solving the technical problems of the skyscraper did not resolve how the building should look.

New York's early skyscrapers relied heavily on historical decoration. A good early example in the Beaux Arts mode is the **American Surety Company,** at 100 Broadway (Bruce Price, 1895). The triangular **Flatiron Building,** at Fifth Avenue and 23rd Street (Daniel H. Burnham & Co., 1902), has strong tripartite divisions and Renaissance Revival detail. And, finally, the later **Woolworth Building** (Cass Gilbert, 1913), on Broadway at Park Place, dubbed the "Cathedral of Commerce," is a neo-Gothic skyscraper with flying buttresses, spires, sculptured gargoyles, and pointed arches.

BEAUX ARTS (1890–1920)

This style takes its name from the Ecole des Beaux-Arts in Paris, where a number of prominent American architects (including **Richard Morris Hunt** [1827–95], **John Mervin Carrère** [1858–1911], and **Thomas Hastings** [1860–1929], to name only a few) received their training, beginning around the mid–19th century. These architects adopted the academic design principles of the Ecole, which emphasized the study of Greek and Roman structures, composition, and symmetry, and the creation of elaborate presentation drawings. Because of the idealized origins and grandiose use of classical forms, the Beaux Arts in America was seen as the ideal style for expressing civic pride.

New York has several exuberant Beaux Arts buildings, exhibiting the style's key features. The **New York Public Library,** at Fifth Avenue and 42nd Street (Carrère & Hastings, 1911), is perhaps the best example. Others of note are **Grand Central Terminal,** at 42nd Street and Park Avenue (Reed & Stem and Warren & Wetmore, 1903–13), and the **U.S. Customs House** (Cass Gilbert, 1907), on Bowling Green between State and Whitehall streets.

INTERNATIONAL STYLE (1920–45)

In 1932, the Museum of Modern Art hosted its first architecture exhibit, titled simply "Modern Architecture." Displays included images of International Style buildings from around the world, many designed by architects from Germany's Bauhaus, a progressive design school. The structures shared a stark simplicity and functionalism, a definite break from historically based, decorative styles.

The International Style was popularized in the U.S. through the teachings and designs of **Ludwig Mies van der Rohe** (1886–1969), a German émigré based in Chicago.

Interpretations of the "Miesian" International Style were built in most U.S. cities, including New York, as late as 1980.

Two famous examples of this style are the **Seagram Building,** at 375 Park Ave. (Ludwig Mies van der Rohe, 1958), and **Lever House,** 390 Park Ave., between 53rd and 54th streets (Skidmore, Owings & Merrill, 1952). The latter is credited for popularizing the use of plazas and glass curtain walls.

Another well-known example is the Secretariat building in the **United Nations** complex, at First Avenue and 46th Street (1947–53), designed by an international committee of architects.

ART DECO (1925–40)

Art Deco is a decorative style that took its name from a Paris exposition in 1925. The jazzy style embodied the idea of modernity. One of the first widely accepted styles not based on historic precedents, it influenced all areas of design from jewelry and household goods to cars, trains, and ocean liners.

Art Deco buildings are characterized by a linear, hard edge, or angular composition, often with a vertical emphasis and highlighted with stylized decoration. The New York zoning law of 1916, which required setbacks in buildings above a certain height to ensure that light and air could reach the street, gave the style its distinctive profile.

Despite the effects of the Depression, several major Art Deco structures were built in New York in the 1930s, often providing crucial jobs. **Rockefeller Center** (Raymond Hood, 1932–40), a complex that sprawls from 48th to 50th streets, between Fifth and Sixth avenues, includes 30 Rockefeller Plaza, a tour de force of Art Deco style, with a soaring, vertical shaft and aluminum details. The **Chrysler Building,** Lexington Avenue at 42nd Street (William Van Alen, 1930), is a towering tribute to the automobile (see illustration). The Chrysler's needle-like spire with zigzag patterns in glass and metal is a distinctive feature on the city's skyline. The famous **Empire State Building,** Fifth Avenue at 34th Street (Shreve, Lamb & Harmon, 1931), contains a black- and silver-toned lobby among its many Art Deco features.

POSTMODERN (1975–90)

After years of steel-and-glass office towers in the International Style, Postmodernism burst on the scene in the 1970s with the reintroduction of historical precedents in architecture. With many feeling that the office towers of the previous style were too cold, Postmodernists began to incorporate classical details and recognizable forms into their designs—often applied in outrageous proportions.

The **Sony Building,** at 550 Madison Ave. (Philip Johnson/John Burgee, 1984), brings the distinctive shape of a Chippendale cabinet to the New York skyline. The **Morgan Bank Headquarters,** 60 Wall St. (Kevin Roche, John Dinkeloo & Assoc., 1988), resembles a classical column, with modern interpretations of a base, shaft, and capital. The base of the column mirrors the style of the facade of the 19th-century building across the street.

Chrysler Building

The new building boom at the beginning of the 21st century has brought edifices designed by such modern architectural giants as Frank Gehry, who designed the **IAC**

Building on West 18th Street with the look of billowing curtains; and Renzo Piano designed the 52-story headquarters of the ***New York Times*** at 620 Eighth Ave. at 42nd Street, which opened in November 2007 (and was climbed by not one but two "human spiders" on the same day in June 2008!).

4 SHOW AND TELL: GETTING THE KIDS INTERESTED IN NYC

Several corny old songs come in handy as memory guides for New York City geography: Start with "I'll take Manhattan / The Bronx and Staten Island too" to teach your kids about the city's five boroughs, the other two being Brooklyn and Queens. Then there's "New York, New York, a wonderful town / The Bronx is up and the Battery's down / The people ride in a hole in the ground." Discuss the subway lines—rendered in different colors on the map—and talk about the neighborhoods and sights they pass through. New York's subways have been cleaned up incredibly since the early 1980s, and it's perfectly safe to take your kids for rides on these underground trains.

Current TV shows tend to present New York either as a hangout for navel-gazing singles or as a gritty battlefield for cops. For a more fun image of Manhattan, try two of my favorite New York kids' movies, *Ghostbusters* and *Splash. Crocodile Dundee* is a lighthearted look at how an outsider might view New York. *The Muppets Take Manhattan* captures the city in its own wacky, cartoony spirit. *Stuart Little* and *Home Alone II* show kids adventuring in NYC; the Olsen twins' *New York Minute* is a 'tweens' fantasy of NYC escapades. For a kids'-eye view of grown-up New York, try the Tom Hanks classic *Big* or its more recent girl equivalent, *13 Going on 30.* Older kids interested in downtown lifestyle might like *Desperately Seeking Susan* or Adam Sandler's *Big Daddy.* Digging deep into the classics vaults, you could get *Miracle on 34th Street,* the musical *On the Town,* or the priceless *Breakfast at Tiffany's.*

For particular neighborhoods, *You've Got Mail* is a love letter to the Upper West Side; *Crossing Delancey* captures the Lower East Side; and *Everybody Says I Love You* (along with most other Woody Allen films) serenades the Upper East Side. For outer-borough views, consult *Moonstruck* or *Saturday Night Fever* (Brooklyn) or *Raising Helen* (Queens).

New York City's skyline is a famous sight—prime your youngsters for that first glimpse of it. Buildings to identify include the Empire State Building, with its tall antenna tower up which the original King Kong climbed; the Chrysler Building's chrome-tipped Art Deco spire, looking for all the world like a spectacular hood ornament; the riverside United Nations, a vertical plane of sheer glass anchored by the dome of the General Assembly; the slant-roofed white Citibank Building; and the Chippendale-style crest on the Sony Building. The Statue of Liberty is another indelible New York landmark to show your kids pictures of ahead of time. Yet another is Rockefeller Plaza, where a giant gilded statue overlooks an ice-skating rink in winter and an outdoor cafe in summer—and where the even-more-giant Rockefeller Center Christmas tree sparkles during the holiday season.

Older kids may have strong associations with New York's battery of sports teams—depending on the season, watch some innings of Yankees or Mets baseball; a Jets or Giants football game; a Rangers, Devils, or Islanders hockey match; or a Knicks or Nets basketball game.

Top Kids' Books Set in New York City

Picture Books

- *The Adventures of Taxi Dog* by Debra and Sal Barracca (Dial; ages 2–6). This, or any of the Barraccas' books about Maxi the Taxi dog, is a lovable look at the city from the seat of a yellow cab.
- *Tar Beach* by Faith Ringgold (Crown; ages 2–5). This charming book recounts evocative memories of a Harlem childhood and hot summer nights up on the roof.
- *The Escape of Marvin the Ape* by Caralyn and Mark Buehner (Dial; ages 3–6). This book portrays a fugitive gorilla happily losing himself in New York City's parks, museums, stores, and ballparks.
- *The Little Red Lighthouse and the Great Gray Bridge* by Hildegarde H. Swift and Lynd Ward (Harcourt Brace; ages 4–7). A Hudson River lighthouse feels superseded by the new George Washington Bridge, until one dark and stormy night. . . . Kids can still see both landmarks today.
- *Eloise* by Kay Thompson (Simon & Schuster; ages 4–8). This irrepressible 6-year-old growing up in the Plaza Hotel definitely has an exotic view of life. Perfect for the precocious.

Chapter Books

- *The Cricket in Times Square* by George Selden (Farrar, Straus, and Giroux or Yearling paperback; ages 6–10). A Connecticut cricket winds up in the Times Square subway station and becomes the toast of Manhattan.
- *Stuart Little* by E. B. White (Harper & Row; ages 7–10). The Little family's mouse-size young son has adventures in and around Central Park.
- *All of a Kind Family* by Sydney Taylor (Dell Yearling; ages 7–10). This portrait of a Jewish family living on the Lower East Side is a window into turn-of-the-20th-century New York.
- *The Saturdays* by Elizabeth Enright (Puffin Books; ages 7–10). Four siblings pool their resources to explore New York City on weekends; it's set in the 1940s but is not as dated as it may seem.
- *Harriet the Spy* by Louise Fitzhugh (HarperTrophy; ages 8–11). Spunky sixth grader Harriet M. Welch keeps tabs on her East Side friends and neighbors.
- *From the Mixed-Up Files of Mrs. Basil E. Frankweiler* by E. L. Konigsburg (Simon & Schuster or Aladdin paperback; ages 8–12). A 12-year-old Connecticut girl and her younger brother hole up in the Metropolitan Museum and become involved in an art mystery.
- *Gossip Girls* by Cecily von Ziegesar (Little Brown; ages 13 and up). This is a paperback series depicting the lives and loves of Upper East Side private-school brats; trashy and a little risqué, it's like *Sex and the City* for teens.

Planning a Family Trip to New York City

New York City is much more kid-friendly than most visitors anticipate—the trick lies in planning your trip to take advantage of it. Timing is everything, as is fortifying yourself with all the printed information you can snare.

For additional help in planning your trip and more on-the-ground resources (including the best ways to get around town), please turn to chapter 4.

1 VISITOR INFORMATION

Before you leave home, your best information source (besides this book, of course) is **NYC & Company,** the organization that fronts the New York Convention & Visitors Bureau (NYCVB), located at 810 Seventh Ave., New York, NY 10019. You can call *C* **800/NYC-VISIT** (692-8474) to request the *Official NYC Guide* detailing hotels, restaurants, theaters, attractions, events, and more. The guide is free and should arrive in 7 to 10 days.

You can find a wealth of free information on the bureau's website, **http://nycvisit. com**. To speak with a live travel counselor, call *C* **212/484-1222,** which is staffed weekdays from 8:30am to 6pm EST, weekends from 8:30am to 5pm EST.

Other useful websites to consult are www.timessquarenyc.org, www.gocitykids. com, and www.nycgovparks.org. The local parents' monthly **Big Apple Parent** (9 E. 38th St., 4th Floor, New York, NY 10016,

C 212/889-6400) has a very useful site at www.parentsknow.com. Parents of infants may want to go online to check out **Urban Baby.com** (http://newyork.urbanbaby. com), which zeros in on topics such as maternity clothing stores, nursery furnishings, havens for nursing mothers, and baby-friendly playgrounds.

For visitor-center and information-desk locations once you arrive, see "Visitor Information," in chapter 4.

FOR U.K. VISITORS The **NYCVB Visitor Information Center** is at 36 Southwark Bridge Rd., London, SE1 9EU (*C* **020/7202-6367**). You can order the Official NYC Visitor Kit by sending an A5-size self-addressed envelope and 72p postage to the above address. For New York–bound travelers in London, the center also offers free one-on-one travel-planning assistance.

2 ENTRY REQUIREMENTS

New regulations issued by the Department of Homeland Security now require virtually every air traveler entering the U.S. to show a passport. As of January 23, 2007, all persons, including U.S. citizens, traveling

by air between the United States and Canada, Mexico, Central and South America, the Caribbean, and Bermuda are required to present a valid passport. As of January 31, 2008, U.S. and Canadian

citizens entering the U.S. at land and sea ports of entry from within the western hemisphere will need to present a passport for admission to the U.S.

For information on how to obtain a passport (for both U.S. citizens and international visitors), go to **"Passports"** in the **"Fast Facts"** section of chapter 4.

VISAS

The U.S. State Department has a **Visa Waiver Program (VWP)** allowing citizens of the following countries to enter the United States without a visa for stays of up to 90 days: Andorra, Australia, Austria, Belgium, Brunei, Denmark, Finland, France, Germany, Iceland, Ireland, Italy, Japan, Liechtenstein, Luxembourg, Monaco, the Netherlands, New Zealand, Norway, Portugal, San Marino, Singapore, Slovenia, Spain, Sweden, Switzerland, and the United Kingdom. (*Note:* This list was accurate at press time; for the most up-to-date list of countries in the VWP, consult **www.travel.state.gov/visa**.) Canadian citizens may enter the United States without visas; they will need to show passports (if traveling by air) and proof of residence, however. *Note:* Any passport issued on or after October 26, 2006, by a VWP country must be an **e-Passport** for VWP travelers to be eligible to enter the U.S. without a visa. Citizens of these nations also need to present a round-trip air or cruise ticket upon arrival. E-Passports contain computer chips capable of storing biometric information, such as the required digital photograph of the holder. (You can identify an e-Passport by the symbol on the bottom center cover of your passport.) If your passport doesn't have this feature, you can still travel without a visa if it is a valid passport issued before October 26, 2005, and includes a machine-readable zone, or between October 26, 2005, and October 25, 2006, and includes a digital photograph. For more information, go to **www. travel.state.gov/visa**.

Citizens of all other countries must have (1) a valid passport that expires at least 6 months later than the scheduled end of their visit to the U.S. and (2) a tourist visa, which may be obtained without charge from any U.S. consulate.

As of January 2004, many international visitors traveling on visas to the United States will be photographed and fingerprinted on arrival at Customs in airports and on cruise ships in a program created by the Department of Homeland Security called **US-VISIT.** Exempt from the extra scrutiny are visitors entering by land or those that don't require a visa for short-term visits. For more information, go to the Homeland Security website at **www. dhs.gov/dhspublic**.

For specifics on how to get a visa, go to **"Visas"** in **"Fast Facts,"** in the appendix.

MEDICAL REQUIREMENTS

Unless you're arriving from an area known to be suffering from an epidemic (particularly cholera or yellow fever), inoculations or vaccinations are not required for entry into the United States.

CUSTOMS
What You Can Bring into the U.S.

Every visitor more than 21 years of age may bring in, free of duty, the following: (1) 1 liter of wine or hard liquor; (2) 200 cigarettes, 100 cigars (but not from Cuba), or 3 pounds of smoking tobacco; and (3) $100 worth of gifts. These exemptions are offered to travelers who spend at least 72 hours in the United States and who have not claimed them within the preceding 6 months. It is forbidden to bring into the country almost any meat products (including canned, fresh, and dried meat products such as bullion, soup mixes, and so on). Generally, condiments including vinegars, oils, spices, coffee, tea, and some cheeses and baked goods are permitted. Avoid rice products, as rice can often harbor insects.

Bringing fruits and vegetables is not advised, though not prohibited. Customs will allow produce depending on where you got it and where you're going after you arrive in the U.S. Foreign tourists may carry in or out up to $10,000 in U.S. or foreign currency with no formalities; larger sums must be declared to U.S. Customs on entering or leaving, which includes filing form CM 4790. For details on U.S. Customs and Border Protection, consult your nearest U.S. embassy or consulate, or **U.S. Customs (www.customs.ustreas.gov)**.

What You Can Take Home from New York

Canadian Citizens: For a clear summary of Canadian rules, write for the booklet *I Declare,* issued by the Canada Border Services Agency (© **800/461-9999** in Canada, or 204/983-3500; www.cbsa-asfc.gc.ca).

U.K. Citizens: For information, contact **HM Customs & Excise** at © **0845/010-9000** (from outside the U.K., 020/8929-0152), or consult their website at **www.hmce.gov.uk**.

Australian Citizens: A helpful brochure available from Australian consulates or Customs offices is *Know Before You Go.* For more information, call the **Australian Customs Service** at © **1300/363-263,** or log on to **www.customs.gov.au**.

New Zealand Citizens: Most questions are answered in a free pamphlet available at New Zealand consulates and Customs offices: *New Zealand Customs Guide for Travellers, Notice no. 4.* For more information, contact **New Zealand Customs,** The Customhouse, 17–21 Whitmore St., Box 2218, Wellington (© **04/473-6099** or 0800/428-786; **www.customs.govt.nz**).

3 WHEN TO GO

New York buzzes every day, with pretty much everything open year-round. All school vacation seasons—late December, spring vacation, and summer—tend to be busy times; lots of museums schedule special programs then, because New York schoolchildren are looking for something to do, too. December is particularly jam-packed, with lots of annual holiday entertainment (the *Nutcracker,* the Big Apple Circus, the Radio City Christmas Spectacular). Fall is traditionally the prime season for culture, with new plays opening on Broadway and classical-music venues booked solid, but even in summer, music series at Lincoln Center and star-studded limited-run plays fill the boards. Spring and summer weekends really bustle, with street fairs all over town and what seems like an endless succession of parades, one for every ethnic group in the city, filing down Fifth Avenue. Following are

suggestions on the best times to visit the Big Apple when it comes to weather, crowds, and budgetary considerations.

Weather Many consider those hot and muggy mid-July and mid-August days, when temperatures can go up to as high as 100°F (38°C) with 90% humidity, as New York's worst weather. But don't get put off by this—summer has its compensations, such as wonderful free open-air concerts and other events, as I've mentioned. But if you are at all temperature sensitive, and you plan to spend a lot of your visit outdoors, your odds of getting comfortable weather are better in June or September.

Another period when you might not like to stroll around the city is during January or February, when temperatures are commonly in the 20s (below 0°C) and those concrete canyons turn into wind tunnels. The city looks gorgeous for about a day after a snowfall, but the streets soon become a slushy mess. Again, you never know—temperatures have regularly been in the 30s and mild 40s (single digits Celsius) during the past few "global warmed" winters. If you hit the weather jackpot, you could have a bargain bonanza (see "Money & Costs," later in this chapter).

Fall and spring are the best times in New York. From April to June and September to November, temperatures are mild and pleasant, and the light is beautiful.

With the leaves changing in Central Park and just the hint of crispness in the air, October is a fabulous time to be here—but expect to pay for the privilege.

If you want to know what to pack just before you go, check the Weather Channel's online 10-day forecast at **www.weather.com**; I like to balance it against CNN's online 5-day forecast at **www.cnn.com/weather**. You can also get the local weather by calling © **212/976-1212**.

New York's Average Temperature & Rainfall

	Jan	Feb	Mar	Apr	May	June	July	Aug	Sept	Oct	Nov	Dec
Daily Temp. (°F)	32	34	42	53	63	72	77	76	68	58	48	37
Daily Temp. (°C)	0	1	6	12	17	22	25	24	20	14	9	3
Days of Precipitation	11	10	11	11	11	10	11	10	8	8	9	10

Seasonal Guidelines Hotel prices have gone up the past couple of years, and bargains are harder to find. Therefore, if money is a big concern, you might want to follow these rough seasonal guidelines.

Bargain hunters might want to visit during the post-holidays winter, between the first of the year and early April. Sure, you might have to bear some cold weather, but that's when hotels are suffering from the post-holiday blues, and rooms often go for a relative song—a song in this case meaning a room with a private bathroom for as little as $150. AAA cardholders can do even better in many cases (generally a 5%–10% savings if the hotel offers a AAA discount). However, be aware that the occasional convention or event, such as February's annual Fashion Week, can sometimes throw a wrench in your winter savings plans.

Spring and fall are traditionally the busiest and most expensive seasons after holiday time. Don't expect hotels to be handing you deals, but you may be able to negotiate a decent rate.

The city is drawing more families these days, and they usually visit in the summer. Still, the prospect of heat and humidity keeps some people away, making July and the first half of August a cheaper time to visit than later in the year; good hotel deals are often available.

During the Christmas season, expect to pay top dollar for everything. The first 2 weeks of December—the shopping weeks—are the worst when it comes to scoring an affordable hotel room; that's when shoppers from around the world converge on the town to catch the holiday spirit and spend, spend, spend. But Thanksgiving can be a great time to come, believe it or not: Business travelers have gone home, and the holiday shoppers haven't yet arrived. It's a little-known secret that most hotels away from the Thanksgiving Day Parade route have empty rooms, and they're usually willing to make great deals to fill them.

Also note that hotels are slightly less crowded on weekends, when business travelers clear out of town; many even offer weekend package rates.

KIDS' FAVORITE NEW YORK CITY EVENTS

The following information is always subject to change. Be sure to confirm information before you make plans around a specific event. Call the venue or the NYCVB at ✆ **212/484-1222,** go to **www.nycvisit.com**, or pick up a copy of *Time Out New York* once you arrive in the city for the latest details.

JANUARY

Restaurant Week. Twice a year some of the best restaurants in town offer three-course prix-fixe meals at *almost* affordable prices. At lunch, the deal is $24.07 (as in 24/7), while dinner is $35. It's a great way to sample the menu at some of New York's most heralded restaurants (and not break the bank doing it), especially with older kids with more adventurous palates. Call ✆ **212/484-1222** for info or visit www.nycvisit.com. Late January.

FEBRUARY

Black History Month is observed with some very good programs for kids at museums around town. Throughout February.

Chinese New Year. Every year, Chinatown rings in its own New Year (based on a lunar calendar) with 2 weeks of celebrations, including parades with dragon and lion dancers, plus vivid costumes of all kinds. The parade usually winds throughout Chinatown along Mott, Canal, and Bayard streets, and along East Broadway. Call the NYCVB hot line at ✆ **212/484-1222** or the Asian American Business Development Center at ✆ **212/966-0100.** Chinese New Year falls on January 26 in 2009, and it's the Year of the Ox.

Westminster Kennel Club Dog Show. The ultimate purebred-pooch fest. Some 30,000 dog fanciers from all over the globe congregate at **Madison Square Garden** for the 133rd "World Series of Dogdom." All 2,500 dogs are American Kennel Club Champions of Record, competing for Best in Show. Check the website **www.westminster kennelclub.org** for further info. Tickets are available after January 1 via **Ticketmaster** (✆ **212/307-7171;** www.ticketmaster.com). February 9 and 10, 2009.

MARCH

The **St. Patrick's Day parade** rolls down Fifth Avenue with more than 150,000 marchers—it's the world's largest civilian parade. The parade usually starts at 11am, but go early if you want a good spot. Call ✆ **212/484-1222** for more information. March 17.

The **Ringling Bros. and Barnum & Bailey Circus** begins its annual month-long run at Madison Square Garden. For dates and ticket information, check out the website **www.ringling.com** or contact Madison Square Garden (✆ **212/465-MSG1;** www.thegarden. com). Late March to mid-April.

APRIL

The annual **Central Park Easter egg hunt** is held on Easter weekend near the Bandshell, with activities, giveaways, and visiting celebrities.

The **Easter Parade** is a stroll down Fifth Avenue that anyone can join—the bigger the bonnet, the better. The parade generally runs from about 10am to 3 or 4pm. Call ✆ **212/484-1222.** Easter Sunday.

MAY

Bike New York: The Great Five Boro Bike Tour. The largest mass-participation cycling event in the United States attracts about 30,000 cyclists from all over the world. After a 42-mile (68km) ride through the five boroughs, finalists are greeted with a traditional New

York–style celebration of food and music. Call ℂ **212/932-BIKE** (932-2453) or visit www.bikenewyork.org. First or second Sunday in May.

Ninth Avenue International Food Festival. Street fairs are part of the New York landscape each summer, but this is one of the best. You can spend the day sampling Italian sausages, clams and oysters on the half-shell, homemade pirogi, spicy curries, and other ethnic dishes. Street musicians, bands, and vendors add to the festive atmosphere stretching along Ninth Avenue from 37th to 57th streets. Call ℂ **212/484-1222.** Early to mid-May.

The Brooklyn Botanic Garden's annual **Cherry Blossom Festival** takes a cue from Japanese tradition in celebrating the flowering pink trees around its pond. Call ℂ **718/623-7200** or visit www.bbg.org. Early May.

Fleet Week welcomes a host of U.S. and foreign naval ships to the Hudson River piers around Memorial Day weekend, highlighted by a parade of ships. Call ℂ **212/484-1222.** Late May.

JUNE

Museum Mile Festival. Fifth Avenue from 82nd to 106th streets is closed to cars from 6 to 9pm as 20,000-plus strollers enjoy live music from Broadway tunes to string quartets, street entertainers from juggling to giant puppets, and free admission to nine Museum Mile institutions, including the Metropolitan Museum of Art and the Guggenheim. Call ℂ **212/606-2296** or check www.museummilefestival.org or any of the participating institutions for details. Usually the second Tuesday in June.

SummerStage. A summer-long festival of outdoor performances in Central Park, featuring world music, pop, folk, and jazz artists ranging from Fiona

Apple to the New York Grand Opera (always performing Verdi) to the Chinese Golden Dragon Acrobats. Performances are often free, but certain events require purchased tickets (usually around $35). Call ℂ **212/360-2756** or visit www.summerstage.org. June through August.

JULY

Independence Day Harbor Festival and Fourth of July Fireworks Spectacular. Start the day amid the crowds at the Great July Fourth Festival in lower Manhattan, and then catch Macy's fireworks extravaganza (one of the country's most fantastic) over the East River (the best vantage point is from FDR Drive, which closes to traffic several hours before sunset). Call ℂ **212/484-1222** or Macy's Visitor Center at 212/494-3827. July 4.

Lincoln Center Festival 2009. This festival celebrates the best of the performing arts from all over—theater, ballet, contemporary dance, opera, nouveau circus performances, even puppet and media-based art. Recent editions have featured performances by Ornette Coleman, the Royal Opera, the Royal Ballet, and the New York Philharmonic. Schedules are available in mid-March, and tickets go on sale in May or early June. Call ℂ **212/546-2656** or visit www.lincolncenter.org. Throughout July.

Midsummer Night's Swing. Dancers head to the **Lincoln Center's Josie Robertson Plaza** for evenings of big-band swing, salsa, and tango under the stars to the sounds of top-flight bands. Dance lessons are offered with purchase of a ticket. Call ℂ **212/875-5766** or visit www.lincolncenter.org. July and August.

AUGUST

The **Lincoln Center Out-of-Doors Festival** turns the plaza around the arts complex into one big street fair, with crafts and food stalls and loads of free performances. Call ✆ 212/546-2656 or visit www.lincolncenter.org for this year's schedule. Throughout August.

The **U.S. Open Tennis Championships** are played in Flushing Meadows, Queens, for 2 weeks starting just before Labor Day. If at all possible, be here for **Arthur Ashe Kids' Day,** which kicks off the tournament with appearances by the pros, music, and interactive games and clinics ($10–$20). Tickets for both go on sale in May or early June and often sell out immediately; call ✆ 866/ OPEN-TIX or 718/760-6200 well in advance; visit www.usopen.org for additional information. Late August to early September.

SEPTEMBER

The **Feast of San Gennaro** fills the streets of Little Italy with carnival booths and Italian food stands for 11 days around the saint's day, September 19. Call ✆ 212/768-9320 or visit www. sangennaro.org for more information.

Broadway on Broadway. This free alfresco afternoon show features the songs and casts from nearly every Broadway show, on a stage in the middle of Times Square. Call ✆ 212/768-1560 or visit www.timessquarenyc.org and click on "Events." Sunday in mid-September.

OCTOBER

Feast of St. Francis. Animals from dogs to goldfish to elephants are blessed as thousands of *Homo sapiens* look on at the **Cathedral of St. John the Divine.** It's a magical experience. A festive fair follows the blessing and music events. It's a good idea to buy tickets in advance. For tickets, call the cathedral's box office at ✆ 212/662-2133 or visit www.stjohndivine.org. First Sunday in October.

Ice-Skating. Show off your skating style in the limelight at the diminutive **Rockefeller Center rink** ((✆ 212/332-7654; www.rockefellercenter.com), open from mid-October to mid-March or early April (you'll skate under the magnificent Christmas tree for the month of Dec). In Central Park, spacious **Wollman Rink** has views of the park and the Central Park South skyline; it's on the east side of the park between 62nd and 63rd streets (✆ 212/439-6900; www.wollmanskatingrink.com). **Lasker Rink** lies midpark between 106th and 108th streets (✆ 917/492-3857). Both Central Park skating rinks usually close in early April.

The **Big Apple Circus** settles in for its annual 3-month run at Lincoln Center's Damrosch Park. Call ✆ 212/307-4100 or check out www.bigapplecircus. org. Mid-October through mid-January.

The **Greenwich Village Halloween Parade** marches up lower Sixth Avenue with sass and style. Call the Village Voice Parade hot line at ✆ 212/ 475-3333, ext. 14044, or visit www. halloween-nyc.com. October 31.

NOVEMBER

The **Radio City Christmas Spectacular** at Radio City Music Hall ushers in the holiday season early, beginning a 2-month run. Call ✆ 212/247-4777 or visit www.radiocity.com for exact dates; buy tickets at the box office or via Ticketmaster's Radio City Hotline at ✆ 212/307-1000 or www.ticket master.com.

The Chocolate Show. This burgeoning 4-day event devoted to chocolate takes place each year about 2 weeks before Thanksgiving and is open to the public. The event features booths representing more than 50 of the world's best chocolate makers, tastings, demonstrations, and activities for children. For info, call **866/CHOC-NYC** or 212/889-5112 or visit www.chocolateshow.com.

The **Macy's Thanksgiving Day Parade** runs from 77th Street and Central Park West down to Broadway and 34th Street; sidewalk viewing along the route is first-come, first-served. The night before, it's great fun to watch the parade's mighty balloons being inflated on 77th and 81st streets, around the Museum of Natural History; go early— it gets to be a mob scene by 8pm. Call Macy's Visitor Center at ✆ **212/494-4495.**

DECEMBER

New York National Boat Show. Slip on your Top-Siders and head to the **Jacob K. Javits Convention Center,** which promises a leviathan fleet of boats and marine products from the world's leading manufacturers. Call ✆ **212/984-7000** or visit www.nyboat show.com or www.javitscenter.com. Mid-December.

The **Christmas Tree Lighting** at Rocke-feller Center is accompanied by an ice-skating show and a huge crowd. The tree stays lit around the clock until after the new year. Contact ✆ **212/3326868** or www.rockefellercenter.com for this year's date.

The *Nutcracker* ballet, performed by the New York City Ballet every year at Lincoln Center, is a perpetual delight. Call ✆ **212/870-5570** or visit www. nycballet.com.

The Lighting of the Giant Hanukkah Menorah at Grand Army Plaza (Fifth Ave. and 59th St.) is performed on the world's largest menorah (32 ft. high) each evening during Hanukkah.

New Year's Eve is celebrated famously in Times Square; although this is hardly an event for kids (or for parents who aren't crazy about lunatic crowds), several other events around town capitalize on the holiday. Contact www.times squarenyc.org for details. December 31 to January 1.

4 WHAT TO PACK

It's important to remember that this is preeminently a walking city. There's almost always a bit of a walk from the subway to wherever you're going, and even if you intend to cab it everywhere, you'll have to sprint for a taxi or two or trudge a few blocks when no cabs are in sight—which will happen. So bring your most **comfortable walking shoes,** whether sneakers, hiking shoes, cushioned sandals, or some sort of sturdy hybrid. Lots of shoe companies, among them Rockport, Merrell, Ecco, Mephisto, and Hush Puppies, make good-looking shoes with cushioned soles that can double as walking shoes and dining-out shoes, so you can make a seamless

transition from street to restaurant without having to schlep back to your hotel.

Walking a lot also makes **strollers** a must for any young children who can't hike at least a mile without complaining. Strollers can be a hassle, though, when getting in and out of cabs or up and down subway stairs; make sure you've got one that folds easily. If you have an infant, a **soft carrier** is a better idea.

July and August can be miserably hot and sticky, conditions worsened by the fact that subway platforms are like saunas, thanks to the heat thrown off by the subway trains' air-conditioning (subway cars are glacially cool, by the way). **Short-sleeved**

T-shirts and shorts are best—the roomier, the better. Sun hats are a great idea for the kids.

January and February are cold. Warm gloves, hats, and scarves are advisable if you arrive from November to March (sometimes Apr). If it does snow, the streets are plowed swiftly, and sidewalks get shoveled fast: It takes a really big blizzard to stop Manhattan in its tracks. But plowed banks of snow can stand for weeks, getting filthier and filthier. Boots are a good idea in winter, just in case, because sewers quickly back up, and lake-size puddles form at curbs—too big for kids to jump over.

If you're bringing an infant, call ahead to your hotel to check what baby equipment it can provide—besides a crib, it may help to have a highchair in your room. You may want to pack a few electrical-outlet covers so you can childproof your room when you arrive. Of course, you can buy diapers, wipes, formula, and no-tears shampoo here, but it might be handier to bring your own bottles, sippy cups, feeding dish, infant spoon, and changing pads.

Accidents do happen, so bring extra changes of clothes for your children; for infants and for toddlers who haven't mastered the fine art of using the potty, make that two or three changes of clothes for each day. You'll also want a tote bag full of toys and books. Older kids may want to carry their own backpacks with books, colored markers and pads, a deck of cards, hand-held electronic games, a personal CD player, or whatever keeps them happy.

Few restaurants have real dress codes; it is the rare spot that requires men to wear jackets and ties out to dinner. Bring along a dressy outfit (a jacket and tie for men; boys may be able to get by without the tie) only if you plan to attend a dressy affair. That doesn't mean you should wear jeans or T-shirts out to dinner; bring "casual dressy" outfits that you can wear sightseeing and dining out.

5 GETTING THERE

GETTING TO NEW YORK CITY

By Plane

Three major airports serve New York City: **John F. Kennedy International Airport** (© 718/244-4444) in Queens, about 15 miles (1 hr. driving time) from midtown Manhattan; **LaGuardia Airport** (© 718/533-3400), also in Queens, about 8 miles (30 min.) from Midtown; and **Newark International Airport** (© 973/961-6000) in nearby New Jersey, about 16 miles (45 min.) from Midtown. Information about all three airports is available online at **www.panynj.gov**; click on the "All Airports" tab on the left.

Even though LaGuardia is the closest airport to Manhattan, it has a bad reputation for delays and terminal chaos, in both ticket-desk lines and baggage claim. You may want to use JFK or Newark instead. (JFK has the best reputation for timeliness, such as it is, among New York–area airports.)

Almost every major domestic carrier serves at least one of the New York–area airports; most serve two or all three. Among them are **American** (© 800/433-7300; www.aa.com), **Continental** (© 800/525-3273; www.continental.com), **Delta** (© 800/221-1212; www.delta.com), **Northwest** (© 800/225-2525; www.nwa.com), **United** (© 800/864-8331; www.united.com), and **US Airways** (© 800/428-4322; www.usairways.com).

In recent years, there has been rapid growth in the number of start-up, no-frills airlines serving New York (and 2008

Tips   **Choosing Your NYC-Area Airport**

It's more convenient to fly into Newark than JFK if your destination is Manhattan, and fares to Newark are often cheaper than those to the other airports. Newark is particularly convenient if your hotel is in Midtown West or downtown. Taxi fare into Manhattan from Newark is roughly equivalent to the fare from JFK—both now have **AirTrains** in place (see "Getting into Town from the Airport," below), but the AirTrain to Newark from Manhattan is quicker.

brought the demise of some of them, so definitely check and see whether the following are still flying when you are planning your trip). You might check out Atlanta-based **AirTran** (© 800/AIRTRAN; www.airtran.com), Denver-based **Frontier** (© 800/432-1359; www.flyfrontier.com), Milwaukee- and Omaha-based **Midwest Airlines** (© 800/452-2022; www.midwest airlines.com), or Detroit-based **Spirit Airlines** (© 800/772-7117; www.spiritair. com). The JFK-based cheap-chic airline **JetBlue** ★ (© 800/JETBLUE; www.jet blue.com) has taken New York by storm with its low fares and service to cities throughout the nation. The nation's leading discount airline, **Southwest** (© 800/ 435-9792; www.iflyswa.com), flies into MacArthur (Islip) Airport on Long Island, 50 miles east of Manhattan, although it recently announced plans to begin service to LaGuardia.

Arriving at the Airport

Immigration & Customs Clearance International visitors arriving by air, no matter what the port of entry, should cultivate patience and resignation before setting foot on U.S. soil. U.S. airports have considerably beefed up security clearances in the years since the terrorist attacks of September 11, and clearing Customs and Immigration can take as long as 2 hours.

Getting into Town from the Airport

With young kids in tow, it's best to take a **cab** from the airport into the city. All three

airports have orderly taxi stands where you line up until it's your turn for the uniformed dispatcher to help you into a licensed cab (only yellow cabs are licensed to pick up passengers from JFK and LaGuardia; New Jersey cab companies work from Newark).

Generally, travel time between the airports and Midtown by taxi or car is 45 to 60 minutes for JFK, 20 to 35 minutes for LaGuardia, and 35 to 50 minutes for Newark. Always allow extra time, especially during rush hour and peak holiday travel times.

If your kids are older, you don't have loads of luggage, and you want to save a little money, take a bus or shuttle into town.

For transportation information for all three airports (JFK, LaGuardia, and Newark), call **Air-Ride** (© 800/247-7433), which offers 24-hour recorded details on bus and shuttle companies and car services registered with the New York and New Jersey Port Authority. Similar information is available at **www.panynj.gov**; click on "All Airports" and then on the airport at which you'll be arriving.

The Port Authority runs staffed Ground Transportation Information counters on the baggage-claim level at each airport where you can get information and book various kinds of transport. Most transportation companies also have courtesy phones near the baggage-claim area.

Following are the details on all your ground transportation options to and from the area airports.

Taxis Despite significant rate hikes the past few years, taxis are still a quick and convenient way to travel to and from the airports. They're available at designated taxi stands outside the terminals, with uniformed dispatchers on hand during peak hours at JFK and LaGuardia, around the clock at Newark. Follow the **ground transportation** or **taxi** signs. There may be a long line, but it generally moves pretty quickly. Fares, whether fixed or metered, do not include bridge and tunnel tolls ($4–$6) or a tip for the cab driver (15%–20% is customary). They do include all passengers in the cab and luggage—never pay more than the metered or flat rate, except for tolls and a tip (8pm–6am a $1 surcharge also applies on New York yellow cabs). Taxis have a limit of four passengers, so if there are more in your group, you'll have to take more than one cab. Of course, if you have a little one you can hold in your lap, the cab driver will probably let you take more than four people in one cab. For more on taxis, see "Getting Around," in chapter 4. The taxi fees from each airport are currently as follows:

- **From JFK:** A flat rate of $45 to Manhattan (plus tolls and tip) is charged. The meter will not be turned on and the surcharge will not be added. The flat rate does not apply on trips from Manhattan to the airport.
- **From LaGuardia:** $24 to $28, metered, plus tolls and tip.
- **From Newark:** The dispatcher for New Jersey taxis gives you a slip of paper with a flat rate ranging from $30 to $38 (toll and tip extra), depending on where you're going in Manhattan, so be precise about your destination. New York yellow cabs aren't permitted to pick up passengers at Newark. The yellow-cab fare from Manhattan to Newark is the meter amount plus $15 and tolls (about $69–$75, perhaps a few dollars more with tip). Jersey taxis aren't permitted to

take passengers from Manhattan to Newark.

Private Car & Limousine Services Private car and limousine companies provide convenient 24-hour door-to-door airport transfers for roughly the same cost of a taxi. The advantage they offer over taking a taxi is that you can arrange your pickup in advance and avoid the hassles of the taxi line. Call at least 24 hours in advance (even earlier on holidays), and a driver will meet you near baggage claim (or at your hotel for a return trip). You'll probably be asked to leave a credit card number to guarantee your ride. You'll likely be offered the choice of indoor or curbside pickup; indoor pickup is more expensive but makes it easier to hook up with your driver (who usually waits in baggage claim bearing a sign with your name on it). You can save a few dollars if you arrange for an outside pickup; call the dispatcher as soon as you clear baggage claim and then take your luggage out to the designated waiting area, where you'll wait for the driver to come around, which can take anywhere from 10 minutes to a half-hour. Besides the wait, the other disadvantage of this option is that curbside can be chaos during prime deplaning hours.

Vehicles range from sedans to vans to limousines and tend to be relatively clean and comfortable. Prices vary slightly by company and the size of car reserved, but expect a rate roughly equivalent to taxi fare if you request a basic sedan and have only one stop; toll and tip policies are the same. (**Note:** Car services are not subject to the flat-rate rule that taxis have for rides to and from JFK.) Ask when booking what the fare will be and if you can use your credit card to pay for the ride so there are no surprises at drop-off time. There may be waiting charges tacked on if the driver has to wait an excessive amount of time due to flight delays when picking you up, but the car companies will usually check on your flight to get an accurate landing time.

If You're Flying into MacArthur Airport on Southwest

Southwest Airlines is one of several carriers flying into New York via Long Island's MacArthur Airport, 50 miles east of Manhattan. (The others are Delta, Spirit, Northwest, and US Airways). If you're on one of these flights (because the price was *sooooo* low), here are your options for getting into the city:

Colonial Transportation (✆ 631/589-3500; www.colonialtransportation. com), **Classic Transportation** (✆ 631/567-5100; www.classictrans.com), and **Legends** (✆ 888/LEGENDS or 888/888-8884; www.legendslimousine.com) will pick you up at Islip Airport and deliver you to Manhattan via private sedan, but expect to pay about $125 plus tolls and tip for door-to-door service (which kind of defeats the purpose of flying a budget airline). Be sure to arrange for it at least 24 hours in advance.

For a fraction of the cost, you can catch a ride aboard a **Hampton Jitney** coach (✆ 631/283-4600; www.hamptonjitney.com) to various drop-off points on Midtown's east side. The cost is $29 per person, plus a minimal taxi fare from the terminal to the Hampton Jitney stop. Hampton Jitney can explain the details and arrange for taxi transport.

Colonial Transportation (✆ 631/589-3500; www.colonialtransportation. com) also offers regular shuttle service that traverses the 3 miles from the airport to the Ronkonkoma Long Island Rail Road station, where you can pick up an LIRR train to Manhattan. The shuttle fare is $5 per person, $1 for each additional family member accompanying a full-fare customer. From Ronkonkoma, it's about a 1¹/₂-hour train ride to Manhattan's Penn Station; the one-way fare is $13 at peak hours, $9.50 off-peak (half-fare for seniors 65 or older and kids 5–11). You can also catch the Suffolk County Transit bus no. S-57 between the airport and the station Monday to Saturday for $1.50. Trains usually leave Ronkonkoma once or twice every hour, depending on the day and time. For more information, call ✆ 718/217-LIRR (217-5477) or visit www.mta.nyc.ny.us/lirr.

For additional options and the latest information, call ✆ 631/467-3210 or visit www.macarthurairport.com.

Reliable companies include **Carmel** (✆ 800/922-7635 or 212/666-6666), **Legends** (✆ 888/LEGENDS or 212/888-8884; www.legendslimousine.com), **Allstate** (✆ 800/453-4099 or 212/333-3333), and **Tel-Aviv** (✆ 800/222-9888 or 212/777-7777). (Keep in mind, though, that these services are only as good as the individual drivers—and sometimes there's a lemon in the bunch. If you have a problem, report it immediately to the main office.)

For a bit more luxury and service, one good option is **Luxor Limo** ✆ 866/990-4111; www.luxorlimo.com), where the cars are spacious and the drivers as reliable as you will find and with rates not much higher than the above companies.

These car services are good for rush hour (no ticking meters in rush-hour traffic), but if you're arriving at a quieter time of day, taxis work just fine.

Private Buses & Shuttles Buses and shuttle services provide a comfortable and less expensive (but usually more time-consuming) option for airport transfers than do taxis and car services.

SuperShuttle serves all three airports; **New York Airport Service** serves JFK and

LaGuardia; **Olympia Trails** and **Express Shuttle USA** serve Newark. These services are a good option for getting to and from Newark during peak travel times because the drivers usually take lesser-known streets that make the ride much quicker than if you go with a taxi or car, which will virtually always stick to the traffic-clogged main route.

The familiar blue vans of **SuperShuttle** (© 800/258-3826; www.supershuttle. com) serve all three area airports, providing door-to-door service to Manhattan and points on Long Island every 15 to 30 minutes around the clock. As with Express Shuttle, you don't need to reserve your airport-to-Manhattan ride; just go to the ground-transportation desk or use the courtesy phone in baggage claim and ask for SuperShuttle. Hotel pickups for your return trip require 24 to 48 hours' notice; you can make your reservations online. Fares run $13 to $22 per person, depending on the airport, with discounts available for additional persons in the same party.

New York Airport Service (© 718/875-8200; www.nyairportservice.com) buses travel from JFK and LaGuardia to the Port Authority Bus Terminal (42nd St. and Eighth Ave.), Grand Central Terminal (Park Ave. btwn 41st and 42nd sts.), and to select Midtown hotels between 27th and 59th streets, plus the Jamaica LIRR Station in Queens, where you can pick up a train for Long Island. Follow the GROUND TRANSPORTATION signs to the curbside pickup or look for the uniformed agent. Buses depart the airport every 20 to 70 minutes (depending on your departure point and destination) between 6am and midnight. Buses to JFK and LaGuardia depart the Port Authority and Grand Central Terminal on the Park Avenue side every 15 to 30 minutes, depending on the time of day and the day of the week. To request direct shuttle service from your hotel, call the above number at least 24 hours in advance. One-way fare for JFK is

$15, $27 round-trip; to LaGuardia it's $12 one-way and $21 round-trip.

Olympia Airport Express (© 800/8-Newark or 212/964-6233; www.coach usa.com/olympia) provides service every 15 to 30 minutes (depending on the time of day) from Newark Airport to Penn Station (the pickup point is the northwest corner of 34th St. and Eighth Ave., and the drop-off point is the southwest corner), the Port Authority Bus Terminal (on 42nd St. btwn Eighth and Ninth aves.), and Grand Central Terminal (on 41st St. btwn Park and Lexington aves.). Passengers to and from the Grand Central Terminal location can connect to Olympia's Midtown shuttle vans, which service select Midtown hotels. Call for the exact schedule for your return trip to the airport. The one-way fare runs $13, $22 round-trip; seniors and passengers with disabilities ride for $6.

Subways & Public Buses For the most part, your best bet is to stay away from the MTA when traveling to and from the airport—especially if you have kids in tow. You might save a few dollars, but subways and buses that currently serve the airports involve multiple transfers, and you'll have to drag your luggage up and down staircases. Spare yourself the drama.

The only exception to this rule is the subway service to and from JFK, which connects with the AirTrain (see below). The subway *can* be more reliable than taking a car or taxi at the height of rush hour, but *a few words of warning:* This isn't the right option for you if have very young children in tow or you're bringing more than a single piece of luggage, since there's a good amount of walking and some stairs involved in the trip, and you'll have nowhere to put all those bags on the subway train. And *do not* use this method if you're traveling to or from the airport late at night or super early in the morning—it's not the safest or fastest way then. For complete subway information, see chapter 4.

Getting to the Other Boroughs & the 'Burbs

If you're traveling to a borough other than Manhattan, call **ETS Air Service**
(© **718/221-5341**) for shared door-to-door service. For Long Island service,
call **Classic Transportation** (© **631/567-5100;** www.classictrans.com) for car
service. For service to Westchester County or Connecticut, contact **Connecticut
Limousine** (© **800/472-5466** or 203/878-2222; www.ctlimo.com) or **Prime Time
Shuttle of Connecticut** (© **866/2-TheAir;** www.primetimeshuttle.com).

If you're traveling to points in New Jersey from Newark Airport, call **Olympic
Airporter** (© **800/822-9797** or 732/938-6666; www.olympicairporter.com) for
Ocean, Monmouth, Middlesex, and Mercer counties, plus Bucks County, Pennsylvania; or **State Shuttle** (© **800/427-3207** or 973/729-0030; www.stateshuttle.
com) for destinations throughout New Jersey.

Additionally, **New York Airport Service** express buses (© **718/875-8200;**
www.nyairportservice.com) serve the entire New York metropolitan region from
JFK and LaGuardia, offering connections to the Long Island Rail Road; the Metro-
North Railroad to Westchester County, upstate New York, and Connecticut; and
New York's Port Authority terminal, where you can pick up buses to points
throughout New Jersey.

3

AirTrain A few years back, a new rail link revolutionized the process of connecting by public transportation to New York–area airports: JFK and now Newark International Airport, in New Jersey. *A word of warning for both AirTrains:* Yes, you'll save money, but if you have a bevy of small children, mobility issues, or mountains of luggage, skip the AirTrain. You'll find it easier to rely on a taxi, car service, or shuttle service that can offer you door-to-door transfers.

AirTrain Newark now connects Newark-Liberty International Airport with Manhattan via a speedy monorail/rail link. Even though you have to make a connection, the system is fast, pleasant, affordable, and easy to use. Each arrivals terminal at Newark Airport has a station for the AirTrain, so just follow the signs once you collect your bags. All AirTrains head to **Newark International Airport Station,** where you transfer to a **NJ Transit** train. NJ Transit will deliver you to New York Penn Station at 33rd Street and Seventh Avenue, where you can get a cab or transfer to the subway or bus. The one-way

AirTrain fare is $12 (children 4 and under ride free). NJ Transit tickets can be purchased from vending machines at both the air terminal and the train station (no ticket is required to board the AirTrain).

Note that travelers heading to points beyond the city can also pick up Amtrak and other NJ Transit trains at Newark International Airport Station to their final destinations.

A few bumpy years after opening in 2003, **AirTrain JFK** is beginning to operate more efficiently. Though you can't beat the price—only $5 (plus $2 subway fare if you take a subway to the AirTrain), $12 if you take the Long Island Rail Road—you won't save much on time getting to the airport. From midtown Manhattan, the ride can take anywhere from 40 minutes to an hour, depending on your connections. Only a few lines connect with the AirTrain: the A, E, J, and Z; the E, J, Z to Jamaica Station and the Sutphin Boulevard–Archer Avenue Station; and the A to Howard Beach/JFK Airport Station. The MTA is working hard to clear up the confusion, and though they are contemplating adding connections to the AirTrain in lower Manhattan sometime in the next decade, there's not much they can do now to speed up the trip.

For more information on AirTrain Newark, call ✆ **888/EWR-INFO** (397-4636) or go online to **www.panynj.gov/airtrainnewark**. For connection details, click on the links on the AirTrain website or contact **NJ Transit** (✆ 800/626-RIDE (626-7433); www.njtransit.com) or **Amtrak** (✆ **800/USA-RAIL** [872-7245]; www.amtrak.com).

For more information on AirTrain JFK, go online to **www.panynj.gov/airtrain**. For connection details, click on the links on the AirTrain website or the MTA site, **www.mta.nyc.ny.us/mta/airtrain.htm**.

By Car

From the **New Jersey Turnpike** (I-95) and points west, there are three Hudson River crossings to the city's West Side: the **Holland Tunnel** (Lower Manhattan), the **Lincoln Tunnel** (Midtown), and the **George Washington Bridge** (Upper Manhattan). From **upstate New York,** take the **New York State Thruway** (I-87), which crosses the Hudson River on the Tappan Zee Bridge and becomes the **Major Deegan Expressway** (I-87) through the Bronx. For the East Side, continue to the Triborough Bridge and then down the FDR Drive. For the West Side, take the Cross Bronx Expressway (I-95) to the Henry Hudson Parkway or the Taconic State Parkway to the Saw Mill River Parkway to the Henry Hudson Parkway south.

From **New England,** the **New England Thruway** (I-95) connects with the **Bruckner Expressway** (I-278), which leads to the Triborough Bridge and the FDR Drive on the East Side. For the West Side, take the Bruckner to the Cross Bronx Expressway (I-95) to the Henry Hudson Parkway south.

Note that you'll have to pay tolls along some of these roads and at most crossings. If your state has an **E-ZPass** program (**www.ezpass.com**), as most states in the Northeast do, your pass will allow you to go through the designated E-ZPass lanes.

Once you arrive in Manhattan, park your car in a garage (expect to pay $20–$45 per day) and leave it there. Don't use

---

ⓘ Tips   Coping with Jet Lag

Jet lag is a pitfall of traveling across time zones. If you're flying north-south and you feel sluggish when you touch down, your symptoms will be the result of dehydration and the general stress of air travel. When you travel east-west or vice-versa, your body becomes confused about what time it is, and everything from your digestive system to your brain is knocked for a loop. Traveling east is more difficult on your internal clock than traveling west because most peoples' bodies are more inclined to stay up late than to fall asleep early.

Here are some tips for combating jet lag:

- **Reset your watch** to your destination time before you board the plane.
- **Drink lots of water** before, during, and after your flight. Avoid alcohol.
- **Exercise and sleep well** for a few days before your trip.
- If you have trouble sleeping on planes, **fly eastward on morning flights.**
- **Daylight** is the key to resetting your body clock. At the website for **Outside In** (**www.bodyclock.com**), you can get a customized plan of when to seek and avoid light.

your car for traveling within the city. Public transportation, taxis, and walking will easily get you where you want to go without the headaches of parking, gridlock, and dodging crazy cabbies.

By Train

Train travel can be great fun for kids. **Amtrak** (© 800/USA-RAIL [872-7245]; www.amtrak.com) runs frequent service to New York City's **Penn Station,** on Seventh Avenue between 31st and 33rd streets, where you can get a taxi, subway, or bus to your hotel. To get the best rates, book early (as much as 6 months in advance) and travel on weekends.

If you're traveling to New York from a city along Amtrak's Northeast Corridor—such as Boston, Philadelphia, Baltimore, or Washington, D.C.—Amtrak may be your best travel bet, particularly on the high-speed Acela trains. The Acela express trains cut travel time from D.C. down to 2½ hours, and travel time from Boston to a lightning-quick 3 hours.

Flying for Less: Tips for Getting the Best Airfare

- Passengers who can book their ticket either **long in advance or at the last minute,** or who **fly midweek** or **at less-trafficked hours** may pay a fraction of the full fare. If your schedule is flexible, say so, and ask if you can secure a cheaper fare by changing your flight plans.
- Search **the Internet** for cheap fares. Among the most popular online travel agencies: **Travelocity** (**www.travelocity. com** or www.travelocity.co.uk); **Expedia** (**www.expedia.com**, www.expedia. co.uk, or www.expedia.ca); and **Orbitz** (**www.orbitz.com**). In addition, most airlines now offer online-only fares that even their phone agents know nothing about.
- Keep an eye on local newspapers for **promotional specials** or **fare wars,**

when airlines lower prices on their most popular routes. You rarely see fare wars offered for peak travel times, but if you can travel in the off months, you may snag a bargain.

- **Consolidators,** also known as bucket shops, are great sources for international tickets, although they usually can't beat Internet fares within North America. Start by looking in Sunday newspaper travel sections; U.S. travelers should focus on the *New York Times, Los Angeles Times,* and *Miami Herald.* U.K. travelers should search in the *Independent, The Guardian,* or *The Observer.* **Beware:** Bucket shop tickets are usually nonrefundable or rigged with stiff cancellation penalties, often as high as 50% to 75% of the ticket price, and some put you on charter airlines, which may leave at inconvenient times and experience delays. Several reliable consolidators are worldwide and available online. **STA Travel** has been the world's lead consolidator for students since purchasing Council Travel, but their fares are competitive for travelers of all ages. **Flights.com** (© 800/TRAV-800; www.flights.com) has excellent fares worldwide, particularly to Europe. They also have "local" websites in 12 countries. **FlyCheap** (© 800/FLY-CHEAP [359-2432]; www.flycheap. com) has especially good fares to sunny destinations. **Air Tickets Direct** (© 800/ 778-3447; www.airticketsdirect.com) is based in Montreal and leverages the currently weak Canadian dollar for low fares; they also book trips to places that U.S. travel agents won't touch, such as Cuba.
- Join **frequent-flier clubs.** Frequent-flier membership doesn't cost a cent, but it does entitle you to better seats, faster response to phone inquiries, and prompter service if your luggage is stolen or your flight is canceled or delayed,

or if you want to change your seat. And you don't have to fly to earn points; **frequent-flier credit cards** can earn you thousands of miles for doing your everyday shopping. With more than 70 mileage awards programs on the market, consumers have never had more options. Investigate the program details of your favorite airlines before you sink points into any one. Consider which airlines have hubs in the airport nearest you, and, of those carriers, which have the most advantageous alliances, given your most common routes. To play the frequent-flier game to your best advantage, consult Randy Petersen's **Inside Flyer** (www.insideflyer.com). Petersen and friends review all the programs in detail and post regular updates on changes in policies and trends.

Flying with Kids

If you plan carefully, you can make it fun to fly with your kids—and, equally important, ensure a positive travel experience for your fellow passengers:

- **Reserve a seat in the bulkhead row** if you have babies or toddlers. You'll have more legroom and your children will be able to play on the floor underfoot.
- **Book the window and aisle seats,** on the chance that no one will book the middle seat (if someone has done so, politely ask if he or she minds moving once you're on the plane). Check at the gate to see if any empty rows are still available. That way, your child will have more room to move in and around his seat and be less tempted to walk in the aisle. Reserving the aisle seat for you or your spouse also protects your child from jostling passersby.
- **Pack items for your kids in your carry-on luggage,** such as books, snacks, and toys. Be sure to bring self-contained compact toys with few pieces. Be aware that electronic games can

interfere with the aircraft navigational system, and their noisiness may annoy your adult neighbors. Small coloring books and crayons work well, as do card games like Go Fish.

- **Have a long talk with your children** before you depart for your trip, explaining to them what to expect at takeoff, at landing, and during the flight. Explain to your kids the importance of good behavior in the air—how their own safety can depend upon their being quiet and staying in their seats during the trip.
- **Pay extra attention to the safety instructions** before takeoff. Consult the safety chart behind the seat in front of you, and show it to your children. Be sure you know how to operate the oxygen masks, as you'll be expected to secure yours first and then help your children with theirs. Locate the emergency exits before takeoff, and plot out an evacuation strategy for you and your children, just in case.
- **Be sure your child's seatbelt remains fastened properly.** Sudden turbulence is a danger to a child who is not buckled into his or her own seat restraint. This will also make it harder for your children to wander off.
- **Bring milk with you on the plane**— few airlines carry milk (other than concentrate for coffee) anymore. The TSA allows formula, breast milk, and juice in containers larger than 3 ounces, but you must declare the liquid at the security checkpoint before you board the plane. (Carry only as much milk as you think you will need on the flight.) If you're carrying regular milk, it's a good idea to use 3-ounce bottles, the maximum-size container the TSA allows onboard— anything larger is prohibited.
- **Always accompany children to the lavatory.**
- Some airlines **serve children's meals first.** When you board, ask a flight

attendant if this is possible, especially if your children are very young or seated toward the back of the plane.

GETTING AROUND

For everything you need to know to get around the city safely and efficiently, go to chapter 4.

6 MONEY & COSTS

KEEPING COSTS LOW

New York is a notoriously expensive destination to visit, but there are definitely ways to keep expenses under control. The first is to aggressively look for **hotel discounts,** through a travel agent or on the Internet. Many Midtown hotels offer excellent weekend or summer packages. Once you arrive, use **public transportation** instead of taxis as often as possible; subways are wonderfully fast and safe, and buses, though prone to traffic slowdowns, are a great way to see the city. Oh, and **walking**—probably the best way to see the city—is free! Use the **TKTS booth** or other theater discount schemes to get half-price tickets to Broadway shows; even though the season's hottest seats may be excluded, you're bound to get into something memorable. And make **smart restaurant choices;** theme restaurants may be exciting for kids, but you'll pay double the price for a mediocre hamburger there. Sample New York's great neighborhood bistros, coffee shops, and ethnic restaurants instead, and if there's no children's menu per se, don't be shy about asking to

have your children share one adult-size entree—that is, if you can get two siblings to agree on an entree. Find **a hotel with self-catering capabilities**—a kitchen or kitchenette—so you can save on meals by having breakfast in, for example (bagels from the local deli, plus fresh orange juice). Or dine in like a real New Yorker— **call for takeout food!**

ATMs

In most Manhattan neighborhoods, you can find a bank with **ATMs** (automated teller machines) every couple of blocks. Many small stores and delis have ATMs with varying fees to withdraw money from your bank account or credit card—but I'd steer clear of these in general; thieves have been known to prey on these machines to access users' card and PIN numbers.

The **Cirrus** (① 800/424-7787; www.mastercard.com) and **PLUS** (① 800/843-7587; www.visa.com) networks span the country; you can find them even in remote regions. Go to your bank card's website to find ATM locations at your destination.

 Easy Money

You'll avoid lines at airport ATMs by exchanging at least some money—just enough to cover airport incidentals and transportation to your hotel—before you leave home.

When you change money, ask for some small bills or loose change. Petty cash will come in handy for tipping and public transportation. Consider keeping the change separate from your larger bills so that it's readily accessible and you'll be less of a target for theft.

What Things Cost in New York City	U.S.$
Hot dog at corner umbrella cart	1.50–2.00
Hot pretzel at corner umbrella cart	1.25–1.50
12-oz. soft drink in a deli	1.25–1.50
16-oz. apple juice in a deli	1.55
Takeout bagel with cream cheese	1.00–1.50
Slice of plain pizza	1.50–2.50
McDonald's McNuggets Happy Meal	3.55–3.99
Local telephone call	0.50
Movie ticket	10.00–11.00 adult, 6.50–8.00 child
Taxi ride from the American Museum of Natural History to American Girl Place	10.00 (plus $2.00 tip)
Taxi ride from South Street Seaport to Rockefeller Center, depending on traffic	17.00 (plus $3.50 tip)
Package of Pampers/Huggies	11.00
32-oz. can prepared Similac formula	6.00

Be sure you know your daily withdrawal limit before you depart.

Note: Many banks impose a fee every time you use a card at another bank's ATM, and that fee is often higher for international transactions than for domestic ones (which is creeping up; I've seen a $3 fee at some major bank ATMs). In addition, the bank from which you withdraw cash may charge its own fee. To compare banks' ATM fees within the U.S., use **www.bankrate.com**. Visitors from outside the U.S. should also find out whether their bank assesses a 1% to 3% fee on charges incurred abroad.

Credit Cards & Debit Cards

Credit cards are the most widely used form of payment in the United States: **Visa** (Barclaycard in Britain), **MasterCard** (EuroCard in Europe, Access in Britain, Chargex in Canada), **American Express, Diners Club,** and **Discover.** They also provide a convenient record of all your expenses, and offer relatively good exchange rates. You can withdraw cash advances from your credit cards at banks or ATMs, but high fees make credit card cash advances a priccy way to get cash.

(Make sure you have your credit card PIN number before you leave home.)

It's highly recommended that you travel with at least one major credit card. You must have a credit card to rent a car, and hotels and airlines usually require a credit card imprint as a deposit against expenses.

ATM cards with major credit card backing, known as **"debit cards,"** are now a commonly acceptable form of payment in most stores and restaurants. Debit cards draw money directly from your checking account. Some stores enable you to receive cash back on your debit card purchases as well (which can save you money on ATM fees). The same is true at most U.S. post offices. Be sure to find out what, if any, fees your bank imposes when you use your debit card in New York City.

Traveler's Checks

Though credit cards and debit cards are more often used, traveler's checks are still widely accepted, and international visitors should make sure that traveler's checks are denominated in U.S. dollars; foreign-currency checks are often difficult to exchange.

You can buy traveler's checks at most banks. Most are offered in denominations of $20, $50, $100, $500, and sometimes $1,000. Generally, you'll pay a service charge ranging from 1% to 4%.

The most popular traveler's checks are offered by **American Express** (② 800/807-6233, or ② 800/221-7282 for cardholders—this number accepts collect calls, offers service in several foreign languages, and exempts Amex gold and platinum cardholders from the 1% fee); **Visa** (② 800/732-1322—AAA members can obtain Visa checks for a $9.95 fee for checks up to $1,500 at most AAA offices or by calling ② 866/339-3378); and **MasterCard** (② 800/223-9920).

Be sure to keep a copy of the traveler's checks' serial numbers separate from your checks in the event that they are stolen or lost. You'll get a refund faster if you know the numbers.

7 HEALTH

STAYING HEALTHY

New York City has no less healthy an environment than that of any other large city: The climate is temperate, public hygiene is relatively good, and the water supply is highly drinkable (in fact, in blind taste tests, New York tap water often scores higher than bottled waters). Although most visitors don't think of New York as an outdoor destination, if you plan to be in the parks a good deal during warm weather, insect repellent is advised, as mosquito- and tick-borne illnesses like the West Nile virus and Lyme disease can be contracted here almost as readily as anywhere in the Northeast.

If you or your child suffers from conditions like epilepsy, diabetes, or heart problems, wear a **MedicAlert identification tag** (② 888/633-4298; www.medicalert. org), which will immediately alert doctors to your condition and give them access to your records through MedicAlert's 24-hour hot line.

What to Do If You Get Sick Away from Home

There is one great advantage to getting sick in the city that never sleeps: Drugstores and hospital emergency rooms are open 24 hours a day, should you need them, and the quality of medical care is very high. (See "Fast Facts," in the appendix, for the one nearest you, as well as **emergency numbers.**)

If you get sick, ask your hotel concierge to recommend a local doctor—even his or her own. This will probably yield a better recommendation than any toll-free telephone number would.

The **NYU Downtown Hospital** offers physician referrals at ② 888/698-3362 or 212/312-5000. You can also try the emergency room at a local hospital. Many hospitals also have walk-in clinics for emergency cases that are not life-threatening; you may not get immediate attention, but you won't pay the high price of an emergency room visit. **DOCS at New York Healthcare,** 55 E. 34th St., between Park and Madison avenues (② 800/673-3627 or 212/252-6001), for non-emergency illnesses, is affiliated with Beth Israel Medical Center and is open Monday through Thursday from 8am to 8pm, Friday from 8am to 7pm, Saturday from 9am to 3pm, and Sunday from 9am to 2pm. We list hospitals and emergency numbers under "Fast Facts," in the appendix.

Bring an extra supply of any **prescription medications** you or your child may be taking, and carry them in their original containers, with pharmacy labels—otherwise, they may not make it through airport security. Divide them between carry-on and checked luggage so that if you lose a

Avoiding "Economy Class Syndrome"

Deep vein thrombosis, or as it's known in the world of flying, "economy-class syndrome," is a blood clot that develops in a deep vein. It's a potentially deadly condition that can be caused by sitting in cramped conditions—such as an airplane cabin—for too long. During a flight (especially a long-haul flight), get up, walk around, and stretch your legs every 60 to 90 minutes to keep your blood flowing. Other preventive measures include frequent flexing of the legs while sitting, drinking lots of water, and avoiding alcohol and sleeping pills. If you have a history of deep vein thrombosis, heart disease, or another condition that puts you at high risk, some experts recommend wearing compression stockings or taking anticoagulants when you fly; always ask your physician about the best course for you. Symptoms of deep vein thrombosis include leg pain or swelling, or even shortness of breath.

bag, you won't be left in the lurch. It's also a good idea to contact your pediatrician before you leave to get a written prescription for any medicines you might lose or run out of and to obtain a reference for a New York City pediatrician in case of a sudden illness. Failing that, your hotel's front desk should be able to put you in touch with a local doctor if illness flares up during your New York City stay. To be on the safe side, bring a supply of any over-the-counter medication your child often needs—why waste vacation time looking for the one brand of diaper ointment that works on your baby's bottom or searching for the only flavor of Tylenol your child is willing to take?

If you have dental problems on the road, a service known as **1-800-DENTIST** (© **800/336-8478**) will provide the name of a local dentist.

8 SAFETY

STAYING SAFE

The FBI consistently rates New York City as one of the safest large cities in the United States, but it is still a large city and crime most definitely exists. Here are a few tips for staying safe in New York:

- Trust your instincts, because they're usually right.
- You'll rarely be hassled, but it's always best to walk with a sense of purpose and self-confidence. Don't stop in the middle of the sidewalk to pull out and peruse your map.
- Anywhere in the city, if you find yourself on a deserted street that feels unsafe, it probably is; leave as quickly as possible.

- If you do find yourself accosted by someone with or without a weapon, remember to keep your anger in check and that the most reasonable response (maddening though it may be) is to not resist.

Subway Safety Tips In general, the subways are safe, especially in Manhattan. There are panhandlers and questionable characters like anywhere else in the city, but subway crime has gone down to 1960s levels. Still, stay alert and trust your instincts. Always keep a hand on your personal belongings.

When using the subway, **don't wait for trains near the edge of the platform** or on extreme ends of a station. During non–rush hours, wait for the train in view of the token-booth clerk or under the yellow DURING OFF HOURS TRAINS STOP HERE signs, and ride in the train operator's or conductor's car (usually in the center of the train; you'll see his or her head stick out of the window when the doors open). Choose crowded cars over empty ones—there's safety in numbers.

Avoid subways late at night, and splurge on a cab after about 10 or 11pm—it's money well spent to avoid a long wait on a deserted platform. Or take the bus.

9 SPECIALIZED TRAVEL RESOURCES

FAMILY TRAVEL

To locate accommodations, restaurants, and attractions that are particularly kid-friendly, refer to the "Kids" icon throughout this guide.

Good bets for the most timely information include the "Weekend" section of Friday's *New York Times,* which has a section dedicated to the week's best kid-friendly activities; the weekly *New York* magazine (www.nymag.com), which has a full calendar of children's events in its listings section; and *Time Out New York* (www.timeout.com/newyork), which also has a weekly kids' section with a bit of an alternative bent. The *Big Apple Parents' Paper* is usually available, free, at children's stores and other locations in Manhattan; you can also find good information from the folks behind the paper at **www. parentsknow.com**.

The first place to look for **babysitting** is in your hotel (better yet, ask about babysitting when you reserve). Many hotels have babysitting services or will provide you with lists of reliable sitters. If this doesn't pan out, call the **Baby Sitters' Guild** (© 212/682-0227; www.babysitters guild.com). The sitters are licensed, insured, and bonded, and can even take your child on outings.

Recommended family travel websites include **Family Travel Forum** (www.family travelforum.com), a comprehensive site that offers customized trip planning; **Family Travel Network** (www.familytravel network.com), an award-winning site that offers travel features, deals, and tips; **Traveling Internationally with Your Kids** (www.travelwithyourkids.com), a comprehensive site offering sound advice for long-distance and international travel with children; and **Family Travel Files** (www. thefamilytravelfiles.com), which offers an online magazine and a directory of off-the-beaten-path tours and tour operators for families.

For a list of more family-friendly travel resources, turn to the experts at frommers.com.

TRAVELERS WITH DISABILITIES

Most disabilities shouldn't stop anyone from traveling in the U.S. Thanks to provisions in the Americans with Disabilities Act (ADA), most public places are required to comply with disability-friendly regulations. Almost all public establishments (including hotels, restaurants, museums, and so on, but not including certain National Historic Landmarks) and at least some modes of public transportation provide accessible entrances and other facilities for those with disabilities.

New York is more accessible to travelers with disabilities than ever before. The city's bus system is wheelchair-friendly, and most of the major sightseeing attractions are easily accessible. Even so, **always call first** to be sure that the places you want to go to are fully accessible.

Most hotels are ADA-compliant, with suitable rooms for wheelchair-bound travelers as well as those with other disabilities. But before you book, **ask specific questions based on your needs.**

Many city hotels are in older buildings that have had to be modified to meet requirements; still, elevators and bathrooms can be on the small side, and other impediments may exist. If you have mobility issues, you'll probably do best to book one of the city's newer hotels, which tend to be more spacious. At **www.access-able. com** (see below), you'll find links to New York's best accessible accommodations (click on "World Destinations"). Some Broadway theaters and other performance venues provide total wheelchair accessibility; others provide partial accessibility. Many also offer lower-priced tickets for theatergoers with disabilities and their companions, though you'll need to check individual policies and reserve in advance.

Hospital Audiences, Inc. (© 212/575-7676; www.hospitalaudiences.org) arranges attendance and provides details about accessibility at cultural institutions as well as cultural events adapted for people with disabilities. Services include "Describe!," which allows visually impaired theatergoers to enjoy theater events; and the invaluable **HAI Hot Line** (© 212/575-7676), which offers accessibility information for hotels, restaurants, attractions, cultural venues, and much more. This nonprofit organization also publishes *Access for All,* a guidebook on accessibility, available free of charge on the website, www.hospitalaudiences.org.

Another terrific source for travelers with disabilities who are coming to New York City is **Big Apple Greeter** (© 212/669-8159; www.bigapplegreeter.org). All of its employees are extremely well versed in accessibility issues. They can provide a resource list of city agencies that serve those with disabilities, and sometimes have special discounts available to theater and music performances. Big Apple Greeter even offers one-to-one tours that

pair volunteers with visitors with disabilities; they can even introduce you to the public transportation system if you like. Reserve at least 1 week ahead.

SuperShuttle (© 800/Blue-Van or 212/258-3826; www.supershuttle.com) operates minibuses with lifts from Newark airports to Midtown hotels by reservation; arrange pickup 3 or 4 days in advance. **Olympia Trails** (© 877/894-9155; www. coachusa.com/olympia) provides service from Newark Airport, with half-price fares for travelers with disabilities (be sure to prepurchase your tickets to guarantee the discount fare, as drivers can't sell discounted tickets). Not all buses are appropriately equipped, so call ahead for the schedule of accessible buses (press "0" to reach a real person).

Taxis are required to carry people who have folding wheelchairs and service dogs. However, don't be surprised if they don't run each other down trying to get to you; even though you shouldn't have to, you may have to wait a bit for a friendly (or fare-desperate) driver to come along.

Public buses are an inexpensive and easy way to get around New York. All buses' back doors are supposed to be equipped with wheelchair lifts (though the city has had complaints that not all are in working order). Buses also "kneel," lowering their front steps for people who have difficulty boarding. Passengers with disabilities pay half-price fares ($1). The **subway** isn't fully wheelchair accessible, but a list of about 30 accessible subway stations and a guide to wheelchair-accessible subway itineraries is on the MTA website. Call © **718/596-8585** for bus and subway transit info or go online to www.mta.nyc.ny.us/nyct and click on the wheelchair symbol.

You're better off not trying to rent your own car to get around the city. But if you consider it the best mode of transportation for you, **Wheelchair Getaways** (© **800/642-2042** or 800/344-5005;

www.wheelchairgetaways.com) rents specialized vans with wheelchair lifts and other features for travelers with disabilities throughout the New York metropolitan area.

Organizations that offer a vast range of resources and assistance to travelers with disabilities include **MossRehab** (© 800/CALL-MOSS;** www.mossresourcenet.org); the **American Foundation for the Blind (AFB;** © 800/232-5463;** www.afb.org); and **SATH** (Society for Accessible Travel & Hospitality; © 212/447-7284;** www.sath.org). **AirAmbulanceCard.com** is now partnered with SATH and allows you to preselect top-notch hospitals in case of an emergency.

Access-Able Travel Source (© 303/232-2979;** www.access-able.com) offers a database on travel agents from around the world with experience in accessible travel; destination-specific access information; and links to such resources as service animals, equipment rentals, and access guides.

Many travel agencies offer customized tours and itineraries for travelers with disabilities. Among them is **Flying Wheels Travel** (© 877/451-5006;** www.flyingwheelstravel.com).

Flying with Disability (www.flying-with-disability.org) is a comprehensive information source on airplane travel.

Also check out the quarterly magazine *Emerging Horizons* (www.emerginghorizons.com), available by subscription ($16.95 a year in the U.S.; $21.95 outside the U.S.).

British travelers should contact **Holiday Care** (© 0845-124-9971 in the U.K. only; www.holidaycare.org.uk) to access travel information and resources for travelers with disabilities and seniors.

GLBT TRAVELERS

Gay and lesbian culture is as much a part of New York's basic identity as yellow cabs, high-rises, and Broadway theater. Indeed,

in a city with one of the world's largest, loudest, and most powerful GLBT populations, homosexuality is squarely in the mainstream. So city hotels tend to be neutral on the issue, and gay couples with kids shouldn't have a problem.

All over Manhattan, but especially in neighborhoods like the **West Village** (particularly Christopher St., famous the world over as the main drag of New York gay-male life) and **Chelsea** (especially Eighth Ave. from 16th to 23rd sts., and W. 17th to 19th sts. from Fifth to Eighth aves.), shops, services, and restaurants have a lesbian and gay flavor.

The **Oscar Wilde Bookshop,** 15 Christopher St. (© 212/255-8097;** www.oscarwildebooks.com), is the city's best gay and lesbian bookstore and a good source for information on the city's gay community.

The **Lesbian, Gay, Bisexual & Transgender Community Center,** familiarly known as "The Center," is at 208 W. 13th St., between Seventh and Eighth avenues (© 212/620-7310;** www.gaycenter.org). The center is the meeting place for more than 400 lesbian, gay, and bisexual organizations. You can check the online events calendar, which lists hundreds of happenings—lectures, dances, concerts, readings, films—or call for the latest. Their site offers links to gay-friendly hotels and guesthouses in and around New York, plus tons of other information; the staff is also friendly and helpful in person or over the phone.

Other good sources for lesbian and gay events are the two free weekly newspapers, *Gay City News* (www.gaycitynews.com) and the *New York Blade* (www.nyblade.com), and the free magazines *HX* (www.hx.com), *Next* (www.nextmagazine.com), and *GONYC* (www.gomag.com), which is lesbian-oriented. You'll also find lots of information on their websites.

The weekly *Time Out New York* (www.timeoutny.com) boasts a terrific gay and lesbian section. The Center (see above) publishes a monthly guide listing many events (also listed on its website).

In addition, there are lesbian and gay musical events, such as performances by the **New York City Gay Men's Chorus** (℗ 212/344-1777; www.nycgmc.org); health programs sponsored by the **Gay Men's Health Crisis** (**GMHC;** ℗ **800/ AIDS-NYC** or Hotline 212/367-1000; www.gmhc.org); the **Gay & Lesbian National Hot Line** (℗ **888/TheGLNH;** www.glnh.org), offering peer counseling and information on upcoming events; and many other organizations.

The International Gay and Lesbian Travel Association (**IGLTA;** ℗ **800/448-8550** or 954/776-2626; www.iglta.org) is the trade association for the gay and lesbian travel industry, and offers an online directory of gay- and lesbian-friendly travel businesses and tour operators.

Many agencies offer tours and travel itineraries specifically for gay and lesbian travelers. **Gay.com Travel** (℗ **800/929-2268** or 415/644-8044; www.gay.com/travel) provides regularly updated information about gay-owned, gay-oriented, and gay-friendly lodging, dining, sightseeing, and shopping establishments in destinations worldwide.

Also check out **Out Traveler** magazine, which in 2008 published *The Out Traveler: New York City* guidebook (Alyson Books). The website, **OutTraveler.com** (www.outtraveler.com), has an extensive online backlog of travel stories on New York City.

British travelers should click on the "Travel" link at **www.uk.gay.com** for advice and gay-friendly trip ideas.

The Canadian website **GayTraveler** (**gaytraveler.ca**) offers ideas and advice for gay travel all over the world.

SENIOR TRAVEL

Members of **AARP**, 601 E St. NW, Washington, DC 20049 (℗ **888/687-2277;** www.aarp.org), get discounts on hotels, airfares, and car rentals. AARP offers

members a wide range of benefits, including *AARP: The Magazine* and a newsletter. Anyone over 50 can join.

New York subway and bus fares are half-price ($1) for people 65 and older. Many museums and sights (and some theaters and performance halls) offer discounted admittance and tickets to seniors, so don't be shy about asking. Always bring an ID card, especially if you've kept your youthful glow.

Many hotels offer senior discounts; **Choice Hotels** (which include Comfort Inns), for example, gives 30% off their published rates to anyone over 50, provided you book your room through their nationwide toll-free reservations number (that is, not directly with the hotels or through a travel agent). For a complete list of Choice Hotels, visit **www.hotelchoice.com**.

Many reliable agencies and organizations target the 50-plus market. **Elderhostel** (℗ **800/454-5768;** www.elderhostel.org) arranges worldwide study programs (including some in New York City) for those age 55 and over.

Recommended publications offering travel resources and discounts for seniors include the quarterly magazine *Travel 50 & Beyond* (www.trave150andbeyond.com) and the bestselling paperback *Unbelievably Good Deals and Great Adventures That You Absolutely Can't Get Unless You're Over 50 2005–2006, 16th Edition* (McGraw-Hill), by Joan Rattner Heilman.

STUDENT TRAVEL

Check out the **International Student Travel Confederation** (**ISTC**) (www.istc.org) website for comprehensive travel services information and details on how to get an **International Student Identity Card** (**ISIC**)**,** which qualifies students for substantial savings on rail passes, plane tickets, entrance fees, and more. It also provides students with basic health and life insurance and a 24-hour help line. The card is valid for a maximum of 18 months.

Frommers.com: The Complete Travel Resource

Planning a trip or just returned? Head to **Frommers.com,** voted Best Travel Site by *PC Magazine*. We think you'll find our site indispensable before, during, and after your travels—with expert advice and tips; independent reviews of hotels, restaurants, attractions, and preferred shopping and nightlife venues; vacation giveaways; and an online booking tool. We publish the complete contents of more than 135 travel guides in our **Destinations** section, covering more than 4,000 places worldwide. Each weekday, we publish original articles that report on **Deals and News** via our free **Frommers.com Newsletters.** What's more, **Arthur Frommer** himself blogs 5 days a week, with cutting opinions about the state of travel in the modern world. We're betting you'll find our **Events** listings an invaluable resource; it's an up-to-the-minute roster of what's happening in cities everywhere—including concerts, festivals, lectures, and more. We've also added weekly **podcasts, interactive maps,** and hundreds of new images across the site. Finally, don't forget to visit our **Message Boards,** where you can join in conversations with thousands of fellow Frommer's travelers and post your trip report once you return.

You can apply for the card online or in person at **STA Travel** (✆ **800/781-4040** in North America; ✆ 132 782 in Australia; ✆ 0871 2 300 040 in the U.K.; www. statravel.com), the biggest student travel agency in the world; check out the website to locate STA Travel offices worldwide. If you're no longer a student but are still under 26, you can get an **International** **Youth Travel Card (IYTC),** which entitles you to some discounts, from the same people. **Travel CUTS** (✆ **800/592-2887;** www.travelcuts.com) offers similar services for both Canadians and U.S. residents. Irish students may prefer to turn to **USIT** (✆ **01/602-1904;** www.usit.ie), an Ireland-based specialist in student, youth, and independent travel.

10 PACKAGES FOR THE INDEPENDENT TRAVELER

Package tours are simply a way to buy the airfare, accommodations, and other elements of your trip (such as car rentals, airport transfers, and sometimes even activities) at the same time and often at discounted prices.

One good source of package deals is the airlines themselves. Most major airlines offer air/land packages, including **American Airlines Vacations** (✆ 800/321-2121; www.aavacations.com), **Delta Vacations** (✆ 800/654-6559; www.deltavacations. com), **Continental Airlines Vacations** (✆ 800/301-3800; www.covacations.com), and **United Vacations** (✆ 888/854-3899; www.unitedvacations.com). Several big **online travel agencies**—Expedia, Travelocity, Orbitz, and Lastminute.com—also do a brisk business in packages.

Travel packages are also listed in the travel section of your local Sunday newspaper. Or check ads in the national travel magazines such as *Arthur Frommer's*

Budget Travel Magazine, Travel + Leisure, National Geographic Traveler, and *Condé Nast Traveler.*

47

11 ESCORTED GENERAL-INTEREST TOURS

Escorted tours are structured group tours with a group leader. The price usually includes everything from airfare to hotels, meals, tours, admission costs, and local transportation.

If you're not a big-city person, or it's your first time in New York City, you might find your comfort level in an escorted group.

Despite the fact that escorted tours require big deposits and predetermine hotels, restaurants, and itineraries, many people derive security and peace of mind from the structure they offer. Escorted tours let travelers sit back and enjoy the trip without having to drive or worry about details. They take you to the maximum number of sights in the

minimum amount of time with the least amount of hassle. They're particularly convenient for people with limited mobility and they can be a great way to make new friends.

On the downside, you'll have little opportunity for serendipitous interactions with locals. The tours can be jampacked with activities, leaving little room for individual sightseeing, whim, or adventure—plus they often focus on the heavily touristed sites, so you miss out on many a lesser-known gem.

For more information on escorted general-interest tours, including questions to ask before booking your trip, see Frommers.com.

12 STAYING CONNECTED

TELEPHONES

Generally, hotel surcharges on long-distance and local calls are astronomical, so you're better off using your **cellphone** or a **public pay telephone.** Many convenience stores and drugstores sell **prepaid calling cards** in denominations up to $50; for international visitors these can be the least expensive way to call home. Many public pay phones at airports now accept American Express, MasterCard, and Visa credit cards. **Local calls** made from pay phones cost either 25¢ or 50¢ (no pennies, please).

That said, there aren't as many pay phones on the streets of New York City as there used to be because of the prevalence

of cellphones, and the ones that are there are often out of order.

For details on making calls to and from New York City, go to "Fast Facts," in the appendix.

CELLPHONES

Just because your cellphone works at home doesn't mean it'll work everywhere in the U.S. (thanks to our nation's fragmented cellphone system). It's a good bet that your phone will work in major cities, but take a look at your wireless company's coverage map on its website before heading out. If you need to stay in touch at a destination where you know your phone won't work, **rent** a phone that does from **InTouch**

(Tips) Hey, Google, Where's That Restaurant Again?

It's bound to happen: The day you leave this guidebook back at the hotel for an unencumbered stroll through the West Village, you'll forget the address of the lunch spot you had earmarked. If you're traveling with a mobile device, send a text message to © **46645 (GOOGL)** for a lightning-fast response. For instance, type "pink teacup new york" and within 10 seconds you'll receive a text message with the address and phone number. This nifty trick works in a range of search categories: Look up weather (type in "weather New York City"), language translations, currency conversions, movie times, and more. If your search results are off, be more specific ("the apple store meatpacking district"). For more tips, see **www.google.com/intl/en_us/mobile/sms/**. Regular text-message charges apply.

USA (© **800/872-7626;** www.intouchglobal.com) or a rental-car location, but beware that you'll pay something like $1 a minute or more for airtime.

If you're not from the U.S., you'll be appalled at the poor reach of the **GSM (Global System for Mobile Communications) wireless network,** which is used by much of the rest of the world. Your phone will probably work in most major U.S. cities; it definitely won't work in many rural areas. To see where GSM phones work in the U.S., check out www.t-mobile.com/coverage. And you may or may not be able to send SMS (text messaging) home.

VOICE-OVER INTERNET PROTOCOL (VOIP)

If you have web access while traveling, consider a broadband-based telephone service (in technical terms, **Voice over Internet Protocol,** or **VoIP**) such as Skype (www.skype.com) or Vonage (www.vonage.com), which allow you to make free international calls from your laptop or in a cybercafe. Neither service requires the people you're calling to also have that service (though there are fees if they do not). Check the websites for details.

INTERNET & E-MAIL
With Your Own Computer

More and more hotels, resorts, airports, cafes, and retailers are going Wi-Fi (wireless fidelity), becoming "hotspots" that offer high-speed Wi-Fi access for free or charge a small fee for usage. Most laptops sold today have built-in wireless capability. You should have no trouble finding Wi-Fi hotspots throughout the city, including free coverage in many hotels (and hotel public spaces) and airports. To find public Wi-Fi hotspots in New York City, go to **www.jiwire.com**; its Hotspot Finder holds the world's largest directory of public wireless hotspots.

For dial-up access, most business-class hotels in the U.S. offer dataports for laptop modems, and a few thousand hotels in the U.S. and Europe now offer free high-speed Internet access.

Without Your Own Computer

Most major airports have **Internet kiosks** or Wi-Fi areas that provide basic Web access for a per-minute/hour/day fee that's usually much higher than cybercafe prices. Check out copy shops like **FedEx Office**

Where to Check Your E-mail in the City That Never Sleeps

If your hotel doesn't offer free access to its business center or a terminal in the lobby to check your e-mail (and many do), where can you go to check it if you don't have a computer with you?

All branches of the **New York Public Library** (www.nypl.org) feature computers that offer free access to the Internet, electronic databases, library catalogs, and Microsoft Office. They are also supposed to offer Wi-Fi, but we've found that having it listed on their website and actually having it operative can be two different things.

More free access is available at the **Times Square Visitors Center,** 1560 Broadway, between 46th and 47th streets (✆ **212/768-1560;** daily 8am–8pm); you can use computer terminals to send e-mails courtesy of Yahoo!, and you can even send an electronic postcard with a photo of yourself home to Mom.

Open 24/7 in the heart of Times Square, **easyInternetCafé** ★, 234 W. 42nd St., between Seventh and Eighth avenues (✆ **212/398-0775;** www.easy everything.com/map/nyc1.html), is the first stateside branch of a worldwide chain of Internet cafes. Boasting flatscreen monitors and a superfast T3 connection, this mammoth place makes accessing the Internet cheap through the economy of scale: Access is available for as little as $1, and the length of time that buck buys you fluctuates depending on the occupancy at the time you log on. This will generally work out to the cheapest Web time you can buy in the city.

CyberCafe (www.cyber-cafe.com), in Times Square at 250 W. 49th St., between Broadway and Eighth Avenue (✆ 212/333-4109), is more expensive at $6.40 per half-hour, with a half-hour minimum (you're billed $3.20 for every subsequent 15 min.). But their T1 connectivity gives you superfast access, and they offer a full range of other cyber, copy, fax, and printing services.

FedEx Office (www.fedex.com) charges 30¢ per minute ($15 per hour) and there are dozens of locations around town. In addition, an increasing number of delis and copy shops frequently stick an INTERNET sign in the window, and you can log on in a unit wedged into a corner next to the ATM for a couple bucks, while you drink your genuine New York City deli coffee.

which offers computer stations with fully loaded software (as well as Wi-Fi).

For help locating cybercafes and other establishments where you can go for Internet access, see the box "Where to Check Your E-mail in the City That Never Sleeps," below.

Getting to Know
New York City

At first glance, New York can be a very intimidating town, especially when you have a flock of youngsters under your wing. Take time from the outset to get a grasp of the city layout and the best navigating methods.

---

1 ORIENTATION

VISITOR INFORMATION

New York City visitor centers are scattered around Manhattan; the main one is the newly renovated **NYC Official Visitor Information Center** at 810 Seventh Ave. between 52nd and 53rd streets (© **212/484-1222;** open daily 7am–7pm). There are also kiosks in **City Hall Park** (Broadway and Park Row, downtown) and **Chinatown** (at the triangle where Canal, Walker, and Baxter sts. meet). Stop by to pick up maps, brochures, and sightseeing suggestions, along with "twofers" for savings on Broadway and Off-Broadway plays. You can call the 24-hour information hot line of **NYC & Company** (the official New York Convention & Visitors Bureau) at © **800/NYC-VISIT** (692-8474) or visit its website, **http://nycvisit.com.** Helpful staff members at © **212/484-1222** will answer questions during daily office hours.

The **Times Square Alliance** (www.timessquarenyc.org) is a good source for information about Broadway theater, Midtown hotels and restaurants, and special events; it operates the **Times Square Information Center** (Seventh Ave. btwn 46th and 47th sts.; open 8am–8pm). For recorded listings of **Lincoln Center** events, call © **212/546-2656** or visit its website at www.lincolncenter.org. For upcoming **events in city parks,** call © **888/NY-PARKS** or visit www.nycgovparks.org; for **Central Park events,** go to www. centralpark.com.

CITY LAYOUT

Major Arteries in Manhattan The limited-access **FDR Drive** runs along Manhattan's East River shore, from the Brooklyn Battery Tunnel (which links to Brooklyn) north to the Triborough Bridge (which links to Queens and to I-95. It was officially renamed the Robert F. Kennedy Memorial Bridge in 2008). The **West Side Highway** goes from Battery Park up along the Hudson, eventually becoming the limited-access **Henry Hudson Parkway** running all the way to Manhattan's northern tip and on through the Bronx (Riverdale), where it becomes the **Saw Mill Parkway.**

Broadway is Manhattan's spine, beginning at Battery Park and angling north all the way through Washington Heights (from there on, as U.S. 9, it continues all the way to Albany). Since Manhattan's axis is skewed to the northeast, Broadway—which runs due north—seems to run at an angle, and every time it crosses a major avenue in the Manhattan grid, there's a significant traffic junction: **Union Square** at 14th Street, **Madison**

HARLEM ↑   ↑ EAST HARLEM (EL BARRIO)   ↑ THE BRONX

YORKVILLE

86th St.

American Museum of Natural History

Metropolitan Museum of Art

Central Park

79th St.

UPPER EAST SIDE

72nd St.

QUEENS

West End Ave.

Broadway

Columbus Ave.

Central Park West

Fifth Ave.

Lexington Ave.

First Ave.

FDR Drive

Roosevelt Island

UPPER WEST SIDE

West Side Hwy.

Lincoln Center

59th St.

Queensboro Bridge

CLINTON (HELL'S KITCHEN)

Rockefeller Center

MIDTOWN EAST

ⓘ

Eighth Ave.

ⓘ

TIMES SQUARE

42nd St.

Grand Central Terminal

Queens-Midtown Tunnel

Lincoln Tunnel

Port Authority Terminal

MURRAY HILL

34th St.

Eleventh Ave.

Seventh Ave.

BROOKLYN

Penn Station

Empire State Building

GRAMERCY PARK

23rd St.

Broadway

FDR Drive

East River

CHELSEA

FLATIRON DISTRICT

Union Square

MEATPACKING DISTRICT

14th St.

Hudson River

GREENWICH VILLAGE

Washington Square Park

EAST VILLAGE

NOHO

The Bowery

Houston St.

THE LOWER EAST SIDE

Williamsburg Bridge

SOHO

NOLITA

Delancey St.

Hudson St.

Broadway

LITTLE ITALY

Grand St.

East Broadway

Canal St.

Canal St.

West St.

Holland Tunnel

TRIBECA

CHINATOWN

Manhattan Bridge

Chambers St.

Park Row

Brooklyn Bridge

Battery Park City

World Trade Center site

ⓘ Information

FINANCIAL DISTRICT

South Street Seaport

BROOKLYN

0   1/2 mi

0   0.5 km

Brooklyn-Battery Tunnel

Battery Park

STATEN ISLAND ↓

A Street by Any Other Name

When the street sign says ...	It's the same as ...
Amsterdam Avenue	Tenth Avenue (above 59th St.)
Avenue of the Americas	Sixth Avenue
Central Park North	West 110th Street (btwn Fifth Ave. and Central Park West)
Central Park South	59th Street (btwn Fifth and Eighth aves.)
Central Park West	Eighth Avenue (from 59th to 110th sts.)
Columbus Avenue	Ninth Avenue (above 59th St.)
Fashion Avenue	Seventh Avenue (from 34th to 42nd sts.)
Park Avenue	Fourth Avenue (above 14th St.)
St. Mark's Place	8th Street (from Third Ave. to Ave. A)
West End Avenue	Eleventh Avenue (from 59th to 107th sts.)

Square at 23rd Street, **Herald Square** at 34th Street, **Times Square** at 42nd Street, **Columbus Circle** at 59th Street, **Lincoln Square** at 66th Street, **Verdi Square** at 72nd Street, and **Straus Park** at 106th Street. Above 59th Street, where Central Park divides Manhattan, Broadway is the West Side's main drag.

The other big avenues in the grid are one-way, with the exception of the Upper West Side's **Central Park West** and the East Side's **Park Avenue.** The avenues that run uptown (north) are **First Avenue, Third Avenue, Madison Avenue, Sixth Avenue** (also called **Ave. of the Americas**), **Eighth Avenue,** and **Tenth Avenue** (called **Amsterdam Ave.** above 59th St.). To go downtown (south), take **Second Avenue, Lexington Avenue, Fifth Avenue, Seventh Avenue, Ninth Avenue** (called **Columbus Ave.** above 59th St.), or **Eleventh Avenue** (called **West End Ave.** from 59th to 107th sts.).

In the older areas of town, below 8th Street, the grid doesn't apply, and you'll need a map to navigate. **Hudson Street** is a major northbound thoroughfare on the West Side; on the East Side it's **Fourth Avenue** (the southern section of Park Ave.), which is created when the **Bowery** splits into Third and Fourth avenues.

Most cross streets in the grid are one-way; generally, in Manhattan even-numbered streets are eastbound and odd-numbered streets are westbound. The following major cross streets, however, are two-way: **Canal Street,** which cuts across the island from the Manhattan Bridge to the Holland Tunnel; **Houston Street,** which funnels traffic from the Williamsburg Bridge to the Holland Tunnel; and **14th Street, 23rd Street, 34th Street, 42nd Street, 57th Street, 59th Street** (aka Central Park South), **72nd Street, 79th Street, 86th Street, 96th Street,** and **110th Street** (aka Central Park North). Above the park, **125th Street** is Harlem's major two-way commercial street.

Central Park bisects Manhattan between 59th Street and 110th Street, dividing the Upper East Side from the Upper West Side. To cross Central Park **from the Upper East Side,** your choices are 66th Street, 72nd Street (open weekday rush hours only), 79th Street, 85th Street, and 97th Street. If you're going east **from the Upper West Side,** your options are 65th Street, 81st Street, 86th Street, and 96th Street. All other car entrances to the park feed into the circular drive, open only during weekday rush hours.

Tips   **Getting Oriented**

Cross streets are listed for every destination in this book, but be sure to ask for the cross street (or avenue) if you're ever calling for an address.

When you give a taxi driver an address, always specify the cross streets. New Yorkers, even most cab drivers, probably wouldn't know where to find 994 Second Ave., but they do know where to find 51st and Second. If you're heading to the restaurant La Bonne Soup, for example, tell them that it's on 55th Street between Fifth and Sixth avenues. The exact number (in this case, no. 48) is given only as a further precision.

Major Arteries in the Outer Boroughs   The **Grand Central Parkway** leads from the Triborough Bridge to LaGuardia Airport, in northern Queens, and on to Long Island. The **Long Island Expressway (I-495)** goes from the Queens Midtown Tunnel across Queens, through Forest Hills and Flushing, and out to Long Island. **Northern Boulevard** is one of Queens's major commercial thoroughfares.

The **Brooklyn-Queens Expressway**—known as the BQE—runs north-south, linking Brooklyn and Queens; you can get on it from the Grand Central Parkway, from the 59th Street Bridge (also called the Queensboro Bridge), from the Queens-Midtown Tunnel, and from the three Brooklyn-Manhattan bridges: the Williamsburg, the Manhattan, and the Brooklyn. At the southern end of Brooklyn, the BQE links with the **Verrazano Bridge** (toll $9 westbound only) from Staten Island, then (as the **Belt Parkway**) swings around the coast past Coney Island and the Rockaways, feeding into **Southern Parkway,** which heads out to Long Island. Radiating out from Brooklyn Heights, **Atlantic Avenue, Flatbush Avenue,** and (starting near Prospect Park) **Ocean Parkway** fan out across Brooklyn.

The **Cross-Bronx Expressway (I-95)** is the major highway cutting across the Bronx; the **Bronx River Parkway** runs up through Bronx Park, where you'll find the Bronx Zoo and the Botanical Garden.

MANHATTAN NEIGHBORHOODS IN BRIEF

Manhattan was settled from its southern tip northward, so the oldest area is **Lower Manhattan,** roughly everything south of Canal Street. Within this, the **Financial District,** concentrated around Wall Street and lower Broadway, has pretty much obscured traces of the early colonial settlement with its battery of skyscrapers, but you'll still find a few venerable churches tucked away, and some of the skyscrapers themselves are early-20th-century landmarks. The only really historic quarter left is on the East River waterfront at

South Street Seaport. Southwest of the Seaport, you'll find **City Hall,** other municipal buildings, and an imposing set of courthouses clustered around **Foley Square.** Over on the Hudson side of the narrow island, you'll get some open green space at Battery Park and the planned community of **Battery Park City,** which has a great riverside promenade. **Ground Zero,** the site of the World Trade Center tragedy, lies just inland from Battery Park City. The nickname **TriBeCa** derives from *Tri*angle *Be*low *Ca*nal Street, but the label is

Value Free New York City Tours

If you'd like to tour a specific neighborhood with an expert guide, call **Big Apple Greeter** (© **212/669-8159;** www.bigapplegreeter.org) at least 1 week ahead of your arrival. This nonprofit organization has specially trained volunteers who take visitors around town for a free 2- to 4-hour tour of a particular neighborhood. And they say New York isn't friendly!

used for only the northwestern chunk of that triangle, a cool neighborhood of spacious, uncrowded streets and converted industrial lofts dotted with kid-friendly restaurants, parks, and shops.

Above South Street Seaport and the courts, **Chinatown** occupies the East River side of the below-Canal area, but it burst its boundaries long ago to spill north of Canal Street, engulfing the old tenements of **Little Italy,** which still clings to Mulberry Street as its main drag. East of Little Italy lays the **Lower East Side,** for years the Jewish immigrant district, more recently a hot spot for young urban bohemians. To the west of Little Italy, a derelict 19th-century industrial zone was converted in the 1970s to the lofts and boutiques of artsy **SoHo** (*So*uth of *Ho*uston St.— pronounced, by the way, "*How*-stun," never "*Hew*-stun").

Above Houston Street you enter the Villages—**Greenwich Village,** from Broadway west to the Hudson River; and the **East Village,** from Broadway on east across Avenues A, B, C, and D. Greenwich Village still has a certain bohemian cachet, and its quiet side streets, with their vintage architecture, make a fine place to ramble. The East Village is funkier and grittier, just the place to bring teenagers who think their parents are so uncool they don't want to be seen with them. (Just walk five paces behind, okay?) Teens may also want to hang out in the New York University area, which sprawls around the Village's

focal point, Washington Square Park, or in the now-chic northwest corner of the West Village, still called the Meatpacking District for its (ever-dwindling) butchers' trade.

Above 14th Street the Manhattan grid falls into place, and the city starts to get more buttoned-down. Between 14th and 30th streets, **Chelsea** occupies the area from Sixth Avenue west. This is a very hot area for art galleries, fashion-industry types, and gays; at its far west end, the Chelsea Piers sports complex on the river is a major draw for families. East of Sixth Avenue is what's called the **Flatiron District** (named after the famous Flatiron Building at 23rd St. and Broadway), a trendy area for restaurants and nightlife, and the quiet older neighborhoods around **Gramercy Park,** the city's only private park. North of Gramercy lays **Murray Hill,** a largely residential neighborhood.

Midtown is the major business district, sprawling across the island from about 34th Street to 59th Street. Big department stores and elegant shops march up Fifth Avenue, with a handful of museums set on side streets; the **Theater District** clusters around Times Square (42nd St. and Broadway). By far the greatest number of Manhattan hotels is in Midtown, and many restaurants as well. But with its crowded sidewalks and restaurants packed with impatient workaday New Yorkers, it's not necessarily where families want to concentrate their time. Come here to

Tips ## Manhattan's Bridges & Tunnels

Manhattan's an island—to get on or off it, you have to go over or under the water. Going clockwise around the island, starting from the northern tip, you can take the **Henry Hudson Bridge** (on the Henry Hudson Pkwy.; $2.25 toll), the **Triborough Bridge** ($4.50 toll), the **59th Street/Queensboro Bridge** (no toll), or the **Queens-Midtown Tunnel** (part of I-495; $4.50 toll). A trio of toll-free bridges into Brooklyn—the **Williamsburg,** the **Manhattan,** and the **Brooklyn**—all connect handily with the Brooklyn-Queens Expressway, as does the **Brooklyn Battery Tunnel** ($4.50 toll) at the island's southern tip. Two big tunnels cross the Hudson on Manhattan's west side—the **Holland Tunnel** ($6 toll only into Manhattan), which funnels into Canal or Houston Street; and the **Lincoln Tunnel** ($6 toll only into Manhattan), which funnels into 40th Street—and the **George Washington Bridge** (part of I-95; $6 toll only into Manhattan) crosses above the water up at 175th Street.

Drivers can zip through bridge and tunnel tollbooths much faster if they have **E-ZPass,** a small device that drivers can post on their windshields to have tolls electronically deducted from a credit card account. Certain lanes at toll stations are designated for E-ZPass users only, so stay alert (there are no toll attendants at those booths). To set up an account, call © **800/333-TOLL** (333-8655) or go online at **www.e-zpassny.com**. Note that E-ZPass devices are also compatible with the New Jersey, Pennsylvania, and Massachusetts turnpikes; the New York State Thruway; Delaware River bridges; and the Atlantic City Expressway.

shop and to gawk at the tall buildings; but venture away from Midtown, and you'll get a better idea of how New York families experience the city.

The **Upper West Side** occupies the part of Manhattan directly west of Central Park—here you'll find great museums for kids, lots of kid-friendly restaurants, toy stores, and playgrounds in both Central and Riverside parks. The **Upper East Side,** everything east of Central Park, is also very child-oriented but less casual; you'll see packs of uniformed kids from tony private schools gathering in pizza parlors and Gaps. The East Side is rich in museums, especially along the park on Fifth Avenue.

Above Central Park to the west is **Morningside Heights,** dominated by Columbia University and two magnificent churches—Riverside Church and the Cathedral of St. John the Divine. East of Morningside Park, **Harlem** takes over the island north of Central Park. Many tourists visit Harlem as part of a guided tour, though you can certainly check it out on your own. However, your kids' interest in the social-history aspects of a Harlem guided tour may lag if they're under 10. Unless you're visiting The Cloisters (the Metropolitan Museum's medieval-art branch in Fort Tryon Park), there's not much reason for you to tour **Washington Heights,** which lies above Harlem.

THE OUTER BOROUGHS IN BRIEF

New York City's other four boroughs surround the island of Manhattan. To the north and east lies the **Bronx,** which only partly deserves its bad rap as a crime-infested slum. Parts of the Bronx are rotten indeed, but the Bronx also includes suburban Riverdale, along the Hudson, and the middle-class Fordham area, anchored by Fordham University and Bronx Park (where the Bronx Zoo and the New York Botanical Garden are). Arthur Avenue is home to a small but choice Little Italy enclave of wonderful restaurants, food markets, and Italian pastry shops. The New York Yankees are called the Bronx Bombers because Yankee Stadium is at 161st Street in the Bronx; crowds of baseball fans make it safe around game time, and the subway takes you directly to the stadium.

The landmass directly east of Manhattan (the western end of Long Island) contains the two most populous boroughs: Brooklyn and Queens. Immortalized (rightly or wrongly) as Archie Bunker territory, **Queens** is the city's great middle-class borough, where hardworking immigrant groups have colonized various neighborhoods from Astoria to Flushing. Directly across the river from Manhattan, Long Island City and Williamsburg are havens for young artists, and Forest Hills in the middle of Queens is a manicured residential area. Farther-out areas of Queens, like St. Albans, Little Neck, and Douglaston, are basically suburban neighborhoods.

Brooklyn on the whole is more urban and edgy, though it has some of the city's loveliest residential areas, notably brownstone-lined Brooklyn Heights, right across the Brooklyn Bridge from Manhattan, and nearby gentrified row house neighborhoods such as Cobble Hill, Carroll Gardens, Fort Greene, and Park Slope (the last has the advantage of bordering Prospect Park, Central Park's Brooklyn cousin). Facing Staten Island across the Narrows, Bay Ridge is a vast middle-class enclave; Brighton Beach, on Brooklyn's southern shore, is a former Jewish area now heavily colonized by immigrant Russians. But other Brooklyn neighborhoods, like Bedford-Stuyvesant, Brownsville, and East New York, aren't for the uninitiated. If you visit Brooklyn, know where you're going.

That leaves **Staten Island,** the most suburban of the boroughs, the one that's always threatening to secede from the city—which actually makes sense, because Staten Island is geographically part of New Jersey. Staten Island's attractions for visitors—the restored historic village at Richmond Town, a

---

⦅Fun Facts⦆ Fun Fact

Population-wise, even if they were counted as separate cities, New York City's five boroughs would still rank high in the list of U.S. cities. Brooklyn on its own would be the nation's third-largest city, right after Los Angeles and Chicago; Queens would be fourth-largest, and Manhattan sixth (just after Houston), with the Bronx ranking ninth right after Phoenix. Even relatively less populous Staten Island would come in 40th, after Albuquerque, New Mexico, and before Kansas City, Missouri.

zoo, a children's museum, a couple of historic houses—don't lure many New Yorkers across the water, which suits most Staten Islanders just fine. Still, the Staten Island Ferry ride is one of those classic New York things to do, a pleasant way to spend an hour or so crossing the harbor—and it's free.

2 GETTING AROUND

Frankly, Manhattan's transportation systems are a marvel. It's simply miraculous that so many people can gather on this little island and move around it. For the most part, you can get where you're going pretty quickly and easily using some combination of subways, buses, and cabs.

But between traffic gridlock and subway delays, sometimes you just can't get there from here—unless you **walk.** New York is one of the great walking cities of the world, and walking can sometimes be the fastest way to navigate the island. During rush hours, you'll easily beat car traffic while on foot, as taxis and buses stop and groan at gridlocked corners. You'll also see a lot more by walking than you will if you ride beneath the street in the subway or fly by in a cab. So pack your most comfortable shoes and hit the pavement—it's the best, cheapest, and most appealing way to experience the city.

BY SUBWAY

Not only are subway stations brighter and better lit than they used to be, but the trains themselves are also now cleaner, graffiti-free, and blessedly air-conditioned in summer. Rush-hour crowds can still be pushy, and derelicts, panhandlers, and thugs still disturb riders' peace from time to time. Trains don't run as often as they should, either. But the subway is truly a viable, fast alternative, especially for long daytime rides, when you'll save time as well as money by gliding under the streets instead of getting mired in city traffic.

The **Metropolitan Transit Authority** (𝄢 718/330-1234; www.mta.nyc.ny.us) operates the city's buses and subways, which run 24 hours. Even mildly adventurous visitors should feel comfortable underground from 7am to 8pm—however, the morning and evening rush hours (generally 8–9:30am and 5–6:30pm weekdays) make the trains so crowded you'd be better off not traveling then, especially with a family to squeeze in. Currently the **fare** is $2, and for your two bucks you can ride as long and far as you like, changing lines at any of more than 50 transfer points. Children under 44 inches tall ride free; in practice, kids under 6 can just duck under the turnstile bar, and no one challenges them. (In some neighborhoods, even 12-year-olds can duck under the turnstile and no one will blink.)

New Yorkers use multiride **MetroCards,** with magnetic strips that automatically deduct one fare every time you slip them through a groove in a turnstile; each time you run your card through a turnstile, your remaining balance is displayed. MetroCards can be bought in various denominations from $3 to $80 and can be refilled at fare booths or at vending machines in many stations. Up to four passengers traveling together can use the same MetroCard—just slide it through the turnstile once for each rider.

Bonuses of 20% are offered for buying MetroCards of $10 or more; unlimited-ride passes are also available, costing $76 for 30 days, $24 for 7 days, and $7 for 1 day (expires at 3am). All of these except the 1-day pass (the Fun Pass) are available at fare booths and vending machines; the Fun Pass can be bought only in the vending

4

Art Down Under

Many Manhattan subway stations were renovated in the 1990s, and more will be in the new century. The tile walls along waiting platforms often feature work by local artists or symbols appropriate for that particular neighborhood. Some of our favorites: the fossils and critters crawling over the walls of the **West 81st Street** stop on the B, C lines (beneath the American Museum of Natural History); the artwork by local schoolchildren at the **West 86th Street** stop on the 1, 9 line and at the **Columbus Circle** station (A, B, C, D, 1, 9 trains); the scenes from famous operas and ballets at **West 66th Street/Lincoln Center** station on the 1, 9 line; the fanciful cartoon characters peeking out from the floors and ceilings of the **14th Street** stop on the A, C, E lines; the sea creatures slithering over the **Houston Street** station (1, 9 line), and the scurrying beavers at the **Astor Place** stop on the 6 line (obscure reference: Astor Place is named after 19th-c. tycoon John Jacob Astor, whose fortune originally came from beaver furs).

machines or at newsstands and shops around town (look for blue-and-yellow METRO-CARDS SOLD HERE signs). *Only one catch:* Unlimited-ride passes cannot be used by more than one passenger, so to take advantage of the discounts, you'll have to buy each member of your family a separate card.

MetroCards allow riders **free transfers** to and from city buses. If you're coming from a city bus, just slide your card through the subway turnstile's groove, and the machine should indicate that this is a transfer. Note that transfers do expire after a certain amount of time; sometimes you'll be pleasantly surprised when you reenter the system half an hour after one ride to find that your second ride registers as a transfer, but don't count on it.

Maps are posted inside stations (usually out by the token booths, so you can make sure where you're going before you enter) and in most cars. Near the token booths, many stations now also feature detailed street maps of the immediate area, so you can get oriented before you hit the street.

BY BUS

There are two ways to pay your $2 bus fare: with a **MetroCard** (the same one you use for the subway) or $2 in exact change (no pennies). You can't buy MetroCards onboard, however; you have to get them at a subway station. Children under 44 inches tall ride free (there's a line near the driver's seat against which to measure your child), but in practice kids under 6 are usually allowed to ride free, regardless of height.

To transfer for free to a second bus, dip your MetroCard into the farebox slot; if you've just come from the subway or another bus, the machine will register this as a transfer (reading "XFER OK" or "2 XFERS OK" if two passengers are using the same card). Transfers expire after a certain amount of time, but you probably can slip into a shop between buses and still have your second ride count as a transfer. *Note:* If more than one passenger is using the same MetroCard, when you are transferring to a second bus or train, *dip only once for the transfer.* (Dip a second time, and an additional fare will be deducted.)

If you're using coins, request a transfer card from the driver of the first bus *when you pay your fare.*

Each bus's destination is displayed above its front windshield; routes are posted at most bus stops. Look for blue-and-red bus-stop signs along sidewalks; at transfer points, a glassed-in shelter often accompanies them. Within Manhattan, bus stops are stationed every 2 or 3 blocks along avenues or major crosstown streets. Once you're riding a bus, if you wish to get off at the next stop, press any one of several electronic strips posted around the bus. A sign at the front of the bus should light up, reading STOP REQUESTED, and the driver will then pull over at the next stop.

If you're trying to get around the downtown area, you should also know about the free **Downtown Connection** bus service organized by the Downtown Alliance (℃ **212/566-6700;** www.downtownny.com). Running about every 10 to 15 minutes between 10am and 7:30pm, these buses travel from the northern end of Battery Park City around Manhattan's southern tip to South Street Seaport, making 16 stops en route. For a downloadable bus-route map, go to the website, and click on "Plan Your Visit," then "Getting Around," and then "Downtown Connection."

BY TAXI

The only taxis authorized to pick up passengers hailing them on the street are **yellow cabs,** which have an official Taxi and Limousine Commission medallion screwed onto the hood. So-called gypsy cabs, working for car services, sometimes stop illegally for passengers on the street; but because they have no meter, you'll have to negotiate your own fare with the driver, and you'll have no legal recourse if there's a problem. To know whether a yellow taxi is available, look for the lit-up center sign on the roof of the cab; off-duty cabs (side sections of the roof sign lit) may pick up passengers at their own discretion.

Taxi meters calculate the fare: currently $2.50 when you get in, plus 40¢ for each one-fifth of a mile or 120 seconds of waiting time in traffic. The meter should "click" every 4 blocks in normal traffic or once every crosstown block. There's an extra 50¢ charge from 8pm to 6am, a $1 surcharge for peak weekday service (Mon–Fri 4–8pm), and passengers pay any bridge or tunnel tolls. A 15% to 20% tip is expected, unless the service is bad. For complaints or inquiries about lost property, dial ℃ **311** or go online at **www. nyc.gov/taxi**.

Technically, a taxi doesn't have to take more than four passengers (with adults, this is possible only if one sits in the front seat next to the driver). But if your kids are small, most cabbies will let you all squeeze in, which is good news for families of five. All New York yellow cabs are supposed to have working seat belts. If your kids are car-seat-size, technically you could haul around a car seat and strap it in every time you get in a cab, but the only person I've ever known to do this did it only once, when cabbing her newborn home from the hospital. Most cabbies are cool about letting kids sit on laps or even kneel on the seat to look out the cab window. Occasionally you'll get one who'll hassle you about your 2-year-old getting his sneakers on the backseat upholstery. I never fight the cabbies on this one—hey, it's their cab.

BY FERRY

The free **Staten Island Ferry** (℃ **718/727-2508**) at Battery Park remains the best way to enjoy views of the Manhattan skyline, New York Harbor, and the Statue of Liberty. To reach the South Ferry terminal, take the R, W train to Whitehall Street or the 1, 9 to South Ferry. If you don't have any business on Staten Island, simply disembark from the ferry, go through the turnstiles, and turn around for the return trip.

The **New York Waterway Ferry System** (ⓒ **800/53-FERRY;** www.nywaterway.com) runs a number of commuter ferries. Most cost $3 to $5 one-way; they link New Jersey (from Jersey City, Weehawken, Hoboken, or Liberty Harbor) to Midtown (W. 39th St.) and Downtown (the World Financial Center in Battery Park City or Pier 11 at Wall St.).

New York Water Taxi offers a seasonal weekend hop-on, hop-off water-taxi experience on the New York waterways (ⓒ **201/985-8000;** www.nywatertaxi.com). It makes stops all over Manhattan at regular intervals. Stops include the South Street Seaport, World Financial Center, Chelsea Piers, West 44th Street, and East 35th Street—check the website for the full schedule of stops. A 1-day pass is $20 adults, $15 children. You can purchase tickets on the boat or online. New York Water Taxis also runs commuter ferries at rush hours ($3–$10 one-way) and harbor cruises.

BY CAR

First of all, I do not recommend getting around the city by car—it's the least efficient way to get around town. But if you must drive, keep in mind that car-rental rates at the airports are often lower than those in Midtown. All the big national chains operate several locations, including at all three major airports: **Avis** (ⓒ 800/331-1212; www.avis. com), **Budget** (ⓒ 800/527-0700; www.budget.com), **Dollar** (ⓒ 800/800-3665; www. dollar.com), **Enterprise** (ⓒ 800/261-7331; www.enterprise.com), **Hertz** (ⓒ 800/654-3131; www.hertz.com), and **National** (ⓒ 800/227-7368; www.nationalcar.com).

If you're visiting from abroad and plan to rent a car in the United States, you probably won't need the services of an additional automobile organization. If you're planning to buy or borrow a car, automobile-association membership is recommended. **AAA, the American Automobile Association** (ⓒ **800/222-4357;** http://travel.aaa.com), is the country's largest auto club and supplies its members with maps, insurance, and, most important, emergency road service. *Note:* Foreign driver's licenses are usually recognized in the U.S., but you should get an international one if your home license is not in English.

Parking   On the streets, look for parking signs stating what days or hours you can park curbside. In Midtown and other spots where police feel it's vital to keep traffic flowing, your illegally parked car will be towed in minutes, so don't even think of violating parking laws. In residential neighborhoods, "alternate side of the street parking" means that everybody's expected to shift their cars to the opposite curb once a day. Officers are required to complete any parking ticket they start to fill out, so pleading will do no good. If your car does get towed, call the **Borough Tow Pound** at ⓒ **212/971-0770** to find out where it is; you'll have to pay $185 in cash to retrieve it.

Space is so tight in New York that some residents are willing to pay over $400 a month for parking-garage spaces. Public garages dot Manhattan streets every 2 blocks or so, with rates averaging about $12 to $15 for less than 2 hours, $20 to $30 for half a day, and $40 overnight. Better-known commercial parking-garage operators include **Rapid Park, Manhattan Parking,** and **GMC.** Prices are sometimes lower at night or on weekends in business districts and during the day in residential areas; outdoor lots are less expensive, when you can find them. Few hotels offer parking. Some Midtown hotels provide valet parking at about $35 per night, often with the requirement that guests not take their cars from the garage between arrival and final departure. The city government's website at **www.nyc.gov** provides maps of licensed parking facilities, as well as information about how to obtain the **NYC Parking Card** (ⓒ **718/786-7042**), which gives you access to certain municipal metered parking. Otherwise, street metered parking costs 25¢ for 10 minutes—if you can find a free space, which isn't easy.

Driving Rules   Every passenger is supposed to wear a seat belt, and all kids 5 and under should be in car seats of some kind. Except for major crosstown streets and a few north-south avenues (Broadway, Park Ave.), most of Manhattan's streets are one-way, so sometimes you'll have to circle around a couple of blocks to get to a specific address. Right turns on red are *not* legal, and left turns are prohibited in some major intersections (watch for signs). Several major avenues have designated bus lanes (marked on the pavement), which are off-limits to cars during rush hours.

Midtown Manhattan streets are prone to the phenomenon known as *gridlock*. Beware of edging into an intersection in slow-moving traffic—if you don't manage to get through the intersection before the light changes, you can get stranded in the path of oncoming cross-traffic. If a police officer's watching, you may be ticketed for "blocking the box."

3 PLANNING YOUR OUTINGS

Everything is relatively close together in Manhattan, but if you're traveling by cab, traffic jams can make even a few blocks' travel take half an hour; waiting for frequent changes of buses or subways can add up to lots of wasted time; and plodding long distances on foot could tire out the kids (or you) before you get to the sights you want to see. Instead, plan carefully and you may be able to spend the entire day within a few blocks' radius, wasting little time on street travel. If you do have to hop from one part of town to another, don't underestimate travel time—snarled traffic or sluggish subways or buses can make a 40-block journey seem to take forever.

Prime areas for families are the **Upper West Side,** with the American Museum of Natural History and the Children's Museum of Manhattan; **SoHo,** with the Children's Museum of the Arts and the Fire Museum; **Midtown,** where you'll find the Sony Wonder Technology Lab, Rockefeller Center, the Empire State Building, and the Museum of Modern Art; **Lower Manhattan,** with South Street Seaport; and the Upper East Side stretch of Fifth Avenue known as **Museum Mile.** If you're going to **Brooklyn** to see the Botanic Garden or Prospect Park Zoo, take in the Transit Museum and Brooklyn Heights on the same day. The same ferry goes to both the **Statue of Liberty** and **Ellis Island,** so it's a natural to do both the same day—but after waiting in all those lines, you probably won't have time to do much else that day. The **Bronx Zoo** and the **New York Botanical Garden** are right next to each other, but it'd be pretty exhausting to do both sprawling venues in a day.

FINDING A RESTROOM
If you've got a recently toilet-trained toddler in tow, better think ahead, because in Manhattan it's not easy to find a bathroom at sudden notice. The **Times Square subway**

A Museum Note

One thing to take into account is museum closing days—many are closed on Monday. For a list of those that will be open, see "Rainy Days & Mondays," in chapter 7.

station does have four clean attended bathrooms, for which there's often a line; **Grand Central Terminal** has a few, but they're not what you'd call clean. Restrooms can be found in **Central Park** and **Riverside Park** (see chapter 8 for locations), as well as in **Bryant Park,** which is at 42nd Street and Sixth Avenue behind the **New York Public Library;** the library itself has nice large bathrooms. Another option may be to use the bathrooms at various skyscrapers' shopping atriums, notably those at the **Sony Building** (56th St. and Madison Ave.), **Trump Tower** (56th St. and Fifth Ave.), the **Citicorp Building** (btwn Lexington and Third aves. and 53rd and 54th sts.), and the **Time-Warner Center** at Columbus Circle (59th St. and Columbus Ave.). **Barnes & Noble** bookstores, which are all around the city (see chapter 10), usually have decent bathrooms available. And here's one good thing about the number of **Starbucks** coffee shops dotting Manhattan: Nobody seems to mind if you stroll in just to use the bathroom. Major hotel lobbies are other good bets, although some of them require guest-room card keys for entry. In a pinch, if your child looks very distressed, you may be able to talk sympathetic waiters or store owners into letting you use their facilities.

Best advice: Always use the potty at your hotel before you leave, and stop in the restroom before you leave any museum or restaurant.

Family-Friendly Accommodations

One big problem families have had with New York hotels is that most are in Midtown, between 30th and 59th streets—just about the least desirable part of town for parents to stay in with their children. There's traffic, there's noise, there's hardly any greenery, and there's little resident population to fill the sidewalks at night. Besides, Midtown's tourist attractions—the Theater District, Fifth Avenue and Madison Avenue shopping, gourmet restaurants—don't matter so much when you've got kids in tow. Of course, Midtown does have some superb hotels whose facilities and service level more than compensate for the location; there are also decent moderately priced hotels that cater well to families. But the list of hotels I recommend is deliberately skewed to include more choices in other neighborhoods. If you can, why not stay near Central Park or the American Museum of Natural History or the Metropolitan Museum of Art? Lower-Manhattan hotels are close to South Street Seaport, the Statue of Liberty/Ellis Island ferry, and Hudson River Park, and they often have incredible weekend discount packages.

Which brings us to the other big problem: cost. Manhattan hotels sit on some very expensive real estate, pay staff wages in a top urban job market, and, because they're often the flagships of various lodging chains, definitely tilt toward the high end of the luxury spectrum. New York City has one of the highest average room rates in the country, and hotels here don't have to discount to fill their beds—citywide occupancy rates regularly hover in the 90% range and up. Many hotels are designed to target business travelers and conventioneers, whose expense accounts presumably cover those hotel bills—so why court cost-conscious families? (Never mind that more and more business travelers and conventioneers are trying to bring their families with them, turning a business trip into a family vacation as well.)

If a swimming pool is important to you and your kids, I warn you now: Few Manhattan hotels have them, and some that do have pools sell memberships to adult New Yorkers, who may resent having a bunch of kids doing cannonballs in the deep end when they're trying to get some laps in on their lunch hour. I've listed nearly every hotel that does have a pool but tried to give you an idea of how welcoming those pools really are for families.

One thing a family can always use when traveling is a kitchenette—if you can throw together breakfasts and lunches in your room, you can easily save $100 a day, not to mention keep your children happy by not requiring them to use their restaurant manners three times a day. Suite hotels in general get my vote whenever they include some kind of kitchen facilities; they're also great with younger kids because you can put toddlers to bed at 8pm and retreat to the other room for a room-service dinner, a movie on cable TV, whatever. Seems a shame to spend your evening this way when you're in Manhattan, but for a couple of evenings of a 1-week stay, it can be just the ticket to de-stress after a long day.

Affinia Gardens **14**
The Carlyle **13**
Comfort Inn on
  Central Park West **8**
Days Hotel Broadway **2**
Excelsior Hotel **3**
Gracie Inn **10**
Hotel Beacon **7**
Hotel Newton **1**
Hotel Wales **9**
Loews Regency **15**
The Lucerne **4**
The Mark **11**
Milburn Hotel **6**
On the Ave Hotel **5**
Surrey Hotel **12**

Ⓜ Subway stop

Best Hotel Bets

See chapter 1 for a list of my hotel favorites—the most family-friendly, the best views, and more.

On this built-up island, there just isn't the range of properties you'd find even in other expensive markets like London and Paris. You've got fleabags, you've got palaces—and not a whole lot in between. But face it: In between is where most families need to be. I've concentrated on ferreting out midrange hotels that are at least decent, if not always charming and atmospheric. When I do include some of the high-priced four-stars, it's because they offer something families especially value—not necessarily stunning decor, hushed privacy, and meticulous valet service (three things that don't mix well with small children anyway), but a pool, a kids' program, or a family-friendly location.

WHEN IS HIGH SEASON? Some hotels report that their slow time is January to early March; others say that July and August are their slow times. Just about all hotels, however, are booked way in advance from Thanksgiving to mid-December. When a big convention hits town, it can be impossible to find a room for love or money. Moral of the story: Call for reservations as soon as you know you're coming to New York to make sure you won't get shut out. But the other side of the coin is also true—call at the last minute, and you may get lucky even at one of the most popular properties.

Because New York attracts lots of business visitors as well as tourists, some hotels, especially those in Midtown or downtown, are more likely to have rooms free on weekends. Always ask about weekend packages if that's when you plan to check in.

RESERVATION SERVICES Quikbook (© 800/789-9887; www.quikbook.com)

will book you into any of more than 80 hotels, including all the Affinia Group suite hotels, the Doubletree Guest Suites, the Crowne Plazas, and Le Parker Meridien; there's no charge, and they can often get you discounts of 25% to 40%. The nationwide **Central Reservation Service** (© 800/873-4683; www.reservation-services.com) also offers a discount, quoted as 10% to 40%, when they help you book rooms in New York. **Hotels.com** (© 800/246-8357; www.hotels.com) offers discount hotel booking in several large cities across the country, including New York.

A NOTE ABOUT HOTEL SERVICES Certain services are so standard in Manhattan hotels that I haven't noted them in individual reviews. Because tall buildings here interfere badly with TV reception, every hotel that offers in-room TVs—and that's virtually all of them—offers **cable TV**, which means you'll have a range of channels to surf. Most hotels also have Spectravision or pay-per-view or some other **in-room movie service** feeding into the TVs. In the past couple of years, **high-speed Internet service** has become standard in most hotels; a number of accommodations charge a daily fee to use it in your room—another tacky way to tack on extra fees, if you ask me—or offer it on a terminal in the lobby, but it's generally available somewhere on-site. **Dry-cleaning** and **laundry services** are usually available. Nearly all hotels have some type of **business services;** if these are important to you, verify before booking that a hotel has the business capabilities you need.

Just about every concierge or front desk has a list of **babysitters** they've used, usually provided by one of the city's many

FAMILY-FRIENDLY ACCOMMODATIONS

5

FAMILY-FRIENDLY ACCOMMODATIONS

Embassy Suites Hotel **3**

Hotel Gansevoort **1**

Marriott New York Downtown **6**

New York Marriott at the Brooklyn Bridge **5**

Ritz-Carlton New York, Battery Park **7**

Seaport Inn **4**

Washington Square Hotel **2**

Ⓜ Subway stop

Ⓜ Closed indefinitely

0   1/4 mi

0   0.25 km

bonded child-care agencies. Rates can be steep—from $15 to $20 per hour, with additional fees for more children, plus cab fare to get home afterward ($15–$20). What you'll get will be professional babysitters, many of them from Europe, Asia, or South America, as well as North America. They'll come to your hotel room and take care of your children there.

Parking at just about all these Manhattan hotels, whether the hotel has its own garage or merely gives you a discount at nearby garages (the latter being more usual), is based on a per-night rate that assumes you won't be taking your car in or out during the day. Once you start moving the car, you'll have to pay more. Just another reason not to use your car while you're visiting.

A NOTE ABOUT PRICES I've categorized hotels according to a fairly basic rate for a family of four. In some hotels, that'll be the price for a double room with two double beds. In others, it may require a connecting pair of double rooms (though hardly any hotels will guarantee you'll get two rooms that connect—they're covering themselves in case the folks next door don't check out as expected—but in general, if you request connectors, you'll get them). In some hotels I've had to base

things on the assumption that a small suite will be the best family deal. At any rate, I call a hotel **inexpensive** if that fictional family of four can stay for less than $225 a night; **moderate** if their bill will run $225 to $300; **expensive,** $300 to $400; and **very expensive,** over $400. (Those terms are, of course, relative to the Manhattan lodging price structure in general—and remember, that's for four people.) Quoted rates don't include the 13.375% New York City hotel tax or the occupancy tax, which is $3.50 per room per night.

These are based on "rack rates," the hotel's standard rates for peak times: Corporate discounts and package deals can bring them in at as much as $100 lower a night, so I've also noted which hotels regularly offer good discounts. Some hotels regularly offer summer packages, while others are likely to activate package deals at the last minute, when occupancy rates appear to be falling short of projected levels. (Yield management is the name of the game.) Even if you've already secured a room at rack rates in a lower-priced hotel, just before you arrive, you might call a couple of pricier places to see if any special deals have kicked in. You could get a premium room for less, if you're lucky.

1 THE UPPER WEST SIDE

VERY EXPENSIVE

Excelsior Hotel ★★ This longtime neighborhood hotel—perfectly situated right across the street from the city's top family attraction, the American Museum of Natural History—has been transformed from a bargain lodging into a smart upscale hotel, with a French Provincial motif in soothing greens and soft rosy browns. The bathroom fixtures are up-to-date, with nice country-French tile accents. The rooms are good-sized—a family of four could fit into one of the double-doubles (double room with two double beds), though a one-bedroom suite, with its queen-size pullout couch in the smallish sitting room, would give even more privacy (one-bedroom suites have one queen-size or two double beds; two-bedroom suites have all queen-size beds). The small but handsome wood-paneled lobby has an ornate plasterwork ceiling, much like many of the grand old apartment houses around the corner up Central Park West. Unfortunately, there's no

Apartments & B&Bs

Yes, hotel prices are high in New York, and the costs climb even higher for families paying for extra people in the room or even extra rooms. Save big bucks, enjoy more space, and live among the locals by staying in a B&B or a short-stay apartment in New York. The city has plenty of reliable operators offering a range of lodgings, from elegant rooms in prewar apartment buildings to sunny, fully furnished apartments in historic brownstones. Fully equipped kitchens help save big on dining out. Prices can start as low as $90 a night. Check out **City Sonnet** (www.citysonnet.com; $135–$700 double) for both hosted and unhosted lodging in apartments and artists' lofts; or **Manhattan Getaways** (www.manhattan getaways.com; $130–$150 rooms; $200–$750 apts.) for furnished rooms or private apartments. The New York page at **BedandBreakfast.com** (www.bedand breakfast.com/manhattan-new-york.html) lists B&Bs, inns, guesthouses, and apartments for rent.

room service, but complimentary continental breakfast is available on-premises in a breakfast room.

The location is superb—facing the wooded side yard of the American Museum of Natural History, on a clean and relatively quiet West Side block of luxury apartment buildings. (Ask about the hotel's Natural History Museum package.) You're half a block from Central Park, and there are loads of good restaurants and stores nearby on Columbus Avenue. The Excelsior is popular, particularly on weekends—reserve a couple of months ahead, if you can.

The hotel restaurant, **eighty one,** opened in 2008, with a modern American menu and an emphasis on local, seasonal foods and fresh greenmarket produce. The chef, Ed Brown, was most recently the executive chef at the Sea Grill at Rockefeller Center.

45 W. 81st St. (btwn Central Park West and Columbus Ave.), New York, NY 10024. ℂ **800/368-4575** or 212/362-9200. Fax 212/721-2994. www.excelsiorhotelny.com. 198 units. $375–$395 double; $544–$579 suite. Children 13 and under stay free in parent's room. Rollaway $20; crib free. AE, DC, DISC, MC, V. Parking garages nearby. Subway: B, C to 81st St./Museum of Natural History. **Amenities:** Restaurant; fitness center; concierge; conference room; Wi-Fi; library. *In room:* A/C, TV, safe.

On the Ave Hotel ★ Definitely the hip choice on the Upper West Side. The trendy lobby looks very minimalist, with pale stone walls, a slick dark-wood floor, and a few scattered pieces of black leather furniture. It's been smartly renovated upstairs as well, with a Zen-like simplicity—neutral carpet, gauze curtains, stainless steel sinks, a sleek panel of varnished wood morphing from headboard into canopy over the bed. Rooms, however, are smallish and contain only a king or queen bed, which means that a family will need to snag connecting rooms (of which there are about 30 in the hotel) or go for the penthouse suites, which have sitting areas and, often, balconies. This stylish hotel is very popular, especially with younger travelers; the location is convenient, with the American Museum of Natural History only 2 blocks away and Lincoln Center a 10-block stroll down Broadway. There's also a marvelous cityscape view accessible to all guests from a common-area balcony. In 2008 On the Ave went from having no restaurants to having two, with the arrival of **West Branch,** serving American cuisine and offering 24-hour room service dining; and the uptown branch of **Fatty Crab,** the celebrated downtown Malaysian restaurant. A new fitness center was also added in 2008. The hotel is also pet-friendly. Ask about the hotel's many seasonal packages.

2178 Broadway (entrance on 77th St.), New York, NY 10023. © **800/509-7598** or 212/362-1100. Fax 212/787-9521. www.ontheave.com. 253 units. $399–$559 double; $529–$589 suite; $639–$709 penthouse suite. Rollaway $20. AE, DC, MC, V. Parking $37 in nearby garage. Subway: 1 to 79th St. **Amenities:** 2 restaurants; concierge; 24-hr. business center; 24-hr. room service; laundry service; dry cleaning; 24-hr. valet parking. *In room:* A/C, plasma TV, CD player, Wi-Fi (for fee), minibar, mini-fridge (for fee), coffeemaker, hair dryer, iron/ironing board, ergonomic chair, robes.

EXPENSIVE

The Lucerne ★★ Just a block from the American Museum of Natural History, in an area rich with restaurants and shopping, the Lucerne has all the earmarks of a chic boutique hotel, but it still works well for families. It's set in a gorgeous 1904 landmark building of plum-colored brownstone with baroque ornamentation running riot around its columned entrance; the small lobby sparkles like a jewel, with marble floors, big potted plants, and deep settees. Glossy, traditional room decor features striped and floral fabrics, thick carpeting, and framed prints. The good-size marble-and-granite bathrooms gleam with top-of-the-line fixtures. For dramatic views, be sure to ask for a room that looks out onto the Hudson River.

Fire laws prohibit rollaways in the double rooms, so unless you've only got one infant, you'll need a suite; but the Lucerne has 42 of these, with either two queen-size beds or a king-size bed plus a queen foldout couch, and all the suites have kitchenette areas. You'll be happy (or not) to know that the in-room TV options include Nintendo games. The service level of this hotel lifts it above other neighborhood options, with a concierge in the lobby, a recently upgraded business center, and a pocket-size fitness center. Hotel guests get a 15% discount at the downstairs **Nice Matin** restaurant, a popular neighborhood restaurant serving French-Mediterranean cuisine; it's open for breakfast, lunch, and dinner.

201 W. 79th St. (at Amsterdam Ave.), New York, NY 10024. © **800/492-8122** or 212/875-1000. Fax 212/721-1179. www.thelucernehotel.com. 186 units. $440–$490 double; $550–$690 suite. Crib free. AE, DC, DISC, MC, V. Parking $30 (valet parking $45). Subway: 1 to 79th St. **Amenities:** Restaurant; fitness center; concierge; Wi-Fi; 24-hr. room service; laundry service; dry cleaning; valet parking. *In room:* A/C, TV w/Nintendo, Wi-Fi, fridge, microwave, coffeemaker, iron/ironing board, newspaper.

MODERATE

Comfort Inn on Central Park West Despite the tony-sounding name, this budget-priced chain hotel isn't on classy Central Park West, but on a side street just off the park, in a narrow converted apartment building clad in a dour gray stone. But it *is* near the park, and close to the American Natural History Museum, and within walking distance of Lincoln Center—a handy location that, given the price, is hard to beat. The small, modern lobby hasn't got much charm, nor do the rooms—floral bedspreads, bland traditional furniture with a shiny cherrywood finish, new but small standard bathrooms—and the doubles are too tight to accommodate more than three guests, once you've wedged in a crib. Still, at the right season these rooms are cheap enough that you can book two for your family and still be in the moderate range, and the free continental breakfast (limited as it is) is a nice bonus. It's a decent choice for a short stay if you plan to be out on the town most of the time anyway.

31 W. 71st St. (btwn Central Park West and Columbus Ave.). © **877/424-6423** or 212/721-4770. Fax 212/579-8544. www.comfortinn.com. 90 units. $160–$300 double. Rates include continental breakfast. AE, DC, DISC, MC, V. Parking $30–$40 nearby. Subway: 1, 2, 3 to 72nd St. **Amenities:** Fitness center; concierge; Wi-Fi. *In room:* A/C, hair dryer, iron/ironing board, newspaper.

Hotel Beacon ★ Converted from an apartment building in the early 1990s, the
Beacon offers just what we need more of in this city: clean, respectably furnished rooms
with all the important amenities and none of the glitzy frills, in a neighborhood great for
kids. Riverside Park is 2 blocks west and Central Park is 3 blocks east; the American
Museum of Natural History and the Children's Museum of Manhattan are just a few
blocks up the street, and Lincoln Center isn't far down Broadway. You'll find a quiet
marble-clad lobby; wide, well-lit corridors; and good-size rooms freshly done up in a
traditional decor (glossy dark Queen Anne–style furniture, muted rose and tan color
schemes, and framed botanical prints on the walls). There's a full kitchenette with a
microwave in every room; the marble bathrooms aren't large but look sparkling clean and
have tidy little amenities baskets.

Even the doubles are big enough for a family, because they have a king or two double
beds and enough space for a crib or rollaway. Suites add on a sitting room with a foldout
couch. There's no room service, but a coffee shop is right on the corner. Though this is
a busy stretch of Broadway, the windows are pretty well soundproofed (internal walls
could use a little more soundproofing, unfortunately); since the 25-story hotel is one of
the tallest buildings in the neighborhood, the upper-floor rooms facing west have nice
views over Riverside Park and the Hudson. The Beacon gets a steady stream of business,
so reserve as far in advance as possible, especially in June and October; weekdays tend to
be less busy than weekends, so plan accordingly. Ask about theater packages.

2130 Broadway (at 75th St.), New York, NY 10023. (℃) **800/572-4969** or 212/787-1100. Fax 212/724-0839.
www.beaconhotel.com. 237 units. $235–$325 double; $295–$550 suite; $650 and up 2-bedroom suite.
Children 12 and under stay free in parent's room. Rollaway $15; crib free. AE, DC, DISC, MC, V. Parking $31.
Subway: 1, 2, 3 to 72nd St. **Amenities:** 24-hr. restaurant; business center; laundry room; dry cleaning. *In
room:* A/C, TV, Wi-Fi, kitchenette, fridge, coffeemaker, hair dryer, iron/ironing board, safe.

INEXPENSIVE

Days Hotel Broadway   Don't let the unglamorous upper Broadway environs put you
off: You're half a block from an express subway stop, where trains can whisk you to the
Theater District in minutes, and with several good casual restaurants nearby (not to mention top playgrounds and sports facilities in both Riverside and Central parks), this
neighborhood works very well for families.

The hotel itself is unexceptional, with tight corridors, a ho-hum chain-hotel decor,
and window air-conditioners (not that there's any view to block). Bathrooms, though
neatly modernized, are on the small side, but any way you look at it, a stay here puts you
in the inexpensive rate category. All rooms with two beds have double beds. Junior suites
have one queen bed and a pullout double-size sofa. Lots of tour operators know about
this place, so book well ahead. Weeknights are considerably cheaper than weekends, and
summer means lower rates, though even then rooms book up fast. There's no room service, but there are plenty of nearby coffee shops. It's a sensible, no-fuss option for families
who plan to be out and about most of the time anyway.

215 W. 94th St. (btwn Broadway and Amsterdam Ave.). (℃) **800/228-5151**, 800/834-2972, or 212/866-
6400. Fax 212/866-1357. www.daysinn.com. 365 units. $220–$280 double. Rollaway $20; crib free. AE, DC,
MC, V. Parking $30–$40 in nearby garages. Subway: 1, 2, 3 to 96th St. **Amenities:** Fitness center; business
center; Wi-Fi. *In room:* A/C, TV, fridge ($15 extra), coffeemaker, hair dryer, iron/ironing board, safe.

Hotel Newton   With a cheerful, eager-to-please staff and newly refurbished rooms,
the Newton has moved up a notch from basic budget lodging to pleasant good-value
hotel, with such newfangled amenities as Wi-Fi and flatscreen TVs. The lobby is bright
and has a comfy seating area, whereas restful guest rooms are neatly done up in beige and

Cool Pools

You'll get fabulous views year-round at the snazzy, glass-enclosed atrium pool at **Le Parker Meridien** (p. 79), which is 42 stories up, with panoramas of Central Park and the Midtown skyline. The enclosed pool at the **Millennium U.N. Plaza Hotel** (p. 86) may be only 27 stories up, but it's right on the East River, which means not only river views but also unobstructed skyline views south. What's more, the Millennium U.N. Plaza's pool features gorgeous tile work and a canopy overhead. Also in Midtown, the **Crowne Plaza Times Square** (p. 80) has a gleaming 50-foot indoor lap pool with a nice view, if that matters to you.

Farther west, the **Skyline Hotel** (p. 82) has a smallish enclosed rooftop pool of an earlier vintage, squirreled away in a hard-to-find upstairs nook; the plus here is big windows grabbing a bit of a Hudson River view. Hours are limited, however. The largest hotel pool in town is the blue Olympic-size one at the **Travel Inn** (p. 83), which is outdoors (hence open seasonally only), surrounded by wings of the hotel; a very pleasant patio area provides space for lounging poolside. The **Holiday Inn Midtown 57th Street** (p. 82) has a small outdoor rooftop pool, open Memorial Day through Labor Day.

Downtown, the outdoor rooftop pool at the **Hotel Gansevoort** (p. 88) in the Meatpacking District is a pretty spectacular spot to watch sunsets over the Hudson River. The glass-enclosed pool has underwater music and morphs into an indoor heated pool in the winter. The 50-foot indoor pool at **Marriott New York Downtown** (p. 91) has no views but is sparkling clean and quiet. Across the East River in Brooklyn, the **New York Marriott at the Brooklyn Bridge** (p. 92) has a 75-foot-long lap pool where kids can cavort after a day of sightseeing.

rose hues with soft carpeting and functional wooden furniture. A deluxe room with two double beds would accommodate a family, but for a little more you could upgrade to the junior suite, which also has a sitting area and kitchenette. Bathrooms are small, but housekeeping keeps them sparkling. So what if the only views are of other buildings, the elevator is tiny, and the hallways are narrow; there's an express subway stop right outside the hotel door, the neighborhood is friendly and safe, and you weren't planning to spend all your time in your hotel room anyway, were you? The **Key West Diner** downstairs is a shiny, up-to-date coffee shop with a huge menu, serving three meals a day, and the nearby area has loads of other family-friendly dining options.

2528 Broadway (btwn 94th and 95th sts.), New York, NY 10025. (**C**) **800/643-5553** or 212/678-6500. Fax 212/678-6758. www.thehotelnewton.com. 105 units. $179–$235 double; $250 suite. Rollaway $28; crib free. AE, DC, MC, V. Parking $27. Subway: 1, 2, 3 to 96th St. **Amenities:** Restaurant; business center; Wi-Fi; 24-hr. room service. *In room:* A/C, TV, Wi-Fi, kitchenettes in suites.

Milburn Hotel ★ As a happy mother checking out reported to me the day I visited, "What's not to like? It's clean, cheap, and friendly to kids." The Milburn Hotel has a lot to offer at a great price. The hallways are narrow, but the rooms are decent-sized (a few even have small outdoor terraces), with simple, traditional furnishings crisply maintained. Adding a crib or rollaway would make one of the doubles seriously snug; a family should probably go for a suite, which adds a sitting room with foldout couch. Kitchenettes have been smartly tucked into all rooms, with a microwave, minifridge, and tiny sink. Keeping kids happy in the room becomes easier with the in-room VCRs (with a free video library downstairs) and PlayStations available from the front desk. Plus: The hotel has complimentary Wi-Fi in both the rooms and the public spaces—hooray!

The Milburn's entrance is just around the corner from Broadway, making it incredibly convenient for shopping and restaurants; though the Milburn has no restaurant, it offers a dining plan with discounts at good local restaurants. Considering you'll have a kitchenette, it's good to know that food shopping is especially great in this neighborhood, with the Fairway market and Citarella's fish store a couple blocks south, and H&H Bagels and Zabar's gourmet emporium a few blocks north. Riverside Park is only 2 blocks away, too. All told, an excellent deal.

242 W. 76th St. (btwn Broadway and West End Ave.), New York, NY 10023. ℂ **800/833-9622** or 212/362-1006. Fax 212/721-5476. www.milburnhotel.com. 122 units. $179–$299 double; $199–$399 suite. Rollaway $15; crib free. Rates include continental breakfast Mon–Thurs. AE, DC, MC, V. Parking $25. Subway: 1 to 79th St.; 1, 2, 3 to 72nd St. **Amenities:** Pool privileges nearby; fitness room; conference/meeting room; 24-hr. room service; video library. In room: A/C, TV/VCR, CD player, Wi-Fi, kitchenette, fridge, coffeemaker, safe.

2 THE UPPER EAST SIDE

VERY EXPENSIVE

The Carlyle ★★★   The roster of celebrity guests includes everyone from Jack Nicholson to JFK, Brooke Astor to David Bowie, Harry Truman to Princess Diana. Many of the staff, from the bellmen to the concierges, make working at The Carlyle a lifetime career, delivering white-glove service that's rare indeed. Surprisingly enough, all this makes The Carlyle a great family hotel, if the prices aren't beyond your budget. The neighborhood is wonderfully quiet and well behaved, and the rooms are huge—even a double is big enough for a smaller family, with a crib or rollaway brought in.

Rooms are elegant and classically beautiful, with sumptuous chintzes and thick carpets draping the hotel's fine Deco bones. From its first decorator in the 1930s, Dorothy Draper, to more recent refurbishments by Thierry Despont and Cameron Barnett, The Carlyle has been furnished by Manhattan society's top residential designers. "Residential" is the key word—if a room has shelves, they'll be stocked with books; vases and china dishes and ormolu clocks are set out on the occasional tables; every sitting room and bedroom has its own entertainment center with a VCR and CD player. More than a dozen rooms even have Steinway or Baldwin grand pianos. Suites have sleek modern kitchens, while even the double rooms at least have an alcove with a sink and well-stocked minibar. The bathrooms are big and gleaming, with Kiehl's toiletries, thick towels and terry-cloth robes, and makeup mirrors; most tubs have whirlpools.

The Carlyle's dining choices have always attracted locals, from the plush and intimate **Carlyle Restaurant** decorated in the style of an English manor (breakfast, lunch, and dinner, with a lavish Sun brunch) and the newly redesigned **Café Carlyle,** a renowned cabaret venue, to the **Gallery,** a Turkish-style red-velvet lobby area with a few small tables—just the place for breakfast coffee and afternoon tea, as well as post-theater snacks. But best of all for kids is the atmospheric **Bemelmans Bar,** with its fanciful murals painted by Austrian artist Ludwig Bemelmans, creator of the *Madeline* books ("In an old house in Paris that was covered in vines lived twelve little girls in two straight lines . . ."), where the charming **Madeline's Tea Party** is held on weekends (p. 118).

The hotel is 35 stories tall, so if you're lucky enough to snag a room overlooking Central Park, you'll have a view to die for. Carlyle guests are near enough to the park to scamper right over and play, as well as being close to the Fifth Avenue museums and the glorious children's shops on upper Madison Avenue. All in all, a swellegant way to experience New York.

35 E. 76th St. (at Madison Ave.), New York, NY 10021. ℂ **800/227-5737** or 212/744-1600. Fax 212/717-4682. www.thecarlyle.com. 187 units. $755–$1,135 double; $1,135–$6,000 suite. AE, DC, MC, V. Valet parking $50. Subway: 6 to 77th St. **Amenities:** Restaurant; cafe/cabaret; bar; lounge; small fitness center w/sauna and steam room; concierge; secretarial services; 24-hr. room service; babysitting; pet care. *In room:* A/C, TV/DVD, Wi-Fi, kitchen in suites, minibar, hair dryer, safe, bathrobes and slippers, CD player, fax machine, iPod docking station, scale.

The Mark ★★   After a spectacular new redesign by one of France's most celebrated interior designers, Jacques Grange, this classic 1927 hotel was scheduled to open for business in late 2008 as a combination hotel/co-op with properties for sale in prices ranging from $2 million up and hotel rooms starting at $1,000 a night. In the process, the hotel has shrunk from 180 to 118 rooms. Designer Grange has given it a bold, playful look, with jazzy stripes on the lobby floor and other Deco-inspired grace notes. Frederick Fekkai, one of the city's top hairstylists, will open a full-service salon in the Mark.

25 E. 77th St. (at Madison Ave.), New York, NY 10021. ℂ **800/843-6275,** 800/526-6566, or 212/772-1600. Fax 212/744-2749. www.themarkhotel.com. 118 units. Doubles start at $1,000. AE, DC, DISC, MC, V. Call for parking rates. Subway: 6 to 77th St. **Amenities:** Restaurant; bar; small fitness center; concierge; business services; Wi-Fi; 24-hr. room service. *In room:* A/C, TV/VCR, kitchenette in many units, minibar, safe.

Surrey Hotel ★   If you haven't got the dough to stay nearby at The Carlyle or The Mark (see above), you can still enjoy this ace East Side neighborhood with a somewhat more affordable suite at the Surrey. Its clean, well-maintained rooms are positively huge—you could easily fit a crib or rollaway into the so-called studio suites. The one-bedroom suites could sleep six, with two double beds in the bedroom and a foldout sofa in the sitting room. The decor is tasteful, if not fussy, with Chippendale-ish reproductions. The bathrooms are sparkling clean, though the fixtures aren't necessarily luxurious. Every unit has a kitchen or kitchenette with cutlery and plates, and guests here really do seem to use their kitchens—the staff will even do your food shopping for only $5 (plus the cost of the groceries, of course). If cooking is not your idea of a vacation, there are scads of restaurants within a short walk, and room service is provided by the kitchen of one of Manhattan's most stellar chefs, Daniel Boulud, whose **Café Boulud** is downstairs.

The ample reception area, with marble columns, a chandelier, and a genteelly faded Oriental rug, resembles many Upper East Side apartment building lobbies—indeed, staying here is one way to discover what it's like to live in New York as a family, as you troll the Madison Avenue children's shops and hang out at the East 76th Street Playground in Central Park. The Surrey's residential air is enhanced by the fact that many guests are on long stays—corporate relocations, local families holing up during apartment renovations. Nevertheless, the Surrey welcomes short-stay guests, especially on weekdays and in the July/August slow period, so don't hesitate to check if there's a room, even on short notice.

20 E. 76th St. (at Madison Ave.), New York, NY 10021. ℂ **866/AFFINIA** or 212/288-3700. www.affinia.com. Fax 212/628-1549. 131 units. $369–$619 studio suite/1-bedroom suite; $990–$2,060 2-bedroom suite. Rollaway $30; crib free. Weekly and monthly discount rates available. AE, DC, DISC, MC, V. Valet parking

EXPENSIVE

Affinia Gardens   The all-suites Affinia Gardens attracts a lot of business from the cluster of hospitals around 68th Street and York Avenue, but this relatively residential neighborhood also makes sense for families on a short stay. From the stylish small lobby, with its tranquil waterfall wall, the decor is spare, Zen-like, and contemporary—serene surroundings to crash in after a long day. Request a junior suite with a pullout couch as well as a king or two double beds, or go for the one- or two-bedroom suites, which have separate bedrooms and sitting rooms, with sleeper sofas. In general, the staff seems helpful and friendly, accommodating whatever requests guests have.

215 E. 64th St. (btwn Second and Third aves.), New York, NY 10021. © **866/AFFINIA** or 212/355-1230. Fax 212/758-7858. www.affinia.com. 130 units. $379–$679 suite. Children 10 and under stay free in parent's room. Rollaway $20; crib free. AE, DC, DISC, MC, V. Valet parking $38. Subway: 4, 5, 6 to 59th St.; 6 to 68th St.; N, R, W to Lexington Ave./59th St. **Amenities:** Fitness center; spa services; concierge; Wi-Fi; pillow menu. *In room:* A/C, TV, kitchenette.

Hotel Wales ★   There's more than a touch of Edwardian Kensington to this charming century-old hotel in Carnegie Hill, a historic Upper East Side neighborhood full of top-notch private schools and well-off families. Only a block from Central Park and Museum Mile, the hotel is smack in the middle of upper Madison's strip of upscale children's shops. The lobby looks like the entry hall in a private mansion, with its marble staircase, carved wood banisters, dark wainscoting, and striped wallpaper, and the room decor is tastefully traditional—beautiful restored woodwork, original cabinets, and cedar-lined closets. The Pied Piper Room, where guests can help themselves to a granola-and-muffins breakfast, is a big comfy space with potted palms and Victorian settees where chamber music is played at teatime and on Sunday evening.

Rooms have been recently renovated and are very comfortable, with Belgian linens, handsome wood accents and armoires, and soft hues. Absolutely the only drawback to staying in this hotel is that the rooms are so small you can barely fit a crib in—better to go for a suite, which consists of a fair-size bedroom and an adjoining sitting area with a pullout sofa. (There are no connecting doubles.) The bathrooms are tiny yet outfitted with top-quality fixtures. Kids get a kick out of the hotel's Puss-in-Boots theme, discreetly carried out with framed prints on the walls and designs on the bath toiletries. Every room has a VCR, and you can tell how popular the Wales is with families when you see how many kids' movies there are in its video library. It's pet-friendly, to boot; ask about the For the Love of Dog! package. **Johanna's Italian Restaurant** is now located in the Hotel Wales, as is the separately owned **Sarabeth's Restaurant,** rightly popular for its delicious brunch.

1295 Madison Ave. (at 92nd St.), New York, NY 10128. © **212/876-6000.** Fax 212/876-7139. www.waleshotel.com. 88 units. $270–$399 double; $370–$699 suite. Rates include continental breakfast. Extra person $20. Rollaway $20; crib free. AE, DC, DISC, MC, V. Valet parking $40–$42. Subway: 6 to 96th St. **Amenities:** 2 restaurants; breakfast room; fitness room; concierge; room service; roof terrace. *In room:* A/C, TV/VCR, CD player, Wi-Fi, fridge on request, iron/ironing board, safe.

Loews Regency ★★   This place has star power, with famous folks wandering in and out on a regular basis. But the Regency staff likes to sprinkle stardust on everyone who stays here, including children. This is one of the most kid-friendly hotels in town, believe it or not. Kids are given welcome gifts, and they even have their own kids' concierge to set up tours and recommend places to see. In the summer, the hotel has lemonade in the lobby; in the winter, hot chocolate. Bring your dog along with you, too—Fido will get a menu of treats, a water bowl, and a mat to soak up the slop. Rooms are big and roomy (kids 17 and under stay free in parent's room), with supremely comfy beds. The hotel has a gracious elegance that's not stuffy and a winning staff.

540 Park Ave. (at 61st St.), New York, NY 10128. (C) 212/759-4100. Fax 212/826-5674. www.loewshotels. com. 353 units. $419–$699 double. Children 17 and under stay free in parent's room. Rollaway $25; crib free. AE, DC, MC, V. Valet parking $56. Subway: N, R, 4, 5, 6 to 59th St. **Amenities:** 2 restaurants; lounge/ cabaret; fitness room; concierge; salon; 24-hr. room service; laundry service; dry cleaning. In room: A/C, flatscreen TV/VCR, CD player, Wi-Fi, minibar, hair dryer, iron/ironing board, safe, bathrobes.

INEXPENSIVE

Gracie Inn (Finds)   If only New York had more places like the Gracie Inn! First off, there's the neighborhood: the Upper East Side, on a side street near the East River, not far from Carl Schurz Park—the part of the East Side where middle-class families live and shop and go to school. Then there are the thoughtful service and quiet un-hotel-like atmosphere, which make this a welcome retreat from Manhattan bustle—the sort of bed-and-breakfast boutique hotel you can find all over Europe but rarely in the States.

Once you get past the unprepossessing exterior and minuscule lobby, the five-story townhouse (with elevator) has individually decorated suites. Antiques, stenciled wallpapers, rag rugs, hardwood floors, and lace curtains go for a country-inn look that's never too frilly or precious; fresh flowers are set out in the rooms, and plump snowy duvets are on the beds. Every suite has a tidy little kitchen with all utensils, and a continental breakfast is brought to your room each morning. Cribs or rollaways could fit handily even in the studios, though a one- or two-bedroom suite would be better for a family, especially the penthouse duplex (kids will have a blast running up and down the snug wooden staircase). With skylights, a greenhouse wall, and weathered wood terraces, the penthouse suites get loads of sun, but even rooms on the lower floors are fairly light. Don't expect to walk to the subway—York Avenue is a long way east from the subway line—but buses and taxis are easy to find, and the neighborhood has plenty of good, reasonably priced restaurants.

502 E. 81st St. (btwn York and East End aves.), New York, NY 10028. (C) 212/628-1700. Fax 212/628-6420. www.thegracieinn.com. 13 units. $199 studio suite; $225 1-bedroom suite; $299–$350 penthouse. Rates include continental breakfast. Discounts offered for weekly and monthly stays. Rollaway or crib free. AE, DISC, MC, V. Parking garages nearby. Subway: 6 to 77th St. In room: A/C, TV, dataport, kitchen.

3 MIDTOWN WEST

At press time, the grandest of dames, the **Plaza,** at Fifth Avenue and Central Park South ((C) 212/759-3000; www.fairmont.com/thePlaza) was just re-opening. After a $400 million, 2-year renovation, the Plaza, like so many other hotels, is part condo, and part hotel. There are now 282 guest rooms ranging from a roomy 482-square feet guest room to suites of almost 1,500 square feet, some with terraces, and all rooms and suites feature white glove butler service. The world famous **Palm Court** is open once again for high (expensive) tea, and the **Oak Room** and Oak Bar for cocktails and dinner. New at the Plaza are the lobby's **Champagne Bar** and the **Rose Club** overlooking the lobby and a fitness club helmed by trainer to the stars, Radu. Rates start at (gulp) $1,000 per night. What would Eloise think?

EXPENSIVE

Doubletree Guest Suites ★★ Quite possibly the most family-oriented hotel in Manhattan, the all-suite Doubletree more than makes up for what might be an off-putting location, smack-dab on Times Square. For families with younger children, two entire floors have been outfitted with plastic drinking cups, childproof power outlets, padded bump guards on furniture edges, and spout covers in the tubs. The suite concept is a natural for families anyway, because you automatically get sleeping space for four or six, depending on whether you request a king-size bed or two doubles in the bedroom (there's a foldout sofa in the sitting room). All suites have kitchenettes with a microwave, a stocked minibar, and TVs in both rooms. The low-key contemporary decor features calm grays and subdued geometric designs that don't show spills.

Now let's get to the really unusual ways the Doubletree provides for families: There's no charge for cribs, playpens, and strollers, and you can request that the cable movie service be shut off if you're worried your kids will go wild with the remote. Next to the restaurant and health club is a delightful large playroom with a stunning Statue of Liberty design on the carpet; it's equipped with well-chosen picture books, big stuffed animals, colorful large foam blocks, and a clever wall-mounted city maze around which kids can steer small taxis. Security is good, though not forbidding: There's a ground-floor foyer with monitored elevators leading up to the guest lobby, and a separate bank of elevators goes up to guest-room floors. After 11pm guests have to show their key card to be admitted into the guest-room elevators. At 45 stories, the Doubletree does have some high-floor rooms with Midtown views; but what's more important about the height is that it means there are lots of rooms, so more families can take advantage of this great deal.

The recently refurbished **Center Stage Café** has whimsical wall murals carrying out its Broadway theater theme—face one way, and you'll feel like an audience watching the stage; face the other, and you'll feel like performers looking up at the audience in the painted balcony. The restaurant serves a breakfast buffet, lunch, and dinner and has a kids' menu, naturally. A new fitness center is another great perk.

1568 Broadway (at 47th St. and Seventh Ave.), New York, NY 10036. **⦿ 800/222-8733** or 212/719-1600. Fax 212/921-5212. www.hilton.com. 460 units. $299–$640 suite. Children 17 and under stay free in parent's room. Crib free. AE, DC, DISC, MC, V. Valet parking $35–$40. Subway: 1 to 50th St.; N, R, W to 49th St.; B, D, F, V to 47th–50th sts./Rockefeller Center. **Amenities:** Restaurant/lounge; fitness center; children's playroom; concierge; business center; room service (6am–midnight). *In room:* A/C, TV, VCR by request, high-speed Internet access, kitchenette, minibar, fridge, coffeemaker, hair dryer, iron, safe.

Le Parker Meridien ★★★ ✓ The 731-room property looks chic enough, with a marble-columned lobby and Zen-like guest rooms—but Le Parker Meridien does a superlative job of making families feel welcome. On arrival, kids are given the hotel's own hand-drawn coloring book; the elevators play continual cartoons and classic silent slapstick comedies; and kids can borrow a Razor scooter from the front desk to whiz around the neighborhood. Not only does the concierge know what's on for kids, but guests can also consult an online concierge even before arrival to scope out kid-friendly activities. Naturally, items like highchairs, night lights, bottle warmers, and safety plugs are available on request.

With its splendid glass-enclosed atrium pool, sun deck, ⅛-mile rooftop jogging track, and top-notch health club, this family-owned hotel is a super choice for any athletic family. The 57th Street location is close to Midtown attractions, yet only 2 blocks from Central Park; several rooms on the 42-story hotel's upper floors—say, from 20 on up—offer green park views. The artfully uncluttered guest rooms are clad in cherry and cedar wood and are spacious by Manhattan standards—a double with two double beds could accommodate a family for a short stay—though the Tower Suites aren't a bad deal, with a king-size bed in one room, a pullout couch in the other, a bathroom, a kitchenette, and an awesome skyline view on upper floors. The suites have full kitchenettes with pots, plates, and condiments available upon request. But best of all, at least from my son's point of view, is the rotating blond-wood entertainment console—which, naturally, has video games on tap as well as movies.

Norma's serves gargantuan gourmet breakfasts, all the way through lunchtime, and **Seppi's** is an atmospheric wine bar/bistro. But face it, the restaurant that kids will dig the most here is the no-name **burger den** hidden off the lobby, which serves nothing but dang good burgers, cheeseburgers, and fries. Look for a neon burger hung discreetly near the concierge desk, and follow.

118 W. 57th St. (btwn Sixth and Seventh aves.), New York, NY 10019. ✆ **800/543-4300** or 212/245-5000. Fax 212/307-1776. www.parkermeridien.com. 731 units. $439–$519 double; $569 and up suite. Rollaway or crib $30. Weekend packages available. AE, DC, DISC, MC, V. Valet parking $50. Subway: N, Q, R, W to 57th St./Seventh Ave. **Amenities:** 2 restaurants; bar; indoor pool; fitness center w/squash and racquetball courts; spa; sauna; concierge; courtesy car to Wall St.; business center; 24-hr. room service; shoeshine; jogging track. *In room:* A/C, TV/DVD, CD player, high-speed Internet access, kitchenette in suites, minibar, hair dryer, iron/ironing board, safe.

Renaissance New York Hotel Times Square ★

Sleek and corporate-looking as it is, the 26-floor Renaissance isn't the kind of hotel families automatically gravitate to, but those who do wind up here should be very pleasantly surprised. First, you're right in the thick of the Times Square action, but in a good way—the famous Coca-Cola sign hangs on the hotel's south wall; the TKTS discount ticket booth is a few steps away; many rooms look out onto one or another of the fabled supersigns; and the hotel's new restaurant, Chop Suey, with windows on three sides, offers the best panoramic view of the Times Square intersection. (You couldn't ask for a better ringside seat on New Year's Eve.) Yet the riffraff get screened out by the ground-floor security lobby (the guest lobby is up on the third floor), and double-paned windows do an amazing job of keeping out traffic noise.

Inside, everything is mahogany and brass and marble and truly handsome. Families can fit nicely into the doubles, which are roomier than most Midtown doubles—go with a king-size-bedded room with a rollaway or a room that has two double beds. Suites consist of a king-size-bedded sleeping room and a sitting room with a pullout couch. Minibars are set under a marble countertop, which makes a handy place for fixing snacks or lunches. The hotel isn't too buttoned down to have a sense of fun: Instead of pillow mints, you get apples at turndown (because you're in the Big Apple, get it?), and there are board games at the front desk to while away the time. The hotel restaurant, **Chop Suey,** serves Asian-inspired cuisine (from Fatty Crab chef Zak Pellacio) and is open for breakfast, lunch, and dinner.

714 Seventh Ave. (btwn 47th and 48th sts.), New York, NY 10036. ✆ **888/236-2427** or 212/765-7676. Fax 212/765-1962. www.marriott.com. 310 units. $329–$729 double. Children 15 and under stay free in parent's room. Rollaway or crib free. AE, DC, DISC, MC, V. Valet parking $54. Subway: N, R, W to 49th St.; B, D, F, V to 47th–50th sts./Rockefeller Center; 1 to 50th St. **Amenities:** Restaurant; breakfast room; lounge; small fitness center; concierge; Wi-Fi; 24-hr. room service. *In room:* A/C, flat-panel TV/VCR, Wi-Fi, minibar, coffeemaker, hair dryer, iron/ironing board.

MODERATE

Crowne Plaza Times Square Manhattan ★

In the new, spiffed-up Times Square, the newly spiffed-up 46-story Crowne Plaza is nicely positioned to be a major player.

With a reception area one floor up from Broadway (security is thorough but not oppressive) and tight soundproofing, you can feel removed from the tumult but not bunkered in—many windows overlook the razzmatazz, including some around the pool and at the end of every corridor. The guest floors begin on the 16th story (several floors of offices are in between the lobby and the guest rooms), giving many rooms great skyline or river views. Yet this contemporary 46-story building sticks firmly to the middle of the road, in style as well as rates. Its lobby has some marble and brass and plush touches, but it's not overbearing; the room decor is traditional and corporate, with greens and browns and lots of table lamps; the restaurants are generally casual, with a breakfast buffet (or if you really want to get going fast in the morning, pick up coffee, juice, and muffins to go from the lobby bar).

Families have several layout options: a double room with two double beds; connecting doubles; a smallish sitting room with your choice of one or two bedrooms connecting; or a large sitting room (complete with a minibar/serving area and dining table) with your choice of one or two bedrooms connecting. Along with pullout sofas, the Crowne Plaza has some pull-down Murphy beds, which kids might enjoy. Some extra amenities (terry bathrobes, a jar of hard candies) are offered on Crowne Plaza Club floors, but it might be worth it if only because you can get continental breakfast free in the lounge, a huge windowed parlor with dynamite views; once the corporate travelers have cleared out at 9am or so, the room is virtually empty. The health club is an obvious attraction for families, though there are some caveats: The fitness center is run by the New York Sports Club, whose members get priority over hotel guests weekdays at lunchtime and after work. The 50-foot lap pool, however, is open to guests at all times; if you want to make sure there's room, call ahead to reserve a lane.

1605 Broadway (btwn 48th and 49th sts.), New York, NY 10019. ✆ **800/2-CROWNE**, 800/980-6429, or 212/977-4000. Fax 212/333-7393. www.ichotelsgroup.com. 770 units. $239–$479 double; $599–$1,200 suite. Children 18 and under stay free in parent's room. Rollaway $30; crib free. AE, DC, DISC, MC, V. Valet parking $39–$49. Subway: 1 to 50th St.; N, R, W to 49th St. **Amenities:** 3 restaurants; bar; indoor pool; fitness center w/classes; sauna; concierge; theater and tour desk; business center; Wi-Fi; shopping arcade; room service (6am–2pm and 5–10pm); massage; concierge-level rooms. *In room:* A/C, TV, Wi-Fi, minibar, coffeemaker.

– looks good

Novotel Times Square ★ At this warm, well-run hotel, the prices are fantastic for a stay in a prime location. What makes it even more appealing to families is that two children 15 and under eat free at the on-site **Café Nicole** (breakfast, lunch, and dinner and a children's menu) and stay free in parent's room, and the "family rooms" nicely fit two adults and two children. The Novotel also has a children's game room and welcome gifts—all in all, it's a winning choice for families. The room decor is perfectly fine, bland but comfortable, with a vaguely Scandinavian blond-wood minimalism and nice firm mattresses with good linens.

226 W. 52nd St. (at Broadway), New York, NY 10019. ✆ **800/668-6835**, or 212/315-0100. Fax 212/765-5365. www.novotel.com. 480 units. $229 double. 2 children 15 and under eat free and stay free in parent's room. AE, DC, DISC, MC, V. Parking $30. Subway: 1, 9 to 50th St.; C, E to 50th St.; N, R to 49th St. **Amenities:** Restaurant; cafe; fitness center; children's game room; concierge; business center; Wi-Fi; room service (6am–midnight); babysitting; dry cleaning. *In room:* A/C, TV/VCR, Wi-Fi, minibar, hair dryer.

The Paramount Hotel Times Square ★ The aggressively cool "pop nouveau" Philippe Starck decor seems almost dated now, but it's still fun to step into the minimalist gray lobby with its asymmetrical rug, cartoonishly shaped armchairs, and free-standing stairway of brushed stainless steel. Young singles who look like *Gossip Girl* extras stare meaningfully at each other at the **Library Bar** or sip coffee at the **Dean & Deluca** cafe. Heading upstairs, you may be disoriented by the deeply colored lighting inside the elevators. The spartan white rooms would almost resemble a doctor's office if not for the whimsical black-and-white checkerboard carpets, the stylized furnishings, and giant Vermeer reproductions in gilt-framed headboards; the bathrooms have an inverted cone of brushed stainless steel for a sink. Beds are pillowed in soft Egyptian cotton linens and down comforters—all in white, of course.

Truth to tell, though, it's stunning, and most kids really get into its self-consciously stagy decor. And who would have expected it would have a children's playroom, with an almost psychedelic Looney Tunes decor? One big drawback is size—some double rooms do have two double beds, but that doesn't leave a whole lot of space. Suites go fast, so book early. The west-of–Times Square location is close to Broadway theaters and Eighth Avenue's mixed bag of restaurants. All in all, I think this is a super place for a few nights' stay.

235 W. 46th St. (btwn Broadway and Eighth Ave.), New York, NY 10036. ✆ **866/760-3174** or 212/764-5500. Fax 212/354-5237. www.nycparamount.com. 597 units. $269–$639 double. Rollaway $25; crib free. AE, DC, DISC, MC, V. Parking $45. Subway: A, C, E to 42nd St./Port Authority; C, E to 50th St.; N, Q, R, S, W, 1, 2, 3, 7 to 42nd St./Times Square. **Amenities:** 2 restaurants; coffee bar; 2 bars; fitness center; children's playroom; concierge; business center; 24-hr. room service. *In room:* A/C, flatscreen TV/VCR, Wi-Fi, minibar, hair dryer, iron, iHome docking station.

INEXPENSIVE

Holiday Inn Midtown 57th Street Ⓥ alue   This reassuring 18-floor motor inn in a residential area of Midtown's far west fringe is a very workable option for families, and a 2008 renovation means the decor has been refreshed and everything's in good working order. If you're driving into Manhattan, the low parking rate for the attached garage may appeal to you, especially because this property is close to the West Side Highway. And if your kids can't survive a vacation without a pool handy, the outdoor rooftop pool (open in summer only) may be a draw. Yes, it's a bit of a walk from here to Midtown attractions, but the relative quiet and calm may make all the difference, and the immediate neighborhood has lots of casual, locals-only restaurants that'll welcome you and your kids. But then again, kids eat free in the hotel restaurants (the **Gotham Café** for breakfast and lunch and **Via Strada** for dinner)—a great deal in a city where practically nothing comes free.

The paneled front-desk area is low-key and pleasant, with a lobby bar (the restaurant and breakfast room are down a hallway). Although the guest room layouts are chain-motel-predictable, with large windows looking out at nothing particularly scenic, the double rooms are of decent size by Manhattan standards—they do hold two double beds comfortably, which means a whole family may be able to fit in. There are a number of connecting doubles, if your family wants more space to spread out. Those who are interested in swimming might try to snag a room in the south tower, where the pool is.

440 W. 57th St. (btwn Ninth and Tenth aves.), New York, NY 10019. ✆ **888/465-4329** or 212/581-8100. Fax 212/581-7739. www.ichotelsgroup.com. 597 units. $178–$399 double. Rollaway $15; crib free. AE, DC, DISC, MC, V. Valet parking $25. Subway: A, B, C, D, 1 to 59th St./Columbus Circle. **Amenities:** 2 restaurants; bar; outdoor pool; fitness center; concierge; room service (6:30am–9pm); gift shop. *In room:* A/C, TV, Wi-Fi, minibar, coffeemaker.

Skyline Hotel Ⓥ alue   With the transformation of the gritty Hell's Kitchen neighborhood into respectable Clinton, the Tenth Avenue location of the Skyline is no longer a drawback. Guest rooms are tastefully decorated—green carpets, mottled rosy walls, flowered bedspreads—with up-to-date bathrooms (though small, most have bathtubs); so-called deluxe floors have a newer, more contemporary decor and added amenities, including a minifridge. Most rooms are large enough to hold two double beds, which means that families may be able to get by with one room; junior and one-bedroom suites comfortably sleep six. We're talking bargain here (parking is just $10 a day), and many European travelers have already found it; so book well ahead. The small rooftop indoor pool is freshly tiled and has lots of surrounding windows, but there's a catch: It's open mornings and evenings only. However, for these prices, people are happy to work around such minor inconveniences.

Off the lobby, **Restaurant 1050** is a casual spot serving American bistro-style food, three meals a day, and it will deliver to your room (though you can't charge it to your room bill). There's a wealth of fun restaurants just a block away on Ninth Avenue, too. Yes, it's a trek from here to most sights, but it's generally easy to hail a cab outside the hotel door. Now that it's no longer scary to walk this far west on 49th or 50th streets, the Skyline makes a lot of sense if you're trying to save a buck or two.

725 Tenth Ave. (btwn 49th and 50th sts.), New York, NY 10019. ⓒ **800/433-1982** or 212/586-3400. Fax 212/582-4604. www.skylinehotelny.com. 230 units. $159–$445 double. Rollaway $20; crib free. AE, DC, DISC, MC, V. Parking $10 (no in/out during stay). Subway: A, C, E to 50th St. **Amenities:** Restaurant; lounge; indoor pool; concierge. *In room:* A/C, TV, Nintendo, Wi-Fi, minifridge (in deluxe rooms only, hair dryer), iron/ironing board, safe.

Travel Inn ★ (Value)   One of New York's very best deals is this bright, clean, sprucely decorated motor inn way at the end of 42nd Street—beyond Theater Row, in an area of warehouses and parking lots and not much else. One reason to stay here is that you get free parking; of course, what you save in parking you could easily spend in taxi fare, because the only attractions close at hand are the Circle Line boat tours. Still, the Travel Inn remains very busy—there are many times when it's sold out months and months in advance—partly because it's handy for the nearby Javits Convention Center; partly because it has a pool; and, well, did we mention that the parking is *free?*

If you don't mind the concrete surroundings (the hotel certainly seems secure enough), you could save a whole lot by staying here: A family could fit comfortably in these rooms, which have two double beds, a desk, a dresser, and upholstered chairs. The decor is standard hotel-room traditional but very nicely kept; the bathrooms are spotless. And as befits a true motor inn, there's a big lap pool (open May–Oct), set in a spacious tiled area with lots of lounge chairs and room to stroll around. A number of rooms overlook the pool area from balconied walkways—request one of these, as opposed to the ones overlooking the street. The fitness room with weights and exercise machines is small but serviceable. The attached **Broadway Deli** will deliver up to your room, and a host of other area delis are happy to deliver as well.

515 W. 42nd St. (btwn Tenth and Eleventh aves.), New York, NY 10036. ⓒ **800/869-4630** or 212/695-7171. Fax 212/967-5025. www.thetravelinnhotel.com. 160 units. $175–$250 double. Rollaway $15; crib free. AE, DC, DISC, MC, V. Free parking. Subway: A, C, E to 42nd St./Port Authority. Bus: M42. **Amenities:** Coffee shop; outdoor pool; fitness room; tour desk; 24-hr. room service. *In room:* A/C, TV, dataport, iron/ironing board.

4 MIDTOWN EAST

VERY EXPENSIVE

Four Seasons ★   Now owned by Ty Warner of Beanie Baby fame, this handsome 52-story hotel designed by I. M. Pei sets high standards for service, upscale chic, and high prices. The tortoiseshell onyx skylight and soaring octagonal limestone columns in the cathedral-like foyer instill a sense of awe, and everything from there on is hushed and knowingly subtle. Smartly dressed guests wander through the lobby toting designer shopping bags; the attentiveness of the staff is wonderful, without a trace of fawning or condescension. This hotel manages to be decorous without being uptight (and kid radar can register uptightness a mile away). The guest rooms are outfitted with understated but sleek modern furnishings, beautifully streamlined stuff Frank Lloyd Wright would approve of. The marble bathrooms are huge and superbly appointed, with roomy adjacent dressing areas.

The room layouts aren't particularly handy for families: A maximum of one extra bed is allowed per room (crib or rollaway), and there are only a few adjoining doubles that could be set off by shutting a common door to the corridor. If connecting rooms are booked up, larger families will have to go for one of the 63 suites, which knocks you up and over the $1,000 range. Some of the suites are on the higher floors, 31 and above, which gives many of them stunning Central Park views. But the Four Seasons chain is known for valuing its young guests; special amenities for kids include a well-focused kids' menu, kid-size bathrobes, baby toiletries, and a collection of toys, videos, and DVDs to borrow.

57 E. 57th St. (btwn Madison and Park aves.), New York, NY 10022. ✆ **800/819-5053** or 212/758-5700. Fax 212/758-5711. www.fourseasons.com. 368 units. $625–$850 double; from $1,550 suite. Extra person $50. Rollaway or crib free for 18 and under. AE, DC, DISC, MC, V. Parking $60. Subway: 4, 5, 6 to 59th St. **Amenities:** 2 restaurants; 2 lounges; fitness center; spa; Jacuzzi; sauna; concierge; business center; 24-hr. room service. *In room:* A/C, TV/DVD, CD player, Wi-Fi, minibar, fridge, hair dryer, safe, robes.

EXPENSIVE

Beekman Tower Hotel ★ In many respects, the circa-1928 Beekman Tower offers the best of all worlds. You're fairly convenient to Midtown but in the posh residential East 50s, where peace and quiet reign. You have all the roominess of a small apartment but with lots of hotel services. You get some super views but don't have to pay through the nose for them.

This orange-brick Deco tower rising on a slope just north of the United Nations is known to New Yorkers for the **Top of the Tower,** a pleasant and unpretentious restaurant and lounge with a stunning view of the skyline and East River. What New Yorkers don't seem to know is what a great deal this all-suites hotel is. Its smallest suite, the studio, will work only for a small family—it has a queen- or full-size bed and a small sofa (not all of them fold out)—but there's plenty of room for a crib or rollaway, and it has a kitchenette. The one-bedroom suites are perfectly fine, with a foldout couch in the spacious living room and a separate bedroom with a king- or queen-size bed. And they have full kitchens—a four-burner stove; a full refrigerator; a big sink; a microwave; pots and pans; and, incredibly enough, a dishwasher. With clean, up-to-date appliances and a grocery-shopping service, these are kitchens people really can use. Ask for a "C-line suite" and you'll also get a dynamite East River view. The traditional room decor is easy to live with; deluxe suites also have VCRs, in-room fax machines, and, on top floors, balconies. July and August are particularly good times to snag a room; and significant discounts may be offered all times of year, so inquire when you book.

3 Mitchell Place (First Ave. at 49th St.), New York, NY 10017. ✆ **866/298-4806** or 212/355-7300. Fax 212/753-9366. www.thebeekmanhotel.com. 176 units. $249–$429 studio suite; $279–$439 1-bedroom suite; $540 and up 2-bedroom suite. Rollaway $20; crib free. AE, DISC, MC, V. Valet parking $42. Subway: E, V to Lexington Ave./53rd St.; 6 to 51st St. **Amenities:** Restaurant; cafe; fitness center; concierge; room service until 6:30pm. *In room:* A/C, TV, Wi-Fi, kitchenette, coffeemaker.

> ### (Tips) A Family of Hotels
>
> Affinia is a very good company to know about because their suite layouts are so convenient for families. Affinia hotels in Midtown are the **Surrey Hotel** (p. 76); **Affinia Gardens** (p. 77); **Affinia Dumont,** 150 E. 34th St., between Third and Lexington avenues (© **212/481-7600**); **Eastgate Tower,** 222 E. 39th St., between Second and Third avenues (© **212/687-8000**); the **Affinia 50 Suite Hotel,** 155 E. 50th St., at Third Avenue (© **212/751-5710**); the **Shelburne Murray Hill Suites,** 303 Lexington Ave., at 37th Street (© **212/689-5200**); and the **Southgate Tower,** 371 Seventh Ave., at 31st Street (© **212/563-1800**). All are in roughly the same price category, and you can make reservations at any of them by calling © **866/ AFFINIA.**

The Kimberly ★ (Finds)   More people ought to know about this plush smaller hotel on a spruce Midtown East block heading toward the townhouses of Turtle Bay. The small lobby, full of shiny marble and gilt rococo furnishings, has pizazz but not a high snobbery quotient, thanks to a friendly, unpretentious veteran staff. Because the 30-story building was designed in the mid-1980s as an apartment building (it was turned into a hotel immediately), the rooms are all big—even the standard doubles don't feel crowded when they have two double beds in them (a great setup for families on a short visit). The closets are sizable, as are the nicely appointed bathrooms. Most units in the hotel are suites; the one-bedroom suites could sleep six, with two double beds in the bedroom and a pullout couch in the sitting room. The decor has been newly refreshed, and the look is one of comfortable elegance, with quality furniture in dark woods, pillowy featherbedding, and Italian linens. All suites have galley kitchens with cooking burners, pots and pans, and full-size refrigerators. The new Kimberly Luxury Suites, on the 22nd and 23rd floors, are sumptuous one- and two-bedroom suites or doubles with antique-reproduction furniture and 42-inch plasma TVs. Almost every room has a balcony, where you can sit and have breakfast or cocktails while watching the Manhattan ad execs, lawyers, and publishing types scurry to or from their offices far below. Though there's no pool on-site, guests get free use of the New York Health & Racquet Club's pool, where there's a Saturday-morning swim session just for families. Even better: On Sundays, the Kimberly offers a 4-hour family brunch cruise on the *Kimberley Yacht* ($20 per person); the 75-foot yacht sails from May to September.

145 E. 50th St. (btwn Lexington and Third aves.), New York, NY 10022. © **800/683-0400** or 212/702-1600. Fax 212/486-6915. www.kimberlyhotel.com. 192 units. $289–$629 1-bedroom suite; $529–$885 2-bedroom suite. Children 17 and under stay free in parent's room. Rollaway or crib free. Weekend rates and summer packages available. AE, DC, DISC, MC, V. Valet parking $30. Subway: 6 to 51st St.; E, V to Lexington Ave./53rd St.; 6 to 51st St. **Amenities:** 2 restaurants; 2 bars; complimentary access to New York Health & Racquet Club; fitness room; concierge; business center; room service (6am–11pm). *In room:* A/C, flatscreen TV, fax machine, dataport, Wi-Fi, kitchenette in suites, fridge, coffeemaker, hair dryer, iron/ironing board, safe, scale.

Waldorf=Astoria ★★   My Aunt Mabel always said that the only place she'd ever go camping was at the Waldorf=Astoria. It was an icon of luxury then, and it's an icon of luxury now. A member of the Hilton chain, the Waldorf gets regular spit-and-polish renovations, with plenty of money and taste devoted to maintaining its character. The wide, stately corridors, the vintage Deco door fixtures, the white-gloved bellmen, the luxe shopping arcade, and that knockout lobby all trumpet Grand Hotel, and there's a certain thrill about being here. Enter from the Park Avenue side and you'll cross a stunning round mosaic under an immense crystal chandelier; in the main lobby, the four-sided free-standing Waldorf clock, covered with bronze relief figures, should fascinate your children.

Upstairs, the wide, plush-carpeted corridors seem to run on forever. The room decor is pleasant, if unremarkable—a sort of traditional English-country-house look. The standard double rooms are plenty spacious; request a room with two double beds if you've got more than one kid. A minisuite, combining one king-size-bedded room with a sitting room, might work better, though not all have foldout couches; some suites have kitchenettes, so ask for one if that's important. There's also a number of connecting doubles you can request. The staff seems unfailingly gracious, though in such a large hotel you won't get the personal service you might at a smaller place. Do inquire about special discounts, because they pop up year-round. There are 244 rooms in the Waldorf Towers, with a separate entrance. The duke and duchess of Windsor and John F. Kennedy are among the guests who've resided here; it's also a favorite of Bill Clinton. Staying in the pricier Towers, which have more distinctive antique-laden decor, snags you some extra amenities, like complimentary continental breakfast and hors d'oeuvres in a lounge on the 26th floor.

The Waldorf's restaurants may no longer be major players in the New York restaurant universe, but they're consistently excellent: **Oscar's,** the ornate **Peacock Alley,** the Japanese **Inagiku,** and the clubby steak-and-seafood (and newly renovated) **Bull and Bear. Sir Harry's Bar,** fitted out in safari style, serves drinks.

301 Park Ave. (btwn 49th and 50th sts.), New York, NY 10022. © **800/WALDORF,** 800/HILTONS, or 212/355-3000. Fax 212/872-7272. http://waldorfastoria.hilton.com. 1,245 units. $499–$519 double; from $549 suite. Children 17 and under stay free in parent's room. Rollaway $25–$50 per stay; Pack 'n Play playards free. DC, DISC, MC, V. Parking $45. Subway: 6 to 51st St. **Amenities:** 4 restaurants; 2 bars; fitness center w/steam rooms (day-use fee $14); concierge; business center; shopping arcade; salon; 24-hr. room service; babysitting; laundry; dry cleaning. *In room:* A/C, TV, high-speed Internet access, minibar, hair dryer, Frette bathrobes.

MODERATE

Millennium U.N. Plaza Hotel
The Millennium U.N. Plaza's neighborhood hardly qualifies as Midtown—across from the United Nations, it's deliciously quiet and residential. When you combine that with the peerless views (all rooms are on the 28th floor or above, overlooking the East River or the skyline, uptown or downtown), the premium prices start to make sense. The clientele is heavily international, with foreign businesspeople as well as some United Nations visitors. Although it's a sleek corporate-style hotel, families may well be attracted not only by the neighborhood but also by the fact that it has a great pool—what may be the prettiest pool in town, with a haremlike canopy hanging overhead and dynamite views from windows on two sides.

There are two towers to choose between, connected by a disconcertingly slick lobby: the original East Tower, built in 1976, and the newer West Tower, built in 1980. While the East Tower is on the same elevator bank as the pool and has a more contemporary decor (think blond wood, opaque glass, and neutral fabrics), the West Tower makes up for it with floor-to-ceiling windows and warm-toned furnishings that feel homelike (homelike, that is, if you're a wealthy international diplomat). The east wing's sleek minimalist design carries into the bathrooms, which feel a bit bigger than those in the

west wing. The wall hangings are framed museum-quality international textile pieces.
Double rooms have only a king-size bed or two twins (two kids could fit in one of these European-size twins), and fire laws permit only one rollaway. Most families go for a junior suite or duplex one-bedroom suite, or spring for a spacious two-bedroom suite.

1 United Nations Plaza (44th St. and First Ave.), New York, NY 10017. © **866/866-8086** or 212/758-1234. Fax 212/702-5051. www.millenniumhotels.com. 427 units. $249–$309 double; $409 and up suite. Rollaway $35; crib free. Weekend packages available. AE, DC, DISC, MC, V. Valet parking $35–$40. Subway: S, 4, 5, 6, 7 to 42nd St./Grand Central. **Amenities:** Restaurant; indoor pool; indoor tennis court; fitness center w/sauna; concierge; business center; 24-hr. room service; babysitting; gift shop. *In room:* A/C, TV, high-speed Internet access, minibar, coffeemaker, hair dryer, iron/ironing board, safe.

Radisson Lexington New York ★

This handsome 1920s vintage property along Lexington's Midtown hotel strip looks and feels like an upscale boutique hotel, especially after a recent $20-million renovation. But at 27 stories and 700-plus rooms, it's much larger than it feels. Look and listen, and you'll notice it has a sophisticated international clientele (not surprising in the U.N. vicinity). The architecture is a heady blend of Art Deco and Gothic elements: Kids will enjoy spotting the terra-cotta figures on the facade, the griffins and dragons prancing over the vaulted ceiling of the Lexington Avenue entryway, and the birds and lizards etched onto the elevator's brass doors. But from the spiffy porte-cochere above the 48th Street entrance to the two-story mahogany-paneled lobby with textured fabrics and brushed-nickel fixtures, the Radisson East Side has been smartly renovated for a contemporary look without sacrificing the property's charm.

The newly renovated guest-room decor shows quiet verve, with a Deco palette of muted earth tones and granite-top work desks. Bathrooms have been tidily modernized, with gray marble floors and modern white fixtures. Amenities like full-length mirrors, large desks, and dataports with high-speed Internet access bespeak the Radisson's attention to traveling executives. What families may appreciate more, though, is room size: The one-bedroom suites are positively rambling, with a huge bedroom and sitting room (some even have little terraces where you can step outside and study the skyscrapers all around). Business-class rooms are large doubles with either two double beds or a king bed and foldout couches; the great thing about these is that they have two bathrooms. Deluxe rooms have a king, a queen, or two single beds, but there's plenty of room for a rollaway. The whole place seems well run, with thoughtful, friendly service; it's dignified enough to be restful, but not at all stuffy.

Breakfast, lunch, and dinner are served in **Raffles,** a cheery dinerlike corner coffee shop; the hotel's upscale restaurant is **Dynasty,** a lovely gourmet Chinese restaurant that does a brisk lunch and dinner business with nonguests as well as guests.

511 Lexington Ave. (at 48th St.), New York, NY 10017. © **800/448-4471** or 212/755-4400. Fax 212/308-0194. www.lexingtonhotelnyc.com. 705 units. $179–$599 double; $239–$799 suite. Rollaway $25; crib free. AE, DC, DISC, MC, V. Parking nearby $40 for 24 hr. Subway: 6 to 51st St.; S, 4, 5, 6, 7 to 42nd St./Grand Central. **Amenities:** 3 restaurants; Starbucks; nightclub; fitness center; concierge; business center; room service (6:30am–10:30pm); babysitting. *In room:* A/C, flat-panel TV, dataport, Wi-Fi, minibar upon request, coffeemaker, hair dryer, iron/ironing board, safe.

Roger Smith Hotel (Value)

The Roger Smith is decidedly quirky, which may be why so many musicians and artists and Europeans choose to stay here. The small oval lobby is a minigallery in itself, with paintings, sculptures, and polished wainscoting (there's more art next door in an actual art gallery run by Roger Smith). Upstairs, however, the look is more like a country inn, with individually decorated rooms featuring such items as four-poster or iron beds, stocked bookshelves, and chintz upholstery and bedspreads.

Lots of hotels boast of a homey feeling, but the rooms here really do qualify. There are a variety of room layouts, including some connecting rooms and a junior suite that has a double bed and a foldout couch in the same room. Bathrooms are somehow homelike as well, not lavish but trim and up-to-date. For the price of a double at the Waldorf or The Plaza, here you can get a suite that includes not only a pullout couch in the sitting room and a double bed in the bedroom, but also a second cozy bedroom with a twin bed.

Though none of the rooms has a full kitchen, all suites have pantries with a refrigerator and coffeemaker. And as if that weren't enough, continental breakfast is included (rare enough in New York hotels), served every morning in **Lily's,** a spunky little bistro with gaudy murals; Lily's also serves an interesting Continental menu for lunch and dinner (closed weekends). This lively, fun hotel does a pretty brisk business, but its slowest months are July and August—peak family travel time—so cross your fingers and call ahead if you're visiting New York in the summer.

501 Lexington Ave. (at 47th St.), New York, NY 10017. $\mathcal{C}$ **800/445-0277** or 212/755-1400. Fax 212/758-4061. www.rogersmithhotel.com. 133 units. $319–$409 double; $339–$619 suite. Rates include continental breakfast. Extra person $20. Rollaway or crib free. AE, DC, DISC, MC, V. Valet parking $35. Subway: S, 4, 5, 6, 7 to 42nd St./Grand Central. **Amenities:** Restaurant; health club access ($25/day); concierge; Wi-Fi; 24-hr. room service; e-mail center; movie library. *In room:* A/C, TV, Wi-Fi, fridge, coffeemaker, hair dryer, iron/ironing board, library.

5 THE FLATIRON, MEATPACKING DISTRICT & GREENWICH VILLAGE

EXPENSIVE

Hotel Gansevoort ★   For many in the Meatpacking District, the construction of this slick hipster hotel represented the beginning of the end of a funky, slightly rough-at-the-edges neighborhood. Since then, there have indeed been many changes to the district, a cobblestoned slice of old New York in the Village's wild west—designer shops, hip restaurants, star salons, even the looming shadow of the Highline Hotel. But the Gansevoort seems to have staying power and is surprisingly accessible, especially when it comes to kids. First off, the hotel has a fabulous rooftop pool, with floats and underwater lighting and music. All children receive Gladys, the Gansevoort goose and the hotel mascot. Kids have access to board games, Xbox, or Nintendo's Wii free of charge and get milk and cookies at turndown. For babies, there's a basket full of baby powder, shampoo, soap, lotion, and a washcloth. Adults should be very happy here, too, with chic rooms highlighted by delicious feather beds, Egyptian cotton linens, and state-of-the-art amenities. Just across the street is Pastis (see chapter 6) and you're close to the Pier 51 Waterpark and Chelsea Piers.

18 Ninth Ave. (at 13th St.). $\mathcal{C}$ **877/426-7386** or 212/206-6700. Fax 212/255-5758. www.hotelgansevoort. com. 187 units. Doubles $435–$675 (duplex penthouse $5,000). AE, MC, V. Subway: A, C, E to 14th; L to 8th Ave. **Amenities:** Restaurant; 2 bars; rooftop pool; spa; Wi-Fi; babysitting; laundry service; dry cleaning; meeting space. *In room:* A/C, LCD TV, CD players, Wi-Fi, hair dryer, iron/ironing board, safe, iPod docking stations.

MODERATE   C. Chute

Gershwin Hotel   This creative-minded, Warholesque hotel caters to up-and-coming artistic types—and well-established names with an eye for good value—with its bold modern art collection and wild style. Standard rooms are clean and bright, with

Picasso-style wall murals and Philippe Starck-ish takes on motel furnishings. Superior rooms are newly renovated and well worth the extra money; all have a queen bed, two twins, or two doubles, plus a newish private bathroom with cute, colorful tile work. The hotel is more service-oriented than you usually see at this price level, and the staff is very professional. Two-room suites are the best option for families, and the bohemian ambience works better for teens than tots.

7 E. 27th St. (btwn Fifth and Madison aves.), New York, NY 10016. ✆ **212/545-8000.** Fax 212/684-5546. www.gershwinhotel.com. 150 units. $109–$300 double; $249–$329 family room. Check website for discounts, 3rd-night-free specials, or other value-added packages. AE, MC, V. Parking $25 3 blocks away. Subway: N, R, W to 28th St. **Amenities:** Bar; tour desk; babysitting; laundry service; dry cleaning; Internet-access PC. *In room:* A/C, TV, dataport, hair dryer, iron.

Washington Square Hotel ★ (**Value**) With its fantastic location at the corner of Washington Square Park, the focal point of Greenwich Village—Bob Dylan and Joan Baez lived here when it was the Hotel Earle in the folkie 1960s—the Washington Square Hotel would probably do well even if it weren't so nice. The good news is that this small hotel is a winner on its own account: clean, cheery, tastefully furnished—and very reasonably priced. Book a room here as soon as you know you're coming to New York, because lots of people have found out about this gem and it's nearly always full, especially on weekends

The rooms are just big enough to accommodate a crib or rollaway, but a family should spring for a quad room, which has two double beds; request no. 902, the largest, which is in front with a superb view of leafy Washington Square Park. (Any front room on the fifth through ninth floors has good park views.) If you need connecting doubles, request rooms 219 and 220, which share a bathroom. All other rooms have their own small but spruce white-tiled bathrooms; the bedrooms sport a snazzy Art Deco look, with rose-colored walls, frosted-glass light fixtures, mahogany and pink granite accents, black leather headboards, and crisp white duvets. There are plenty of generous-size mirrors and reading lamps, operating on the novel assumption that guests might actually like to read in bed.

At the back of the Parisian-looking little lobby, with its wrought-iron gate and marble staircase, there's an atmospheric little bar; the attached **North Square** restaurant draws locals on its own merits. There's no room service, but this part of the Village is crawling with restaurants in all price ranges that stay open all hours, and walking around here is a pleasure at night.

103 Waverly Place (btwn Sixth Ave. and MacDougal St.), New York, NY 10011. ✆ **800/222-0418** or 212/777-9515. Fax 212/979-8373. www.washingtonsquarehotel.com. 150 units. $204–$350 double. Rates include continental breakfast. Crib free. AE, MC, V. Parking nearby $40. Subway: A, B, C, D, E, F, V to W. 4th St. **Amenities:** Restaurant; cafe; small fitness room; meeting space; Wi-Fi. *In room:* A/C, TV, dataport, high-speed Internet access in Deluxe rooms only, hair dryer, iron/ironing board, safe, bathrobes.

6 LOWER MANHATTAN

VERY EXPENSIVE
Ritz-Carlton New York, Battery Park ★ Facing out onto New York Harbor, this luxury high-rise has without a doubt the best views of any Manhattan hotel. It finally opened in January 2002 (its original opening date of Oct 2001 was derailed by the World Trade Center attacks), a much-heralded emblem of downtown's triumphant rebound. A majority of rooms face the harbor, and every room with harbor views has its own telescope

so you can zoom in on each spike in Lady Liberty's crown. Anchoring the lower end of Battery Park City (like a bookend to balance the Embassy Suites a few blocks north), the Ritz-Carlton is marvelously convenient to downtown attractions such as the Ellis Island/ Statue of Liberty ferry, the Museum of Jewish Heritage (right behind the hotel), the new Sports Museum of America, and the National Museum of the American Indian. The beautifully landscaped South Cove portion of Battery Park City is the hotel's backyard.

The signature decor details are lots of warm wood paneling; a discreet Art Deco–inspired lobby; heartwarming tones of gold, ochre, and green; and artworks specially commissioned from living New York artists—that and big windows everywhere, to drink in those wide-open harbor views. Even the standard double rooms are large enough for a family; request one with two double beds, or take advantage of a pullout sofa or rolla-way bed. Suites don't necessarily add bed space so much as they add entertaining space (and a super home-theater system, which would indeed be great for parents relaxing in the room after the kids have gone to sleep). Weeknights are busy here, so weekend visitors may be able to net some serious rate discounts.

The Ritz-Carlton has a well-deserved reputation as a top kid-friendly hotel chain. Every youngster who visits finds his or her own (to keep!) Ritz-Carlton teddy bear waiting on the pillow; the entertainment armoire has Nintendo; you can just phone downstairs to get board games and kid movies; and you can call for the hotel's bath butler to draw a perfectly calibrated bubble bath. On-site restaurants and room service include a well-tailored kids' menu; all meals, including afternoon tea, are served downstairs in either the **2 West Steakhouse** or the Art Deco **Lobby Lounge.** The **Rise** bar on the 14th floor has a grassy outdoor terrace and wraparound views; its casual light menu includes dim sum, tapaslike snacks, and (oh, yes) extravagant desserts.

2 West St. (at Battery Place), New York, NY 10004. (C) **800/241-3333** or 212/344-0800. Fax 212/344-3804. www.ritzcarlton.com. 298 units. $495–$795 double; $850 and up for suites. Children 12 and under stay free in parent's room. Weekend packages available. AE, DC, DISC, MC, V. Parking $60. Subway: 4, 5 to Bowling Green. **Amenities:** Restaurant; bar; lounge; fitness center and spa; concierge; complimentary shuttle around downtown; business center; Wi-Fi; 24-hr. room service; babysitting; laundry service. *In room:* A/C, TV w/Nintendo, dataport, Wi-Fi, minibar, hair dryer, safe, bathrobes, scale.

EXPENSIVE

Embassy Suites Hotel ★ This classy Hilton property in Battery Park City, with views of the harbor on one side and of the downtown skyline on the other, is a great deal for families on weekends, when the rates fall well into the moderate category. (On weekdays, they may slide up into very expensive.) Every unit is totally suitable for a family, with a king-bedded bedroom and a separate living room with foldout couch (larger families may gravitate toward one of the rooms with two double beds in the bedroom). Bathrooms are roomy, with tubs, and there's always a table big enough for paperwork or art projects, not to mention room-service meals. The place has a with-it sort of buzz, from the curvy bright yellow wall behind the reception desk, to the soaring atrium dominated by an 11-story purple-and-blue Sol LeWitt abstract painting, to the sleek room decor, all neutral tones and textured fabrics and striking art prints commissioned expressly for the hotel. A complimentary breakfast buffet is served each morning, always a huge plus for families. Even better: Every suite has a PlayStation.

The Embassy Suites building also contains several other restaurants (Lili's Noodle Shop and Grill; and the somewhat more plebeian Applebee's, Chevy's, and Pizza Bolla), as well as an 11-screen Regal Cinema movie theater. The location is prime: The well-outfitted New York Sports Club is a handy on-site add-on for hotel guests. The excellent playgrounds of Hudson River Park are only steps from the hotel, as is the gorgeous riverside promenade of Battery Park City. Right outside the hotel's door is one of the coolest memorials ever: the Irish Hunger Memorial, a tilting acre of Irish sod complete with a ruined crofter's cottage. You're within decent walking distance of the Museum of Jewish Heritage, the National Museum of the American Indian, and the ferry to Ellis Island and the Statue of Liberty, and across West Street from the former World Trade Center site. No rooms have direct views of World Trade Center construction, as the hotel is slightly north of the site.

102 North End Ave. (btwn Murray and Vesey sts.), New York, NY 10282. (C) **800/EMBASSY** or 212/945-0100. Fax 212/945-3012. www.embassynewyork.com. 463 units. $359–$449 double. Rate includes full breakfast and cocktail reception. Children 17 and under stay free in parent's room; restrictions on rollaways in some rooms. Crib free. AE, DC, DISC, MC, V. Valet parking $55. Subway: A, C, E, 1, 2, 3 to Chambers St. **Amenities:** 5 restaurants; 2 bars; fitness center; concierge; tour desk; business center; Wi-Fi; 24-hr. room service; laundry services; gift shop. *In room:* A/C, TV/VCR, CD player, dataport, Wi-Fi, kitchenette, minibar, microwave, coffeemaker, bathrobes.

MODERATE

Marriott New York Downtown ★

A good downtown choice for families, the 38-floor Marriott Financial Center has wonderful skyline and harbor views and its own 50-foot pool. So what if the pool has no views? When they're splashing in the water, kids don't care if there are glorious vistas at hand.

The small lobby's traditional marble-and-mahogany look is pleasantly unintimidating, almost cozy. Though guest rooms here don't give you the same kind of space to stretch out in as the Embassy Suites, the double rooms with two double beds are roomy enough to take a crib or rollaway, and there are plenty of connecting doubles. The executive suite is a decent option for families. Bathrooms are a good size. Rooms are decorated in glossy reproduction furniture, deep-piled patterned carpeting, and dark print fabrics, and have large windows to drink in those views. The main restaurant, **Roy's New York,** serves a standout Hawaiian fusion cuisine (never fear, the buffet breakfasts are American-style). The other on-site restaurant, **85 West,** serves light grill food. If you're going to be in Manhattan for the weekend, ask if weekend packages are in effect—they could save you nearly $100 a night over the weekday rates, plus throw in a complimentary breakfast. Summer packages plunge even lower. You'll be right across from Battery Park City, within walking distance of the Statue of Liberty/Ellis Island ferry, and not far from South Street Seaport—and have a very comfy hotel room to boot.

85 West St. (at Albany St.), New York, NY 10006. (C) **800/228-9290** or 212/385-4900. Fax 212/227-8136. www.marriott.com. 497 units. $399–$524 double; $549 and up suite. Rollaway or crib free. Weekend and summer packages available. AE, DC, DISC, MC, V. Valet parking $50. Subway: E to World Trade Center/Chambers St.; R, W to Rector St. **Amenities:** 2 restaurants; coffee shop; indoor pool; fitness room; concierge; business center; Wi-Fi; room service (6am–midnight); concierge-level rooms. *In room:* A/C, TV, Wi-Fi, minibar, coffeemaker, iron/ironing board, safe.

Seaport Inn

This spunky little hotel in a converted 19th-century red-brick building has an offbeat location—on a cobbled street just north of the Fulton Fish Market, a couple of blocks up from South Street Seaport, in the lee of the Brooklyn Bridge's Manhattan entrance ramps (a delightful *trompe l'oeil* mural on a brick building just east of the hotel shows you what the view through the bridge's arches would look like if the building weren't in the way). Walk through the front door to find a spruce country-style decor and a cheerful staff. Upstairs are quiet, bright corridors and newly refreshed guest rooms; some have two double beds, while others have a queen-size bed plus a foldout couch. The bathrooms are up-to-date and dazzlingly clean. While you don't get kitchenettes, there's an unstocked minifridge in every room, as well as a VCR (pick up a tape in the lobby). The Terrace Rooms have AstroTurf terraces with lawn furniture and partial views of the East River and Seaport. The complimentary continental breakfast is a nice plus, as are the fresh-baked cookies offered daily and the board games on hand at the front desk for kids to borrow.

The immediate area has been transformed lately by a spate of residential co-op buildings, bringing in its wake more foot traffic and street-level businesses. Pace University is a block away, and there's no trouble getting cabs at night if you walk a block to Pearl Street. Though the inn has no restaurant and no room service, local restaurants will deliver, and Chinatown is just as close as the Seaport for nighttime forays. For what you save on frills, you can easily afford to spend a little money on cabs by staying here.

33 Peck Slip (btwn Front and Water sts.), New York, NY 10038. $\textcircled{C}$ **800/HOTEL-NY** or 212/766-6600. Fax 212/766-6615. www.seaportinn.com. 72 units. $199–$405 double. Rates include continental breakfast and afternoon tea. Children 17 and under stay free in parent's room. Rollaway $25; crib free. AE, DC, DISC, MC, V. Parking $20 nearby. Subway: 4, 5, 6 to City Hall; J, M, Z to Chambers St. **Amenities:** Fitness room; guest pass to NY Sports Club nearby ($15); concierge; tour desk; Wi-Fi. *In room:* A/C, TV/VCR, dataport, Wi-Fi, fridge, coffeemaker, hair dryer, iron/ironing board, safe, flatscreen TV and whirlpool bath in terrace rooms only.

---

7 BROOKLYN

MODERATE

New York Marriott at the Brooklyn Bridge   Brooklyn Heights is said to be America's first suburb, and many Manhattanites still have the notion that Brooklyn is not quite "New York." But anyone who's spent time there knows better. In addition to having its own attractions (including a top-notch children's museum), Brooklyn is very much part of New York City, not to mention wonderfully convenient to downtown Manhattan—the Wall Street area, Battery Park, and the Statue of Liberty ferry are only one subway stop away. Located in downtown Brooklyn, near picturesque Brooklyn Heights, the Marriott is also a mere 7-minute subway ride from trendy SoHo and, of particular interest to families, only a few blocks away from the famous Brooklyn Bridge, with its pedestrian walkway where energetic kids can run off steam while their parents enjoy breathtaking views. Don't be put off by the location on Adams Street, a busy, nondescript thoroughfare feeding the Brooklyn Bridge; the hotel itself is spacious, comfortable, attractive, and well organized without being the least bit uptight or intimidating.

Kids will love the domed ceiling that soars above the entryway and mezzanine lobby, a stunning mural of the sky behind a white trellised gazebo. As you sweep up to the lobby on the escalator between huge potted plants, for a split second you feel as if you're flying. Otherwise, there's a businessy feel to the place, with its network of conference rooms off the main lobby. Guest rooms are pleasant enough, with standard hotel antique reproduction furniture, but high ceilings make rooms feel spacious. There are some connecting rooms, and the doubles themselves have two double beds and just enough extra space to fit a crib or cot. Room decor is reasonably cheery, with red, gold, and green patterned bedspreads and soft green carpeting.

The **Archives** restaurant off the lobby lounge takes its name from the Brooklyn memorabilia it proudly exhibits (on loan from the Brooklyn Historical Society); it serves breakfast, lunch, and dinner. Kids will also enjoy some of the reasonably priced family restaurants on nearby Montague Street in Brooklyn Heights, a 5-minute walk from the hotel. Another plus for families is the 75-foot lap pool; several kids were swimming happily the day we visited.

333 Adams St., Brooklyn, NY 11201. ℂ **888/436-3759** or 718/246-7000. Fax 718/246-0563. www. marriott.com. 665 units. $299–$349 double; $499 and up suite. Rollaway or crib free. AE, DC, DISC, MC, V. Parking $30. Subway: A, C, F to Jay St./Borough Hall; 2, 3, 4, 5 to Borough Hall; M, R to Court St. **Amenities:** Restaurant; bar; indoor pool; health club/fitness center; concierge; car-rental desk; business center; Wi-Fi; salon; room service (6am–1am); concierge-level rooms. *In room:* A/C, TV, Wi-Fi, minibar, coffeemaker, iron/ ironing board, safe.

Family-Friendly Dining

One of the great pleasures of being in New York is dining out in one of the city's many world-renowned restaurants. You don't have to be a long-time resident to make the most of the culinary opportunities either: Visitors are giving locals stiff competition for seats—and that includes vacationing families. In fact, statistics from NYC & Company (the city's official tourism bureau) show that more families visit New York City than any other group. And what, you may ask, do families like to do in the Big Apple? For domestic travelers, eating out is *tops* on visitors' to-do lists—beating out sightseeing, museum-going, and shopping—and for international visitors, dining out is topped only by shopping.

These days, families are a huge part of the city's restaurant scene. From an early age, New York kids are indoctrinated into this dazzling culinary stew—and more and more restaurants are finding ways to welcome children. Plus, the city is filled with solid midrange choices—Italian trattorie, French bistros, and all-American neighborhood favorites—that welcome children with open arms and offer great-tasting dishes for you and the comfort food that kids love. So don't think that just because you have kids in tow in one of the world's top culinary capitals you have to spend your mealtimes in a purgatory of chicken fingers and french fries. Do like the locals do: Bring the kids along on your gastronomic adventures.

First, some common-sense caveats. No, we do not expect you to breeze into Le Bernardin on a Friday night with a passel of toddlers. This is a bad idea on many levels. To begin with, not many adults

who've reserved a table for a leisurely (and not inexpensive) 2- or 3-hour dining experience in a fine restaurant will be thrilled to share their dining space with boisterous children. Then there's the weekend factor. New York City is a major restaurant town, and you can bet that the most popular restaurants will be swamped with serious diners on Friday and Saturday nights. If you're going to try to dine in a nice or trendy restaurant, reserve a table on a **less-busy night** (Sundays are always fun). Keep in mind that **summer** is a great, family-friendly time to try out (and actually snag a reservation at) some of the city's trendiest restaurants (the natives have gone to the beach). And unless your kids are gold-star graduates of the Emily Post school of mealtime manners, avoid reserving a table **at the height of the dinner service.** It's always a good idea to **eat early,** before the restaurant is packed with patrons.

Of course, one way to circumvent the previous caveats is to choose a restaurant with **sidewalk seating.** The open-air arrangement minimizes the impact of noisy children on other diners, provides endless distraction, and makes messes less important. A restaurant with **other divertissements,** such as eye-popping decor, big picture windows, even a jukebox, can not only distract the kids but prove to be a memorable experience for all.

If your children are squeamish or picky eaters, **play it safe:** Don't choose a place that is too exotic or thoroughly unfamiliar.

If your kids are not ready for prime time and you still want to dine well, **call room service.** Most NYC hotels are fortunate to have highly rated restaurants, and

Peggy Post: The Finer Points of Dining Out with Kids

It's a question that etiquette expert **Peggy Post** (Emily Post's great-grand-daughter-in-law) is asked all the time: *At what age can we take our kids out to a restaurant?* "By all means, take your children out to dinner," Post says. "It's great to get kids used to going out." Post suggests using the following guidelines when dining out to ensure that everyone has a positive experience—and you've put consideration for other diners at the forefront and diminished the potential for ruining someone else's special night.

- **Pick the right place for your family.** Always ask the reservations person if the restaurant is kid-friendly. Many restaurants have kids' menus, kids' diversions, even dining sections for families. Others may not have kid-specific bells and whistles, but welcome kids nonetheless.
- **Assess your child's preparedness.** At what age can you take a child to a nice restaurant? Some kids are really well-behaved early on; others are unpredictable—there's no black and white. But for the most part, very young children don't sit still naturally for long, so try to select a place where the meals don't go on forever. Toddlers can be unpredictable, and sometimes the experience is simply too much pressure for them, and you—not to mention other patrons, whose dining experience can be easily ruined by an unruly or ill-mannered child.
- **Prep your children.** Teach them about sitting still and using their "inside" voices. Bring "quiet toys" to keep kids occupied, crayons and coloring books, say, or books. Before going, tell the child that she'll be given a menu and is expected to stay at the table until the meal ends. Maybe bring some favorite snacks to eat.
- **Be efficient.** Order as soon as possible and ask if the waiter can bring an appetizer or bread right away to keep the child occupied. And make sure you figure out what the child wants *before* the server comes to the table.
- **Be aware of other patrons.** A child kicking the back of someone's chair does not endear himself to anyone. Make sure your child stays put and is not running around—it drives people crazy and is a hazard to the staff. If your child makes a mess, do the best you can to help the waitstaff clean up. You don't have to crawl under the table to pick up crumbs, but do help pitch in where it makes sense.
- **Take a break.** If your child is getting restless, leave the dining area for a minute. Walk around outside or an area away from other diners so you aren't driving anyone crazy or getting in the way of the waitstaff.
- **Don't linger over dessert and coffee.** Start getting the check as you're finishing the meal.
- **Have your wits about you.**
- **Be ready to make an exit if you have to.**

you can easily enjoy superlative meals in the comfort of your hotel room.

Finally, remember that **some restaurants are simply not suitable for kids 12 and under.** This is a generalization, I know, but something to keep in mind when choosing a place to eat.

For the last word on dining out with kids, see "Peggy Post: The Finer Points of Dining Out with Kids," below, straight from etiquette expert Peggy Post.

HOURS & RESERVATIONS Most Manhattan restaurants serve continuously—you can generally order dinner as early as 5pm if that's what you're used to, though most New Yorkers eat around 7 or 8pm. Again, if you have small children in tow, it's a good idea to dine earlier rather than later. If you're dining anywhere in the Theater District (the W. 40s) or near Lincoln Center (the W. 60s), you'll be competing with lots of other people trying to finish dinner before an 8pm curtain time; unless you're trying to make that curtain, too, delay your arrival until 7:30pm or so, when most of these restaurants are ready to draw a sigh of relief and relax. Similarly, Midtown and Lower Manhattan restaurants can be very busy from 11:30am to 2:30pm.

I've noted in this chapter if a given restaurant doesn't take **reservations** or if reservations are generally necessary to ensure a table. If there's no notation about reservations, you have a fair chance of being seated even if you haven't called ahead, but making a reservation is always smart.

DRESS CODES Although a few posh Manhattan restaurants still cling to formal dress codes, requiring men to wear a jacket and tie, none of the restaurants listed here do. Many New Yorkers do like to dress it up a bit for a night out, but "casual-chic" is the general buzzword for restaurant dining.

THE CHAIN GANG Besides the restaurants covered in detail below, a number of kid-friendly chains—some local, some national—have properties in New York

City that can be handy if you're in the neighborhood. I don't indicate a specific price category for them, but their prices are uniformly low. Head to their website to find locations near you.

Among the local burger restaurant chains, **Jackson Hole** (www.jacksonhole burgers.com) offers burgers so thick and juicy they'll make your buns soggy (whatever that means), as well as grilled-chicken sandwiches, some salads, and less successful Mexican dishes. If you want your fast food organic, check out the various branches of **Better Burger** (www.better burgernyc.com), which also adds a number of salads, pastas, meatloafs, and veggie burgers to its burgers-fries-and-dogs menu. For the lowdown on the best burgers in town, see the sidebar "The Best Burger Joints in the Big Apple," later in this chapter.

Blockheads Burritos (www.blockheads. com) is a fun addition to the city's dining scene, with a menu of tortilla-wrapped meals that go well beyond the Mexican standards (like the West Indian vegetable casserole tortilla or the Bar-B-Cuban Chicken); teenagers in particular like its hipster decor and healthy emphasis on fresh vegetables, lean meats, and lard-free cooking. Bargain hunters like the casual **Dallas BBQ** restaurants (www.bbqnyc. com), where you can get big portions for under $10. The menu holds no surprises: barbecued chicken, barbecued baby back ribs, barbecued sliced beef, half-pound burgers (turkey or beef). Just beware if you see a tour bus parked out front.

Expanding beyond its original East Harlem location, the chain branches of **Patsy's Pizzeria** (www.patsyspizzeriany. com) have discarded the married-to-the-mob ambience in favor of wood paneling and potted plants and marble-topped tables, perfect for serving up savory pizza pies, crisp salads, and satisfying pastas. The Upper West Side branch is only a few blocks from the American Museum of Natural History.

A Note About Prices

The following reviews include a range of specific menu prices as often as possible; the restaurants are categorized as expensive, moderate, or inexpensive, based on rough estimates of what it would cost to feed a family of four—two parents and two children, assuming that one of the kids is young enough to be satisfied with either a kids' meal or a half portion or just an appetizer. If this mythical family would have to spend $80 or more for dinner (excluding any bar tab), I've classed that restaurant as **expensive;** between $60 and $80, **moderate;** under $60, **inexpensive.**

Uno Chicago Grill (formerly known as Pizzeria Uno; www.unos.com) is a known commodity: swift, cheery service; child-friendly amenities (kids' menu, crayons, flimsy activity booklet, drinks served in lidded plastic cups); and a saloonish decor with wooden booths, black-and-white tiled floors, and exposed-brick walls. Both the deep-dish and the thin-crust pizzas are decent; it's when they go beyond pizzas that you can't always be sure of what you'll get.

A NOTE ABOUT FAST FOOD The reality of eating out with small children is that fast-food joints are sometimes a blessing. Most of those in high-traffic areas of Manhattan are spanking clean and recently renovated; somehow, there's always a McDonald's or a Burger King or a Sbarro just where you need one. There's also a McDonald's delivery service operating in Manhattan (how New Yorkers do love to phone out for their food!): Call ℭ **212/337-3278** to get your Happy Meals and Big Macs brought to your door.

A NOTE ABOUT BROOKLYN Brooklyn is undergoing a restaurant renaissance, with numerous small, artisanal restaurants serving some of the best food in the city—and many of them welcome children with open arms. Unfortunately, for reasons of space, this book does not include Brooklyn restaurants. For information about dining out in Brooklyn, check out *Time Out New York*'s restaurant listings when you get to town.

1 RESTAURANTS BY CUISINE

American

American Girl Café ★★ (Midtown, $$$ p. 118)

Barking Dog Luncheonette ★ (Upper East Side, $$, p. 114)

Blue Ribbon Bakery ★★ (Greenwich Village, $$$, p. 130)

Blue Smoke ★ (Gramercy Park, $$, p. 128)

Boat Basin Café ★★ (Upper West Side, $, p. 112)

Bubby's ★★ (TriBeCa, $, p. 143)

Chat 'n' Chew ★ (Flatiron District, $, p. 129)

City Bakery ★★ (Chelsea, $$, p. 128)

ESPN Zone (Midtown, $$, p. 122)

Fetch Bar & Grill ★(Upper East Side, $$, p. 114)

Good Enough to Eat ★ (Upper West Side, $$, p. 109)

Hard Rock Cafe (Midtown, $$, p. 123)

Key to Abbreviations: $$$$ = Very Expensive $$$ = Expensive $$ = Moderate $ = Inexpensive

FAMILY-FRIENDLY DINING

RESTAURANTS BY CUISINE

6

Alice's Tea Cup 21, 41
Artie's Delicatessen 11
Barking Dog Luncheonette 26, 39
Barney Greengrass 8
Barron's Pizza 27
Bella Luna 6
Boat Basin Café 13
Brother Jimmy's 15, 28, 40
California Pizza Kitchen 44
Carmine's 5
Fetch Bar & Grill 29
Gabriela 3
Good Enough to Eat 9
Gray's Papaya 20
Henry's 1
H&H Bagels 16
H&H Midtown Bagels East 36
Homer's World Famous
    Malt Shop 12
John's Pizzeria Eastside 42
Lexington Candy Shop 34
Lili's Noodle Shop & Grill 33
Luke's Bar and Grill 37
Mary Ann's 4
O'Neals' 25
Ollie's Noodle Shop 10, 23
Papaya King 31
Pizzabolla 2
Popover Café 7
Rain 14
Ruby Foo's 18
Sassy's Sliders 30
Serendipity 3 43
T & R Pizzeria 17
Tavern on the Green 24
Tony's di Napoli 35
Trattoria Sambucca 22
Two Little Red Hens 32
Vinnie's Pizzeria 19

FAMILY-FRIENDLY DINING

6

RESTAURANTS BY CUISINE

American Girl Café 28
Angelo's Coal Oven
  Pizza 19, 24
Benihana 22
Blue Smoke 36
Brgr 13
Buttercup Bake Shop 27
Carmine's 9
Carnegie Deli 3
Chat 'n' Chew 45
Chelsea Market 16
The City Bakery 43
Comfort Diner 33, 40
Cupcake Café 12
Dougie's Bar-B-Que
  & Grill 29
Ellen's Stardust Diner 5
Empire Diner 14
ESPN Zone 10
F&B 15
The Grand Central
  Dining Concourse 32
The Great American
  Health Bar 21
Hard Rock Café 1
Jekyll & Hyde Club 20
John's Times Square 8
Kelley & Ping 38
Kosher Delight 34
La Bonne Soupe 23
Mickey Mantle's 18
Pete's Tavern 44
Planet Hollywood 7
Prime Burger 25
Rock Center Café 35
Rodeo Bar 37
Ruby Foo's 6
Sarabeth's Central Park
  South 17
Shake Shack 39
Stage Deli 4
Tony's di Napoli 30
Virgil's Real Barbecue 31

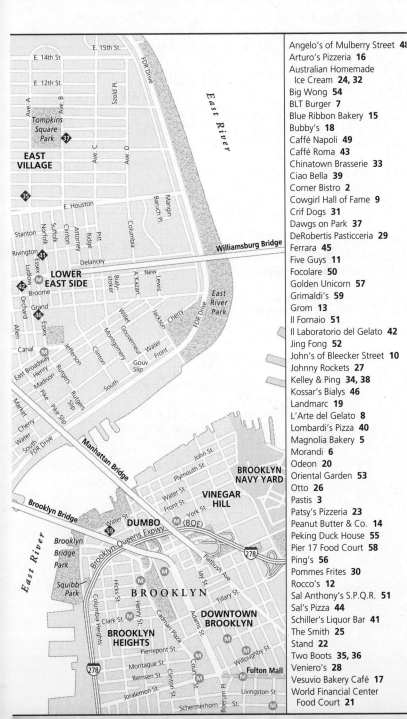

Angelo's of Mulberry Street **4**[

Arturo's Pizzeria **16**

Australian Homemade
  Ice Cream **24, 32**

Big Wong **54**

BLT Burger **7**

Blue Ribbon Bakery **15**

Bubby's **18**

Caffé Napoli **49**

Caffé Roma **43**

Chinatown Brasserie **33**

Ciao Bella **39**

Corner Bistro **2**

Cowgirl Hall of Fame **9**

Crif Dogs **31**

Dawgs on Park **37**

DeRobertis Pasticceria **29**

Ferrara **45**

Five Guys **11**

Focolare **50**

Golden Unicorn **57**

Grimaldi's **59**

Grom **13**

Il Fornaio **51**

Il Laboratorio del Gelato **42**

Jing Fong **52**

John's of Bleecker Street **10**

Johnny Rockets **27**

Kelley & Ping **34, 38**

Kossar's Bialys **46**

Landmarc **19**

L'Arte del Gelato **8**

Lombardi's Pizza **40**

Magnolia Bakery **5**

Morandi **6**

Odeon **20**

Oriental Garden **53**

Otto **26**

Pastis **3**

Patsy's Pizzeria **23**

Peanut Butter & Co. **14**

Peking Duck House **55**

Pier 17 Food Court **58**

Ping's **56**

Pommes Frites **30**

Rocco's **12**

Sal Anthony's S.P.Q.R. **51**

Sal's Pizza **44**

Schiller's Liquor Bar **41**

The Smith **25**

Stand **22**

Two Boots **35, 36**

Veniero's **28**

Vesuvio Bakery Café **17**

World Financial Center
  Food Court **21**

FAMILY-FRIENDLY DINING

6

RESTAURANTS BY CUISINE

Henry's ★ (Upper West Side, $$, p. 110)

Homer's World Famous Malt Shop ★ (Upper West Side, $, p. 112)

Jekyll & Hyde Club (Midtown, $$$, p. 119)

Landmarc ★ (TriBeCa, $$$, p. 142)

Luke's Bar and Grill ★★ (Upper East Side, $$, p. 115)

Mickey Mantle's (Midtown, $$, p. 123)

Odeon ★★ (TriBeCa, $$$, p. 142)

O'Neals' ★ (Upper West Side, $$, p. 110)

Peanut Butter & Co. (Greenwich Village, $, p. 132)

Planet Hollywood (Midtown, $$, p. 124)

Popover Café (Upper West Side, $$, p. 110)

Prime Burger ★ (Midtown, $, p. 125)

Sarabeth's Central Park South ★★ (Midtown, $$, p. 124)

The Smith ★ (East Village, $$, p. 133)

Tavern on the Green (Upper West Side, $$$, p. 107)

Vesuvio Bakery Café (SoHo $, p. 140)

Virgil's Real Barbecue ★ (Midtown, $$, p. 124)

Bagels

H&H Bagels (Upper West Side, $, p. 108)

H&H Bagels East (Upper East Side, $, p. 108)

Ess-a-Bagel (Murray Hill and Midtown East, $, p. 108)

Kossar's Bialys (Lower East Side, $, p. 108)

Barbecue

✓ Blue Smoke ★ (Gramercy Park, $$, p. 128)

Brother Jimmy's Bait Shack (Upper East Side, $, p. 115)

Brother Jimmy's BBQ (Upper West Side and Upper East Side, $, p. 112 and p. 115)

Rodeo Bar (Flatiron District, $, p. 129)

Virgil's Real Barbecue ★ (Midtown, $$, p. 124)

British

Alice's Tea Cup ★★ (Upper West Side and Upper East Side, $, p. 111 and p. 115)

Burgers

BLT Burger (Greenwich Village, $, p. 126)

Brgr (Chelsea, $, p. 126)

Corner Bistro (Greenwich Village, $, p. 126)

Five Guys Burgers and Fries (Greenwich Village, $, p. 126)

Hard Rock Cafe (Midtown, $$, p. 123)

Homer's World Famous Malt Shop ★ (Upper West Side, $, p, 112)

Johnny Rockets ★★ (Greenwich Village, $, p. 132)

Luke's Bar and Grill ★★ (Upper East Side, $$, p. 115)

Prime Burger ★ (Midtown, $, p. 125)

Sassy's Sliders (Upper East Side, $, p. 116)

Shake Shack (Madison Park, $, p. 126)

Stand (Greenwich Village, $, p. 126)

Chinese

Big Wong ★ (Chinatown, $, p. 142)

Chinatown Brasserie ★ (NoHo, $$$, p. 139)

Golden Unicorn ★ (Chinatown, $$, p. 141)

Jing Fong (Chinatown, $, p. 142)

Lili's Noodle Shop & Grill (Upper East Side, $, p. 116)

Ollie's Noodle Shop (Upper West Side, $, p. 113.)

Oriental Garden ★ (Chinatown, $$, p. 141)

Peking Duck House ★★ (Chinatown, $$$, p. 140)

Ping's ★ (Chinatown, $$, p. 141)

Continental

Madeline's Tea Party at the Carlyle
Hotel (Upper East Side, $$, p. 118)
Schiller's Liquor Bar ★ (Lower East
Side, $$, p. 133)
Tavern on the Green (Upper West
Side, $$$, p. 107)

Deli

Artie's Delicatessen ★ (Upper West
Side, $, p. 111)
Barney Greengrass ★★ (Upper West
Side, $S, p. 108)
Carnegie Deli (Midtown, $$, p. 122)
Stage Deli ★ (Midtown, $, p. 127)

Desserts

Alice's Tea Cup ★★ (Upper West Side
and Upper East Side, $, p. 111 and
115)
Australian Homemade Ice Cream
(Greenwich Village, $, p. 133)
Buttercup Bake Shop (Midtown, $,
p. 117)
Caffe Dante (Greenwich Village, $,
p. 133)
Caffé Roma ★ (Little Italy, $, p. 139)
Capogiro (Midtown, $, p. 133)
Ciao Bella (Nolita/Little Italy, $,
p. 139)
Crumbs (Upper West Side, Down-
town, and Upper East Side, $,
p. 117)
Cupcake Cafe (Midtown, $, p. 117)
DeRobertis Pasticceria (East Village,
$$, p. 136)
Ferrara (Little Italy, $, p. 139)
Grom (Greenwich Village, $, p. 133)
Il Laboratorio del Gelato (Lower East
Side, $, p. 136)
L'Arte del Gelato (Greenwich Village,
$, p. 133)
Magnolia Bakery (Greenwich Village,
$, p. 117)
Serendipity 3 ★ (Upper East Side, $$,
p. 115)
Two Little Red Hens (Upper East Side,
$, p. 117)
Veniero's (East Village, $$, p. 136)

Diner

Comfort Diner ★ (Midtown$, p. 125)
Ellen's Stardust Diner ★ (Midtown,
$$, p. 122)
Lexington Candy Shop ★★ (Upper
East Side, $, p. 116)
Prime Burger ★ (Midtown, $, p. 125)
Serendipity 3 ★ (Upper East Side, $$,
p. 115)

Eclectic

Ellen's Stardust Diner ★ (Midtown,
$$, p. 122)
Fetch ★(Upper East Side, $$, p. 114)
Tavern on the Green (Upper West
Side, $$$, p. 107)

French

La Bonne Soupe ★ (Midtown, $$,
p. 123)
Pastis ★★ (Meatpacking District,
$$$, p. 136)
Pommes Frites (East Village, $, p. 135)

Hot Dogs

Crif Dogs (East Village, $, p. 134)
Dawgs on Park (East Village, $,
p. 134)
F&B (Chelsea, $, p. 134)
Gray's Papaya (Upper West Side, $,
p. 134)
Papaya King (Upper East Side, $,
p. 134)

Indian

Mitali East (East Village, $, p. 121)

Italian

Angelo's Coal Oven Pizza ★
(Midtown, $, p. 127)
Angelo's of Mulberry Street (Little
Italy, $$, p. 137)
Arturo's Pizzeria (Greenwich Village,
$$, p. 131)
Bella Luna ★ (Upper West Side, $$,
p. 109)
Caffé Napoli (Little Italy, $$, p. 137)
Carmine's ★ (Upper West Side and
Midtown, $$, p. 109 and 120)

Focolare ★ (Little Italy, $$, p. 138)

Il Fornaio (Little Italy, $, p. 138)

John's of Bleecker Street ★★ (Greenwich Village, $, p. 132)

John's Times Square ★★ (Midtown, $, p. 127)

Morandi ★★ (Greenwich Village, $$$, p. 130)

Patsy's Pizzeria (Greenwich Village, $, p. 132)

Pete's Tavern ★ (Gramercy Park, $, p. 129)

Pizza Bolla ★ (Upper West Side, $, p. 113)

Rock Center Café ★ (Midtown, $$$, p. 119)

Sal Anthony's S.P.Q.R. (Little Italy, $$$, p. 137)

Tony's di Napoli (Upper East Side and Midtown, $$$, p. 114 and 119)

Trattoria Sambuca ★ (Upper West Side, $$, p. 111)

Two Boots ★ (East Village, $, p. 135)

V & T Pizzeria-Restaurant (Upper West Side, $, p. 113)

Vinnie's Pizzeria (Upper West Side, $, p. 113)

Japanese

Benihana ★★ (Midtown, $$$, p. 118)

Kosher

Great American Health Bar (Midtown, $, p. 135)

Kosher Delight (Midtown, $, p. 135)

Dougie's Bar-B-Que & Grill (Midtown, $$, p. 135)

Mexican

Gabriela's (Upper West Side, $$, p. 109)

Middle Eastern

Kalustyan's (Midtown, $, p. 121)

Pan-Asian

Kelley & Ping ★(Gramercy Park, East Village, and SoHo, $$, p. 129, 134, and 140)

Rain (Upper West Side, $$, p. 110)

Ruby Foo's (Upper West Side and Midtown, $$$, p. 107 and 119)

Pizza

Angelo's Coal Oven Pizza ★★ (Midtown, $, p. 127)

Arturo's Pizzeria (Greenwich Village, $$, p. 131)

Barron's Pizza (Upper East Side, $, p. 116)

California Pizza Kitchen (Upper East Side, $, p. 117)

Famous Ray's Pizza of Greenwich Village (Greenwich Village, $, p. 125)

Grimaldi's (Brooklyn, $, p. 143)

Il Fornaio (Little Italy, $, p. 138)

John's of Bleecker Street ★★ (Greenwich Village, $, p. 132)

John's Pizzeria Eastside ★★ (Upper East Side, $, p. 117)

John's Times Square ★★ (Midtown, $, p. 127)

Lombardi's Pizza (Little Italy, $, p. 138)

Otto ★ (Greenwich Village, $$, p. 131)

Patsy's Pizzeria (Greenwich Village, $, p. 132)

Pizza Bolla ★ (Upper West Side, $, p. 113)

Sal's Pizza (Little Italy, $, p. 139)

T & R Pizzeria (Upper West Side, $, p. 113)

Two Boots ★ (East Village $, p. 135)

V & T Pizzeria-Restaurant (Upper West Side, $, p. 113)

Vinnie's Pizzeria (Upper West Side, $, p. 113)

Southern

Brother Jimmy's Bait Shack (Upper East Side, $, p. 115)

Brother Jimmy's BBQ (Upper West Side and Upper East Side, $, p. 112 and p. 115)

2 THE UPPER WEST SIDE

EXPENSIVE

Ruby Foo's ★ PAN-ASIAN   The red-lacquer Suzy Wong–style decor of this bi-level rice palace is eye-popping, and the menu hits all the high notes of Asian cuisine, from dim sum to sushi to maki rolls to Thai curries. Compared to more authentic Chinese, Japanese, or Thai restaurants, the food is only competent, but the stunning setting makes up for it—you'll feel like you're inside a jewel-toned lacquered box, with Chinese lanterns glowing overhead, your linen napkin crisply folded into a fan, chopsticks set before you in a gleaming metal stand. Don't expect to get in without a reservation, and don't expect the service to be speedy. The restaurant does, however, offer a coloring sheet and crayons to keep the kids busy. A new cafe menu at lunch has lots of interesting small plates, soups, salads, and stir-fries; the lunch kids' menu is irresistible, with "samurai sword" chicken fingers, "long life" noodles, dumplings, and popcorn shrimp. They will even make a good ol' PB&J or grilled-cheese sandwich for those kids who will not try the Asian cuisine.

2182 Broadway (at 77th St.). © 212/724-6700. www.brguestrestaurants.com. Kids' menu, high chairs, boosters. Reservations recommended. Lunch $10–$12; dinner $27–$40; kids' menu $9–$15 (average per person, including drinks). AE, DISC, MC, V. Sun–Mon 11:30am–10pm; Tues 11:30am–10:30pm; Wed–Thurs 11:30am–11pm; Fri–Sat 11:30am–midnight. Subway: 1 to 79th St.

Tavern on the Green AMERICAN/CONTINENTAL/ECLECTIC   Local wisdom has it that only tourists go to Tavern on the Green, drawn by scores of movies featuring this iconic Central Park site with its crystal chandeliers, gardens and topiary, and twinkling outdoor lights. But on temperate evenings when the starry lights beckon, even New Yorkers find themselves considering this undeniably enchanting place. Tavern also now has a serious chef, Brian Young, who was once chef de cuisine for the late Gilbert Le Coze at Le Bernardin. So things should be picking up—although with seating for 1,500, the job may be more about herding 'em in and out than actual cooking. The menu changes seasonally, but expect such American dishes as roasted cod, grilled double pork chop, and prime rib with mashed potatoes, along with seafood starters and an assortment of salads. The children's menu is surprisingly ordinary—pasta with tomato sauce, chicken fingers, hot dogs—but it does indicate a commitment to family business. I'd save this place for a special-occasion lunch or a nighttime meal (so you can see the twinkling lights and Japanese lanterns on the patio outside the window), and only with kids old enough to appreciate the glitz and glamour, because the service can be deadly slow and careless—and you know how fatal that is when you've got restless children.

In Central Park at W. 67th St. © 212/873-3200. www.tavernonthegreen.com. Kids' menu, sassy seats. Reservations recommended. Lunch $22–$34; dinner $26–$45; kids' menu $18–$20. AE, DC, DISC, MC, V. Mon–Fri 11:30am–3pm; Sun–Thurs 5–10pm; Fri–Sat 5–10:30pm; Sun 10am–3pm. Subway: 1 to 66th St.; B, C to 72nd St.

The Best of the Bagels

Why is it that bagels in other cities just don't taste as good as New York bagels? There can't be such a mystery, after all, to baking what's essentially a chewy bread doughnut. Yet we know many transplanted New Yorkers who beg us to bring real bagels along when we come to visit. (Even New Jersey suburbanites make special treks into the city to get their bagels.) And bagels are such a great kid-pleasing food—New Yorkers even use them to pacify teething infants—that we'd hardly know what to do without them.

In my opinion, the premier outlet is **H&H Bagels** (www.hhbagels.com; call 🕐 **800/NY-BAGEL** for shipping anywhere), which has two 24-hour retail shops in Manhattan: (1) 2239 Broadway, at 80th Street (🕐 **212/595-8000**), and (2) 639 W. 46th St., between Eleventh Avenue and the West Side Highway (🕐 **212/765-7200**). Besides selling bagels hot out of the oven to the public, H&H supplies bagels to delis and grocery stores all around the city, so look for signs boasting WE HAVE H&H BAGELS. The problem with H&H is that it has no seating and doesn't serve bagels with any spread (in local parlance, a "schmear"), though you can buy separate little tubs of cream cheese, chopped liver, egg salad, herring in cream sauce, whatever. At least the store has finally installed a coffee machine so you can get a cup of coffee to go. **H&H Midtown Bagels East,** 1551 Second Ave., near 80th Street (🕐 **212/717-7312;** www.hhmidtown bagelseast.com), is a former branch that had to litigate for the right to keep using the name; it too has wonderfully chewy bagels, with the added convenience of a deli counter where countermen can cut and dress your bagels. I know many people who'd award the crown to **Ess-a-Bagel,** 359 First Ave., at 21st Street (🕐 **212/260-2252;** www.ess-a-bagel.com), and 831 Third Ave., at 51st Street (🕐 **212/980-1010**), a full-service bagel deli where you can sit down and eat. But if you really want to get authentic, you might journey down to the Lower East Side to try **Kossar's Bialys,** 367 Grand St., between Essex and Norfolk streets (🕐 **212/473-4810**).

—Holly Hughes

MODERATE

Barney Greengrass ★★ (Finds) DELI As authentic as Artie's is contrived, Barney Greengrass has been a West Side institution since 1908, and it looks like it hasn't been redecorated in half a century—the vintage dairy cases, chipped Formica tabletops, stained brownish wallpaper, and fluorescent lighting are an aggressive statement of the fact that the food's so good, you come here anyway. The fish here is so silky, so meltingly tender, it converted me for life (problem is, nobody else's lox is ever gonna live up to this standard). The service is famously laconic, even gruff, but food arrives quickly. Sodas come in cans; the plates are plain white institutional china—who cares? Your kids may not get the time warp charm of this place, but if they're at all inclined to try classic deli food—lox, chopped liver, cold borscht, chopped herring, whitefish salad, with omelets and bagels as safe alternatives—they'll love it. It's especially good for breakfast, but on weekends you may have to wait in line.

Bella Luna ★ ITALIAN   This sunny restaurant with art-hung yellow walls looks like it'd be strictly for grown-ups, but from day one the place has been extremely easygoing about young diners, always happy to bring them a small portion of plain pasta. The Tuscan-style pasta dishes are truly delicious, as are the veal and fish dishes, the bruschetta, and the mixed antipasto starter (practically a meal in itself); the kids often fill up on the crusty, dense bread. Prices are gentle on the wallet, too.

584 Columbus Ave. (btwn 88th and 89th sts.). ☏ **212/877-2267.** www.bellalunanyc.com. High chairs, boosters. Reservations recommended. Main courses $9.95–$19. AE, MC, V. Daily noon–10:30pm (11pm Fri–Sat). Subway: B, C, 1 to 86th St.

Carmine's ★ ITALIAN   The original location of this popular northern Italian eatery (see also p. 120) is still tough to get into, so be sure to make a reservation. That said, this lively, hearty restaurant is fun, with a decor that's a 1960s throwback (dark wood trim, chrome bar stools) and the aroma of garlic hanging in the air. The menu features superbly executed standards like shrimp scampi, rigatoni with sausage, chicken Marsala, veal scaloppine, and big thick steaks. The dining room can be noisy, but it's a cheerful rumble so conversation isn't impossible. Portions are served family-style and are legendarily huge, so order accordingly—insist on your children splitting a dish with you, even if they're big eaters. We always over-order, though; the menu's so tempting, we just can't help it.

2450 Broadway (btwn 90th and 91st sts.). ☏ **212/362-2200.** www.carminesnyc.com. High chairs, boosters. Reservations recommended. Family-style main courses (serve 2–4 people) $21–$35 (more for porterhouse steaks and lobsters). AE, DC, MC, V. Sun–Thurs 11:30am–11pm; Fri–Sat 11:30am–midnight. Subway: 1 to 86th St.

Gabriela's ★★ MEXICAN   Gabriela's serves up astonishingly good regional dishes that go well beyond rote Mexican combo platters. The roast chicken is a marvel, succulent and delicately spiced; quesadillas are light, crisp, and flavorful; and you can't go wrong with any of the spicy casseroles and soups. As for kids, there are simple tacos (served without hot red sauce—hooray!), accompanied by rice and beans, as well as a number of fruit drinks, fruit shakes, and exotic Mexican soft drinks. The staff is cordial and accommodating; the softly lit stucco walls have a golden glow that's very relaxing, even when the restaurant is packed to the gills, as it usually is. The kids' meal includes one entree, a side dish, and a drink.

688 Columbus Ave. (btwn 93rd and 94th sts.). ☏ **212/961-9600.** www.gabrielas.com. Subway: B, C, 1, 2, 3 to 96th St. Kids' menu, high chairs, boosters. Reservations recommended. Main courses $15–$23; kids' menu $6.95. AE, DISC, MC, V. Mon–Thurs 11:30am–11pm; Fri–Sat 11:30am–midnight; Sun 11:30am–10pm.

Good Enough to Eat ★ AMERICAN   This charming little restaurant grew out of a bakery, so you can bet the pies and cakes are excellent. Tables are small, with weathered wood pickets around to strike a rustic note; cut flowers add another farmhouse touch. Breakfasts are to die for: How about apple pancakes, banana-walnut pancakes, or Peter Paul pancakes (Belgium chocolate and coconut)? Though the menu focuses on old-fashioned American dishes like mac 'n' cheese, meatloaf, and a classic turkey dinner (with homemade cornbread), chef/owner Carrie Levin trained at the Russian Tea Room and the Four Seasons, and is perfectly capable of turning out stunning daily fish specials, lemon Parmesan chicken breast, and a vegetable Napoleon that's memorable indeed. Its kids' menu, "designed and tested by kids," has pasta, burger bites, chicken fingers, and mac 'n' cheese—a hit parade of children's faves.

483 Amsterdam Ave. (btwn 83rd and 84th sts.). ✆ **212/496-0163.** Kids' menu. No reservations. Main courses $15–$24; kids' menu $4–$6.75. AE, MC, V. Mon–Thurs 8am–10:30pm; Fri 8am–11pm; Sat 9am–4pm and 5:30–11pm; Sun 9am–4pm and 5:30–10pm. Subway: 1 to 86th St.

Henry's ★ AMERICAN   This popular spot features solid versions of all-American standards in a handsome dining room that was patterned after the Gamble House, a major Arts and Crafts landmark in Pasadena, California. The woody inside is roomy, and an outdoor cafe offers even more space. It's a family favorite for Upper West Siders and Columbia University profs, and don't think they don't know it—you and your kids will be warmly welcomed and well taken care of. The usual kid-friendly dishes—pasta, burgers, fries—are all here.

2745 Broadway (at 105th St.). ✆ **212/866-0600.** www.henrysnyc.com. High chairs, boosters. Reservations recommended. Main courses $10–$30. AE, DC, DISC, MC, V. Mon–Thurs noon–11pm; Fri noon–midnight; Sat 11am–4pm and 5pm–midnight; Sun 11am–4pm and 5–11pm. Subway: 1, 9 to 103rd St.

O'Neals' ★ AMERICAN   Opened in 1964 as the Ginger Man, this perennial Lincoln Center–area favorite is a great place, so long as you can steer around the pre-performance rush. The staff is adept at getting diners out in time for the 8pm curtain; but if you want a relaxed meal, come for dinner after 8pm, or do weekday lunch or an early weekend brunch. The rambling dining rooms have the authentic look of a turn-of-the-20th-century saloon—brass fittings, wood trim, tile floors—and the unpretentious menu runs the gamut from burgers to seafood with more than a bit of panache. The shrimp curry is a winner, but the daily specials are always worth considering. The burgers are some of the best in town.

49 W. 64th St. (btwn Broadway and Central Park West). ✆ **212/787-4663.** www.onealsny.com. Kids' menu, high chairs, boosters. Reservations recommended, especially for dinner or brunch. Main courses $22–$34; kids' menu $13. AE, DC, DISC, MC, V. Mon–Fri 11:30am–midnight; Sat 11am–midnight; Sun 10:30am–10:30pm. Subway: 1 to 66th St.

Popover Café AMERICAN   This pleasantly upscale cafe's signature teddy bears lined up in the front windows have always deluded folks into thinking it's a restaurant for kids—but it's not particularly so, and the staff has been burned enough by unsupervised brats that they've added a note on children's manners to their menu. With an unpretentiously handsome decor (red plaid banquettes, cadet-blue walls, granite-speckled Formica tabletops), it serves the West Side equivalent of the East Side ladies-who-lunch crowd, wholesome chic types who appreciate sprout-bedecked salads and soul-warming soups accompanied by a light-as-air baked popover. The owner seems somewhat to have accepted the family fate, serving milk in a lidded paper cup and adding a kids' menu of sorts—yet a grilled cheese cooked on hearty home-baked peasant bread isn't necessarily as good as one made with Wonder Bread if you're 4 years old. Avoid weekend brunch, when the lines can be ridiculous.

551 Amsterdam Ave. (at 87th St.). ✆ **212/595-8555.** www.popovercafe.com. Kids' menu, high chairs, boosters. No reservations. Main courses $8.95–$25; kids' menu $3.95–$6.95. AE, MC, V. Mon–Fri 8am–10pm; Sat–Sun 9am–10pm. Subway: B, C, 1 to 86th St.

Rain PAN-ASIAN/THAI   The dreamy Maughamesque decor of this upscale West Sider perfectly matches its exotic cuisine, principally Thai but borrowing accents from Malaysia and Vietnam—peanut sauces; coconut-milk soups; grilled meats; stir-fries; and lemongrass, chile, and lime flavorings. Though there's no kids' menu, many young diners are happy with the chicken skewers, noodle dishes, and rice. The place certainly is family-friendly, especially at lunch, despite the romantic calm of its softly lit dining room, with lots of drapes and rattan chairs and potted plants and fringed lampshades. *An added plus:* It's very handy to the Natural History Museum—repair here after a morning in the Asian-animals gallery, and you'll feel you've really been to the Far East.

100 W. 82nd St. (at Columbus Ave.). (𝄃) **212/501-0776**. www.rainrestaurant.com. High chairs. Reservations recommended. Lunch $6.50–$15; dinner $15–$29. AE, DC, DISC, MC, V. Mon–Thurs noon–11pm; Fri noon–midnight; Sat noon–midnight; Sun noon–10pm. Subway: 1 to 79th St.; B, C to 81st St./Museum of Natural History.

Trattoria Sambuca ★ ITALIAN   This 20-year-old business is a great place for family birthday celebrations; the waiters are very friendly, you can color on the paper table-cloths, and the food consists of straightforward Italian classics, served in robust portions. (We have to remind our kids not to fill up on the delicious bread beforehand.) Dishes are served in both regular and family-style portions. If you order family-style, don't over-order—a family of five can choose a couple of entrees and still leave a lot of food on the platters. The chicken piccata is a real winner, as is the penne with eggplant and mozzarella. The dining room is pleasantly soft-hued and contemporary, with sponged orange walls, iron sconces, and Tuscan painted pottery on wall brackets. Very casual, but you still get that special dining-out feeling.

20 W. 72nd St. (btwn Columbus Ave. and Central Park West). (𝄃) **212/787-5656**. http://sambucanyc.com. Kids' menu, high chairs, boosters. Reservations recommended. Main courses $23–$39 (family-size portions); kids' menu $13. AE, DC, DISC, MC, V. Mon–Thurs 5–10pm; Fri–Sat 5–11pm; Sun 3–10pm. Subway: B, C, 1, 2, 3 to 72nd St.

INEXPENSIVE

Alice's Tea Cup ★★ (Finds) BRITISH/DESSERTS   My daughter and her friends adore this unique little spot snuggled into a West Side brownstone, with its shabby-chic jumble of secondhand furniture and mismatched china. Lewis Carroll quotes are stenciled onto the walls, and the gift shop in front is full of treasures. While it's perfect for tea parties—the menu of teas is encyclopedic, brownies and cookies arrive freshly baked and buttery, and crumbly scones are served with clotted cream and preserves—Alice's is brilliant for lunch or dinner, too, serving around-the-world favorites like cucumber sandwiches, curried chicken salad, and croque-monsieurs. Eating here is a special treat indeed.

102 W. 73rd St. (btwn Columbus and Amsterdam aves.). (𝄃) **212/799-3006**. www.alicesteacup.com. Kids' menu, high chairs. AE, DISC, MC, V. Salads and sandwiches $8–$14, kids' dishes $5–$8; $23–$38 high tea. Daily 8am–8pm. Subway: B, C, 1, 2, 3 to 72nd St.

Artie's Delicatessen ★ DELI   Pastrami is a cornerstone of the huge menu, though the scrumptious meatloaf is even better. Pickles come standard with table service and the crisp, tangy coleslaw. Teenagers will love the hot chicken wings. Hot dogs, potato pancakes, and grilled-cheese sandwiches are other kid-friendly choices. Service is quick and friendly, and the white-tiled setting is always noisy enough that no one minds if kids add to the din. Okay, so it's only a decade old, as opposed to burnished veterans like the Carnegie Deli or Barney Greengrass; Artie's still has good classic deli food (at reasonable prices), at least a couple of old-timer waiters, and a sort of go-figure nonchalance that's very kid-friendly and very New York.

2290 Broadway (at 83rd St.). (𝄃) **212/579-5959**. www.arties.com. Kids' menu, high chairs, boosters. No reservations. Sandwiches and burgers $7.50–$14; main courses $11–$17; kids' menu $6–$7.75. AE, DISC, MC, V. Sun–Thurs 9am–11:30pm; Fri–Sat 9am–1am. Subway: 1 to 86th or 79th St.

Boat Basin Café ★★ AMERICAN   A stroke of genius, to put an outdoor restaurant here overlooking the houseboat marina in lower Riverside Park. Not only are the views west over the Hudson spectacular (time it right, and you'll get a sunset show to die for), but the vaulted limestone arches of this open-air structure give it a kind of Venetian charm. And the food is head and shoulders above what you'd expect at an outdoor cafe: superb grilled burgers, zestfully seasoned salads and sandwiches, and excellent grilled seafood. The trappings are supercasual: checked vinyl tablecloths, sturdy plastic chairs, folding tables, and fries heaped in a plastic basket on wax paper. The service can dawdle, but our kids didn't seem to mind, they were so busy counting boats on the river. They're smart enough to serve the kids'-menu sandwiches on white bread and not blacken the hot dogs on the grill; the lemonade was too sour for our kids, but once they realized they could pour packets of sugar into their glasses, they were delighted. This cafe is run by the management of **O'Neals'** restaurant (see above), which also operates a similar seasonal restaurant, the **Hudson Beach Café,** in Riverside Park at about 105th Street.

W. 79th St. at the Hudson River, in Riverside Park. ⓒ **212/496-5542.** www.boatbasincafe.com. Kids' menu. No reservations. Burgers and sandwiches $7.95–$16; main courses $16–$26; kids' menu $2.75– $3.50. AE, DC, MC, V. Late Mar to end of Oct. Mon–Wed noon–11pm; Thurs–Fri noon–11pm; Sat 11am– 11:30pm; Sun 11am–10pm. Subway: 1 to 79th St.

Brother Jimmy's BBQ BARBECUE/SOUTHERN   As the evening wears on, this low-lit, cluttered joint becomes a noisy, beery frat party, especially on nights when UNC and Duke square off in basketball. But the three Brother Jimmy's restaurants definitely like kids and prove it by letting the under-12 set eat free (two free kids' meals per each paid adult entree)—a great deal in today's economy. And the barbecue is not bad, with meaty, spicy ribs, pulled pork, and chicken cooked slowly over hickory wood and slathered with a tangy sauce. Add a little cornbread, candied yams, corn on the cob, and black-eyed peas, and it's a welcome break from pizza and burgers.

428 Amsterdam Ave. (btwn 80th and 81st sts.). ⓒ **212/501-7515.** www.brotherjimmys.com. Kids' menu, high chairs, boosters. Reservations accepted for groups of 8 or more only. Main courses $8.50–$23; salads and sandwiches $5.25–$9.25; kids' menu $4.50. AE, DC, DISC, MC, V. Mon–Wed 4pm–midnight; Thurs–Fri 5pm–1am; Sat noon–1am; Sun noon–11pm; Wed–Sun noon–midnight during summer months. Subway: B, C, 1, 9 to 79th St.

Homer's World Famous Malt Shop ★ AMERICAN/BURGERS   This is one of the classic kid-friendly spots where the burgers are just right and the french fries ("Homerfries") are some of the city's best; the chicken tenders are indeed tender, the chili hot and gutsy, shakes and malteds creamy and thick. Hot dogs come in several variations, and the slushies are . . . well, they're *slushies,* which you can't get in most restaurants. There is no kids' menu, precisely because *the entire menu* is basically a kids' menu; check the blackboards for daily specials, which may include offbeat stuff like deep-fried Snickers. Don't worry, grown-ups, there are tasty soups and salads, too. The restaurant name refers to home runs (the owner used to play baseball), not to Homer Simpson, although Homer Simpson would be right at home here, especially with the freshly made doughnuts. You'd expect a place with this sort of throwback menu to be loaded with kitsch, but the decor is streamlined and bright—the better to focus on the big-screen TVs, invariably tuned to either cartoons or sports.

487 Amsterdam Ave. (btwn 83rd and 84th sts.). ⓒ **212/496-0777.** www.homersworldfamous.com. High chairs, boosters. Reservations accepted. Main courses $2.75–$7.75. AE, DC, DISC, MC, V. Daily 10am– 10pm. Subway: 1 to 86th St.

Ollie's Noodle Shop CHINESE The roast poultry hanging in the front window is **113**
a good sign, and the cheery bustle inside the sunny, contemporary interior carries out the promise of tasty, well-prepared Chinese food—nothing too exotic to challenge the taste buds. This is kid-friendly noodle heaven, and it does the standards cleanly and well. Besides the usual spring rolls, dumplings, and steamed buns for appetizers, the menu features lots of fish, grilled or steamed or braised or sautéed, and a fairly classic range of Chinese dishes (lemon chicken, double-sautéed pork, eggplant sautéed in garlic sauce). For the kids, opt for lo mein noodles or the broader chow fun noodles, topped with chunks of chicken and a few shredded vegetables. The service is brisk and tolerant; it can get pretty crowded on weekends, but tables empty quickly.

(1) 2315 Broadway (at 84th St.). ✆ **212/362-3111.** Subway: 1 to 86th St. (2) 1991 Broadway (near 68th St.). ✆ **212/595-8181.** Subway: 1 to 66th St. (3) 2957 Broadway (at 116th St.). ✆ **212/932-3300.** Subway: 1 to 116th St. Reservations not accepted on weekends. Main courses $7–$21; lunch specials $6.45. AE, MC, V. Sun–Thurs 11:30am–midnight; Fri–Sat 11:30am–1am.

PIZZA

Pizza Bolla ★ (Finds) ITALIAN/PIZZA This casual corner spot, with an upscale trattoria decor of brick facing and mustard-colored walls, never fails us. The menu isn't huge, but we still have a hard time choosing—the tangy thin-crust pizza? A meatball hero? The superb chicken tenders? A satisfying Caesar salad? The staff is friendly and responsive; it's just the right place to plunk yourself down and relax after a dizzying day, and so unpretentious you may be surprised to realize how good the food is.

654 Amsterdam Ave. (at 92nd St.). ✆ **212/579-4500.** Kids' menu, high chairs, boosters. Main courses $8–$18, kids' menu $5–$6. AE, DISC, MC, V. Sun–Wed 11:30am–10pm; Thurs–Sat 11:30am–11pm. Subway: 1, 2, 3 to 96th St.

T & R Pizzeria PIZZA Need a pizza near the Natural History Museum? Here's the place for a quick slice or a pie to go—a very dependable neighborhood storefront pizzeria. No fancy airs or graces, just good pizza.

411 Amsterdam Ave. (at 79th St.). ✆ **212/787-4093.** No reservations. Pizzas $12–$16. No credit cards. Mon–Tues 10am–midnight; Wed 10am–1am; Thurs–Sat 11am–3am; Sun 10am–11pm. Subway: 1, 9 to 79th St.

V & T Pizzeria-Restaurant ITALIAN/PIZZA With its brick walls, painted murals, low lighting, and red-checkered tablecloths, V & T looks just like the campus pizza joint it is, the campuses in question being nearby Columbia and Barnard. The pizzas are fabulous, with thin crusts, runny cheese, and robust tomato sauce; other southern Italian dishes, like lasagna and baked ziti, are heartwarmingly good, too. Not much on ambience, but then, you don't get a lot of attitude, either.

1024 Amsterdam Ave. (btwn 110th and 111th sts.). ✆ **212/663-1708.** High chairs. Main courses $6–$17. AE, DC, DISC, MC, V. Daily 11:30am–midnight. Subway: 1 to 110th St.

Vinnie's Pizzeria ITALIAN/PIZZA One of the best by-the-slice walk-in pizzerias in the city, Vinnie's also provides table service if you want to go beyond the wonderful pies and order pasta, antipasti, or salads. At $2 for a plain cheese slice, the pizza is a good deal, flavorful and nicely goopy. The location is handy too.

285 Amsterdam Ave. (btwn 73rd and 74th sts.). ✆ **212/874-4382.** Reservations accepted. Pizza $2–$3 slice, $10–$17 pie; pasta $7–$12. No credit cards. Daily 11am–11:30pm. Subway: 1, 2, 3 to 72nd St.

FAMILY-FRIENDLY DINING

6

THE UPPER WEST SIDE

EXPENSIVE

Tony's di Napoli ITALIAN   Hearty southern Italian food is served family-style at this genial Upper East Side neighborhood spot, which opens onto a big sidewalk cafe in fair weather. Polaroids of satisfied customers in the front window and black-and-white head shots of race-car drivers on the yellowed plaster walls give it the look of a vintage family-owned red-sauce joint, though in fact it's part of the Dallas BBQ restaurant empire. Sunday lunch is the most popular time for families (Tony's doesn't serve lunch on week-days), but you'll find kids sprinkled around the boisterous dining room on weeknights, too. The family-style menu is strong on pasta dishes, with several chicken and veal offerings as well, plus a two-person steak for dedicated carnivores. If your family can't agree on dishes, half portions can be ordered for individuals, as well as kid-size portions of pasta (there's no separate kids' menu). Though I prefer the similar food at Carmine's (p. 109 and 120), the scene here is less frenetic, and the prices are certainly reasonable, considering that you can get away with $20 a head, including wine for adults. Note that there isn't room to park strollers beside tables.

1606 Second Ave. (btwn 83rd and 84th sts.). ✆ 212/861-8686. www.tonysnyc.com. High chairs, boosters. Reservations recommended. Main courses (serve 2–4 people) $18–$50. AE, DC, DISC, MC, V. Mon–Fri 5pm–midnight; Sat–Sun 2pm–midnight. Subway: 4, 5, 6 to 86th St.

MODERATE

Barking Dog Luncheonette ★ AMERICAN   The Barking Dog isn't automatically a family restaurant, but that's what I like about it. Convenient to the 92nd Street Y and Carl Schurz Park, this retro diner welcomes diners with wood-trimmed booths and parchment-shaded lamps at every table. The dog motif amuses most kids: Posters, cookie jars, and even bulldog hood ornaments from Mack trucks put dogs all around the room, and there's a dog bar outside, a blue-tiled corner trough with a polished spigot. But what really makes this place work for families is that it serves breakfast until 4pm—kids can feast on waffles or blueberry pancakes while parents get a chance to eat something suitably grown-up, like a salad of field greens with goat-cheese croutons or a grilled fillet of salmon sandwich. For dinner, there's a good fried chicken with real mashed potatoes, baked ham, pot roast, and a homey meatloaf, as well as more sophisticated stuff like the pan-roasted breast of chicken with piquant Mediterranean-flavored ragout. Old-fashioned ice-cream sodas and sundaes are served from a vintage soda fountain.

(1) 1678 Third Ave. (at 94th St.). ✆ 212/831-1800. Subway: 6 to 96th St. (2) 1453 York Ave. (at 77th St.). ✆ 212/861-3600. Subway: 6 to 77th St. Boosters, sassy seats. No reservations. Main courses $13–$22; sandwiches and salads $6–$13. No credit cards. Daily 7:30am–11pm.

Fetch Bar & Grill ★ AMERICAN/ECLECTIC   A welcoming environment and friendly staff go a long way to make this neighborhood favorite work for kids; what really seals the deal is the dog theme, with snapshots of beloved family pups covering every inch of the warm yellow walls (hence the restaurant's name). The ever-popular burgers and fries, delicious salads, omelets, soups, and pastas give you a decent range of options, with grilled fish and roast chicken added at dinner. Anyone up for Philly cheese steak egg rolls?

1649 Third Ave. (btwn 92nd and 93rd sts.). ✆ 212/289-2700. www.fetchbarandgrill.com. Kids' menu, high chairs, boosters. Reservations recommended. Main courses $9–$19; kids' menu $6–$7. AE, DC, DISC, MC, V. Mon–Fri 11am–3pm and 5–11pm; Sat–Sun 10am–3pm and 5pm–midnight. Subway: 4, 5, 6 to 96th St.

Luke's Bar and Grill ★★ AMERICAN/BURGERS   This is a very civilized place
where children are included as a matter of course. Lots of brick and wood give it a warm,
clubby look that's also somehow young and casual; there's definitely an active bar scene
here, but it never overwhelms the pleasant, relaxing restaurant. Luke's burgers are wonderful, firm and yet juicy, with an ever-so-slightly charred outside, and the salads are big, fresh,
and well conceived. Or you can go for the grilled-cheese sandwich, roast chicken, or one of
the pasta dishes. There's no attitude on the part of the waiters: They seem genuinely happy
to serve youngsters, even babies. If only more restaurants were like this.

1394 Third Ave. (btwn 79th and 80th sts.). ✆ **212/249-7070.** www.lukesbarandgrill.com. Boosters, sassy
seats. Reservations accepted. Main courses $9.95–$21. No credit cards. Mon–Fri 11:30am–1am; Sat
10am–2am; Sun 10am–midnight. Subway: 6 to 77th St.

Serendipity 3 ★ DESSERTS/DINER   This cheery restaurant with its snugly deep
booths and Tiffany-style lamps has an interesting and eclectic menu, with good burgers
and such down-home faves as country meatloaf, chicken potpie, and barbecue chicken.
It also offers parent pleasers like charbroiled Norwegian salmon and curried shrimp
almandine. But it's best known far and wide in the under-12 population as a source for
huge, wickedly rich desserts; fountain sodas; and ice-cream sundaes. The Outrageous
Banana Split is priced at $20 and worth every penny. Because space is tight, strollers and
carriages cannot be accommodated within the restaurant. And it can get packed on the
weekends.

225 E. 60th St. (btwn Second and Third aves.). ✆ **212/838-3531.** www.serendipity3.com. Boosters. Reservations accepted for full meals only. Main courses $12–$20. AE, DC, DISC, MC, V. Sun–Thurs 11:30am–
midnight; Fri 11:30am–1am; Sat 11:30am–2am. Subway: 4, 5, 6 to 59th St.

INEXPENSIVE

Alice's Tea Cup ★★ BRITISH/DESSERTS   Chapter II of the popular West Side
tearoom has the same boho assortment of castoff furniture and china, and the same
delightful menu of sandwiches, omelets, salads, and pastries, with fuller selections available for dinner. The after-school snack menu attracts lots of private-school girls and their
nannies.

156 E. 64th St. (at Lexington Ave.). ✆ **212/486-9200.** www.alicesteacup.com. Kids' menu, high chairs. AE,
DISC, MC, V. Salads and sandwiches $8–$14; kids' dishes $5–$8; $23–$38 high tea. Daily 8am–8pm. Subway: 6 to 68th St.

Brother Jimmy's Bait Shack BARBECUE/SOUTHERN   The rowdy roadhouse
charm of Brother Jimmy's always appeals to kids. Blackened catfish and peel-and-eat
shrimp are featured on a menu otherwise heavy on barbecued chicken, ribs, and pork.
The kitchen doesn't stint on the spices, and beer flows plentifully. But kids are welcomed
warmly, with a kids-eat-free policy that can't be beat anywhere else in town (two under-
12s per parent, so long as the adult buys an entree rather than a sandwich). A variety of
nightly "events" like All-U-Can-Eat-Ribs Sundays make every evening a party here.

1644 Third Ave. (at 92nd St.). ✆ **212/426-2020.** www.brotherjimmys.com. Kids' menu, high chairs, boosters. Reservations accepted for groups of 8 or more only. Main courses $8.50–$23; salads and sandwiches
$5.25–$9.25; kids' menu $4.50. AE, DC, DISC, MC, V. Mon–Wed 4pm–midnight; Thurs–Fri 5pm–1am; Sat
noon–1am; Sun noon–11pm; Wed–Sun noon–midnight during summer months. Subway: 6 to 96th St.

Brother Jimmy's BBQ BARBECUE/SOUTHERN   With a jumble of frat-party
paraphernalia littering the walls, low-lit Brother Jimmy's brings hickory-smoked Carolina
barbecue—both Northern and Southern versions—to New York City. Thick 'n' meaty

ribs, brisket, and chicken are served up in hefty dinners that also include cornbread and a choice of country sides; if your kids aren't into collard greens (yeah, right), you can satisfy them with creamed corn, french fries, or macaroni and cheese. As with the Upper West Side location (p. 112), it may be best to get here early, before the frat party swings into high gear.

1485 Second Ave. (btwn 77th and 78th sts.). © **212/288-0999.** www.brotherjimmys.com. Kids' menu, high chairs, boosters. Reservations accepted for groups of 8 or more only. Main courses $8.50–$23; salads and sandwiches $5.25–$9.25; kids' menu $4.50. AE, DC, DISC, MC, V. Mon–Wed 4pm–midnight; Thurs–Fri 5pm–1am; Sat noon–1am; Sun noon–11pm; Wed–Sun noon–midnight during summer months. Subway: 6 to 77th St.

Lexington Candy Shop ★★ (Finds) DINER   Walking through the door of the Lexington Candy Shop is like passing through a time warp: Inside is a perfectly preserved old luncheonette that's been around since 1925 and looks it. There's a counter with chrome-rimmed stools, along with a handful of wooden booths, where you can down creamy milkshakes and malteds, fresh lemonade, buttery grilled-cheese sandwiches, BLTs, outstanding cheeseburgers, pancakes, and crinkle fries. For the adults, there's fresh shrimp salad and hearty club sandwiches—as well as a classic New York City egg cream. Best of all, the staff seems to positively perk up when they see kids coming. The front window is crammed full of stuffed animals for sale, which guarantees that children never pass by without stopping.

1226 Lexington Ave. (at 83rd St.). © **212/288-0057.** www.lexingtoncandyshop.net. Boosters, sassy seats. Main courses $5.75–$12. AE, DC, DISC, MC, V. Mon–Sat 7am–7pm; Sun 9am–6pm. Subway: 4, 5, 6 to 86th St.

Lili's Noodle Shop & Grill CHINESE   The food in this classic noodle-shop/rotisserie is delicately spiced and not too greasy, a feat considering how fatty barbecue-roasted pork and chicken can be. The noodle dishes, even plain lo mein, are good; the soups come in enormous bowls and can be a challenge to finish, but the broth is light and flavorful, filled with fresh noodles and vegetables. Light varnished woods and streamlined shapes give the decor a smart, modern feel, and the service is efficient, casual, and friendly.

1500 Third Ave. (btwn 84th and 85th sts.). © **212/639-1313.** High chairs, boosters. Main courses $8.95–$20. AE, DC, DISC, MC, V. Daily 11am–11pm. Subway: 4, 5, 6 to 86th St.

Sassy's Sliders (Value) BURGERS   If New York City has drained you dry—your wallet, that is—this is the place for you. The decor is very 1950s—wall tiles, Formica tables, and linoleum, all in Fiestaware colors—and so is the fast-food concept: 2-inch hamburgers steamed with onions, so small and moist they slide whole down your throat, hence the name "sliders." If you're thinking White Castle (which also specializes in miniburgers), think again: Sassy's Sliders are much better, and with other choices like grilled chicken, ground turkey, and veggie burgers, this nifty little spot should satisfy everyone in the family. The hamburger slider ($1.09) is a perfect-size burger for a small kid anyway, and at these low prices, you may be able to feed the whole gang for, gulp, less than $20. Hey, you can panhandle for that kinda dough in no time! Most of its business is takeout and delivery, but there are a few tables inside.

1530 Third Ave. (at 86th St.). © **212/828-6900.** www.sassyssliders.com. No reservations. Burgers $1.09. AE. Mon–Tues 11:30am–10pm; Wed–Thurs 11:30am–11pm; Fri 11am–midnight; Sat 11:30am–midnight; Sun 11:30am–10pm. Subway: 4, 5, 6 to 86th St.

PIZZA

Barron's Pizza (Finds) PIZZA   We stumbled into this pizzeria one Sunday noontime and had some of the best pie of our lives—tangy sauce, fresh mozzarella, crisp chewy

The Cupcake Craze

Whether it's the crowns of butter cream frosting, the portable charm of a cake that fits in your palm, or an automatic response to fond childhood memories, Manhattanites old and young alike crave cupcakes. And cupcakes abound. Scattered throughout the city, bakeries that feature shiny glass cases full of these beloved treats have multiplied, with some small shops drawing not only neighborhood crowds but also citywide fame.

Among the most popular are **Magnolia Bakery,** located at 401 Bleecker St. (at W. 11th St.; ✆ **212/462-2572**), and the **Cupcake Cafe,** on the outskirts of midtown (522 Ninth Ave., at 40th St.; ✆ **212/465-1530**), as well as inside one of the city's best children's bookstores, Books of Wonder (18 W. 18th St.; ✆ **212/465-1530**). (Frequent mentions and cameos on *Sex and the City* didn't hurt Magnolia's fame any—witness the long lines.) For these bakeries, the story is in the frosting; whether piled on in flowerets or cloudlike curls, there's always enough to trump the cake. Both shops produce and sell thousands of the miniature cakes daily and have loyal customer followings. Farther north, **Two Little Red Hens** on the Upper East Side (1652 Second Ave., at 85th St.; ✆ **212/452-0476**) and the five city locations of **Crumbs** (www.crumbsbakeshop.com) feature decadent goods—we're talking frosting you can really sink your teeth into. And in the middle of it all, the **Buttercup Bake Shop,** a descendent of Magnolia located at 973 Second Ave. (at 51st St.; ✆ **212/350-4144**), offers a challenge to even the most determined sweet tooth. Both cake and frosting are overwhelmingly sweet—combined, they could send you into sugar shock.

—*Connor Puleo*

crust—along with friendly counter service. The decor is a little different from your standard storefront pizza shop, with mosaic tile designs and wrought-iron cafe chairs. This is the sort of place you might not seek out without a recommendation, so take it from me: It's well above average. We go back whenever we're in the neighborhood.

1426 Lexington Ave. (at 93rd St.). ✆ **212/410-6600.** Slice $2.25; plain pie $14–$16. No credit cards. Daily 7am–11pm. Subway: 6 to 96th St.

California Pizza Kitchen PIZZA   This cheery chain restaurant, which populates a number of U.S. airports (not to mention the frozen-pizza section of many grocery stores), remains a kid-friendly fave. The menu features pizza topped with such "California style" items as barbecued chicken as well as more traditional pizzas, all of which are cooked in a brick oven. You can also order salads, soups, and pasta dishes.

201 E. 60th St. (at Third Ave.). ✆ **212/755-7773.** Kids' menu, high chairs, boosters. Reservations accepted for parties of 8 or more only. Main courses $10–$16; kids' menu $5. AE, DC, MC, V. Sun–Thurs 11:30am–10pm; Fri–Sat 11:30am–11pm. Subway: 4, 5, 6 to 59th St.; E, N, R, V, W to Lexington Ave.

John's Pizzeria Eastside ★★ PIZZA   The great Village pizzeria chain (p. 127 and 132 later in this chapter) has opened this East Side branch for thin-crust, brick-oven pies, substantial green salads, and a few well-executed pasta dishes. The menu's limited, but every dish on it is delectable.

408 E. 64th St. (btwn First and York aves.). ✆ **212/935-2895.** www.johnspizzerianyc.com. Reservations accepted for groups of 5 or more only. Pizzas $12–$18, toppings $2–$4.75; pastas $8.95–$14. AE, DISC, MC, V. Daily 11:30am–11:30pm. Subway: 4, 5, 6 to 59th St.

AFTERNOON TEA

Madeline's Tea Party at the Carlyle Hotel ★★ CONTINENTAL   Beneath the charming murals by Ludwig Bemelmans (the creator of the *Madeline* children's books) in the luxe surroundings of Bemelmans Bar, this tony East Side hotel (p. 75) offers a storybook **Madeline's Tea Party** every Saturday and Sunday (two seatings: 10am and 12:30pm). Finger sandwiches and delicate little pastries from Payard's Patisserie accompany finely brewed tea and other beverages, not to mention a singalong.

In the Carlyle Hotel, 35 E. 76th St. (at Madison Ave.). ✆ **212/570-7192.** www.thecarlyle.com. AE, DC, DISC, MC, V. Full tea $40 adults and kids. Sat and Sun seatings 10am and 12:30pm; closed in Aug. Subway: 6 to 77th St.

---

4 MIDTOWN

EXPENSIVE

American Girl Café ★★ AMERICAN   Girls would have begged to come to American Girl Place's house restaurant anyway, but parents will be gratified to discover that the food is actually good. Advance reservations are essential, up to 6 months ahead in busy seasons, but it never hurts to stop by the front desk as you enter the store just to see if there are any free slots. Prix-fixe pricing simplifies everything, as does the small, well-chosen menu. As soon as you sit down, you're offered warm, gooey cinnamon buns (don't bypass these). At lunch and dinner there's one choice of appetizer (an arrangement of crudités, dips, cheeses, and breads that's already on the table when you arrive), and everybody gets the same dessert, a yummy little pudding in a chocolate cup. Special touches make all the difference, as with the kids' pizza, decorated with veggies to look like tic-tac-toe, or the baby-size hamburgers with the side of creamy mac 'n' cheese. Best of all, there are special doll seats where girls can prop their American Girl dolls while they eat (the dolls get their own tea sets, and you wouldn't believe how many girls carefully feed their dolls). If you haven't brought a doll, they'll kindly lend you one for the meal. The waitstaff is unfailingly patient and kind, and the decor is sophisticated yet girly. The experience will make your daughter's day, and—surprise, surprise—yours too.

609 Fifth Ave. (at 49th St.). ✆ **877/AG-PLACE.** www.americangirl.com. High chairs, boosters. Reservations required. Brunch $19; lunch $24; tea $20; dinner $26. AE, DISC, MC, V. Subway: E, V to Fifth Ave./53rd St.

Benihana ★★ JAPANESE   Watching the Benihana chefs at work with their flying knives, slicing and dicing the meat, seafood, and vegetables they'll grill on the teppanyaki right at your table, is endlessly fascinating to kids. (Best trick: the onion transformed into a smoking volcano or the shrimp tail flipped into the top of the chef's hat.) As far as Japanese food goes, this doesn't require as adventurous a palate as, say, sushi does, so it's a great choice for kids. For adults, the grilled food is a hearty, healthy meal (and, I admit, delicious). Yes, the operation is clearly tourist-oriented, and some of the chefs look slightly bored—but is the experience any less authentic than a Southern roadhouse or Mexican cantina plopped down on the streets of Manhattan? I think not. What with the teahouse decor, dramatic lighting, and food-flying floor show, kids feel they're getting an exotic experience, and it's great, cornball fun for everyone. And just try to take your eyes off the cook at work. . . .

47 W. 56th St. (btwn Fifth and Sixth aves.). ⓒ **212/581-0930**. www.benihana.com. Boosters. Reservations recommended. Lunch $8.75–$18; dinner $18–$44. AE, DC, DISC, MC, V. Mon–Fri 11:30am–2:30pm; Mon–Thurs 5–10pm; Fri 5–11pm; Sat noon–11pm; Sun noon–10pm. Subway: E, V to Fifth Ave./53rd St.; F to 57th St.; N, Q, R, W to 57th St./Seventh Ave.

Jekyll & Hyde Club AMERICAN   Other theme restaurants have staid display cases full of memorabilia; Jekyll & Hyde delivers a thrill-ride experience, from the crashing ceiling in the vestibule to the creepy artwork that stares back at you from the walls. The waiters all look decked out for Halloween, and there's a continual floor show of ghastly figures telling even ghastlier jokes—expect an extra $2.50 per person slapped onto your bill to cover the entertainment. The food is somewhat beside the point, but for the record, I'll tell you that they serve burgers, popcorn shrimp, pizzas, pastas, baby back ribs, and more. The kitchen's general strategy seems to be to smother things with cheese if at all possible and to grill anything that's grillable.

1409 Sixth Ave. (btwn 57th and 58th sts.). ⓒ **212/541-9505**. www.jekyllandhydeclub.com. Kids' menu. Reservations accepted for groups of 15 or more only. Main courses $14–$32; kids' menu $13. AE, DC, DISC, MC, V. Mon–Thurs 11:30am–11pm; Fri 11:30am–1am; Sat 11am–1am; Sun 11:30am–11pm. Subway: F, N, Q, R, W to 57th St./Seventh Ave.

Rock Center Café ★ ITALIAN   If it weren't in the very heart of Midtown, this restaurant might have cause to be snooty about children, with its sleek, mahogany-trimmed contemporary decor and upscale Italian food (stylish pastas, roasted chicken, fish, and steak). But as they say in the real estate biz, location is everything, and this location couldn't be more of a tourist magnet: set right on the lower plaza of Rockefeller Plaza, where you can watch the ice skaters in winter and sit out under Prometheus in summer. (And you can ride a tiny glass-enclosed elevator down from sidewalk level to the restaurant.) Where tourists flock, there are bound to be children, and the Rock Center Café has shrewdly decided to make the most of them with a decent children's menu—a petite filet mignon, handmade penne pasta, and a grilled-cheese sandwich. Everything about this place spells Special Event.

20 W. 50th St. (at Rockefeller Center). ⓒ **212/332-7620**. www.rapatina.com/rockCenterCafe. Kids' menu, high chairs. Reservations recommended, especially for lunch. Lunch $19–$40; dinner $20–$32; kids' menus $13–$18. AE, DC, MC, V. Mon–Fri 7:30–10am and 5–10pm; Mon–Sat 11:30am–3pm; Sat 4–10pm; Sun 10am–3pm and 4–9pm. Subway: B, D, F, V to 47th–50th sts./Rockefeller Center.

Ruby Foo's ★ PAN-ASIAN   This Theater District location of the Asian-themed chain (p. 107) is good for special events—the decor is as stunning as a movie set, the food precisely presented, the whole atmosphere trendily abuzz. The menu ranges all over Asia, with dim sum, sushi, hand rolls, and Thai curries. Best for older kids who can appreciate the setting and are willing to sample exotic dishes.

1626 Broadway (at 49th St.). ⓒ **212/489-5600**. www.brguestrestaurants.com. Kids' menu, high chairs, boosters. Reservations recommended. Lunch and dinner $19–$39; kids' menu $5–$6.50. AE, DISC, MC, V. Daily 11:30am–5pm; Sun–Mon 5–11pm; Tues–Thurs 5–11:30pm; Fri–Sat 5pm–midnight. Subway: 1 to 50th St.

Tony's di Napoli ITALIAN   Heaping platters of satisfying Italian food are served family-style at this boisterous, good-natured Theater District branch of the Upper East Side favorite (p. 114). The menu offers lots of pasta choices, but also veal, chicken, fish, and Tuscan-style steaks; the waiters really bustle to get folks out in time for their theater curtain.

Around the World in, Oh, a Week

You can sample a different culture every day you're in the city simply by turning a corner. That's because Manhattan is blessed with a number of ethnic enclaves that bring color and flavor to the streets of the city (and don't even get me started on Queens). In all of them, you can find wonderful, exotic places to eat. In addition, you can sample Brazilian specialties like *feijoada* (bean and meat stew) in restaurants pocketing **Little Brazil** on West 45th and 46th streets between Fifth and Sixth avenues; or Filipino fast-food *turo-turos* in **Little Manila,** on First Avenue between 12th and 14th streets.

- **Chinatown.** Whether you choose one of the big, Hong Kong–style banquet restaurants or a modest dumpling house, your family will be welcomed in Chinatown. This is one of the country's largest Chinatowns, a sprawling enclave of restaurants and businesses that has bled into neighboring Little Italy and the Lower East Side. The food is good, cheap, and plentiful—and it's great fun for kids to be in a place that feels and sounds so utterly exotic. Yes, the streets and sidewalks are crowded with people, but the bustle of commerce is palpable. It's easily one of my favorite places in the city. For suggestions on where to eat, see the "Chinatown" listings, later in this chapter.

- **Little Italy.** This is a great place for a lunch or a family dinner, especially on weekends when Mulberry Street is closed to traffic and becomes a strolling pedestrian mall, with Frankie Sinatra crooning from every storefront. Some places stray a little too close to theme park Italian, but the pasta is red-sauce hearty, it's piled high on the plate, and kids eat up the show. For suggestions on where to eat, see the "Little Italy" listings, later in this chapter.

- **Koreatown.** Close to Macy's and the Empire State Building, Koreatown is located in the low 30s between Sixth and Madison avenues, but its locus is 32nd Street between Fifth Avenue and Broadway. Turn a corner and you're in another world: Neon signs and billboards in Korean tout restaurants, snack shops, and late-night karaoke lounges. The Korean barbecue restaurants are fun and delicious; basically, marinated meat is cooked on a grill right at your table. The waterfall in the two-story **Kum Gang San,** at 49 W. 32nd St. (© **212/967-0909;** www.kumgangsan.net), should be enough to draw kids,

147 W. 43rd St. (btwn Sixth and Seventh aves.). © **212/221-0100.** www.tonysnyc.com. High chairs, boosters. Reservations recommended. Main courses (serve 2–4 people) $18–$50. AE, DC, DISC, MC, V. Mon–Fri 5pm–midnight; Sat–Sun 2pm–midnight. Subway: B, D, F, V to 42nd St.; N, Q, R, S, W, 1, 2, 3, 7 to 42nd St./Times Square.

MODERATE

Carmine's ★ ITALIAN   Northern Italian, and lots of it—and the quality is amazing considering the volume of meals they prepare here. The linguine with shrimp in red sauce is light and delicious; the chicken scarpariello in wine sauce is a wonder of garlicky flavor;

but come for reliably good barbecue and Korean favorites like *bimbimbap* and rice-flour pancakes filled with scallions and seafood.

- **Little Tokyo.** In the East Village, along and around 9th Street between Second and Third avenues, Japanese restaurants, stores, and sake bars have flourished. I like to buy Japanese snacks (like tasty shrimp chips) at the **Sunrise Mart** (4 Stuyvesant St., near Third Ave.; ℂ 212/598-3040) Japanese grocery store. For soul-warming ramen-noodle soup, head over to 10th Street between First and Second avenues to **Rai Rai Ken** (214 E. 10th St.; ℂ 212/477-7030); it's really little more than a cozy soup counter with 14 stools, but find your kids a seat and watch them slurp. The owners have opened a Japanese curry shop, **Curry-Ya,** next door (214 E. 10th St.; ℂ 866/602-8779), which serves nine kinds of Japanese curry.

- **Little India.** Two areas in Manhattan qualify as Little India enclaves. Little India in the East Village, along 6th Street between First and Second avenues, is just 1 block long, but its numerous Bengali restaurants compete side by side for diners' attention. These restaurants have several things in common: They're cheap, the food is decent, and they have atmosphere to burn, with colorful Indian fabrics draping the walls, dramatic lighting, and a background of seductive sitar or raga music. As you would expect, kids eat it up. One of the most dependable choices is **Mitali East** (334 E. 6th St.; ℂ 212/533-2508), a cozy downstairs spot where a water fountain splashes at the back of the dining room. Reliable choices include the spicy curries, *murgha tikka* (boneless chicken pieces cooked in a tandoori oven), *biryanis* (meats and vegetables mixed with rice), and masalas. The *papadoms* (thin, crisp lentil wafers) are downright addictive.

  The neighborhood of Murray Hill has a larger, more sprawling Little India, this one on and around Lexington Avenue from 26th to 29th streets, with restaurants, grocery stores, and sari shops. One of my favorite spots is **Kalustyan's** (123 Lexington Ave.; ℂ 212/685-3451; www.kalustyans.com), a Middle Eastern market that sells nuts, dried fruits, and spices out of big barrels and has a little cafe on the second floor selling homemade Indian and Middle Eastern specialties; it's famous for its delicious *mujadarra* (a traditional lentil-and-rice dish with caramelized onions, served as a salad or in pita bread).

and salads are fresh and tasty. Family-style dinners make this a natural if you're eating out with kids, especially if yours are the kind to suck up spaghetti with gusto. The noisy, casual atmosphere absorbs a lot of tantrums, and once you've got a table, service is prompt (if you can't move customers in and out quickly in the Theater District, you're done for). The original branch is on the Upper West Side (p. 109).

200 W. 44th St. (btwn Broadway and Eighth aves.). ℂ **212/221-3800.** www.carminesnyc.com. High chairs, boosters. Reservations after 6pm accepted for groups of 6 or more only. Family-style main courses (serve 2–4 people) $21–$35 (more for porterhouse steaks and lobsters). AE, DC, DISC, MC, V. Sun 11am–11pm;

Mon 11:30pm–11pm; Tues and Thurs–Fri 11:30am–midnight; Wed and Sat 11am–midnight; Sun 11am–11pm. Subway: N, Q, R, S, W, 1, 2, 3, 7 to 42nd St./Times Square.

Carnegie Deli DELI   A classic delicatessen restaurant, straight out of Woody Allen's *Broadway Danny Rose*, the Carnegie Deli may borrow its name from nearby Carnegie Hall, but the atmosphere is anything but refined and stuffy. Every table has a little bowl of crisp dill pickles on it, and the sandwiches are piled so high you can hardly get your mouth around them—corned beef, pastrami, brisket, chopped liver, the works, with Russian dressing the condiment of choice. You can also get kosher dairy dishes like blintzes, pirogi, and matzo brei, or eastern European home cooking like chicken paprikash, Hungarian goulash, and stuffed cabbage. The menu is as huge as the servings. Ya wanna know what New York was like in the '40s and '50s? Come here; order an egg cream, borscht, or gefilte fish; and schmooze away.

854 Seventh Ave. (btwn 54th and 55th sts.). ⓒ 212/757-2245. www.carnegiedeli.com. High chairs, boosters. No reservations. Breakfast $8–$13; sandwiches and main courses $16–$23. No credit cards. Daily 6:30am–4am. Subway: B, D, E to Seventh Ave.

Ellen's Stardust Diner ★ DINER/ECLECTIC   Enter this *Happy Days*–style diner through what looks like a vintage red subway car, and you're in a nostalgic time warp—streamlined chrome trim, turquoise vinyl and Formica, vintage movie posters and ads, and a wall full of subway posters introducing a bevy of Miss Subways (owner Ellen Hart was herself voted Miss Subways in 1959). A model train zips around on an elevated track above diners' heads and TV monitors show old black-and-white TV shows. The food—your basic grab bag of burgers and fries, salads, omelets, tacos, and club sandwiches—tastes decent and comes in good-size portions; Nick at Niters may get a kick out of the cutesy names for menu items, like Fred Mertz-arella Sticks or the Cesar Romero Salad. The waitstaff is supercongenial, and Wednesday through Saturday nights they even sing, as part of a slightly goofy dinner-hour floor show.

1650 Broadway (at 51st St.). ⓒ 212/956-5151. www.ellensstardustdiner.com. Kids' menu, high chairs, boosters. Reservations accepted only for groups of 10 or more. Breakfast $3–$10; lunch and dinner entrees $7–$24; kids' menu $8. AE, DISC, MC, V. Mon–Thurs 7am–midnight; Fri–Sat 7am–1am; Sun 7am–11pm. Subway: 1 to 50th St.

ESPN Zone AMERICAN   It's definitely a theme-restaurant scene, with a line out front, a gift shop, multiple floors, an arcade upstairs, and big-screen TVs putting sports in your face everywhere you turn. But the streamlined blond-wood decor is not too cluttered; the noise level is tolerable; and the menu offers a decent range of standard dishes, with salads and pizzas and lighter food amid all the fried stuff that kids and jock types are expected to love. Meat is, however, a linchpin of the menu: steaks, ribs, cheese steak, burgers, and barbecued pork, along with tailgate-party-worthy appetizers like chicken wings, queso chips, and cheese fries. Though the kids' menu is pretty standard, there are two unusual items—sliders (mini-hamburgers) and a chicken breast with broccoli. Maybe the best thing about the place is the upstairs game room, which is the city's best arcade—clean, well-lit, and spacious, with tons of great sports-themed games to play. That alone makes it worth the visit.

1472 Broadway (at 42nd St.). ⓒ 212/921-3776. www.espnzone.com/newyork. Kids' menu, high chairs, boosters. Sandwiches $11–$13; main courses $12–$26; kids' menu $6. AE, DC, DISC, MC, V. Mon–Thurs 11:30am–11pm; Fri 11:30am–midnight; Sat 11am–midnight; Sun 11am–11pm. Subway: N, Q, R, S, W, 1, 2, 3, 7 to 42nd St./Times Square.

Pizza Etiquette

Sometimes it seems there's a narrow little neighborhood pizzeria on every corner in New York City (though, of course, when you really need one you may not find one for blocks). Most kids like pizza, and between the tomato sauce and the cheese, it actually makes a fairly well-balanced meal. In most neighborhood pizzerias, a single slice of plain cheese pizza will cost between $2 and $3, with higher prices for additional toppings. But the New York preference for huge triangles of thin-crust pizza with satiny thin sauce can make it hard to eat without utensils. The local solution: Fold the triangular slice in half lengthwise, hold it by the thick end, and eat it like a sandwich from the narrow end up. Younger kids may need to have their pizza cut up, which is tricky when you're sawing away on a thin paper plate with a plastic knife. Try slicing it into long, triangular strips.

Hard Rock Cafe AMERICAN/BURGERS   Right in the pulsing heart of Times Square, under a big revolving neon guitar, this brassy burger joint promotes its rock-'n'-roll theme with such stellar memorabilia as a pair of John Lennon's wire-rims with a cracked lens, a red feather boa of Janis Joplin's, Jimi Hendrix's purple velvet suit, and a complete set of collarless suits worn by the Beatles on the *Ed Sullivan Show.* Various trippy 1960s slogans pepper the place, scripted in neon or proclaimed on posters, but the target audience isn't baby boomers nostalgic for Woodstock: It's teenagers, who regard the place as a museum of their parents' goofy past. Despite its lowbrow Disneyland-ish cachet, the Hard Rock is really not so bad; the burgers and milkshakes are perfectly fine, the prices aren't out of sight, and there's something infectious about the blaring rock soundtrack. And if you've got teenagers in tow, the fact that the place is packed with callow teenagers might even be a plus. (Unless, of course, your teenager is too sophisticated for the place already.)

1501 Broadway (btwn 43rd and 44th sts.). (C) **212/343-3355.** www.hardrock.com. Reservations accepted for groups of 15 or more only. Main courses $7.95–$14. AE, DC, DISC, MC, V. Sun–Thurs 11am–12:30am; Fri–Sat 11am–1:30am. Subway: N, Q, R, S, W, 1, 2, 3, 7 to 42nd St./Times Square.

La Bonne Soupe ★ (Finds) FRENCH   This is a cozy, charming bistro, French but not snooty, that truly welcomes *les enfants.* The quiches are splendid, as is the onion soup gratinée, and there are a few fine fondue dishes (talk about throwbacks). Omelets, salads, and filet mignon fill out the menu. The "junior menu" offers hamburger, cheeseburger, or chicken breast with french fries and dessert. There are two floors, the lower one softly lit and paneled, the cheery upper floor more like an Alpine chalet, checkered tablecloths and all. Service isn't speedy, but it's pleasant. This is a nice change of pace from the pounding, pulsating theme-restaurant experience.

48 W. 55th St. (btwn Fifth and Sixth aves.). (C) **212/586-7650.** www.labonnesoupe.com. Kids' menu. Reservations recommended. Main courses $14–$26; kids' menu $11. AE, MC, V. Mon–Sat 11:30am–11pm; Sun 11:30am–10pm. Subway: F, N, Q, R, W to 57th St./Seventh Ave.

Mickey Mantle's AMERICAN   Young fans hungering for a brush with 21st-century athletic celebrity may not get the point of this sleek blond-wood sports shrine owned by the late, great baseball star Mickey Mantle: The autographed jerseys hung on the walls belonged to Ted Williams, Hank Aaron, Stan Musial, Yogi Berra, and Joe DiMaggio, names from long-ago baseball cards, back in the days when they gave you bubble gum with your cards. Oh, yeah, there's a Shaquille O'Neal autographed basketball, but who's this Johnny Unitas whose name is scrawled on the football next to it? Of course, with 28 high-def LCD screens transmitting daily sports events, it's hard to live in the past. Still, the atmosphere is friendly and casual, and the menu has a sprinkling of grown-up dishes like grilled yellowfin tuna, New York strip, three-pepper-crusted chicken, and lobster ravioli with grilled shrimp. Most of the food is studiedly down-home, however, including Mick's own picks: chicken-fried steak, Texas barbecued ribs, and grilled sirloin chili with blue-corn tortillas. The Little League menu has the usual range of chicken fingers, grilled cheese, spaghetti, and burgers.

42 Central Park South (btwn Fifth and Sixth aves.). (C) **212/688-7777.** www.mickeymantles.com. Kids' menu, high chairs, boosters. Reservations recommended. Main courses $14–$30; kids' menu $9.95. AE, DC, DISC, MC, V. Sun–Thurs 11:30am–10pm; Fri–Sat 11:30am–11pm. Subway: N, R, W to Fifth Ave./59th St.

Planet Hollywood (Overrated) AMERICAN   The Times Square location makes this movie-themed restaurant more convenient for tourists than when it was on 57th Street, but it has lost much of its pizazz. Large display cases in the high-ceilinged rooms feature a thinned-out collection of film memorabilia (with the nationwide proliferation of Planet Hollywoods, there must have been little to go around); what's left is mostly costumes and weapons from movies you never heard of. Forget the classics: We're talking music videos and action movies (no surprise, considering that the founders were Bruce Willis, Sylvester Stallone, and Arnold Schwarzenegger). Service is lackluster, and the menu is squarely middle-of-the-road, with hamburgers, steaks, and grilled fish. On the plus side, the restaurant is big enough that you may not have to wait in line to get in, especially if you go before 8pm, and there's a kids' menu of standards like spaghetti and meatballs, chicken tenders, and pizza. The dramatic central room still has a bit of buzz, though the upstairs bar seems to be where it's happening.

1540 Broadway (at 45th St.). (C) **212/333-7827.** www.planethollywood.com. Kids' menu, high chairs, boosters. No reservations. Main courses $13–$26; kids' menu $8. AE, DC, DISC, MC, V. Sun–Thurs 11am–midnight; Fri–Sat 11am–1am. Subway: N, Q, R, S, W, 1, 2, 3, 7 to 42nd St./Times Square.

Sarabeth's Central Park South ★★ AMERICAN   This warm, handsome restaurant is a welcome break from the Midtown glut of theme eateries. It has more than a touch of smart Deco decor, with swanky zebra-pattern banquettes and chairs. It's part of the Sarabeth's Kitchen empire, which began in 1981 as a bakery and jam shop on the Upper West Side. It's open for breakfast, lunch, and dinner, and I recommend them all—the food here is delicious, made with fresh, seasonal ingredients, and comforting all at once. You and the kids will love the free-range-chicken potpie, the mini bacon-cheeseburgers, the pizza margheritas. The Central Park Cobb salad here comes with lobster, crabmeat, and shrimp—zowie! And the breads, baked goods, and desserts, of course, are divine. Finish with a Sarabeth's cookie plate for the kids and a double chocolate pudding for yourself.

40 Central Park South (btwn Fifth and Sixth aves.). (C) **212/826-5959.** www.sarabethscps.com. High chairs, boosters. Reservations recommended. Main courses $15–$29. AE, MC, V. Mon–Sat 8am–11pm; Sun 8am–4pm and 5:30–10pm. Subway: N, R, W to Fifth Ave./59th St.

Virgil's Real Barbecue ★ AMERICAN/BARBECUE   Your cutlery is wrapped in a maroon hand towel atop the plastic tablecloth, which tells you all you need to know about Virgil's—this is barbecue, and you're expected to get messy eating it. Along with the wood-smoked barbecued specialties, you get sides of down-home stuff like turnip greens, a slaw made with mustard greens, and buttery cornbread, as well as more mainstream choices like

> **Fun Facts**   **Who Is Ray & Why Does He Own So Many Pizza Joints?**
>
> You may have noticed that an overwhelming number of pizza places in New York have the name *Ray* somewhere in the title: Famous Ray's, World Famous Ray's, Famous Original Ray's, Original Ray's, Ray's Famous, Ray's House of Pizza, Ray's Real Pizza. Most of these are trying to cash in on the success of **Famous Ray's Pizza of Greenwich Village,** where you'll often have to stand in line just to buy a slice to go. (Considering the equal popularity of the Village's **John's of Bleecker Street,** it could just as easily have been that every pizzeria in town was named John's.) Litigation has been useless in trying to convince these lesser Rays to change their names. Just for fun, ask your kids to keep a running log of Ray sightings as they ramble around the city—you may be surprised by how many they'll turn up.

french fries and coleslaw for folks whose home isn't below the Mason-Dixon line. Kids who can't handle ribs are offered some safer choices, like grilled cheese and hot dogs. The decor is roadhouse chic, with polished wood paneling, ceiling fans, and a clutter of vintage livestock photos. Casual and friendly as it is, Virgil's has a postmodern self-consciousness—come on, that woodpile inside the front door is not there just to stoke the barbecue. But you might as well play along with the game when the food is this good and this hearty.

152 W. 44th St. (btwn Broadway and Sixth Ave.). (C) **212/921-9494.** www.virgilsbbq.com. Kids' menu, high chairs, boosters. Reservations recommended. Main courses $17–$32; kids' menu $5.95. AE, DC, MC, V. Sun–Mon 11am–11pm; Tues–Fri 11:30am–midnight; Sat 11am–midnight. Subway: N, Q, R, S, W, 1, 2, 3, 7 to 42nd St./Times Square.

INEXPENSIVE

Comfort Diner ★ DINER   This chain diner is a great place to know about if you're visiting the U.N. or staying in one of the Midtown East hotels. The Comfort Diner certainly lives up to its retro name, with generous portions of satisfying diner classics— mac 'n' cheese, open-faced hot turkey sandwiches, chili, tuna melts, BLTs, and burgers, as well as a substantial breakfast menu served all day. The clean, cheery look is classic, too, with booths and banquettes and a long chrome-trimmed counter with stools; you almost expect the waitress to call you "honey." Service is quick, and kids are welcomed with a joke-laden menu they can color. The kids' menu is wonderfully sensible, with PB&J sandwiches, pancakes, and buttered noodles ("with no green stuff") along with the usual burger/grilled-cheese/macaroni-and-cheese stuff. Somebody running this place must have young children.

214 E. 45th St. (btwn Second and Third aves.). (C) **212/867-4555.** www.comfortdiner.com. Kids' menu, high chairs, boosters. No reservations. Main courses $6–$20; kids' menu $5.75–$6.50. AE, DC, DISC, MC, V. Mon–Fri 7:30am–9pm; Sat–Sun 9am–9pm. Subway: S, 4, 5, 6, 7 to 42nd St./Grand Central.

Prime Burger ★ Finds AMERICAN/BURGERS/DINER   Behind an unprepossessing Midtown coffee shop facade is this amazing slice of the 1950s (Truman Capote mentions it in *Breakfast at Tiffany's* under its former name, Hamburg Heaven). The decor is all chrome and Formica and fake wood paneling, with a long counter and spinning stools. Food is served on melamine plates; drinks come in plastic tumblers; and your

The Best Burger Joints in the Big Apple

Some say the city has gone meat mad, with steakhouses turning up on every other block and barbecue pits in every neighborhood. But it's the burger joints that are really cooking, with competition for the best patties a boon for burger lovers all over New York. Even top chefs like Daniel Boulud have come up with exquisite (and expensive) versions of the all-American burger at their upscale eateries—but I don't include those fancy joints here. Following are some of the tastiest, juiciest burgers (and kid-friendly burger venues) in the Big Apple.

- **BLT Burger,** 470 6th Ave., at 12th St. (✆ **212/243-8226;** www.bltburger. com). Super-chef Laurent Tourondel has created BLT ("Bistro Laurent Tourondel") restaurants all over the city—BLT Fish, for one, and BLT Steak. This is his most casual, family-friendly spot, with succulent burgers. You can order the Classic (5 oz. of certified Black Angus beef), a Kobe beef version, or one made with Colorado lamb.

- **Brgr,** 287 Seventh Ave., at 26th St. (✆ **212/488-7550;** www.brgr.us). These burgers are made to order with top-quality ingredients and all-natural, humanely raised livestock, and it shows. A number of the toppings are even homemade.

- **Corner Bistro,** 331 W. 4th St., btwn Jane St. and Eighth Ave. (✆ **212/242-9502**). This place is a bar, the kind where people huddle in wooden booths and initials have been carved into the tabletops. Which is precisely why some kids will think it's totally cool to come here; others will simply dig into the thick, juicy burgers and piles of fine fries. And if that's not enough, there's a pretty darn good jukebox.

- **Five Guys Burgers and Fries,** 296 Bleecker St., at Barrow St. (✆ **212/367-9200;** www.fiveguys.com). The first Manhattan outpost of the celebrated D.C. burger chain (more are on the way) is reliably good, with free toppings and french fries cooked in flavorful peanut oil. And free refills on your soft drink.

- **Shake Shack,** Madison Square Park, at 23rd St. and Madison Ave. (✆ **212/889-6660;** www.shakeshacknyc.com). During the week, a long line of office workers snakes outside Danny Meyer's "roadside food stand" in Madison Square Park. What are they waiting for? Terrific hamburgers, hot dogs, and milkshakes. Come on weekends or during off-hours and enjoy an alfresco picnic on a park bench—this is one of the city's nicest pockets of green.

- **Stand,** 24 E. 12th St., University Place and Fifth Ave. (✆ **212/488-5900;** www.standburger.com). Not only can you get a regular-size classic burger here, but you can also order the mini version, a perfectly cooked, kid-size slider on a brioche roll for $4.

order gets to your table unbelievably fast, all of which makes this great for young ones. But what kids may remember best are the seats at the front, which have wooden trays you swing in front of you in lieu of a table. The hand-formed hamburgers are small—maybe 5 inches in diameter—a welcome relief from most diners' too-big-to-finish wads of ground beef. French fries are crisp, tasty, and perfectly salted. The menu has many other offerings (chicken in a basket, BLTs, club sandwiches, grilled cheese, omelets, even retro choices like canned peaches with cottage cheese) but burgers—and the seats with the trays—are the main event.

5 E. 51st St. (btwn Madison and Fifth aves.). ℂ **212/759-4729.** www.primeburger.com. Kids' menu, high chairs, boosters. No credit cards. Mon–Fri 6am–7pm; Sat 6am–5pm; closed Sun. Main courses $4.25–$13; kids' menu $5. Subway: 6 to 51st St.

Stage Deli ★ DELI   Doggedly trying to compete with the Carnegie Deli up the street (p. 122), the Stage Deli promotes more of a theatrical connection; besides the requisite black-and-white glossies of stars plastered all over the place, near the door there's a large display case of Polaroids taken of more recent stars (I use the term loosely for folks like Pauly Shore and David Faustino, along with old reliables like Dom DeLuise—who, judging from the number of pictures posted in restaurants around town, must've eaten his way through the city). On many factors—the overstuffed sandwiches, dill pickles on every table—the Stage Deli competes head-to-head with its rival, and there are some who even claim its corned beef is better; the cheesecake here is smooth as satin and of heroic proportions. The menu is more limited than Carnegie's, sticking mostly to sandwiches. On the whole, the Stage Deli is less atmospheric than the Carnegie, if vintage ambience is what you're after. Lunch and pre-theater hours are crazed, which may mean impatient service, something you don't need when you're with young kids.

834 Seventh Ave. (btwn 53rd and 54th sts.). ℂ **212/245-7850.** www.stagedeli.com. Kids' menu, high chairs. Reservations accepted only for parties of 8 or more. Sandwiches $10–$17; main courses $14–22; kids' menu $6–$11. AE, DISC, MC, V. Daily 6am–2am. Subway: B, D, E to Seventh Ave.

PIZZA

Angelo's Coal Oven Pizza ★ ITALIAN/PIZZA   Yet another claimant to the title of New York's most authentic pizza. With ties to the Patsy's dynasty, Angelo's (which is actually run by Angelo's nephew, John) is an upscale two-level pizzeria dishing up crisp thin-crust pies as well as calzones, salads, and pastas. The glossy decor features wood trim, green marble-topped tables, and parchment yellow walls; you can't get just a single slice of pizza here, but you can get a superb cannoli. I still wouldn't rate it as high as John's (see below), but it's an excellent choice for a Midtown meal. You can order pastas individual or family-style.

(1) 117 W. 57th St. (btwn Sixth and Seventh aves.). ℂ **212/333-4333.** Subway: F, N, Q, R, W to 57th St./ Seventh Ave.; B, D, E to Seventh Ave. (2) 1045 Second Ave. (at 55th St.). ℂ **212/521-3600.** Subway: E, V to Lexington Ave./53rd St. (3) 1697 Broadway (at 53rd St.). ℂ **212/245-8811.** Subway: E, V to Lexington Ave./53rd St. www.angelospizzany.com. Pizzas $15–$17; pasta courses (individual) $9.95–$17. AE, MC, V. Daily 11:30am–11pm.

John's Times Square ★★ ITALIAN/PIZZA   As good as all the John's Pizzeria branches are (p. 117 and 132), this one deserves special mention because it fills such a need in the Theater District for a quick, unpretentious, fabulous meal. The simple, white-walled space is stunning, too, a two-story dining room converted from a church, with a stained-glass dome in its upper reaches. Pizzas slide out of the brick ovens with incredibly thin, crisp crusts; the satisfying green salads are huge enough for two; and the stuffed homemade rolls are a special treat. They don't take reservations, so expect up to an hour's waiting time in the height of the pre-theater crush; but the food's worth it, and service is prompt enough to get you out before your curtain.

260 W. 44th St. (btwn Broadway and Eighth Ave.). ℂ **212/391-7560.** High chairs, boosters. No reservations. Pizzas $12–$18, toppings $2–$4.75; pastas $8.95–$14. AE, MC, V. Daily 11:30am–11:30pm. Subway: N, Q, R, S, W, 1, 2, 3, 7 to 42nd St./Times Square; A, C, E to 42nd St./Port Authority.

FOOD COURT *ikctic*

The **Grand Central Dining Concourse** ★★ (Mon–Sat 7am–9pm; Sun 11am–6pm) is definitely a smart option, even if you're not taking a train into or out of the city. The globe-spanning assortment of vendors aren't the usual tired food-court chains but respected New York restaurants coaxed into this high-profile location, so expect to eat well. There's loads of seating under the cool marble arches, and a few of the participating restaurants, like **Two Boots** (pizza and Cajun food), **Zocalo** (trendy Mexican), and **Junior's** (classic deli), have sit-down table-service areas as well as carryout. I highly recommend it.

---

5 CHELSEA, THE FLATIRON DISTRICT & GRAMERCY PARK

MODERATE

Blue Smoke ★ AMERICAN/BARBECUE   Danny Meyer set out to make an authentic barbecue restaurant in New York City, and even devised a way to smoke his own barbecue on the premises, a near-impossible trick to pull off in a city of 1,001 permits. The result is a bustling, high-ceilinged space where the scent of barbecued meats is frankly irresistible and big, wide booths are just right for families. It's a casual, sunny place with a menu that represents the best of regional American barbecue, with Memphis-style ribs, Texas beef ribs, Carolina pulled pork, and Kansas City spareribs. The kids' menu includes one entree (tuna sandwich, grilled salmon, grilled cheese, elbow pasta with butter or mac 'n' cheese, or Memphis baby backs), one side, dessert, and a drink.

116 E. 27th St. (btwn Park and Lexington aves.). ℂ **212/447-7733.** www.bluesmoke.com. Kids' menu, high chairs. Reservations recommended. Main courses $12–$35; kids' menu $9.50. Sun–Mon 11:30am–10pm; Tues–Thurs 11:30am–11pm; Fri–Sat 11:30–1am. Subway: 6 to 28th St.

The City Bakery ★★ AMERICAN   How about a place that fuses our best and most endearing impulses? Where you can dine on delicious comfort food that is healthful and environmentally sustainable, much of it from the morning's greenmarket in Union Square? Where gigantic, hot-out-of-the-oven chocolate chip cookies are not a guilty indulgence but an essential part of living, like air? Even better: This award-winning bakery/restaurant is one of the most kid-friendly lunch spots in town, with homemade fried chicken, syrup-soaked slabs of French toast, mac 'n' cheese, minipizzas, and an actual spinning wheel of chocolate. City Bakery is officially a "salad bar," but I bet you've never seen one like this one, piled high with bowls of homemade vegetables, pastas, fish, and chicken. I love the green beans dressed in mustard oil, curry leaf, and shaved coconut; the Old Bay chicken wings; the jasmine rice tossed with preserved Asian beans and Thai basil; and the pretzel croissants. On weekends the place is jumping with merry bands of kids, their Bugaboo strollers tucked neatly under the stairs.

INEXPENSIVE

Chat 'n' Chew ★ AMERICAN   Here's another one of those places with (nudge, nudge) "down-home" decor—red-painted floors, dark-stained wood, farm implements and road signs on the walls—and a painfully goofy menu, with dishes like the Cesar Romero Salad, Uncle Red's Addiction (honey-dipped fried chicken), 110% Veggie Chili, and the Holy Cow (a 9-oz. hamburger). Still, it's hard to stay grumpy with food this good and a staff this friendly. The fried catfish po' boy is especially moist and delicious, and the meatloaf comes with "skin on" smashed potatoes. Kids get offered a fairly standard menu of favorites, but the names will intrigue them: Flying Saucer Pancakes, for example, or Tarzan Sticks (chicken fingers).

10 E. 16th St. (btwn Fifth Ave. and Union Square W.). ℭ 212/243-1616. http://chatnchew.ypguides.net. Kids' menu, high chairs, boosters. No reservations. Main courses $11–$17; kids' menu $3.95 at brunch, $4.95 at lunch and dinner. AE, MC, V. Mon–Fri 11am–midnight; Sat 10am–midnight; Sun 10am–11pm. Subway: N, Q, R, W, 4, 5, 6 to 14th St.; L to Union Square.

Kelley & Ping PAN-ASIAN   Over in the Gramercy Park area, this low-key noodle shop offers a change of pace for families who've had too many burgers and chicken fingers; like its urban-chic SoHo parent (p. 140), it's sophisticated, but not too snobbish to welcome kids who don't mind a few spices.

340 Third Ave. (at 25th St.). ℭ 212/871-7000. Kids' menu (dinner only), high chairs, boosters. Reservations accepted for parties of 6 or more. Lunch $4–$13; dinner $6.50–$22; kids' menu $7. AE, MC, V. Daily 11:30am–11pm. Subway: 6 to 33rd St.

Pete's Tavern ★ ITALIAN   If authenticity means something to you (and it does to me), then bypass those artificially concocted theme joints and discover a real slice of old New York. The restaurant has been a tavern since 1864, when it entertained such luminaries as O. Henry, who, in the first booth by the front doors, wrote his classic short story "Gift of the Magi"—a delicious story-time tale for kids if ever there was one. Pete's food is basic red-sauce Italian, and the bar can get a bit rowdy when the frat boys take over; but it's a grand place for kids—even if, as the salty manager said, "we got no balloons, no coloring books." There's no kids' menu, either, just gen-u-ine kids' food: spaghetti with meatballs, burgers, chicken wings, fried zucchini, and fries. It's stroller central during weekend brunches (10:30am–4pm).

129 E. 18th St. (at Irving Place). ℭ 212/473-7676. www.petestavern.com. High chairs. Reservations accepted. Dinner main courses $9.95–$25; lunch main courses $6.95–$15; brunch $7.75–$9.95. AE, DISC, MC, V. Mon–Fri 11:30am–4pm; Sun–Tues 4–11:45pm; Wed–Sat 4pm–12:45am; Sat–Sun 10:30am–4pm. Subway: 4, 5, 6 to 14th St.

Rodeo Bar BARBECUE/TEX-MEX   Someone had a lot of fun decorating this bi-level space, with the feed-grain silo on the upper landing and the huge stuffed bison on a ledge above the bar. The weathered-wood walls are hung with old highway signs and lots of animal horns; Western music twangs, and a basket of taco chips arrives on your table in a flash. Children are a welcome part of the mix—on Monday night they even eat free. The menu is heavy on burgers, steaks, barbecue, fajitas, and burritos, but there are a fair number of vegetarian items and a short list of salads as well. French fries come piled high.

375 Third Ave. (at 27th St.). ℭ 212/683-6500. www.rodeobar.com. Kids' menu, high chairs, boosters. Reservations accepted. Main courses $12–$26; kids' menu $3.50. AE, DC, DISC, MC, V. Daily noon–2am. Subway: 6 to 28th St.

FOOD COURT

Definitely the coolest place to eat in Chelsea is at **Chelsea Market ★★**, 75 Ninth Ave., between 15th and 16th streets (www.chelseamarket.com; Mon–Fri 7am–9pm; Sat–Sun 10am–8pm), a rambling series of food shops set in a rehabbed Nabisco factory. Older kids with a sense of style will appreciate the industrial-chic look, with scrubbed brick walls, exposed pipes, and utilitarian light fixtures; the focal point is a ripped-open water main gushing into a crumbling brick cavity in the floor. Among fish stores and produce stalls, you'll find hip little takeout eateries like Hale and Hearty Soups, Amy's Bread, Sarabeth's Bakery, Buon Italia, Fat Witch Bakery, and the Lobster Place, all with tiny cafe tables nearby where you can enjoy the food.

6 GREENWICH VILLAGE

EXPENSIVE ✓

Blue Ribbon Bakery ★★ AMERICAN   This neighborhood favorite is rarely anything but a sure thing when it comes to flavorful American-bistro food—the standards here are cooked to perfection. Blue Ribbon Bakery is part of the Blue Ribbon mini-empire, with Blue Ribbon Brasserie and Blue Ribbon Sushi nearby. All are worthy dining experiences, although the Bakery feels like the most kid-friendly of the bunch. It's set in a casual, candlelit space with glass windows surveying narrow Village streets. I was there on a Friday night, when the place was packed with couples and groups of young professionals—and smack-dab in the center was a table with small kids who were comfortable and happy and generally fawned over by the excellent waitstaff. The menu features plenty of dishes grown-ups will love (rack of lamb, duck confit, New Orleans–style barbecue shrimp), but it also manages to have lots of kid-pleasing food on hand, such as fried chicken and hamburgers. You could make a dinner out of the extensive selection of small plates, and the excellent wine list is three pages deep. If you have a large group, ask for one of the rooms downstairs, an atmospheric enclave enveloped in 19th-century brick walls. The 135-year-old brick oven was discovered in the basement in 1995; it was beautifully restored, and the restaurant was basically built around it. The oven still cranks out homemade breads, crostini, and other baked delicacies.

35 Downing St. (at Bedford St.). ℭ 212/337-0404. www.blueribbonrestaurants.com. High chairs. Reservations accepted for parties of 5 or more. Main courses $19–$34. AE, DC, DISC, MC, V. Mon–Thurs noon–midnight; Fri noon–2am; Sat 11:30am–2am; Sun 11:30am–midnight. Subway: A, B, C, D, E, F, V to W. 4th St.

Morandi ★★ ITALIAN   I admit: Eating at restaurateur Keith McNally's 2007 re-creation of a rustic Italian trattoria makes me really happy. It's a sunny spot, both inside and out, with a congenial staff, hearty regional Italian cooking, and the easygoing feel of an outdoor cafe on a Roman piazza. It's become a real neighborhood spot, with a sprinkling of actors, models, and European moguls relaxing with their families and having a good time. Lunchtime is a fine time to come on a sun-dappled day; the evening becomes more of a scene, but really, this one of those places that isn't trying so hard to scale the hip-o-meter—which makes it pretty cool in my book. I love the pesto pasta with green beans and potatoes, and the fried artichokes are first-rate. Kids of all ages are welcome here—dogs, too (outside only, of course)—and the tagliatelle Bolognese is a surefire winner for the little ones. It's now open for real Italian-style breakfasts—how about crepes with Nutella to start your day?

211 Waverly Place (at Charles St.). ✆ **212/627-7575**. www.morandiny.com. High chairs. Reservations
recommended. Main courses $16–$29. AE, MC, V. Mon–Fri 8:30–11:30am and noon–midnight; Sat–Sun
10am–4pm; Sat 5:30–midnight; Sun 4:30–11pm. Subway: 1, 2, 3 to 14th St.; 1 to Christopher St.; A, B, C,
D, E, F, V to W. 4th St.

MODERATE

Arturo's Pizzeria ITALIAN/PIZZA   Crowded, dimly lit, and busy, this vintage
hangout is right on the border between the Village and SoHo around Father Demo
Square. It's a fun place to bring the family because it's the opposite of buttoned-down:
It's a little raucous (some say lively), a little cramped (some say cozy), and old-school
colorful, with corny still-life paintings a-kilter on the walls. Kids fit right in with the mix.
Arturo's serves decent thin-crust pizzas; they're slung on your table fresh from a coal-fired
oven, so hot the mozzarella could burn the roof of your mouth. You can get various pasta
dishes, too (go for the baked stuff like ziti and lasagna), but it's the pizzas you're here for.
It's a casual sort of red-checkered-tablecloth place where drinks come in plastic tumblers
and side salads come in plastic fake-wood bowls, which bodes well if you've got kids in
tow. You may have to wait in line, though, and at particularly frantic mealtimes, it can
be hard to get your waiter's attention. There's live jazz every night, which may make
waiting easier. Arturo's is certainly as authentic as any place officially in Little Italy—and
a good deal less touristy.

106 W. Houston St. (at Thompson St.). ✆ **212/677-3820**. High chairs, boosters. Reservations not
accepted on weekends. Pizzas $14 and up; main courses $16–$24. AE, DC, MC, V. Mon–Thurs 4pm–1am;
Fri–Sat 4pm–2am; Sun 3pm–midnight. Subway: 1 to Houston St.

Cowgirl Hall of Fame TEX-MEX   Think the Old West motif of this West Village
theme spot is corny? You're darn tootin' it's corny, and that's why kids get into it. Cowboy
hats, boots, and lassos adorn the walls; steer horns poke from the mirrors and antlers
from the chandeliers; younger customers are handed crayons to color a paper Indian
headdress. Passable barbecue, hearty chili, and a mess of fried catfish are included in the
menu roundup; kids' options feature some offbeat items such as corn dogs and Frito pie
along with the obligatory chicken fingers. You can sit outdoors in nice weather.

519 Hudson St. (at 10th St.). ✆ **212/633-1133**. www.cowgirlnyc.com. Kids' menu, high chairs, boosters.
Reservations recommended. Lunch entrees $7.95–$14; dinner entrees $13–$18; kids' menu $4.50–$6.25.
AE, MC, V. Mon–Thurs 11am–midnight; Fri 11am–2am; Sat 10am–2am; Sun 10am–11pm. Subway: 1 to
Christopher St./Sheridan Square.

Otto ★ PIZZA   This sprawling, handsome space is always bubbling with chatter. It's
a bustling place, with groups of friends and families happily munching on thin-crust
pizza at big, round tables. Star chef Mario Batali and Company made an instant success
of this space, which despite its sleek Deco bones, never quite made it in its previous
incarnations (remember One Fifth? Clementine?). Despite the prevalence of smart-
looking young professionals, this is a great family restaurant (it was even named for the
owners' combined eight children: *otto* is Italian for 8), with bubbling-hot pizzas, a sprinkling of simple pastas, *contorni* such as eggplant caponatina, Tuscan lentils, roasted beets,
and fabulous handmade gelato to finish. The kitchen is happy to do a basic pasta with
marinara sauce for children. The front of the restaurant is an *enoteca* designed to look like
an Italian train station—and it's a beaut.

One Fifth Ave. (entrance on 8th St.). ✆ **212/995-9559**. www.ottopizzeria.com. High chairs, boosters.
Reservations recommended. Pizza $7–$14; pasta $7; salad $8. AE, DISC, MC, V. Daily 11:30am–midnight.
A, B, C, D, E, F, V to W. 4th St.

Johnny Rockets ★★ BURGERS It's a chain, of course, but the formula works pretty well: The 1950s soda-shoppe look is executed smartly, with lots of gleaming white tile and chrome, and the menu is nicely slanted toward kids. You get decent burgers, creamy milkshakes, good fries that aren't too greasy—and get this, a jukebox at every table. With $4.40 to $5.50 kids' meals and menus to color, this is a good bet to please the little ones. The staff seems cheerful enough (and they break into choreographed song and dance every now and then), and it's just too corny for NYU hipsters.

42 E. 8th St. (at Greene St.). ℂ **212/253-8175.** www.johnnyrockets.com. Kids' menu, high chairs, boosters. Burgers $5.20–$7. AE, DC, DISC, MC, V. Daily 10:30am–midnight. Subway: N, R, W to 8th St./NYU; 6 to Astor Place.

John's of Bleecker Street ★★ ITALIAN/PIZZA This is the kind of place that's often described as having no ambience, when in fact it has plenty—classic Village pizzeria ambience, with wooden booths, a faded mural of Olde Italy, a vintage tin ceiling, and an open view of the brick ovens where the pizzas are baked. Folks in the Village lament that John's doesn't sell pizza by the slice, but families should have no problem polishing off a whole pie. The crust is crunchy thin, with savory tomato sauce, bubbly melted mozzarella, and a host of fresh toppings to pick among (nothing too trendy, though)—the sausage and mushroom pizzas are particularly good. After eating at John's, you can say you've truly sampled New York pizza at its best. This branch takes no credit cards, but there's a cash machine in the back.

278 Bleecker St. (btwn Seventh Ave. and Morton St.). ℂ **212/243-1680.** No reservations. Pizzas $12–$18, toppings $2–$4.75; pastas $8.95–$14. No credit cards. Mon–Sat 11:30am–midnight; Sun noon–midnight. Subway: 1, 9 to Christopher St./Sheridan Square.

Patsy's Pizzeria ITALIAN/PIZZA On this restaurant strip just north of the New York University campus, this branch of the Patsy's chain gives Village pizza lovers a good alternative if their legs are too tired to walk west to the original John's Pizza on Bleecker Street (see above). It has a classic pizzeria look and a spacious, informal atmosphere that works great with kids. You can order your pasta in individual portions or family-style, for the whole table.

67 University Place (btwn 10th and 11th sts.). ℂ **212/533-3500.** www.patsyspizzeriany.com. High chairs, boosters. Pizzas $15–$17; pasta $9.95–$17 (individual). AE, MC, V. Sun–Thurs 11:30am–11pm; Fri–Sat 11:30am–midnight. Subway: N, R to 8th St./NYU; N, Q, R, W, 4, 5, 6 to 14th St.; L to Union Square.

Peanut Butter & Co. AMERICAN Born of owner Lee Zalben's obsession, this is a quirky little store/restaurant that serves mostly, you guessed it, peanut butter. Peanut butter memorabilia decorates the golden-hued little cafe, and jars of the house brand are for sale, along with jam and Marshmallow Fluff and other suitable accompaniments. The menu's a hoot, with items like Ants on a Log (a celery stalk coated with peanut butter and raisins), your traditional Fluffernutter, and the Elvis (grilled peanut butter sandwich with bananas and honey—top it with bacon if you really want to eat like the King). If you must, you can also get a grilled cheese, a tuna-fish sandwich, or a baloney sandwich, you spoilsport you. But the peanut butter is superb, freshly ground from high-quality peanuts with just enough oil to make it spreadable. Every sandwich is served with potato chips and carrot sticks, and they'll even cut off the crusts for you. You should be drinking milk with your PB&J, but Welch's grape juice is also available, as are fountain treats such as egg creams and milkshakes. And for dessert, what else but peanut butter cookies or chocolate peanut butter pie?

240 Sullivan St. (btwn Bleecker and W. 3rd sts.). ℂ **212/677-3995.** www.ilovepeanutbutter.com. Kids' menu, high chairs, boosters. Sandwiches $5–$9. AE, DC, DISC, MC, V. Sun–Thurs 11am–9pm; Fri–Sat 11am–10pm. Subway: A, B, C, D, E, F, V to W. 4th St.

SWEET STUFF

ICE CREAM   The West Village has become ground zero for superb ice cream and gelato. Getting fevered press since its 2008 opening is **Grom** (233 Bleecker St., at Carmine St.; ℂ **212/206-1738;** www.grom.it/eng), the Turin-based Italian gelato shop whose product *New York* magazine described as having "the purest, cleanest, freshest flavors." See for yourself, or head down the street to another heralded gelato purveyor, **L'Arte del Gelato** (75 Seventh Ave. S., btwn Bleecker St. and W. 4th St.; ℂ **212/924-0803;** www.lartedelgelato.com), where gelato is made fresh daily. Over on 8th Street, which is fast becoming a mini foodie block, the locals are flocking to **Australian Homemade Ice Cream** (33 E. 8th St.; ℂ **212/677-7787**), for rich, dense ice cream made fresh daily. What do the Australians know about making ice cream? Who knows? This chain is based in the Netherlands. In summer, **Capogiro** (www.capogirogelato.com), sells superb gelato on the skating-rink steps at Rockefeller Center (20 W. 50th St.).

PASTRIES & COOKIES   Fans of Italian pastries and cookies will find bliss on the traditional Italian strip of Bleecker Street between Sixth and Seventh avenues, where **Rocco's** (243 Bleecker St.; ℂ **212/242-6031;** www.roccospastry.com) still sells pignola cookies, cannoli, and napoleons. Nearly a century old, **Caffe Dante** (79–81 MacDougal St., btwn Bleecker and Houston sts.; ℂ **866/681-0299;** www.caffe-dante.com) is a vintage Italian cafe where you can sit and rest your feet over strong espresso and Italian pastries.

---

7 THE EAST VILLAGE & THE LOWER EAST SIDE

MODERATE

Schiller's Liquor Bar ★ CONTINENTAL   Keith McNally does it again, creating an instant neighborhood favorite in this excruciatingly faithful re-creation of a French bistro. It's a neat trick, coming up with a place that is both hipster- and family-friendly; but, hey, how can you go wrong with warm, stylish surrounds and solid food? McNally has a knack, says *New York* magazine, for creating "fun, atmospheric places that grow old gracefully," and this is no exception. Set in an old Jewish enclave that has been rediscovered by hepcats, musicians, and trendsters, Schiller's is a congenial, attitude-free zone where you can order satisfying renditions of roast chicken, steak frites, French onion soup, and Cobb salad. For kids, there are burgers, mac 'n' cheese, fish and chips, and homemade gnocchi.

131 Rivington St. (at Norfolk St.). ℂ **212/260-4555.** High chairs. www.schillersny.com. High chairs. Reservations recommended. Main courses $13–$29. AE, DISC, MC, V. Mon–Fri 11am–midnight; Sat–Sun 10am–5pm and 6pm–midnight. Late supper Sun–Wed midnight–1am; Thurs midnight–2am; Fri–Sat midnight–3am. Subway: F to Delancey St.; V to Second Ave.

The Smith ★ AMERICAN   Where, oh where did all these folks go before The Smith showed up on this nondescript block on Third Avenue? An immediate hit since its opening in early 2008, The Smith cannily hit upon the right formula in a location that never quite gelled with other businesses. Now the spot is packed with diners, a lively, casual, and very congenial place to dine out, with surprisingly good food and a thoughtful

Hot Dog!

The ubiquity of the New York hot dog may be due to the century-old Coney Island frankfurter shrine of **Nathan's Famous,** 1310 Surf Ave., Brooklyn (✆ **718/946-2202**), site of the annual world hot-dog-eating contest. But a recent crop of East Village hot dog emporiums have been standing Nathan's franks on their ends. **Dawgs on Park,** 178 E. 7th St., near Avenue B (✆ **212/598-0667**), has a dog-centric theme, posting photos of customers' dogs; its signature offering is the deep-fried chili dog (beef, turkey, or tofu franks). Its rival is **Crif Dogs,** 113 St. Mark's Place, between First Avenue and Avenue A (✆ **212/614-2728**), which has wacky slogans scrawled on the walls and offers over-the-top treats like a deep-fried bacon-wrapped hot dog topped with avocado and jalapeños. The frankfurters dished out at Chelsea's **F&B,** 269 W. 23rd St., between Seventh and Eighth avenues (✆ **646/486-4441**), put a European spin on the standard hot dog; a few dollars will buy you beignets and *pommes frites* along with specialties like the Great Dane (a hot dog with rémoulade, roasted onions, and cucumber slices).

Uptown, your hot doggery choices are more limited and less retro-chic. **Gray's Papaya,** 2090 Broadway, at 72nd Street (✆ **212/799-0243**), may not tempt youngsters with its milky, sweet, refreshing papaya juice (there's also fruit punch and soda), but you can't complain about the plump, succulent hot dogs, which still cost about a buck—an absurdly quick and cheap meal, which you can eat stand-up at the counter or on the go as you walk on down the street. Gray's Papaya's Upper East Side counterpart is **Papaya King,** at the northwest corner of 86th Street and Third Avenue (✆ **212/369-0648**).

menu, with grown-up choices such as braised beef short ribs, roasted cod, and tuna tartare. Kids get crayons to start doodling with almost before they sit down, and the menu is kiddie heaven, especially at breakfast or brunch—the pancakes are killer. At night Mom and Dad can sip a brew from the restaurant's smart selection (Duvel, Allagash White, Bluepoint Toasted Lager) or toast with a glass of good wine while the kids chow down on spaghetti and meatballs, mac 'n' cheese, or the house specialty, beer-battered string beans. Prices are reasonable, too.

55 Third Ave. (btwn 10th and 11th sts.). ✆ **212/420-9800.** High chairs. www.ctrnyc.com/thesmith. Reservations recommended. Main courses $16–$29. AE, DISC, MC, V. Mon–Tues 8:30am–midnight; Wed–Thurs 8:30am–1am; Fri 8:30am–2am; Sat 10am–2am; Sun 10am–midnight. Subway: L to Third Ave.; 6 to Astor Place.

INEXPENSIVE

Kelley & Ping PAN-ASIAN   This cafeteria-style noodle shop, a branch of the original SoHo Kelley & Ping's, is a smart lunchtime option in the East Village—casual and hip, with noodles as spicy (or not) as you want them.

325 Bowery (at 2nd St.). ✆ **212/475-8600.** Kids' menu (dinner only), high chairs, boosters. Reservations accepted for parties of 6 or more. Lunch $4–$13; dinner $6.50–$22; kids' menu $7. AE, MC, V. Daily 11:30am–11pm. Subway: 6 to Bleecker St.

Pommes Frites FRENCH   Not really a restaurant but a narrow storefront takeout joint with a bill of fare that's pretty straightforward: nothing but thin, crispy, Belgian-style french fries with all manner of sauces to dip them into. Considering that many children often eat nothing but fries anyway at sit-down restaurants, this isn't such a bad option for a lunchtime pit stop.

123 Second Ave. (at 9th St.). ℂ **212/674-1234.** French fries $4–$7.50. No credit cards. Sun–Thurs 11am– 1am; Fri–Sat 11am–3:30am. Subway: 6 to Astor Place.

Two Boots ★ ITALIAN/PIZZA   This dandy East Village restaurant couldn't be better for kids—in fact, it's one of the city's pioneers in serving kid-friendly food in a welcoming environment. To start, you've got witty junk-shop decor (strings of Christmas lights

---

Eating Kosher

Even if you don't maintain a kosher diet, New York offers the best kosher family dining outside of Israel. The important thing to remember is that a kosher restaurant will be meat, dairy, or pareve (*pareve* means the food doesn't contain either meat or dairy products)—you won't find a cheeseburger or chicken parmigiana on any menu unless either the meat or the cheese is really an imitated product. This may sound restricting, but restaurants have learned to make do and become extremely creative in the process.

In Midtown, **Kosher Delight,** 1365 Broadway, at 36th Street (ℂ **212/563-3366;** www.kdexpress.com; meat), is the kosher answer to McDonald's and Burger King. Grilled burgers and chicken sandwiches are standard, but you can also choose from a small Chinese menu and Middle Eastern specialties like falafel. Kosher Delight also has free delivery to any location in Manhattan (although it's not guaranteed your food will arrive hot or within a reasonable amount of time). The **Great American Health Bar,** 35 W. 57th St., between Fifth and Sixth avenues (ℂ **212/355-5177;** www.greatamericantogo.com; dairy), proves that healthy food doesn't have to be boring and flavorless, offering a varied menu from salads to vegetarian chili to pastas. There are wonderful fresh-fruit health shakes blended with milk and yogurt, and kids may get a kick out of the pita pizza—tomato sauce, melted cheese, and vegetables baked on top of pita bread. Unlike most of these restaurants, the Health Bar also serves breakfast, opening at 8am; it's also the only one of these restaurants that doesn't close Friday night and Saturday for the Sabbath.

Dougie's Bar-B-Que & Grill, 74 W. 47th St., between Fifth and Sixth aves. (ℂ **212/398-7070;** meat), offers crayons on all tables to keep kids occupied while they're waiting for their food. Burgers and hot dogs are popular items, but the ribs and pasta dishes shouldn't be passed up.

Note: Because of the Sabbath, most kosher restaurants vary their hours on Friday and Saturday, depending on when sundown is on Friday night and when the Sabbath ends on Saturday night. (Some simply close all day Fri.) Call ahead to be sure when they'll be open if you plan to dine on Friday or Saturday.

shaped like red chiles, old movie posters, and a pair of cowboy boots hanging on a pink wall); then when you're seated, the kids are handed coloring books. You know these people are used to dealing with kids when you see that the milk is served in plastic cups; grown-ups get their drinks in glass mugs shaped like boots. The service can be pretty casual, but the waitresses relate to kids instantly, which always seems to make children behave better. For kids, probably the most popular choice is the Pizza Face, an individual-sized pizza with vegetables arranged to form eyes, nose, and grin. Bigger pizzas are served on cake stands, which is a kick. For the adults, there's a range of salads, heroes, and Cajun-style po' boys.

(1) 37 Ave. A (at 2nd St.). ✆ **212/254-1919.** Subway: F, V to Lower East Side/Second Ave. (2) 74 Bleecker St. (btwn Broadway and Crosby St.). ✆ **212/777-1033.** Subway: B, D, F, V to Broadway/Lafayette St. (3) 200 W. 11th St. (at Seventh Ave.). ✆ **212/633-9096.** Subway: 1 to Christopher St./Sheridan Square. www. twoboots.com. High chairs, boosters. Reservations accepted for groups of 6 or more only. Main courses $7.50–$13; pizzas $7.50–$24. AE, DISC, MC, V. Sun–Tues 11:30am–11pm; Wed–Thurs 11:30am–midnight; Fri–Sat 11:30am–2am.

SWEET STUFF

ICE CREAM As the clinical-sounding name suggests, **Il Laboratorio del Gelato** (95 Orchard St., btwn Broome and Delancey sts.; ✆ 212/343-9922; www.laboratoriodel gelato.com) takes its ice cream very seriously, and good thing—it's absolutely delicious, with creative flavors like apple cinnamon, bourbon pecan, and Thai chili chocolate. **Australian Homemade Ice Cream** (115 St. Mark's Place, at First Ave.; ✆ 212/228-4539; www.australianhomemade.nl; see above), with its rich and flavorful ice creams made fresh daily, has a location on St. Mark's Place.

ITALIAN PASTRIES Two family-owned Italian pastry shops have held on in the East Village for a century, vestiges of an earlier immigrant community—and there's a reason they've survived. The better-known one is **Veniero's,** 342 E. 11th St., between First and Second avenues (✆ 212/674-7070; www.venierospastry.com), a spiffed-up dessert cafe that's open until midnight to accommodate crowds of people craving after-dinner delights from cakes to cookies to cannoli, plus cappuccino and espresso that put Starbucks to shame. With kids, come in the afternoon, when you'll have no trouble getting a table. A more relaxed local crowd skips the lines at Veniero's and drifts over to **De Robertis Pasticceria,** 176 First Ave., between 10th and 11th streets (✆ 212/674-7137), which gives its around-the-corner neighbor a run for its money, serving creamy cannoli and cheesecake along with anise cookies and fruit tarts. The back room, with its pressed-tin ceiling and small marble tables, feels as authentic as any place in Little Italy. It shuts down completely for 2 weeks in July—hey, a family's got to take a vacation.

8 THE MEATPACKING DISTRICT

EXPENSIVE

Pastis ★★ FRENCH   Keith McNally's gorgeous re-creation of a Paris brasserie enjoys a picturesque setting on a wide cobblestone plaza in the Meatpacking District. Its serves terrific bistro fare: steak frites, croques, and salade niçoise. Kids are a big part of the scene, especially at crowded weekend brunches. In the warm months, there's outdoor seating. The waitstaff is cheerful and attitude free, and kids get crayons to doodle with while they're munching on great frites, hamburgers, pasta, or macaroni gratin.

9 Ninth Ave. ⓒ **212/929-4844.** www.pastisny.com. High chairs. Main courses $16–$34. AE, MC, V. Daily **137**
8–11:30am; Sun–Wed 6pm–1am; Thurs 6pm–2am; Fri noon–3am; Sat 6pm–3am; Sat–Sun brunch 10am–
4:30pm. Subway: A, C, E to 14th St.

9 LITTLE ITALY & NOLITA

The tourist trade is the bread-and-butter of this little enclave, and some locals wouldn't be caught dead dining here, pooh-poohing the cookie-cutter pasta-and-red-sauce cuisine, the "O Solo Mio" blaring from storefronts, the Olde Italy decor, the flowery *"grazies"* and *"pregos."* That's a shame, because Little Italy is undoubtedly one of New York's most kid-friendly places to eat, and although the menus are formulaic, the food is generally good quality and sometimes even delicious. The pizzas are surprisingly good. And for a kid, it makes for a great show—and what could be better than pizza and spaghetti for dinner? During the summer, Mulberry Street is closed off to traffic from Friday at 6pm till Sunday night. Expect to get the soft sell up and down Mulberry from maitre d's trying to coax you into their restaurants.

EXPENSIVE

Sal Anthony's S.P.Q.R. ITALIAN   Lots of bustle and elbow room define this vast, high-ceilinged dining hall, where people on all sides are happily digging into Italian food: You can tuck your napkin into your collar here with no fear. Despite the brick walls and potted plants, the look is modern, not vintage trattoria. But what it lacks in coziness and atmosphere, it more than makes up for in efficiency, big portions, and party spirits; it seems there are always a few large tables occupied by extended families, bonding over fusilli and linguine. Pastas are good, as are the hearty meat dishes, especially the macho veal chop.

133 Mulberry St. (btwn Grand and Hester sts.). ⓒ 212/925-3120. www.salanthonys.com. High chairs, boosters. Reservations recommended. Three-course fixed-price dinner $30; dinner entrees $19–$37. AE, MC, V. Sun–Thurs noon–11pm; Fri–Sat noon–midnight. Subway: N, Q, R, W, 6 to Canal St.

MODERATE

Angelo's of Mulberry Street ITALIAN   This crowded Little Italy favorite, which has been around since 1902, turns out an incredibly long list of southern Italian pasta dishes with zestful flavor, most around $13. Don't be put off by the world-weary waitstaff; that's part of the entertainment. Make a reservation so you won't get stuck in the line of tourists waiting to get in, but don't be dissuaded by the place's lowbrow popularity—this is Little Italy, after all, where tourists flock to eat, and no restaurant here that's any good would be without a line. Order anything with garlic, or anything with tomato sauce. If your kids like their pasta plain, even they'll benefit from the fresh, homemade quality of the food.

146 Mulberry St. (btwn Grand and Hester sts.). ⓒ **212/966-1277.** Sassy seats. Reservations recommended. Main courses $12–$17. AE, DC, MC, V. Tues–Thurs and Sun noon–11:30pm; Fri noon–12:30am; Sat noon–1am; closed Mon. Subway: N, Q, R, W, 6 to Canal St.

Caffè Napoli ITALIAN   For a leisurely dinner out with family, Caffè Napoli and its annex, **Trattoria Canta Napoli** (ⓒ 212/226-8705), are recommended for their hearty Italian fare—and everyone seems to know it; this place is perpetually packed (good thing the restaurant stretches around the block). The food is upscale enough to feel like a treat, with seafood alongside the pasta dishes (Naples is a seaport, remember); specialties include the stuffed veal chop and the pasta malafemmina. The softly lit dining room has been tastefully decorated—Neapolitan pictures and artifacts are strewn about, but there's no attempt to make it look like the Old Country. Diners are encouraged to linger over their meals; waiters are attentive but not intrusive. And families are definitely welcome—they'll cheerfully do half portions of pasta for kids.

191 Hester St. (at Mulberry St.). $\textcircled{C}$ **212/226-8705.** High chairs. No reservations. Lunch prix fixe $8.50; dinner entrees $10–$34. AE, DC, DISC, MC, V. Daily 11am–2am. Subway: N, Q, R, W, 6 to Canal St.

Focolare ★ ITALIAN   Some have said this handsome, intimate bistro and bar marks the renaissance of Little Italy, and in its own modest, sure-footed way, it is a step up. Its rustic, dark wood decor has nothing to do with Olde Italy, garish murals, or rococo flourishes (offenders, you know who you are). It's got a homey stone fireplace. And the food is quality, from the Caesar salad to the pastas and pizzas. It's a pleasant respite from the Little Italy carnival—so does it really have to have its own aggressive tout out front pushing the goods like all the other joints?

115 Mulberry St. (at Canal St.). $\textcircled{C}$ **212/993-5858.** High chairs. Reservations recommended. Main courses $13–$31; pizza $12–$14. AE, MC, V. Sun–Thurs 11:30am–11pm; Fri–Sat 11:30am–midnight. Subway: N, Q, R, W, 6 to Canal St.

INEXPENSIVE

Il Fornaio ITALIAN/PIZZA   The sign outside is explicit: KIDS WELCOME. And it goes without saying, no one will get too upset about spills or crying or food left on the plate in this unpretentious spot. It's small enough that you can't miss the shouted exchanges between waiters and cooks; but the pizza here has a long-standing reputation for excellence, so don't be surprised if you have to wait a few minutes for a table on a weekend. (And once you get in, don't be startled if you're hustled back out again fairly soon—not a bad thing if you're with kids.) Pizza, pasta, calzones, and muffalettas are on the lunch menu—who needs a chicken-fingers-and-burgers kids' menu? Pizza is not served at dinnertime, so settle in with a few pastas to feed the brood.

132A Mulberry St. (btwn Canal and Hester sts.). $\textcircled{C}$ **212/226-8306.** www.ilfornaionyc.com. Reservations recommended. Main courses $12–$22; pizzas $7–$18. AE, DC, DISC, MC, V. Daily 11:30am–10:30pm. Subway: N, Q, R, W, 6 to Canal St.

PIZZA

Sometimes all you want is a quick bite of pizza to fuel you up and send you on your way. For a decent slice, check out **Frankie Cee's Pizza** at the **Italian Food Center** (186 Grand St., at Mulberry St.; $\textcircled{C}$ **212/925-2954;** cash only); tables are set up outside in nice weather. You can also order Italian subs or pastas or buy olive oils, cheese, and other Italian delicacies to take home.

Lombardi's Pizza PIZZA   Claiming to be a resurrection of New York's first pizza restaurant, which opened at 53 Spring St. in 1905—and where all the other pizza maestros learned their trade—the new Lombardi's is owned by a grandson of the original Gennaro Lombardi, and it does have an authentic coal oven, taken over from an old bakery. It's a bit far north from the main Little Italy strip along Mulberry Street, but the look is nice and atmospheric, with the obligatory red-checkered tablecloths, brick walls, and white tiled floor. Its wonderful pizzas more than hold their own among the top contenders (John's, Patsy's, Angelo's), with lightly charred thin crusts and totally fresh ingredients. The clam pie is so good that it actually justifies the weird idea of putting seafood on a pizza. Don't expect to just pick up a slice: Sit your family down in a booth, and apply yourselves to consuming a whole pie.

Sal's Pizza (Finds) PIZZA This cozy, modest spot is a little off the beaten track, but it always seems to be packed, and for good reason: The homemade pizzas are tasty and filling. Sal's has been making and serving pizza since 1975, when it was opened by a Neapolitan family in what was then the heart of Little Italy (it's now surrounded by boutiques and Chinese businesses). It serves not only pizzas (and 9-in. minipizzas), but also red-sauce pastas (including lasagna and ravioli), antipasti, and even hearty *secondi* such as shrimp parmigiana and *pollo Marsala.* The walls are filled with photos of the eclectic assortment of celebrities who've dined here, including Sarah Jessica Parker, Mario Batali, Victoria Gotti, and a few wise guys from the *Sopranos.*

369 Broome St. (at Mott St.). (℃ **212/925-0440.** www.salslittleitaly.com. Reservations accepted for parties of 6 or more. Pizzas $6–$14; main courses $9.95–$16. AE, DISC, MC, V. Sun–Thurs noon–9:45pm; Fri–Sat noon–10:45pm. Subway: 6 to Spring St.

SWEET STUFF

ICE CREAM **Ciao Bella,** an award-winning premium ice cream found in stores all over the city, has a gelato shop at 285 Mott St., near Houston Street (℃ **212/431-3591;** www.ciaobellagelato.com) and a block from Old St. Patrick's Cathedral. (Once part of Little Italy, the neighborhood is now referred to as Nolita, but it's mere blocks from the restaurants of Little Italy proper.) The gelato is rich, creamy, and flavorful.

ITALIAN PASTRIES In the heart of shrinking Little Italy, a pair of venerable pastry shops still convey the flavor of the old neighborhood. With its hexagonal-tile floors and tiny wrought-iron cafe tables, **Caffé Roma** ★, 385 Broome St., at the corner of Mulberry Street (℃ **212/226-8413**), is a great place to duck into for cannoli, those ricotta-filled roll-ups of sweet crisp pastry. Kids can drink frothy hot chocolate or chilled lemonade while parents indulge in cappuccino or espresso, made the classic way (no half-caf mocha double latte here). Follow Mulberry down to Grand Street, and you'll find the somewhat larger and brighter (and more crowded) **Ferrara,** 195 Grand St., between Mulberry and Mott streets (℃ **212/226-6150**), its refrigerated display cases crowded with mouthwatering pastries to go or to stay. If your kids want to sample Italian gelato (ice cream), this is a good place for that, too.

10 SOHO & NOHO

EXPENSIVE

Chinatown Brasserie ★ CHINESE This place is a treat for young and old alike. It's a big, glamorous space, staged to look like a vintage Chinese banquet hall, with ornate lamps, brasserie tables and chairs, and sexy lighting. Downstairs is a pond filled with koi fish, which never fails to mesmerize my toddler. It offers a slightly modern take on (largely) Cantonese favorites, with an emphasis on lighter and healthier (and pricier). In other words, it's kid-friendly Chinese, with few strange or exotic ingredients. Recommended dishes include pao pao beef, seasoned strips of beef sautéed with scallions and ginger; delicious roast pork tenderloin, thinly sliced; and kid-pleasing shrimp fried rice. Dim sum is available all day long. Chinatown Brasserie is *not* the place to go on a Friday or Saturday night, when the scenesters take over. Better to come on a weekday evening or lunch. Some families prefer low-key Sunday nights—evidenced by the strollers lining the front bar. There's a very nice outdoor space, where you can sit under wide umbrellas and watch the passing parade. I've put it under the "Expensive" category because the servings are so small you'll need to order a number of dishes, and it adds up.

380 Lafayette St. (at Great Jones St.). ✆ 212/533-7000. www.chinatownbrasserie.com. High chairs, boosters. Reservations recommended. Main courses $12–$34; Peking duck $48. AE, DC, DISC, MC, V. Mon–Fri 11:30am–11:30pm; Sat 11am–midnight; Sun 11am–10pm. Subway: 6 to Bleecker St.

INEXPENSIVE

Kelley & Ping ★ PAN-ASIAN   With its pressed-tin ceiling and wooden factory floor, Kelley & Ping looks very SoHo, but its friendliness to kids is unusual in this hyper-urban-chic neighborhood. It started out as an Asian grocery store but soon added an open kitchen in the center of the room; there are still stocks of bottled sauces and woks for sale along the walls. The noodles, stir-fries, and grilled meats (Vietnamese crispy duck, Thai grilled shrimp) go down well with children, though some dishes can be superspicy—ask for your waiter's guidance. There are also branches in the East Village (p. 134) and Gramercy Park (p. 129).

127 Greene St. (btwn Houston and Prince sts.). ✆ 212/228-1212. Kids' menu (dinner only), high chairs, boosters. Reservations accepted for parties of 6 or more. Lunch $4–$13; dinner $6.50–$22; kids' menu $7. AE, MC, V. Daily 11:30am–11pm. Subway: N, R, W to Prince St.; B, D, F, V to Broadway/Lafayette St.

Vesuvio Bakery Café Finds AMERICAN   When SoHo starts feeling too trendy for words, here's a refuge: a tiny brick-walled cafe at the western edge of the artsy district where you can rest your feet briefly at one of the few tiny tables while fortifying yourself with a salad, wrap, panini, muffin, or omelet. You'll be in and out fast, with a minimum of fuss. The bakery part has been here since the 1920s, and it's still owned by the same family.

160 Prince St. (btwn W. Broadway and Thompson St.). ✆ 212/925-8248. No reservations. Sandwiches $7–$8.50. No credit cards. Sun–Thurs 8am–7pm; Fri–Sat 8am–11pm. Subway: N, R, W to Prince St.

11 CHINATOWN

In Chinatown, children not only are seen and heard, but also have a place at the restaurant table from an early age on. If you come to Chinatown for dim sum on a weekend, you will see generations of families sharing dishes at big, communal tables—it's both tradition and entertaining family pastime. So throughout Chinatown, and even in the very few white-tablecloth restaurants, children are welcomed, fawned over, and treated well.

Finding a place to eat in Chinatown isn't difficult—just stroll along Mott or Mulberry streets south of Canal Street, or along Bayard Street between Mott Street and the Bowery, and you'll pass dozens of decent restaurants with menus posted outside so you can check out what's on offer. They may not accept credit cards, and communicating with your waiter may require a little bit of menu-pointing and sign language; but so long as you order prudently, the food should be good. The following are some tried-and-true options.

EXPENSIVE

Peking Duck House ★★ CHINESE   This is one of the neighborhood's few upscale restaurants, with white linen tablecloths and a minimalist, monochromatic decor. The food in general is fresh and delectable, but the Peking duck is off-the-chart delicious.

Dim Sum

Chinatown is famous for its dim sum palaces, where servers offer choice little delicacies from carts they wheel around the restaurant floor. It's a family ritual during the weekends. Eating dim sum is a novel experience that can be loads of fun for kids who are willing to sample new foods, though no item is really that far from standard Chinese dishes. During dim sum hours, the cart ladies start wheeling out hot, steaming carts laden with tiny dishes containing all kinds of delectable dumplings and skewers and rolls. You don't have to read a menu or speak Chinese with the cart ladies—just point to choose yourself a meal full of mouthwatering dishes. Great for sharing (and a smart economical choice), these offerings often include *har gow* (shrimp dumplings), pork buns, even chicken feet. Among my favorites: **Ping's** (22 Mott St.; ☏ **212/602-9988;** see below), which has exceptionally fresh seafood, and **Oriental Garden** (14 Elizabeth St.; ☏ **212/619-0085;** see below), a smaller, quieter place with consistently fresh and tasty food.

This restaurant is pricier than most, and its service can be brusque; but every time I've gone I've seen family groups enjoying the food.

28 Mott St. (near Pell St.). ☏ **212/227-1810.** www.pekingduckhousenyc.com. Main courses $7.50–$26; Peking duck $40. AE, MC, V. Sun–Thurs 11:30am–10pm; Fri–Sat 11:30am–11pm. Subway: J, M, N, R, Z, 6 to Canal St.

MODERATE

Golden Unicorn ★ CHINESE   This big, two-level Hong Kong–style banquet hall (with giant dragons as background decor) serves good, solid dim sum (some 100 types) from 10am to 4pm. I've also had good noodle dishes, such as the Singapore-style beef chow fun, here. The dining rooms have recently been renovated, and everything looks spiffy and bright. Expect waits for tables on the weekends, with staff on walkie-talkies crisply keeping the crowds moving.

18 E. Broadway (at Catherine St.). ☏ **212/941-0951.** www.goldenunicornrestaurant.com. Main courses $9.95–$25; Peking duck $35. AE, DISC, MC, V. Daily 9am–10:30pm. Subway: F to E. Broadway.

Oriental Garden ★ CHINESE   This is the smaller, quieter, much more understated neighbor of flashy Jing Fong (see below). It's actually a very pleasant place to have a leisurely lunch or dinner. But it's the food that gets consistently high marks, and even though the dim sum carts are considerably fewer and arrive at your table with less frequency than they do at the mega dim sum palaces, Oriental Garden's dim sum delicacies are some of the freshest and tastiest in Chinatown. The seafood is fresh (witness the active fish tanks), and service is fast and no-nonsense.

14 Elizabeth St. (btwn Bayard and Canal St.). ☏ **212/619-0085.** Main courses $11–$29. AE. Daily 10am–10:30pm. Subway: J, M, N, R, Z, 6 to Canal St.

Ping's ★ CHINESE   Ping's is a somewhat scaled-down version of the often overwhelming Hong Kong–style banquet halls, but it crackles with activity the minute the dim sum carts start rolling through the aisles. It's one of the more attractive restaurants in Chinatown, and the dim sum is exemplary. Ping's excels in Cantonese-style seafood and noodle dishes, so you can't go wrong ordering either.

22 Mott St. (btwn Pell and Worth sts.). ✆ **212/602-9988.** Main courses $6.95–$25. MC, V. Daily 10am–midnight. Subway: J, M, N, R, Z, 6 to Canal St.

INEXPENSIVE

Big Wong ★ CHINESE   It certainly doesn't look like much, but this is a reliable spot for flavorful Cantonese food—one blogger called it the "King of Chinatown Cheap Eats." If you like congee (Chinese rice porridge), the version here is hard to beat, and the barbecued meats (you can see them hanging in the window) are exemplary. I thought the dim sum wasn't bad, either. If you're looking for good, basic, inexpensive Chinese, head to Big Wong.

67 Mott St. (near Bayard St.). ✆ **212/964-0540.** Main courses $4–$20; Peking duck $40. No credit cards. Daily 7am–10pm. Subway: J, M, N, R, Z, 6 to Canal St.

Jing Fong CHINESE   It's Vegas come to Chinatown. If you're looking to give the kids an eye-popping Chinatown experience, try this vast, chandeliered Hong Kong–style dim sum parlor. A ride up a *lo-o-o-n-n-g* escalator delivers you into a bustling, gilded football-field-size dining emporium. The place can easily become a madhouse, but the steady stream of dim sum carts keeps the hot food coming.

18 Elizabeth St. (near Canal St.). ✆ **212/964-5256.** Boosters. Reservations accepted for dinner only. Main courses $9–$24. AE, MC, V. Daily 10am–10pm; dim sum daily 10am–3:30pm. Subway: J, M, N, R, Z, 6 to Canal St.

12 TRIBECA & LOWER MANHATTAN

EXPENSIVE

Landmarc ★ AMERICAN   This is just one of those places that does things right, from the consistently delicious American bistro standards to the smart (and astonishingly well-priced) wine list to the easygoing, family-friendly atmosphere and creative kids' menu. The kids' choices reflect a real effort on the part of the kitchen to create fun and delicious variations on the usual suspects, with offerings such as English muffin pizza, spaghetti pie, pigs in a blanket, and grilled-chicken skewers with honey mustard. Grown-ups can enjoy salmon tartare, rock shrimp risotto, mussels (with four different sauces to choose from), and any number of grilled meats, from pork chops to steaks to lamb chops. Every night has a pasta special, from hearty pasta Bolognese to rigatoni alla Genovese.

179 W. Broadway (at Leonard St.). ✆ **212/343-3883.** www.landmarc-restaurant.com. Kids' menu, high chairs. Reservations accepted only for parties of 6 or more. Main courses $15–$38; kids' menu $6–$17. AE, DC, DISC, MC, V. Mon–Fri noon–2am; Sat–Sun 9am–2am. Subway: 1 to Franklin St.

Odeon ★★ AMERICAN   The mellow Art Deco look of Odeon, with its wooden blinds and comfy banquettes, helped make it one of TriBeCa's first hot spots way back in the early 1980s. Standards have been kept up exceedingly well into the 21st century, and now it's a neighborhood fixture that welcomes families. It doesn't have theme nights; there are no TVs blaring sports events. The brasserie menu is inventive and constantly changing, but there's always simple classic food like burgers, roast chicken, steak frites, and pastas. This is also a good place to make a meal of two appetizers, with some excellent salads and a fine country pâté available. While there's no kids' menu, kids' options are available upon request. This is a place where grown-ups come to dine with their children. There's very little attitude and a lot of smart cooking going on here—no wonder Odeon has survived.

MODERATE/INEXPENSIVE

Bubby's ★★ AMERICAN   "Homey" is the word for this comforting TriBeCa restaurant, with its wooden chairs, soft recorded jazz, and kitschy clutter. The food is comforting as well, with sandwiches, burgers, pastas, and a great selection of pies—not to mention breakfast food served until 4pm, good to know if you've got kids who like scrambled eggs and French toast for lunch. There are also more upscale salads and chicken and fish dishes to please adults. It's the sort of place that understands that kids may like their spaghetti with butter and Parmesan instead of tomato sauce and that cooked carrots go down better if you drizzle maple syrup on top. The laid-back ambience somehow makes children willing to linger. The Saturday and Sunday brunch is very popular, and you may have to wait in line for a table. On Sundays, kids 7 and under eat free at dinner.

120 Hudson St. (at N. Moore St.). © 212/219-0666. www.bubbys.com. Kids' menu, high chairs, boosters. Reservations recommended; no reservations accepted for weekend brunch. Lunch $5–$16; dinner $10–$17; kids' menu $2–$6. DC, MC, V. Mon–Thurs 8am–11pm; Fri 8am–midnight; Sat 9am–4pm and 6pm–midnight; Sun 9am–4pm and 6–10pm. Subway: 1 to Franklin St.; A, C, E to Canal St.

PIZZA

Grimaldi's PIZZA   Yet another contender for the title of Best Pizza in New York, Grimaldi's lays legitimate claim to honors in the coal-oven category, with gooey homemade mozzarella and chunky tomato sauce topping a wonderfully thin but not tough crust. Like its rivals Anthony's and Lombardi's, it doesn't serve slices, and there are often lines out the door on summer evenings waiting for a table. Persevere: The line moves quickly enough, and you'll have views of the Manhattan skyline to entertain yourselves while you wait. (Better yet, come in the late afternoon, when there's no crush.) Inside, just as you'd expect, the tables are covered in red-checkered cloths, and Sinatra and Pavarotti dominate the jukebox as well as the photos on the walls. If your kids are into pepperoni, be sure to order some on your pizza—Grimaldi's uses the best in town. Make a Grimaldi's pizza your kids' reward for walking over the Brooklyn Bridge (it sits right beneath the bridge, by the old Fulton ferry landing), and top it off with a post-pizza ice-cream cone down by the river at the Brooklyn Ice Cream Works.

19 Old Fulton St. (btwn Front and Water sts.), Brooklyn. © 718/858-4300. Boosters. No reservations. Pizzas $14 and up. No credit cards. Sun–Thurs 11:30am–10:45pm; Fri 11:30am–11:45pm; Sat noon–11:45pm. Subway: A, C to High St.

FOOD COURTS

On the top floor of the **Pier 17** pavilion at **South Street Seaport,** a big food court enjoys the kind of picture window river views normally reserved for the toniest restaurants. Unfortunately, the food is nothing to write home about, but it's varied, including pizza, Chinese, deli, seafood, and Japanese. The food court in the **World Financial Center** in Battery Park City features a cluster of sit-down, table-service restaurants; but the ambience is casual enough for kids, and there are takeout options.

Exploring New York City with Your Kids

Yes, everyone knows that New York City is a world-class sightseeing destination. Yet visiting parents may be baffled by it at first—many of its top museums are not inherently suited for youngsters (the Frick Museum won't even admit anyone 9 and under), real estate is too tight for anything like a theme park, and though there are four children's museums—one in Manhattan, one in Brooklyn, one on Staten Island, and one out on Long Island (see chapter 12)—none of them is as central to local kids' lives as their counterparts in Boston, Chicago, San Francisco, or even Indianapolis. Many of its famous family attractions get so crowded, especially on weekends and school holidays, that tourists face waiting in long lines. (*Tip:* If you're visiting during the school year, hit the popular museums in the mornings, when the local kids are in school.)

But New York City's charms are inexhaustible, and as soon as you start thinking out of the tourist box, the city will open its best-kept secrets for you. My advice? For one thing, don't sell your children short: They may appreciate those smaller specialty museums, historic houses, and botanic gardens more than you'd expect. For another thing, don't be afraid to get on a subway and zip to the outer boroughs. Remember, kids love subway rides, and on weekends especially it's the way to go. Spend a day in **Brooklyn** in Prospect Park, dividing your time between the Wildlife Center and the Carousel, or pop over to the Brooklyn Botanic Garden and the Brooklyn Museum—incredibly, these are all within a few minutes' walk of one another. Flushing Meadows is my destination of choice in **Queens,** where you can see both the New York Hall of Science and Queens Wildlife Center in one easy go. In the **Bronx,** the huge Bronx Zoo and the equally huge New York Botanical Garden are right across the road from each other. Getting to **Staten Island** is even more fun because you get to take a ferry ride, and the children's museum there is only a short bus ride from the ferry docks.

Many museums court families by designing weekend and holiday workshops for kids— these are detailed in chapter 9, where you'll also find everything you'll need to know about having fun outdoors in New York's great parks, playgrounds, and neighborhoods.

SIGHTSEEING SUGGESTIONS

If you're trying to cram a lot of sightseeing into a short time, you may want to consider buying a **City Pass,** which gives you entry to six popular attractions: the **American Museum of Natural History, the Metropolitan Museum of Art and The Cloisters, the Museum of Modern Art, the Guggenheim Museum, the Empire State Building** observation deck, and the **Circle Line** cruise around Manhattan. Good for a 9-day period, passes cost **$74** for adults and **$54** for youth 12 to 17 and **$16** for children ages 3 to 12. Buy them at the admission desk of any of these attractions or online at www.citypass.com. The Guggenheim might not otherwise be on a family's agenda; but the other four sights all have tremendous kid appeal, and you'd still save money on the

What's in a Name?

Here's a trivia quiz to test your kids' knowledge of New York City history:

1. Who was the Hudson River named after?
2. Who was the Verrazano Bridge named after?
3. Where does the downtown street name Wall Street come from?
4. Where does the name Harlem, for the uptown neighborhood, come from?
5. Why is the street leading down to South Street Seaport named Fulton Street?
6. What does the name of the New York Mets refer to? (**Hint:** Think of the opera and the big art museum.)
7. What other two area sports teams have names that rhyme with the Mets?
8. Why is Times Square called Times Square?
9. Carnegie Hall, the famous concert hall at 57th Street and Seventh Avenue, is named after whom? And how do you get there?
10. Who is buried in Grant's Tomb?

ANSWERS: 1. English explorer Henry Hudson, who sailed up the river in 1609. 2. Italian explorer Giovanni da Verrazano, the first European to enter the Narrows, in 1524. 3. In the original Dutch settlement, a wall was built at that point to keep out invaders. 4. Nieuw Haarlem was a separate Dutch settlement in the mid-1600s, named after the Dutch city of Haarlem. 5. Ferry service, operated by steamship inventor Robert Fulton, crossed the river at that point, linking Manhattan to Brooklyn (until the completion of the Brooklyn Bridge in 1883). 6. It's short for Metropolitans. 7. The New York Jets football team and the New Jersey Nets basketball team. 8. Because the headquarters of the *New York Times* newspaper is there (an earlier paper, the *New York Herald,* lent its name to Herald Square, a few blocks south at 34th St.). 9. It's named for the man who built it, industrialist/philanthropist Andrew Carnegie (his former mansion is now the Cooper-Hewitt Museum). How do you get there? Practice, practice, practice. 10. Duh—it's Grant, of course (that's Ulysses S. Grant, Civil War commander and U.S. president), alongside his wife, Julia.

adult pass if you did only those five (it comes out about even on the kid pass, because the art museums don't charge admission for children).

IF YOU HAVE ONLY 1 DAY

Talk to the animals at the **Central Park Zoo,** followed by a spin on the nearby **Carousel.** Grab a hot dog for lunch in the park; then head up Central Park West to the **American Museum of Natural History,** with its magnificent dinosaur bones and wildlife dioramas. If you've got enough stamina, wind up with an hour or so at the **Children's** **Museum of Manhattan,** a couple of blocks away on West 83rd Street.

IF YOU HAVE 2 DAYS

Spend day 1 as above. On day 2, start out at **Rockefeller Center** (if you're early enough you can join the crowds watching the *Today* show broadcast live), where you can hang over the railing at Rockefeller Plaza and delve into the downstairs concourse to see the underground city in action. Go up to the **Top of the Rock** for a view of Manhattan's glittering cityscape, then cross Fifth Avenue to slip into **St. Patrick's Cathedral.** Swing over to Madison Avenue, where you can grab a sandwich to eat while you wait for your reserved time slot at the **Sony Wonder Technology Lab.** Optional Midtown alternatives, depending on your kids' tastes, are the **Paley Center for Media** (formerly known as the Museum of Television and Radio) and the **American Folk Art Museum.**

After a spell at the museum, head west to the neon razzmatazz of **Times Square,** where, depending on your age, you can either take a spin on the Ferris wheel at **Toys "R" Us** or watch *TRL Live* being broadcast through the windows at the **MTV Studio.** (Interested in the theater? Check out what's being offered at the **TKTS** half-price ticket booth for tonight's shows.) If you've still got the energy, end your day with a visit to the pricey-but-memorable **Madame Tussauds New York** on 42nd Street, capped by dinner at one of Times Square's many theme restaurants (see chapter 6).

If You Have 3 Days

Spend days 1 and 2 as above. On day 3, get up early to be first in line for the Circle Line ferry to the **Statue of Liberty** and **Ellis Island.** If you get out on Liberty Island, know that her inside staircase has been closed indefinitely (although you can visit exhibits inside the base), but viewing her close up is still awesome. Proceed via the ferry to Ellis Island, where you can pick up lunch at the Crown Café or Kiosk Café and browse around the fascinating immigration displays. Catch the ferry back to Manhattan, where you've got three options: Zip over to the **National Museum of the American Indian,** do a lobby-hopping tour around the Wall Street area (see chapter 8), or take a cab

over to **South Street Seaport** for a peek into Manhattan's 19th-century maritime past.

If You Have 4 Days

Spend days 1 to 3 as above. With older kids, start out day 4 by taking the hour-long tour of the **United Nations,** have an early lunch in the Delegates' Dining Room (make reservations in advance), and then cab it uptown for an afternoon at the **Metropolitan Museum of Art.** If you have younger kids, start out at the Metropolitan first thing in the morning (when the crowds are lighter and the guards a trifle more patient), have lunch inside the museum or at an East Side coffee shop, and then go to **Central Park playgrounds** so your youngsters can let off some steam (see chapter 9 for playground details). Work your way up Fifth Avenue to 103rd Street, where you can pop in to check out the toy gallery at the **Museum of the City of New York,** and end your day with a stroll through the **Conservatory Garden.**

If the Weather's Cold

To cram the most into 1 day with a minimum of exposure to the elements, start out at the **American Museum of Natural History;** then scoot across Central Park on the 79th Street crosstown bus (just as quick as a taxi) and dive into the **Metropolitan Museum of Art.** Or do it the other way around, depending on which you think your child will want more time for. Both have good on-site cafes, so you won't have to venture outside to eat.

If the Weather's Hot

East River breezes make **South Street Seaport** a refreshing spot in summer, and you can always duck inside the air-conditioned shops and museums when the sun beats down too strongly. As the sun moves westward, so should you: Cab it across town to **Battery Park**

City, where you can take in an afternoon movie at the Regal Battery Park Stadium 11 multiplex, emerging in time to stroll down the breezy Esplanade along the Hudson and watch the sun set behind Lady Liberty—or even walk down to South Ferry and take a spin on the **Staten Island Ferry.** Another good warm-weather refuge is the **Cloisters,** the Metropolitan's medieval art annex located up in Fort Tryon Park, where you can chill out amid the dim light and cool stone of transplanted European chapels.

Tip: Don't be tempted to do the Statue of Liberty and Ellis Island on a really hot day—though the ferry ride may be refreshing, the wait in line for the boat will be unbearable.

Take advantage of the opportunity to dawdle in one of the art museums kids aren't as happy in—like the **Frick,** the **Whitney Museum of American Art,** or the **Asia Society Galleries,** all on the Upper East Side. Then window-shop along tony **Madison Avenue,** where designer boutiques cluster from the 80s on down to 57th Street. Another child-free option may be to prowl around the Wall Street area: Visit the **New York Stock Exchange,** venerable **Trinity Church,** and the surprisingly small but ornate **City Hall.** Go out to dinner at an elegant restaurant; then catch either a **Broadway show** or a concert at **Carnegie Hall** or **Lincoln Center.** For complete details on all such grown-up activities, pick up a copy of *Frommer's New York City.*

1 KIDS' TOP 10 ATTRACTIONS

American Girl Place ★★ **Ages 4 to 14.** Just a store? Try telling that to the legions of 'tween-age girls, dolls lovingly clasped in their arms, who converge on this Midtown site as if they were pilgrims heading to Mecca. If you've been on Mars for the past few years—or if you only have sons (which is the same thing)—you may not know about these expensive, beautifully made 18-inch dolls, each with her own carefully researched back story presented in a series of middle-grade-level books. Originally developed by Wisconsin-based Pleasant Company, the line has been acquired by Mattel; but the quality level remains high, and there are several good spinoff products like modern-era American Girls of Today, Bitty Babies, and human-child-size clothing to match the dolls' outfits. At American Girl Place New York, as at the original American Girl Place in Chicago and the new Los Angeles branch, this concern shines through.

Technically, it is possible to visit without spending a penny, although if you can swing that, you deserve a medal of some sort. Besides the three floors of American Girl merchandise, there is an excellent **cafe** upstairs (p. 118), and a small **art gallery** displaying original illustration art for the books. On the second floor, detailed and delightful **historical dioramas** present each of the American Girl dolls in her time period. Often, craft activities and special celebrations are on tap, and if your daughter has brought her own Felicity or Kayla or Samantha or whomever, she can have the doll's hair restyled in the **doll salon.**

Warning: Boys may be allergic to this place. If possible, pack them off to the nearby Sony Wonder (later in this chapter), the Top of the Rock observation deck (later in this chapter), or the Build-A-Bear Workshop down the street (see chapter 10), and let your daughter have her day in the sun.

American Folk Art Museum
  Feld Gallery **5**
American Museum
  of Natural History **2**
Belvedere Castle **4**
Bronx Zoo **28**
Central Park Carousel **7**
Central Park Zoo **10**
Children's Museum of Manhattan **1**
The Cloisters **21**
Conservatory Garden **18**
Cooper-Hewitt National
  Design Museum **16**
The Dairy **8**
Dana Discovery Center **26**
Gracie Mansion **14**
The Guggenheim Museum **15**
Henry Luce Nature Observatory **4**
Inwood Hill Urban Ecology Center **20**
Lincoln Center for
  the Performing Arts **6**
Magic Bus **24**
Metropolitan Museum of Art **13**
Morris-Jumel Mansion **22**
Museum of the City of New York **17**
New York Botanical Garden **29**
New-York Historical Society **3**
Riverbank Carousel **23**
Roosevelt Island Tram **12**
The Studio Museum in Harlem **25**
Tisch Children's Zoo **11**
Wave Hill **19**
Wollman Rink/Victorian Gardens **9**
Yankee Stadium **27**

Area of
inset

THE
BRONX

UPPER
MANHATTAN

Area of
main map

Central Park

MIDTOWN

DOWNTOWN

UPPER
WEST
SIDE

Hudson River

RIVERSIDE PARK

Henry Hudson Parkway

Riverside Dr.

West End Ave.

Broadway

Amsterdam Ave.

Columbus Ave.

Central Park West

Manhattan Ave.

West Drive

CENTRAL

The
Lake

Sheep
Meadow

LINCOLN
CENTER **6**

American
Museum
of Natural
History **2**

Freedom Pl.

Columbus
Circle

W. 104th St.
W. 103rd St.
W. 102nd St.
W. 101st St.
W. 100th St.
W. 99th St.
W. 98th St.
W. 97th St.
W. 96th St.
W. 95th St.
W. 94th St.
W. 93rd St.
W. 92nd St.
W. 91st St.
W. 90th St.
W. 89th St.
W. 88th St.
W. 87th St.
W. 86th St.
W. 85th St.
W. 84th St.
W. 83rd St.
W. 82nd St.
W. 81st St.
W. 80th St.
W. 79th St.
W. 78th St.
W. 77th St.
W. 76th St.
W. 75th St.
W. 74th St.
W. 73rd St.
W. 72nd St.
W. 71st St.
W. 70th St.
W. 69th St.
W. 68th St.
W. 67th St.
W. 66th St.
W. 65th St.
W. 64th St.
W. 63rd St.
W. 62nd St.
W. 61st St.
W. 60th St.
W. 59th St.

86th St.
97th St.
79th St.
65th St.

M5

Ⓜ Subway stop
········· M5 bus route

0   1/4 mi
0   0.25 km

American Girl Place **15**
American Folk Art Museum **11**
American Museum of the Moving Image **9**
Le Caroussel in Bryant Park **16**
Chelsea Piers **7**
Chelsea *Screamer* **7**
Circle Line Sightseeing Cruises **4**
Empire State Building/ SkyRide **20**
Gray Line Tours **6**
Intrepid Sea-Air-Space Museum **1**
Madame Tussauds New York **5**
Morgan Library **19**
Mount Vernon Hotel Museum **8**
Museum of Modern Art **12**
New York Hall of Science **9**
New York Public Library (main branch) **17**
The Paley Center for Media **13**
Queens County Farm Museum **9**
Queens Museum of Art **9**
Rockefeller Center **14**
Sony Wonder Technology Lab **10**
Times Square Visitors Center **2**
Top of the Rock **14**
Toys "R" Us **3**
United Nations **18**

EXPLORING NEW YORK CITY WITH YOUR KIDS

KIDS' TOP 10 ATTRACTIONS

7

ⓘ Information
Ⓜ Subway stop
⋯⋯ M5 bus route

0   1/4 mi
0   0.25 km

Where to Eat: The **American Girl Cafe** (p. 118), serving lunch, weekend brunch, afternoon tea, and dinner, is an important part of the total experience. Reserve well in advance (for school vacation times, up to 6 months ahead!).

609 Fifth Ave. (at 49th St.). ℂ **877/AG-PLACE.** www.americangirl.com. Free admission. Sun–Tues 9am–7pm; Wed–Sat 9am–9pm. Closes 5pm Labor Day, Dec 24, and Dec 31; closed Thanksgiving and Dec 25. Subway: E, V to Fifth Ave./53rd St.; B, D, F, V to 47th–50th sts./Rockefeller Center.

American Museum of Natural History ★★★ **All ages.** This is the city's one real don't-miss if you're with kids. The excitement begins even in the subway station below (B and C trains to W. 81st St.), where the walls feature wonderful ceramic bas-reliefs of dinosaurs, insects, birds, and mammals. When you enter the rotunda at the top of the Central Park West steps, a huge rearing skeleton of a mommy dinosaur protecting her baby from a small, fierce predator clues you in that the dazzling fourth-floor **dinosaur halls** are the perennial star attraction; they feature interactive consoles, glass-floored walkways that bring you up to the dino's eye level, and please-touch displays illustrating key points of evolution. But our favorite sights are the superb dioramas in the **North American Mammals** section (first floor)—the grizzly bear raking open a freshly caught salmon, majestic elks lifting their massive antlers, wolves loping through eerie nighttime snow—or, on the floor above, the bi-level **African Mammals Hall,** where you can circle around a lumbering herd of perfectly preserved elephants or check out the giraffes browsing by their water hole.

A circuit of the first floor alone could take a whole day. The PC-but-never-preachy **Hall of Biodiversity** features an immense multimedia re-creation of an African rainforest and a display of Earth's entire family tree, with more than 1,500 specimens and models spread out along a 100-foot wall. We love the dimly lit **Millstein Hall of Ocean Life,** where a gargantuan model of a blue whale swims overhead and water-dappled lights play against the walls; it has informally become known as the place where toddlers can stretch their legs, racing and twirling around the vast open space. Around the corner, the less-well-visited **North American Forest dioramas** are a peaceful part of the museum, where you can hunt for blue jays in oak trees and rattlesnakes behind the cactus. Most people hurry through here to get to the interactive **Human Biology and Evolution** exhibits, which seem always full of busy grade-schoolers. Past that lies the **Mineral and Gem room,** where little kids can thrust their hands into a huge geode while older kids gape in awe at the jewels on display.

The museum is not all animals, by any means (remember that Margaret Mead was only one of many brilliant anthropologists whose research was supported by this museum over the years). Studying Native Americans? On the first floor, by the 77th Street entrance, is the astounding collection of **Northwest Coast Indian** totem poles immortalized by J. D. Salinger in *Catcher in the Rye.* The haunting soundtracks in the **African and Asian peoples** sections (on the second floor) lull you into studying the precisely detailed displays there, too. The stunning **Rose Center for Earth and Space** is a seven-story glass cube that holds the Hayden Planetarium, where you can take a thrilling virtual ride through the Milky Way to the edge of the universe, step on a scale that shows your weight on Saturn, see an eerie phosphorescent model of the expanding universe, and touch cosmic debris. At night the sphere floating inside the Rose Center is lit in an ethereal blue hue.

The **Discovery Room,** on the first floor by the 77th Street entrance (near the immense outrigger canoe), is a special spot where kids 5 and older can touch and feel and fiddle with items related to the displays; it's open weekday afternoons from 1:30 to

Alice Austen House **16**
Battery Park City Esplanade **2**
Castle Clinton National Monument **3**
Children's Museum of the Arts **7**
Circle Line Sightseeing Cruises **11**
Ellis Island Ferry **4**
Forbes Magazine Galleries **5**
Historic Richmond Town **16**
Lower East Side Tenement Museum **8**
Merchant's House Museum **6**
Museum of Chinese in America **9**

Subway stop
Closed indefinitely
M5 bus route
Downtown Connection bus route

National Museum of
 the American Indian **13**
New York City Fire Museum **1**
New York City Police Museum **12**
The *Pioneer* **11**
South Street Seaport Museum **10**
Sports Museum of America **14**
Staten Island Ferry **15**
Staten Island Children's Museum **16**
Staten Island Zoo **16**
Statue of Liberty Ferry **4**
U.S. Customs House **13**

Natural History Museum Treasure Hunt

The American Museum of Natural History is so vast, kids can easily tire if you trudge willy-nilly from hall to hall without a set plan. Make your visit a more interactive one with this treasure hunt, designed by my sons, Hugh and Tom, to keep kids busy exploring. Younger children may get through only one floor in an afternoon, but persist—I swear, it's all here.

First Floor

1. **North American Mammals**—Where is the rabbit hiding from the lynx?
2. **Ocean Life**—Who's talking back to the orca? (**Hint:** Orca is another name for a killer whale.)
3. **New York State Environment**—How many baby chipmunks are sleeping in the spring burrow?
4. **Human Biology and Evolution**—Find the cave of mammoth bones.
5. **Minerals and Gems**—Where are the rocks that glow in the dark?

Second Floor

6. **African Peoples**—Find the xylophone.
7. **Birds of the World**—How many stuffed penguins are there?
8. **Asian Peoples**—Who's getting married?
9. **Rose Center**—How soon after the Big Bang did our solar system start to form?

Third Floor

10. **African Mammals**—Who's watching the ostriches fight the wart hogs?
11. **Reptiles and Amphibians**—Which is the crocodile, and which is the alligator?

Fourth Floor

12. **Saurischian Dinosaurs**—Find the fossil dinosaur teeth.
13. **Ornithischian Dinosaurs**—Touch the triceratops horn.

ANSWERS: 1. Behind the bush. 2. The leopard seal. 3. Four. 4. Toward the end of the exhibit, in the Earliest Architecture display. 5. In the first gem room, the southeast corner. 6. Midway through the hall, on the west wall, across from the guys in straw skirts who look like Cousin Itt from The Addams Family. 7. Twenty in all—16 adults, 4 babies. 8. In the Chinese section, a bride in her ornate ceremonial sedan chair. 9. Eight billion years. 10. The mouselike elephant shrew, behind a dead log. 11. Facing each other by the entrance at the north end of the hall—the gator (on your right) has the snub snout; the croc (on your left) has the pointy snout. 12. On the south wall. 13. On the east wall.

—Holly Hughes

5:10pm, Saturday and Sunday 10:30am to 1:30pm and 2:15 to 5:15pm. "Meet the Scientist" events are held on the first Saturday afternoons of February, April, June, August, October, and December. After Labor Day the Discovery Room hosts Gateway Storytime, where 2- to 5-year-olds explore natural science through story, song, and a visit to a related

7

Brooklyn Academy of Music 5
Brooklyn Botanic Garden 8
Brooklyn Bridge 1
Brooklyn Children's Museum 6
Brooklyn Heights Promenade 3
Brooklyn Museum 7
Coney Island 13
Lefferts Homestead 10
New York Aquarium 13
New York Transit Museum 4
Prospect Park Audubon
  Center 12
Prospect Park Carousel 11
Prospect Park Wildlife Center 9
Stairwell to Brooklyn Bridge
  footpath 2

A Night at the Museum

The nationwide trend of children spending an adventure-filled night in a major museum has arrived in New York City with a bang, at the American Natural History Museum's summer **Sleepovers** (ages 8–12). What could be cooler? (Well, I've always wanted to spend a night at Bergdorf's, but that's another story.) You arrive at the museum with sleeping bag and pillow in tow, and with your trusty flashlight guiding the way, you explore the halls in search of T-Rex, a herd of thundering buffalo, and erupting volcanoes. You sleep under the big blue whale in the Millstein Hall of Ocean Life, next to a lifelike brown bear in the Hall of North American Mammals, or in the Hall of Planet Earth. Just know that you won't be alone: The museum can handle some 465 people for a night's sleepover. Families are welcome; one adult is required to chaperone every one to three children. Pre-registration is required (✆ **212/769-5200;** www.amnh.org/kids/sleepovers; $129 per person, $119 members, including evening snack and light breakfast, cots, IMAX film, and take-home activities).

museum hall (Mon at 10:30am with a second program at 11:15am). Squirreled away in a back corner of the second floor is the **Natural Science Center,** a delightful hands-on workshop where kids 4 and older can explore the natural life of New York City (Tues–Fri 2–4:30pm, Sat–Sun 1–4:30pm).

Here comes my only quibble with the museum: On top of the already significant admission price, there are substantial extra fees, even for members, for special exhibits, and even for regular features such as the space show *Cosmic Collisions* at the **Hayden Planetarium** and the various films shown in the **IMAX theater** (see below for prices). These can add up awfully fast to make a visit here quite expensive. Believe me, there's enough to do here that you don't need to go for the extras (I personally find the space shows a letdown). Shops at every turn lure you to spend more money, though there are always at least a few inexpensive items.

Where to Eat: The excellent **Museum Food Court** (open 11am–4:45pm) offers a wide range of sophisticated sandwiches, salads, fruit, and snacks as well as hot food, including hamburgers and french fries. There's also **Café on One** for gourmet finger food, salads, and sandwiches. On weekends, you can also grab a light meal at the **Café on 4** (on the fourth floor by the 77th St. elevators) and **Cafe 77** (by the 77th St. entrance on the first floor). Since you can reenter the museum with your admission tag, consider popping out into the neighborhood to **Rain, PINCH & S'MAC, Ollie's,** or **T & R Pizzeria** (see chapter 6), only a block or two away.

Central Park West (at 79th St.). ✆ **212/769-5100;** for reserved tickets to Space Show and other special exhibits, ✆ 212/769-5200. www.amnh.org. Suggested admission for **nonmembers:** $15 adults, $11 students and seniors, $8.50 children 2–12; nonmember admission plus IMAX ticket $22 adults, $17 students and seniors, $13 children 2–12; Super Saver Packages Adult nonmember $30, members $15, nonmember children (2–12) $19, member children $10. Admission for **members** free; added fee for Space Show $15 adults, $8.50 children; added fee for IMAX $7 adults, $4.50 children; added fee for both IMAX and Space Show $15 adults, $10 children. Children 1 and under admitted free. Daily 10am–5:45pm (Rose Center open until 8:45pm first Fri each month). Closed Thanksgiving and Dec 25. Limited parking available on-site (enter on W. 81st St. btwn Central Park West and Columbus Ave.). Subway: B, C to 81st St./ Museum of Natural History; 1 to 79th St.

Bronx Zoo ★★ All ages. The big kahuna of New York City's wildlife parks, the
Bronx Zoo is a world-class facility in every way. It covers 265 acres and boasts more than
4,000 animals, from Siberian tigers and snow leopards to condors and vultures to naked
mole-rats and meerkats. Though there's a scattered number of indoor exhibits—the
deliciously creepy **World of Darkness** (nocturnal animals); the **World of Reptiles;** the
Monkey House; the **World of Birds;** the **Giraffe House;** the **Mouse House; Madagas-**
car!; and **Jungle World**—most of the animals live outdoors in large enclosures that re-
create as closely as possible the species' native environment. Kids 4 and under may get
frustrated by the long walks between animals and the fact that certain creatures may be
viewable only at a distance. This doesn't mean they won't love the zoo—it just means
you've got to organize your visit sensibly. Maybe plan to visit **Toddler Time Tuesdays,**
April through October from 10:30am to 12:20pm, where parents and kids up to 3 see
Wildlife Theater shows and attend the Children's Zoo free.

You can run into several added charges once you get inside the gates, so I recommend
opting for the Pay One Price ticket plan—it not only saves you money, it also saves time,
because you can bypass individual ticket booths inside. From April to October several
rides help you navigate the park—the **Zoo Shuttle,** an **open-sided tram** ($3) that rattles
in a big loop around the main part of the zoo; the **Skyfari** cable car ($3) that soars high
over the treetops (handy for cutting across, but hardly any animals are visible); and the
narrated **Bengali Express monorail ride** ($4, May–Oct) in the Wild Asia section. The
monorail is worth the extra money, since it's the only way you can see Wild Asia at all,
and the guide en route helps you spot all the lions and antelopes patrolling their roomy
open-air habitats. There's also a $3-per-person charge for the **Children's Zoo,** open April
to October, which is surprisingly fun even for 8- or 9-year-olds, with lots of learn-by-
doing exhibits (like a spider-web rope climb and a prairie dog burrow that kids can climb
through) and a petting zoo. If you want to take a camel ride in the Wild Asia section,
that's another $5. The zoo also tacks on $3 for each of its two star exhibits, the **Congo**
Gorilla Forest and the **Butterfly Zone** (open June–Sept only). Both of them are fascinating—on a good day you can practically go snout-to-snout with our huge simian
cousins through a wide glass window or have immense tropical butterflies land on your
outstretched hand. (Note that the newer **Tiger Mountain** gives you the same close-up
access to its big striped cats for no extra charge.) With all these extras, you could easily
spend over $100 on a full day for a family of five. Since a 1-year family membership costs
$120 anyway, consider joining, especially if you're likely to visit another of the city's four
Wildlife Conservation parks anytime during the next year; you'll be supporting valuable
conservation efforts as well.

During winter, when many of the outdoor animals aren't on view, the park lures visitors with fanciful animal sculptures spangled with lights, as well as the indoor exhibits
(still enough species on view to fill a smaller zoo); there's a certain pleasure in visiting
during this uncrowded season.

The zoo has several entrances: I recommend the Southern Boulevard/Crotona
entrance, which brings you in near the Children's Zoo and the elephants, or the Asia
entrance (pedestrians only, closest to the subway station), which brings you in near Wild
Asia and Jungle World. In any case, study the zoo map as soon as you enter, and plot
which animals you want to visit and the simplest route to pass them. Operate on the
assumption that you can't see everything in 1 day, even if your kids are good walkers.
Relax, take your time, and enjoy yourselves.

Getting There: By **bus,** BxM11 express buses (call $©$ **718/330-1234**) run about every 15 to 30 minutes from stops along Madison Avenue in Manhattan at 24th, 54th and 99th streets; the fare is $5 per person one-way (free for a child under 45 in. riding on an adult's lap) and $2.50 seniors. By **train,** take Metro-North from Grand Central Terminal to Fordham Road, change to the Bx9 bus, and ride to the zoo's Southern Boulevard entrance. By **subway,** take the no. 2 or 5 to East Tremont Ave./West Farms Square; walk straight ahead on Boston Road, and you're 1 block from the zoo's Asia gate entrance. A **taxi** might cost $20 to $35 one-way, depending on your Manhattan starting point or destination. By **car,** take exit 6 off the Bronx River Parkway.

Where to Eat: The zoo's **Dancing Crane Cafe** is open year-round, and three open-air cafes operate seasonally. Expect fast-food-ish menus, with slightly high (but not outrageous) prices. Stop by the **Grizzlies Goodies Corner** near the grizzly bears or pick up a snack at **Asia Plaza** near Jungle World. Pack a picnic lunch if you can—there are plenty of places to sit and eat outdoors. But why come all the way up and miss Arthur Avenue, the Little Italy of the Bronx? Unlike Manhattan's Little Italy, this neighborhood has some of the best Italian restaurants in the city—and all are extremely family-friendly. It's also very walkable from the Bronx Zoo, but you can also call a cab. You can't go wrong at **Dominick's** (2335 Arthur Ave.; $©$ **718/733-2807**), **Mario's** (2342 Arthur Ave.; $©$ **718/ 584-1188**), or **Pasquale's Rigoletto** (2311 Arthur Ave.; $©$ **718/365-6644**).

In Bronx Park, Bronx River Pkwy. and Fordham Rd. $©$ **718/367-1010.** www.wcs.org or www.bronxzoo. com. Admission $15 adults, $13 seniors, $11 children 2–12, free for children 1 and under; Pay-One-Price (POP) tickets (include 7 exhibits and/or rides) $27 adults, $21 students and children, and $23 seniors; admission fees optional Wed, but charges still apply to ticketed exhibits and rides. Stroller rental $6 single, $10 double stroller with $5 deposit (inquire at park entrances). Apr–Oct Mon–Fri 10am–5pm, Sat–Sun and holidays 10am–5:30pm; Nov–Mar daily 10am–4:30pm. Parking $12.

Central Park Zoo and Tisch Children's Zoo ★★ **All ages.** Beautifully landscaped, this pair of tiny zoos is perfect for young animal lovers—there's nothing bigger than a polar bear here, you can get pretty close to every species on display, and you don't have to walk very far to see everything. The centerpiece of the main zoo is the oval **Sea Lion Pool,** which has glass sides so everyone can watch the sea lions swimming underwater. A few steps to the west is **Monkey Island,** where a troop of snow monkeys scramble over the rocks and swans glide on the water. To the north lies the **Polar Circle,** with a big flock of penguins indoors and polar bears outside, cavorting in and out of their rock-edged pool. Up on the hill behind Monkey Island is the **Temperate Territory,** which stars an otter, some ducks, and a pair of shy red pandas; at the south end you can stand on the bridge over a mucky turtle pond and look for frogs sunning themselves. The greatest number of species in the zoo are inside the **Tropical Zone,** a two-story enclosed aviary with plenty of glass tanks arranged along the wall, featuring exciting creatures like piranhas and bats and snakes—not to mention our favorites, the golden lion tamarins, whose wizened faces remind us of the flying monkeys from *The Wizard of Oz.* Be sure to climb to the upper levels and stand out on the stairways, looking for the bright plumage of tropical birds flitting from tree to tree. Always warm and humid, the Tropical Zone is a great refuge on a chilly day. As soon as you go through the main zoo's gates, check signs near the entrance to see when the sea lion and penguin feedings are scheduled; there's often a crowd for these, but it's fun to see the animals scamper over to their keepers for their fish. (No, they don't do tricks.)

The **Tisch Children's Zoo** is a short stroll north, on the other side of the Delacorte Arch. Much of this friendly hilltop spot is a walk-through aviary. Kids love the waterfall they can stick their hands through, with a dusky little grotto full of fish tanks behind it.

Wooden bridges cross over a tidy central pond, cedar-chip paths circle around, and at the back is a giant spider web kids can clamber over. Children can get right up close to most of the animals here, so who cares if none of them is an exotic species? To many a city kid, pigs, goats, sheep, and baby llamas are (and here you can feed them by hand).

Where to Eat: If you can, pack a picnic lunch and eat it at outdoor tables throughout the park. Otherwise, you'll have to go with the **Leaping Frog Café,** within the Park's Wildlife Center. It has indoor and outdoor seating and "self-serve" standards such as burgers, hot dogs, pizzas, and sandwiches. There's usually also a cart selling drinks and ice cream in the central courtyard. Note that drinks are served without straws, since a straw tossed into an animal's enclosure could be harmful.

In Central Park, near the park entrance at Fifth Ave. and 64th St. ℭ **212/439-6500.** www.nyzoosand aquarium.com. Admission (includes both zoos) $8 adults, $4 seniors, $3 children 3–12, free for children 2 and under. Mon–Fri 10am–5pm; Sat–Sun 10am–5:30pm (closes 4:30pm Nov–Mar). Subway: N, R, W to Fifth Ave./59th St.; 6 to 68th St.

Ellis Island Immigration Museum ★★★   Ages 4 & up. From the mountain of ragtag luggage stacked right inside the front doors, to the cramped dormitories and medical examination rooms upstairs (cough the wrong way, and you could be sent right back to Europe), to the family heirlooms immigrants brought with them in the **Treasures from Home** collection—this place really brings history to life. We can't help but linger over the first-floor **Peopling of America** exhibit, with a life-size "family tree" and huge three-dimensional bar graph tracking immigration patterns over the years. The second-floor **Registry Hall** is awesome, with its soaring vaulted ceiling faced with white tile; this is where new arrivals waited in endless lines to be interviewed by immigration officials. On a **Wall of Honor** outside, some 420,000 immigrants' names are inscribed in steel. There's a self-guided audio tour, or you can pick up handsets at various displays to hear narration; the stirring documentary *Island of Hope, Island of Tears* runs frequently throughout the day, as does a delightful little play with young actors reenacting the immigration experience. You can easily spend 2 hours here.

Getting There: The **ferryboats** make frequent trips, running a loop from Battery Park to Liberty Island to Ellis Island and back to Battery Park (from New Jersey, you can board ferries in Liberty State Park). In Battery Park, you can buy tickets at Castle Clinton, where there are some interesting exhibits to help pass the time before your ferry. The wait in line can take a while, and security procedures include metal detectors, bag searches (bags larger than a milk crate aren't allowed on the ferry), and waiting in several different holding pens—perhaps an appropriate introduction to the immigrant experience. Once on the ferry (best views are from the top deck on the right-hand side), you can disembark at either island and board a later boat to continue your trip. Schedules vary, but the service generally runs daily starting at 9am (the last trip starts around 3:50pm); allow at least half an hour beforehand to clear security. Boats depart every 30 minutes (every 20 min. on busy weekends); sailing time is about 15 minutes to Liberty Island, another 10 minutes to Ellis Island, and 10 minutes back to Manhattan. The Reserve Ticket allows priority entry to security check-in and provides access to Liberty Island and the Ellis Island Immigration Museum, Tickets adults $12, seniors $10, children (ages 4–12) $5. With audio tour add $6 per ticket. For the same price there's the Flex Ticket for one-time use within a 3-day period. A specific start date is required for access to Liberty Island and Ellis Island, including the grounds of Liberty Island and the Ellis Island Immigration Museum. For information and current schedules, call ℭ **877/523-9849** or go to **www. statuecruises.com**. For advance tickets, call ℭ **800/600-1600.**

Where to Eat: There's a big food court on the site, as well as a snack bar on the ferry. Bring a picnic lunch if you can—there are plenty of places to sit out and eat.

On Ellis Island in New York Harbor. ℂ **212/344-0996.** www.ellisisland.com. Free admission. Mon–Fri 9:30am–5pm; Sat–Sun 9am–5:30pm (extended hours in summer). Closed Dec 25. Subway: 4, 5 to Bowling Green; 1 to South Ferry; R to Whitehall Station. Walk through Battery Park to Castle Clinton to purchase tickets.

Madame Tussauds New York ★   Ages 7 & up. Transplanted from London, this wax museum to the stars has adapted its slightly creepy signature attraction to the Big Apple by featuring wax replicas of quintessential New Yorkers such as former mayor Rudolph Giuliani, Woody Allen, Joe DiMaggio, Yoko Ono, Jacqueline Kennedy Onassis, Donald Trump, and Andy Warhol. Newer models include Usher, Derek Jeter and David Wright, and Johnny Depp as Captain Jack Sparrow. (Never fear, they'll still have Tussauds favorites like Princess Di and the Beatles.) The admission fees are outrageous, granted, but you can have a whopping good time here, prowling through room after room of these meticulously crafted effigies. Evening hours mean that you can fit this into your schedule after most of the regular museums have closed for the day. Young children may get freaked out by the all-too-lifelike statues; it's better for kids old enough to recognize the celebrities and the great figures from the past. Be sure to bring a camera so that you can pose next the statue of your choice and show off your new best friend to the folks back home. *Note:* The ghoulish section re-creating the French Revolution is rife with blood and dismemberment (another Tussauds trademark).

234 W. 42nd St. (btwn Seventh and Eighth aves.). ℂ **800/246-8872.** www.nycwax.com. Admission $35 adults, $32 seniors, $28 children 4–12. Mon–Thurs 10am–10pm; Fri–Sun 10am–11:30pm. Subway: A, C, E to 42nd St./Port Authority; B, D, F, V to 6th Ave./42nd St.; N, Q, R, S, W, 1, 2, 3, 7 to 42nd St./Times Square.

Metropolitan Museum of Art ★★   All ages. Even though this is the city's number one tourist attraction, many families we know never take their young kids here. Big mistake. You can have a great time at the Metropolitan, even with toddlers, so long as you remember two rules: Go at their pace, not yours (forget about standing transfixed for 10 min. in front of that wonderfully serene Vermeer), and don't let the gruff museum guards intimidate you. They're the city's most fervent believers that children should be seen and not heard—they'll level stern, disapproving glares if your child so much as skips for joy or exclaims above a whisper. Naturally, don't let youngsters touch the precious works of art or press their fingers against glass cases, but otherwise, let your own common sense prevail.

Granted, the $20 admission price can be off-putting, but remember that children 11 and under get in free. And it's only a suggested donation—if you think your kids' attention spans are too short for a lengthy visit, don't be shy about paying less. A better strategy to get your money's worth, however, is to inquire at the information desk about what children's programs may be available that day—these are free with admission, and they're a brilliant way to get the kids immersed in the collection.

The echoing marble-clad Great Hall tells you as you enter that this is a Serious Art Museum. If there's a long ticket line at the booths in front of the entrance, go to the right, past the cloakroom—the booth at the north end is generally quicker. Kids love to climb the awesome central stairway up to the European painting galleries, the museum's prize jewel, but you may want to skip those galleries—they go on forever, boring the pants off most kids.

Here are the galleries kids are more likely to enjoy: the **arms and armor** (first floor), the extensive **Egyptian rooms** (also on the first floor—make a beeline for the glorious mummies), **musical instruments** (second floor, off the American Wing's courtyard), the

Costume Institute (ground floor—rotating installations will be of varying interest to kids), and the **European** and **American period rooms** (all over the place). On the first floor of the **American Wing,** a side gallery displays vintage baseball cards, and a whole gallery of grandfather clocks tick away on the second floor—but check to see if it's open; renovations of the American Wing were ongoing at press time. The courtyard of the American Wing is a light-filled open space with plantings, benches, and statues kids can actually relate to (a mountain lion and her cubs, a pensive Indian brave). Bring lots of small change for them to throw into the pool here and in the pool in front of the Egyptian Wing's momentous **Temple of Dendur** (but *not* in the Chinese scholars' court goldfish pool in the second-floor Asian art galleries!). In the Japanese galleries, find the room overlooking the Temple of Dendur; off the musical instruments gallery, find the balcony overlooking the mounted knights in armor. Get the idea? Wander around this immense museum, keep your eyes open, and be willing to walk away from anything that doesn't interest your children. Older kids who are beginning to appreciate art may go for the **Impressionist gallery** (second floor) or the **Lehman Pavilion,** set up like the town house of a wealthy collector—it's art in small enough doses that it doesn't overwhelm.

The huge **museum gift shop** has a lot of wonderful stuff for kids (see "A World of Museum Shops," on p. 254).

Where to Eat: The Cafeteria on the first floor behind the Medieval Hall features self-serve dining from a menu of hot entrees, sandwiches, salads, and snacks. Kids' Grill meals (chicken fingers, French fries, juice or milk) come packaged in cute yellow cardboard taxis. Or, since your museum badge allows reentry, go outside and sit on the splendid Fifth Avenue steps (one of the city's best impromptu grandstands) to eat a hot dog bought at a nearby pushcart.

1000 Fifth Ave. (at 82nd St.). ℭ **212/535-7710.** For daily tours and programs call ℭ **212/570-3930.** www.metmuseum.org. Suggested donation (includes same-day admission to the Cloisters) $20 adults, $10 students, $5 seniors, free for children 12 and under with adult. Tues–Thurs and Sun 9:30am–5:30pm; Fri–Sat 9:30am–9pm. Closed Jan 1, Thanksgiving, and Dec 25; open some school-holiday Mon (check website). Baby carriers available at the coat checks and strollers are allowed in all galleries, unless otherwise noted. Subway: 4, 5, 6 to 86th St.

South Street Seaport and the Seaport Museum ★ **All ages.** One of the reasons New York became the biggest city in the United States was its prominence as a port, something that's easy to forget in these days of jet travel and Internet communications. But down here, in this charming jumble of restored warehouses and maritime shops on the cobblestone East River waterfront, you'll go straight back to New York Harbor's clipper-ship heyday. Like its counterparts in Boston and Baltimore, some of South Street Seaport has been converted into a "festival marketplace" with an inordinate number of chain stores and general junk for sale; the food court upstairs has fabulous views of the East River and kid-friendly food. Still, you can spend a fun day here just with the shops and restaurants, pier-side entertainers, and wide-open East River views.

If, however, you fork over admission to the **South Street Seaport Museum** (12 Fulton St., btwn Water and South sts.; ℭ **212/748-8600;** www.southstreetseaportmuseum.org; Fri–Sun 10am–5pm, Mon 10am–5pm Schermerhorn Row galleries only; $10 adult, $8 student, $5 children 5–12), you'll discover a whole new dimension: a **gallery** presenting rotating historic exhibits; a 19th-century **printing shop** at 211 Water St.; a **boat-building shop** at the corner of John and South streets; and, best of all, several **historic ships** to climb onto, including the gallant four-masted barque *Peking* and the imposing wrought-iron sailing ship *Wavertree.* **Harbor cruises** on the *Zephyr* or the historic *Pioneer,* an 1885

The While-Waiting-in-Line-at-Lady-Liberty Quiz

1. The Statue of Liberty weighs
   a. 225 tons.
   b. 25 tons.
   c. 225 pounds (when she's been to her step-aerobics class).

2. The statue's full official name is
   a. The Gatekeeper of Liberty.
   b. Liberty Enlightening the World.
   c. Liberty Looking for a Lost Contact Lens.

3. Sculptor Frédéric-Auguste Bartholdi is said to have modeled the statue after
   a. the Mona Lisa.
   b. Napoleon Bonaparte's girlfriend.
   c. his mommy.

4. Emma Lazarus's poem *The New Colossus* ("Give me your tired, your poor . . .") is engraved
   a. on the tablet Liberty cradles in her arm.
   b. on a plaque inside the base of the statue.
   c. on a tattoo on every park ranger's left biceps.

5. The engineer who designed the statue's tricky steel skeleton is also known for
   a. the Eiffel Tower in Paris.
   b. the Brooklyn Bridge.
   c. the Spaceship Earth sphere at Epcot.

schooner, also leave from here (see "Boat Tours," later in this chapter). Special children's workshops and storytelling hours are organized all over the place—pick up a schedule at the visitor center or call ℭ 212/748-8758. What with the ocean air whipping in off the estuary, you'll feel like old salts before the day is through. *Note:* A major renovation of the Seaport is in the works (complete with pricey condos), so check the website before you arrive to get an update.

Pier 17, Fulton and South sts. ℭ 212/SEA-PORT (732-7678). www.southstreetseaport.com. Free admission to South Street Seaport. Mon–Sat 10am–9pm; Sun 10am–5pm. Subway: 2, 3, 4, 5 to Fulton St.; A, C to Broadway/Nassau St.

Statue of Liberty ★★ **Ages 3 & up.** The symbol of New York is impressive enough from across the harbor, but close up—man, this chick is *big*. It gives me vertigo just to look up at her. (In fact, younger kids may be frightened by the sheer scale of Lady Liberty.) At present, visitors cannot climb up inside the statue, but ranger-led tours explore the promenade (right inside the entrance is displayed her original torch, replaced at the statue's centennial in 1986), or go to the 10th-floor observatory to look at fascinating exhibits and peer up through a glass ceiling into her copper-clad steel skeleton. Timed-pass tickets for these tours must be reserved in advance, although a certain number are

6. The French intellectual who first proposed the idea for the statue was
   a. the Marquis de Lafayette.
   b. Edouard René Lefebvre de Laboulaye.
   c. Pepe Le Pew.

7. Once completed and shipped in sections to the United States, the statue almost wasn't erected because
   a. Americans lost the instructions on how to put it together.
   b. Americans hadn't raised enough money to build a pedestal for it.
   c. everybody thought it was so ugly.

8. Lady Liberty looks green because
   a. the statue's hammered-copper sheathing has oxidized as expected.
   b. pollution from New York Harbor has corroded it.
   c. she gets seasick from watching the ferries chug past all day.

9. The statue's nose is
   a. 4¹/₂ feet long.
   b. 10 feet long.
   c. 100 feet long (she could use some plastic surgery).

10. The Statue of Liberty was given to the people of the United States by the people of France
    a. because there was no room for it in Paris.
    b. in repayment of old war debts.
    c. to symbolize a special friendship between the two countries.

ANSWERS: 1. a 2. b 3. c 4. b 5. a 6. b 7. b 8. a 9. a 10. c

available on a walk-in basis at the ferry ticket office at Castle Clinton. Even if you don't have a tour reservation, it's fun to stroll around Liberty Island to gaze out over the harbor. For some kids, the ferry ride over may be more fun than the statue itself.

Getting There: The **ferryboats** make frequent trips, running a loop from Battery Park to Liberty Island to Ellis Island and back to Battery Park (from New Jersey, you can board ferries in Liberty State Park). In Battery Park, you can buy tickets at Castle Clinton, where there are some interesting exhibits to help pass the time before your ferry. The wait in line can take a while, and security procedures include metal detectors, bag searches, and waiting in several different holding pens—you'll come to appreciate the statue's poem about huddled masses yearning to be free. (Keep in mind that if you're carrying belongings that can't fit into a milk crate, you won't be allowed onto the ferry to Liberty or Ellis islands.) Once on the ferry (best views are from the top deck on the right-hand side), you can disembark at either island and board a later boat to continue your trip. Schedules vary, but the service generally runs daily starting at 9am (the last trip starts around 3:50pm); allow at least half an hour beforehand to clear security. Boats depart every 30 minutes, every 20 minutes on busy weekends; sailing time is about 15 minutes to Liberty Island, another 10 minutes to Ellis Island, and 10 minutes back to Manhattan.

Where to Eat: There's a **snack bar** on the ferry and a food concession on Liberty Island. If you bring a picnic lunch, watch out for marauding sea gulls.

On Liberty Island in New York Harbor. Buy tickets online or in Castle Clinton National Monument. ✆ **212/363-3200** (general info). www.nps.gov/stli. Free admission; ferry ticket to Statue of Liberty and Ellis Island $12 adults, $10 seniors, $5 children 3–17 (✆ 877/523-9849; www.statuecruises.com). Daily 9am–4pm (last ferry departs around 3pm); extended hours in summer. Subway: 4, 5 to Bowling Green; 1, 9 to South Ferry.

United Nations ★★　**Ages 8 & up.** Technically it's not even part of New York City, but an international zone all its own—step onto U.N. property and you can say you visited each of its 192 member nations in 1 day. This stunning East River site, its serene lawns and gardens cantilevered cleverly over the FDR Drive, makes a grand setting for that memorable architectural design: the low dome of the General Assembly building tucked in at the base of the sheer glass plinth of the Secretariat Building. You'll mingle with an international cast of characters, African and Asian and Scandinavian and Middle Eastern and Latin American bureaucrats chattering in a Babel of different tongues: It really brings home how big the world is and what an amazing feat it is to get all these people to agree on *anything*.

Walk past the long line of flagpoles (one for every member nation) to reach the visitors entrance at 46th Street and First Avenue; go through security and proceed through the lobby to get on a **guided tour** in English. These run every 10 to 30 minutes and last nearly an hour (call ✆ 212/963-TOUR [963-8687] to find out about tours in other languages). These information-loaded talks fill you in on the organization's history while you cruise around to the complex's major highlights—the General Assembly Hall, the Security Council chamber, and other major meeting halls. The modernist interiors, mostly furnished in sleek Scandinavian style, look a little worn and frayed since their 1950s inception, but there are many details that will impress the kids—the earpieces for simultaneous translations, the glassed-in booths for TV cameras, the horseshoe-shaped Security Council table, and massive pieces of internationally commissioned art and sculpture. A sobering exhibit of relics from the 1945 bombing of Nagasaki and Hiroshima reminds us of why the U.N. was formed in the first place; an exhibit on the horrors of land mines reminds us why it still is necessary.

The various U.N. agencies operate year-round, so there's always plenty of activity on the grounds. But things heat up when the General Assembly is in session, from the third Tuesday in September to sometime near the end of December. The **Gift Center** downstairs is great for finding unusual international handcrafts, including a delightful collection of dolls of all nations.

Where to Eat: There is a quick coffee shop near the gift shops, but for a more special experience, try the **Delegates Dining Room** ★ (reservations required—call ✆ **212/963-7625,** and be sure to bring a photo I.D.; jackets are required for men, and no sneakers or shorts are allowed), open to the public Monday through Friday from 11:30am to 2:30pm. Even if it's not exactly packed with high-level diplomats, the river views are great. And each week features a different culinary theme.

On the East River from 42nd to 48th sts. (entrance at First Ave. and 46th St.). ✆ **212/963-TOUR** (963-8687). www.un.org. Admission $13 adults, $8 students, $8 seniors, $6.50 ages 5–14; children 4 and under not admitted on tours. Mon–Fri 9:30am–4:45pm. No tours Jan 1, Thanksgiving, Dec 25; limited schedule Sept–Oct. Subway: S, 4, 5, 6, 7 to 42nd St./Grand Central. Bus: M15, M27, M42, M104.

Battery Park City Esplanade   All ages. The Statue of Liberty, Ellis Island, the Verrazano Bridge, and the Jersey City skyline punctuate the harbor views from this landscaped riverside walkway in a stunning residential/office development at the lower edge of Manhattan. People loll on the benches reading the *Times,* coffee mugs in hand; dog owners walk frisky pets on leashes; in-line skaters and cyclists weave patiently around pedestrians; and children hang on the inward-curved railings watching yachts cruise past on their way to the boat basin at the north end. No panhandlers, no T-shirt vendors, no ice-cream carts—it's a wonderfully civil scene.

On the Hudson River, btwn Chambers St. and Battery Place. Subway: A, C to Chambers St.

Brooklyn Heights Promenade ★   All ages. The calm here is so palpable, you'd never know that the Brooklyn-Queens Expressway is rumbling beneath this cantilevered promenade. On one side are the back gardens of lovely Brooklyn Heights town houses; on the other, the East River and a drop-dead view of Lower Manhattan and the harbor. It faces west, which means that the view is especially terrific near sunset. Best of all, if you're with little kids, there's a superb neighborhood playground at the south end, near Pierrepont Street. Combine this with a walk across the Brooklyn Bridge or a visit to the New York Transit Museum (p. 177), and you've got a great day trip.

West of Columbia Heights (btwn Montague and Cranberry sts.), Brooklyn Heights, Brooklyn. Subway: 2, 3 to Clark St., then follow Clark St. west to reach the Promenade.

Empire State Building ★   Ages 6 & up. The Empire State Building is the classic skyscraper observation deck—after all, this is where Cary Grant and Deborah Kerr missed their rendezvous in *An Affair to Remember* and Tom Hanks and Meg Ryan made theirs in *Sleepless in Seattle.* And, of course, this is where Fay Wray and King Kong had their own kind of rendezvous. Shabby as much of the building has become, its Art Deco lobby is still a looker, and the location puts you squarely in the middle of Manhattan, with close-up views to all sides. Tickets for the observation deck are sold up on the second-floor concourse, where you can also waste some money on the **New York Skyride** attraction (see later in this chapter). Elevators whiz you up to the small enclosed observation deck on the 86th floor (change elevators at the 80th floor), which also has narrow outdoor promenades on all sides, though the parapets are too high in many places for youngsters to see over. If you invested the extra $14 downstairs, you can go even farther up to get porthole-type window viewing from the 102nd floor (1,250 ft. up). An excellent tape, available for $6, tells you exactly what you're looking out at—not a bad investment if you're an out-of-towner. Gift shops in the main lobby and on the 86th floor sell all kinds of New York City, Empire State Building, and (of course) King Kong knickknacks.

350 Fifth Ave. (at 34th St.). ℭ **212/736-3100.** www.esbnyc.com. Admission $19 adults, $17 seniors and students 12–17, $13 children 6–11, free for children 4 and under. ESB Express Passes $45 in advance. Observatories daily 8am–2am; last elevator goes up at 1:15am. Subway: B, D, F, N, Q, R, V, W to 34th St./Herald Square.

Top of the Rock ★   Ages 6 & up. Though the Empire State Building deck is higher, I'd recommend the Deco-detailed observation terraces atop Rockefeller Center's GE Building, especially for folks who get uneasy with heights—they're cleaner, roomier, and more securely enclosed with big glass panes that don't hinder the view. The 67th-floor deck is mostly indoors, a boon if the weather's rainy or cold; an escalator takes you on up to floor 69, where wide terraces ring the building (this is the only level where you can

24-Hour Party City

Children's parties are big business in Manhattan, where the competitive stakes are high and the possible venues truly fantastic—among them, Yankee Stadium, Central Park, and the USS *Intrepid*. And you don't have to be a Rockefeller to rent these joints! Following are just a few of the very nifty places you can hold a child's birthday party in the city.

But hey: Simply celebrating a birthday in the fizzy, heady atmosphere of the Big Apple can be a thrill in itself. If you want to do it yourself, in a restaurant, say, or a prime picnic spot in Central Park with the Manhattan skyline for cinematic backdrop, here are a few places to get the supplies you need. For decorations, balloons, party dishware, balloons, and party favors, **Party City** (38 W. 14th St., btwn Fifth and Sixth aves.; ✆ 212/271-7310) is the spot. You can get colorful balloon bouquets created by "Certified Balloon Artists" and fun party favors at the **Balloon Saloon** (133 W. Broadway; ✆ 800/540-0749; www.balloonsaloon.com), in TriBeCa. If you need someone to hunt down just the right gift and come up with creative party favors, contact Hillary Waterous of **Pride and Joy** (✆ 401/743-0814; www.prideandjoynyc.com). Hilary, who has been a nanny in some of the city's most illustrious homes, locates gifts for kids from newborn to teens.

- **Yankee Stadium.** Birthday tours of Monument Park, the baseball field, the dugout, and even the press box, followed by a party in the Adidas Hall of Fame suite with pizza, soft drinks, and cake (✆ 718/579-4531; www.yankees.com; $40 per person, min. 12 people; 1½ hr.).
- **The Carousel, Central Park.** Birthday rides on the vintage Carousel, followed by a party, with balloons and party favors, in an outdoor picnic area with hot dogs, pizza, and apple juice; cake is available at extra charge (✆ 212/879-0244; www.centralparkcarousel.com; $22 per child weekdays, $28 weekends, min. 12 children; 1½ hr.).

take in views to the west), and stairs lead up to the narrower 70th-floor outdoor deck. The elevator ride up is fun—the elevator car has a glass ceiling that allows you to look right up the shaft as you zoom upward; another fun feature is the Target Breezeway on floor 69, where colored lights behind opaque white panels switch on and off in response to people's movements around the room.

30 Rockefeller Center (entrance 50th St. btwn 5th and 6th aves.). ✆ 212/698-2000. www.topoftherocknyc.com. Admission $18 adults, $13 children 6–12, $18 seniors. Daily 8am–midnight. Subway: B, D, F, V to 47th–50th sts./Rockefeller Center.

3 MORE MANHATTAN MUSEUMS

American Folk Art Museum **All ages.** For whatever reason, even young kids get the point of folk art—in fact, young kids sometimes enjoy this stuff more than older kids

- **FAO Schwarz.** Parties for all ages in Fifth Avenue store's celebration room next to the big piano (featured in Tom Hanks's *Big*), with a toy-soldier host, decorations, and a choice of themes (safari, princess, LEGO, and so on). Store will do custom-made goodie bags (767 Fifth Ave.; 📞 **212/644-9400;** www.fao.com; price available on request; 2 hr.).

- **The USS *Intrepid*.** Birthday parties include museum admission, party hosts, food and cake, and a choice of themes, such as "pilot for a day" or "junior astronaut" (Pier 86, W. 46th St.; 📞 **212/957-3701;** www.intrepidmuseum. org; birthday packages $900–$1,800 for 30 guests [15 children/15 adults]; additional guests $40–$70).

- **The NBA Store.** Hoops-crazed celebrants (ages 6–12) will have exclusive use of the store's Center Court, pizza lunch and drink, a basketball cake, personalized team jersey, and video and All-Star Photocard favors (666 Fifth Ave.; 📞 **877/NBA-EVENT** (622-3836); www.nba.com; $4,500 for up to 24 children, additional children $25 each; 2 hr.).

- **New York Fire Museum.** Birthday celebrations for the 4- to 6-year-old crowd at this downtown museum are surrounded by vintage fire engines. Kids get fire-truck-decorated cake, juice, balloons, and One Alarm loot bags with a fire chief hat, medals, and other fire-themed goodies (📞 **212/691-1303,** ext 15; www.nycfiremuseum.org; $40 per person; 2 hr.; Sat–Sun only).

- **Swedish Cottage Marionette Theatre.** Private puppet show followed by party in child-size seats in room adjoining 1876 puppet theater; you'll need to cart in your own food and party favors (📞 **212/988-9093;** www.city parksfoundation.org; $650 for birthday child and 15 guests; 2¹/₂ hr.).

who think they know what "good" art is. The shows here change continually, but every time we've visited, my children have been charmed by the paintings and sculptures and collages, all by untutored artists, past and present—quilts, weather vanes, bottle-cap sculptures, an immense canvas covered with obsessively tiny handwriting, whatever. If your kids are only good for about 20 minutes of museum-going, pop into the small **Feld Gallery** annex on the Upper West Side (2 Lincoln Square, on Columbus Ave. btwn 65th and 66th sts.; 1 train to 66th St./Lincoln Center; open Tues–Sun noon–7:30pm), where admission is free. The gift shop features a selection of toys you won't see everywhere else (see "A World of Museum Shops," on p. 254).

45 W. 53rd St. (btwn Fifth and Sixth aves.). 📞 **212/265-1040.** www.folkartmuseum.org. Admission $9 adults, $7 students and seniors, free for children 11 and under; free to all Fri 5:30–7:30pm. Tues–Sun 10:30am–5:30pm (Fri until 7:30pm). Closed Mon and legal holidays. Subway: B, D, F to 47th–50th sts./Rockefeller Center; V to Fifth Ave./53 St.

Rainy Days & Mondays

Given that Monday is New York City's standard museum closing day, many a visitor on a tight schedule has been disappointed to find sights shuttered up on Monday. A number of family-friendly attractions are open on Monday, however, including the following:

- American Museum of Natural History
- Cooper-Hewitt National Design Museum
- Ellis Island and the Statue of Liberty
- Empire State Building/New York Skyride
- Guggenheim Museum of Art
- Madame Tussauds New York
- Merchant's House Museum
- Museum of Modern Art in Queens
- National Museum of the American Indian
- New York Public Library
- New York Unearthed
- New York Transit Museum's satellite gallery in Grand Central Station
- Queens County Farm Museum
- South Street Seaport Museum
- Top of the Rock
- The Toys "R" Us Ferris Wheel
- United Nations
- Yankee Stadium

All five of the city's zoos are open 7 days a week as well. The New York Botanical Garden and Brooklyn Botanic Garden, while are usually closed on Monday, are open on Monday during 3-day holiday weekends. And to accommodate the schoolchildren who are their core audience, three outer-borough attractions—the Brooklyn Children's Museum, the New York Hall of Science, and Historic Richmond Town—stay open on Mondays during the summer school-vacation period.

Children's Museum of Manhattan ★ Ages 10 & under. Best for the under-8 crew (and perfect for preschoolers), it's full of things they can touch, and has space for them to run and jump, make-believe environments, and opportunities to experiment. The museum's four floors also include a playroom especially for 4-and-unders; a carpeted reading room with a puppet theater where kids can do their own impromptu shows; a few computers for older kids to mess around on; an interactive "TV station" where they can project themselves into a broadcast; and an activity-packed basement area that's periodically remodeled with a new literary theme. Young readers may appreciate the fun upstairs corridor that pays homage to various children's-book authors. There are always daily activities (check schedules when you enter) like face painting, storytelling, and shows in the auditorium. On rainy days and during school vacations, the joint gets pretty crowded, and the high-ceilinged spaces reverberate with noise; but it's still worth checking out.

$10 adults and children, $7 seniors, free for children under 1. Free admission 5–8pm on the first Fri of every month. Tues–Sun 10am–5pm; open school holidays. Subway: 1 to 79th or 86th St.; B, C to 81st St./ Museum of Natural History.

Children's Museum of the Arts   Ages 10 & under. Smaller than the Children's Museum of Manhattan (see above), this is a good alternative if you're downtown, with lots of hands-on stuff for kids. Various art projects are set up; youngsters are encouraged to explore rhythm instruments; a couple of computers loaded with graphics programs are available; children's art from around the world is on display; and there's a small Monet-themed play area where infants and toddlers can work off their extra energy. There are loads of creative workshops scheduled, usually for toddlers in the morning and school-age kids in the later afternoons and on weekends. On rainy or cold weekends, it's crowded to the rafters, so be warned.

182 Lafayette St. (btwn Broome and Grand sts.). © **212/274-0986.** www.cmany.org. Admission $9, free for children under 1; pay what you wish Thurs 4–6pm. Wed–Sun noon–5pm (Thurs until 6pm); open school holidays. Subway: 6 to Spring St.; N, R, W to Prince St.

The Cloisters ★★   All ages. Of course your kids aren't into medieval art—that's not the point. For families, the point of the Cloisters, the Metropolitan's beautiful medieval art annex, is the sheer weirdness of it—a conglomeration of chapels and courtyards and refectories lifted from European convents and monasteries, brought in packing crates to America, and reconstructed here on a bluff-top site in Fort Tryon Park. Wander from room to room, soaking up the time-stands-still atmosphere; go out on the terrace for splendid views of the Hudson River and the New Jersey Palisades; and poke around the monks' herb garden. Talk with your kids about unicorns before you go—there's one fascinating gallery devoted to a series of tapestries depicting a unicorn hunt (a medieval version of an adventure comic strip?).

It's a long trek up here, but your children might actually enjoy the bus ride, which won't take forever if you're coming from the Upper West Side (combine the Cloisters with visits to St. John the Divine and Riverside Church for a full day of Gothic-ness). If you're doing this in the same day as the Metropolitan (which makes sense, since your pricey admission covers both sites), compare what you see up here to the Met's first-floor medieval galleries.

In Fort Tryon Park, at 193rd St. and Fort Washington Ave. © **212/923-3700.** www.metmuseum.org. Suggested donation (includes same-day admission to Metropolitan Museum of Art) $20 adults, $10 students and seniors, free for children 12 and under. Tues–Sun 9:30am–5:15pm (closes at 4:45pm Nov–Feb). Closed Jan 1, Thanksgiving, and Dec 25. Free parking. Subway: A to 190th St. Bus: M4 to the end of line.

Cooper-Hewitt National Design Museum   Ages 5 & up. Check to see what exhibit is currently running at this Smithsonian branch devoted to design and decorative arts: A surprising number of them appeal to kids (clothing, furniture, advertising posters), and the accompanying material is usually so lucid that even a young kid can grasp what's interesting about the displays. What's more, it gives you a chance to get inside industrial tycoon Andrew Carnegie's surprisingly homey neo-Georgian mansion—don't forget to check out the beautiful plaster ceilings, and point out to kids how low some of the doorways are (Carnegie, a short man, wanted the house built to *his* scale). My older son fell in love with the elegant leaded-glass conservatory. There's a nice garden out back and a super gift shop with a number of clever toys and kids' books; it's set in Carnegie's library—look at the inlaid designs in the wood paneling (see "A World of Museum Shops," on p. 254).

What Goes Around Comes Around: New York's Carousels

Most kids are suckers for old-fashioned merry-go-rounds, no matter how corny the music, and New York is well supplied with them. The best-known is probably the vintage hand-carved 1908 **Central Park Carousel** (midpark near 64th St.; $2 ride; April–Oct Mon–Fri 10am–5 or 6pm, Sat–Sun 10am–7pm) with its elaborately carved wooden horses spinning around for 4 minutes to creaky tunes like "Rainy Days and Mondays"; it's not far from either the zoo or the Wollman Rink, another plus. Our other antique choice is also near a good zoo: the **Prospect Park Carousel** (Flatbush Ave. entrance, Prospect Park; $1.50 ride; April–June and Sept–Oct Thurs–Sun noon–5pm; July to Labor Day Thurs–Sun noon–6pm), which has giraffes and zebras and other exotics in addition to horses, all painted in fanciful pastels.

These being postmodern times, however, a new generation of retro carousels has sprung up recently, just as meticulously handcrafted but often with a clever twist. In Bryant Park, **Le Carrousel** (in Bryant Park, btwn 40th and 42nd sts. along Sixth Ave.; $2 ride; Sun–Thurs 11:30am–9pm; Fri–Sat 11:30am–10pm) may be small but it's enchanting, with a riot of pastel floral decorations and a deer, a frog, and a bunny alongside the traditional horses. Though its ornate style is French-inspired, it was manufactured in good old Brooklyn, by the same firm that made the distinctive **Riverbank Carousel** (Riverbank State Park, 145th St. and Riverside Dr.; $1 ride; open Fri–Sun in summer); this one is most memorable, with its wonderfully whacked-out steeds designed by New York City kids themselves. The lucky schoolchildren whose drawings were chosen to be reproduced—fanciful creatures like winged frogs replacing the traditional horses—were awarded free rides for life. Now there's a lottery worth winning.

2 E. 91st St. (at Fifth Ave.). ℂ **212/849-8400.** www.cooperhewitt.org. Admission $15 adults, $10 students and seniors, free for children 12 and under. Mon–Fri 10am–5pm; Sat 10am–6pm; Sun noon–6pm. Closed major holidays. Subway: 4, 5, 6 to 86th St.

Forbes Magazine Galleries Ⓥ**alue** **All ages.** An obsessive collector, publishing magnate Malcolm Forbes had enough money to turn his obsessions into a strange and wonderful little museum. Basically, he collected five things: toy boats, toy soldiers, Monopoly games, medals and trophies, and lavishly bejeweled Fabergé eggs. The eggs were sold, alas, for a princely sum, but that leaves plenty that kids do love. This labyrinth of small galleries won't tax youngsters' attention spans, though they should be warned ahead that this is a sedate don't-touch kind of place. (No strollers permitted inside, either.) The display windows aren't always low enough for small children, so expect to do a lot of lifting. Your kids may not want to linger as long as you do over the minutiae of the collection—remember, Forbes was a grown-up when he collected this stuff, with an adult's idea of what made something valuable. But there's still enough here to make kids press their noses against the glass for a good half-hour or so, more if they're older. Be sure to book a free tour in advance.

60 Fifth Ave. (at 12th St.). ℂ **212/206-5548.** www.forbesgalleries.com. Free admission, but children 15 and under must be accompanied by an adult. Tues–Wed and Fri–Sat 10am–4pm. Closed major holidays. Subway: N, Q, R, W, 4, 5, 6 to 14th St.; L to Union Square.

Guggenheim Museum   Ages 6 & up. The Guggenheim's rotating exhibits of 20th-century art may or may not appeal to your kids—Norman Rockwell maybe yes, Mark Rothko maybe no. No matter. The main reason for including this museum in your NYC itinerary is the museum building itself: Frank Lloyd Wright's glorious, streamlined, totally wacky inverted spiral, which displays the art along one long ramp coiling down around a huge central atrium. I mean, can you imagine doing the Guggenheim on a *skateboard?* Since kids 11 and younger get in free, it may be worthwhile to pay the adult admission just so you can enjoy this visionary interior for half an hour. In any case, the side galleries display some artworks kids might enjoy, by such masters as Degas, Cézanne, and Picasso.

1071 Fifth Ave. (at 89th St.). ℂ **212/423-3500.** www.guggenheim.org. Admission $18 adults, $15 students and seniors, free for children 11 and under. Sat–Wed 10am–5:45pm; Fri 10am–7:45pm. Subway: 4, 5, 6 to 86th St.

***Intrepid* Sea-Air-Space Museum ★★   Ages 5 and up.** *Note:* Following a 2-year refurbishment and restoration, the *Intrepid* reopened on Pier 86 in late 2008. The aircraft carrier known as the "Fighting I" served the U.S. Navy for 31 years, suffering bomb attacks, kamikaze strikes, and a torpedo shot. In 1982 it opened as a sea, air, and space museum on the New York waterfront. You can crawl inside a wooden sub from the American Revolution; inspect a nuclear missile submarine; or enter the cockpit of an A–6 Intruder and manipulate the controls. Summers are crowded; get here early or buy tickets online.

Pier 86, 12th Ave. and 46th St. ℂ **212/245-0072.** www.intrepidmuseum.org. Admission $19.50 adults, $15.50 students and seniors, $14.50 children 6–17, $7.50 children 2–5, free for children under 2. Apr 1–Sept 30 Mon–Fri 10am–5pm, Sat–Sun 10am–6pm; Oct 1–Mar 31 Tues–Sun 10am–5pm. Bus: M42 to 12th St. and Hudson Ave. Subway: A, C, E, S, 1, 2, 3, 7, 9 to 42nd St./Times Square.

Lower East Side Tenement Museum ★★   Ages 5 & up. A collection of 19th-century tenement buildings has been converted into this brilliant small museum that picks up the immigrant story where Ellis Island leaves off—in the poor neighborhoods where the new arrivals landed. Once you've seen these bare, cramped living quarters, all too authentically furnished, your kids may never fight again over sharing a bedroom. (It's the perfect antidote to all those ornate period rooms at the Metropolitan Museum.) The restored tenement apartments can be seen only via hour-long guided tours; book ahead to make sure you get onto the right tour. Furnishings and other artifacts tell the stories of immigrants from different homelands and eras of immigration; the best one for kids would be the living-history tour of the Confino apartment, Sephardic Jews who emigrated from Turkey around 1916, which features costumed interpreters. It's held only on weekend afternoons, and tours are limited to 15 people; so reserve in advance, especially for Sunday. Weekend walking tours widen the scope to include the whole neighborhood—they're wonderful if your kids are old enough to keep up with the pace.

108 Orchard St. (below Delancey St.). ℂ **212/431-0233.** www.tenement.org. Tours $17 adults, $13 students and seniors. Tours daily 11am–5pm. Advance tickets available through TicketWeb (ℂ **866/811-4111;** www.ticketweb.com). Subway: J, M, Z to Essex St.; B or D to Grand St.; F to Delancey St.

The Morgan Library   Ages 8 & up. The Morgan Library's refined gallery space exhibits prints and drawings, which may or may not be of interest to your kids—past shows about A. A. Milne or St. Exupéry's *The Little Prince* were totally delightful for youngsters, but that isn't always the case. What kids will appreciate is the wing J. P. Morgan actually used as a library, especially his elegant wood-paneled study with its ceiling-high shelves of rare books, gorgeously bound in leather.

225 Madison Ave. (at E. 36th St.). ✆ 212/685-0008. www.themorgan.org. Admission $12 adults; $8 students, seniors, and children 16 and under. Tues–Thurs 10:30am–5pm; Fri 10:30am–9pm; Sat 10am–6pm; Sun 11am–6pm. Closed holidays. Subway: 6 to 33rd St.

Museum of Chinese in America **Ages 5 & up.** Now ensconced in a larger space in a new location, this museum mounts fascinating rotating exhibits, mostly drawn from its huge collection of photographs and artifacts—tiny shoes for a Chinese woman's bound feet, tin tea canisters, brocaded Chinese opera costumes, the heavy irons used in a laundry. The gallery is a stunning surprise, with angled translucent walls creating the illusion of being inside a giant Chinese lantern. Saturday afternoons are a great time to visit, to take advantage of free hands-on workshops for kids (teaching about paper folding, shadow puppets, and so on) or in-depth themed walking tours of Chinatown.

211–215 Center St. ✆ 212/619-4785. www.moca-nyc.org. Suggested admission $5 adults, $3 students and seniors, free for children 11 and under. Tues–Sun noon–6pm. Subway: N, Q, R, W, 6 to Canal St.

Museum of Modern Art (MoMA) ★★ **All ages.** The "modern" in the museum's name no longer means cutting edge, but its galleries do provide a retrospective of the best in 20th-century art, from Picasso to Pollock, from Rodin to Rothko, and its newly expanded Midtown space should finally give MoMA room to display more daring stuff. The very young may be blissfully happy here because they don't care whether a painting looks like anything; preschoolers who've just learned how to make a tree look like a tree may be baffled by a canvas covered with mere spatters of paint, but they'll get the bright images of Andy Warhol's pop art or the moody intensity of van Gogh. A favorite spot is the splendid central sculpture garden.

Though the adult entrance fee is high, kids 15 and under get in free, so your visit here may end up costing no more than an afternoon at the American Museum of Natural History (once you've paid AMNH's extra fees for IMAX and the sky show and special exhibits). Saturday activities for kids include special tours for 4-year-olds, gallery talks for ages 5 to 10, interactive activity workshops for the entire family, and programs of classic short films chosen for a family audience.

11 W. 53rd St. (btwn Fifth and Sixth aves.). ✆ 212/708-9400. www.moma.org. Admission $20 adults, $16 seniors, $12 students, free for children 15 and under when accompanied by an adult; pay what you wish Fri 4–8pm. Wed–Mon 10:30am–5:30pm (until 8pm Fri). Subway: E, V to Fifth Ave.

The Paley Center for Media **Ages 5 & up.** Formerly known as the Museum of Television & Radio, this sleek Midtown museum (with a sister branch in L.A.) is where junior couch potatoes can gorge on all kinds of broadcast media, from vintage commercials to 1960s sitcoms to TV coverage of the first moonwalk. Get here early in the day and make a reservation to use the library, where you can search the database on a Mac and then call up a program on an individual console with headphones. If you can't get a reservation, at least stop by the fifth-floor radio-listening room to sample sound bites from timely preselected programs or attend any of the screenings running frequently in a number of cushy small theaters. Weekends are the best time for kids, when there are hands-on workshops in the morning and uncrowded screenings of top international children's TV shows in the afternoon; the staff is genuinely friendly to youngsters. If your child's hooked on TV Land, plan for hours of browsing.

Museum of the City of New York ★ (Finds)   **Ages 3 & up.** If you're on Museum Mile already, your kids may enjoy this more than the art museums farther south (be sure to skip across the street afterward to Central Park's lovely Conservatory Garden—see p. 184). The biggest draw for kids is the spectacular exhibit of dolls and dollhouses in the Toys Gallery, though some kids I know like to come here just to parade up and down the gorgeous staircase in the entrance hall. Perhaps the most famous dollhouse in the collection is the **Stettheimer Dollhouse** ★★, the exquisite creation of Carrie Walter Stettheimer, a theater stage-set designer in the 1920s. The dollhouse has period wallpaper, delicate paper lampshades, and an art gallery featuring original miniatures of famous artworks—done by the artists themselves for their theatrical friend. Prowling through re-created bedchambers and parlors and gazing at displays of famous New Yorkers' fashionable outfits is a great way for kids to peek back in history. Theater lovers won't want to miss the Broadway exhibit, displaying posters and mementos from the Great White Way (including a costume Barbra Streisand wore in *Funny Girl*). Peter Pan fans will be blown away upon seeing the black net "shadow" that Wendy sewed back onto Peter Pan's toes in the old Mary Martin musical—that's the kind of cool stuff this museum has hidden away.

1220 Fifth Ave. (at 103rd St.). 𝄐 **212/534-1672.** www.mcny.org. Suggested admission $9 adults, $5 students and seniors, free for children 12 and under; $20 families. Tues–Sun 10am–5pm. Subway: 6 to 103rd St.; 2 or 3 to Central Park North (110th St.). Bus: M1, M2, M3, M4.

National Museum of the American Indian (Value)   **Ages 5 & up.** A branch of the Smithsonian, this museum enjoys a fabulous setting in the ornate 1907 U.S. Customs House, a Beaux Arts gem that was a principal site in the movie *Ghostbusters II*. To enter the exhibition galleries, you pass through the awesome Great Rotunda—don't miss looking up at the painted dome. The museum has vast holdings, only a small portion of which are on display here (especially now that the Smithsonian has opened its main NMAI museum on the Mall down in Washington, D.C.). It isn't big on interactivity, but wend your way through the series of rooms and you should be able to find something of interest, particularly if your kids have studied Native American culture in school—a hanging bison hide they can stroke, a glass case filled with hundreds of moccasins, mysterious Mesoamerican clay figures, or some eye-opening art by contemporary Native American artists.

1 Bowling Green, beside Battery Park. 𝄐 **212/514-3700.** www.nmai.si.edu. Free admission. Daily 10am–5pm (Thurs to 8pm). Closed Dec 25. Subway: 4, 5 to Bowling Green; R, W to Whitehall St./South Ferry.

New York City Fire Museum   **Ages 3 & up.** Though small, this two-story museum in a converted firehouse is worth the money if your kids are into fire trucks. There's an awesome collection of antique fire engines, including several horse-drawn ones (the horses aren't on display, unfortunately, but there's a stuffed fire dog that used to be the mascot of one Brooklyn firehouse). A lot of the museum is most interesting to adults patient enough to pore over the mementos of 19th-century firefighting, but there are enough bells, alarms, pickaxes, and nozzles to hold the youngsters' interest for 45 minutes or so. Best of all, there are usually retired firefighters on hand eager to explain each apparatus to admiring youngsters.

278 Spring St. (btwn Varick and Hudson sts.). 𝄐 **212/691-1303.** www.nycfiremuseum.org. Suggested admission $5 adults, $2 students and seniors, $1 children 11 and under. Tues–Sat 10am–5pm; Sun 10am–4pm. Subway: 1 to Houston St.; C, E to Spring St.

New York City Police Museum (Value) **Ages 6 & up.** With everything from vintage uniforms to a mock-up of a crime scene and a computer simulation of what it would be like to be confronted with a gun-wielding criminal, this collection of police memorabilia should mesmerize any child who's into cops and robbers. Confiscated weapons (including Al Capone's machine gun), counterfeit money, old patrol cars and motorcycles, badges and radios and alarms and nightsticks . . . the mind boggles. It's staffed by NYPD officers and has a clear bias toward supporting law enforcement.

100 Old Slip (at South St.). ☎ 212/480-3100. www.nycpolicemuseum.org. Suggested admission $7 adults; $5 students, seniors, and children 6–18; free for children 5 and under. Tues–Sun 10am–5pm. Subway: 2, 3 to Wall St.; R, W to Whitehall St.; J, M, Z to Broad St.; 4, 5 to Bowling Green.

New-York Historical Society ★ **Ages 4 & up.** Rotating exhibits here will be of varying interest to children, but several have been noteworthy in recent years—the block-buster Alexander Hamilton exhibit, for example, exhibits of Presidential campaign memorabilia, or the occasional opportunity to gaze upon John James Audubon's stunning original art for his classic *Birds of America.* Older children may be ready to browse through the fourth-floor exhibit space, crammed with treasures from the society's vast holdings—George Washington's camp bed from Valley Forge, the desk where Clement Clarke Moore wrote *A Visit from St. Nicholas,* a glorious collection of Tiffany lamps, and a portrait of an early governor of New York dressed as a woman.

2 W. 77th St. (at 170 Central Park West). ☎ 212/873-3400. www.nyhistory.org. Admission $10 adults, $7 educators and seniors, $6 students, free for children 11 and under. Tues–Sat 10am–6pm; Sun 11am–5:45pm. Subway: B, C to 81st St./Museum of Natural History.

New York Public Library **Ages 10 & up.** Though most little kids fall in love with the noble pair of lions—Patience and Fortitude—poised beside the front steps, the exhibits mounted inside the New York Public Library are usually of interest to older kids only. (But you never know—there was an exhibit on garbage in 1995 that my boys thought was totally cool.) The library does have an extraordinary collection of first editions, manuscripts, letters, prints, maps, and other treasures on paper and often puts together fascinating shows, but whether or not your youngster will be intrigued all depends on the theme. Otherwise, pop in for a few minutes just to gape at the Beaux Arts architecture, from the dignified marble lobby to the extraordinary third-floor Main Reading Room, where anyone can join the scholars and writers at endless ranks of tables poring over research materials from the NYPL's famous stacks. Note that behind the library is **Bryant Park,** which has cafes and its own spiffy little carousel.

One good reason to pop in to the library these days is to see the original **Winnie-the-Pooh animals** ★ displayed in their new home here in the city's main library.

Fifth Ave. at 41st St. ☎ 212/930-0800. www.nypl.org. Free admission. Mon and Thurs–Sat 11am–6pm; Tues–Wed 10am–7:30pm. Subway: B, D, F, V to 42nd St.; 7 to Fifth Ave.

Sony Wonder Technology Lab ★ (Value) **Ages 6 & up.** Though no doubt it helps sell Sony products, this wonderful interactive exploratorium isn't annoyingly self-serving. Sony Wonder actually lets people experiment with all types of high-tech equipment, from TV cameras to industrial robots to ultrasound scanners; you can play at being a game designer, a movie director, or an electronic musician or just mess around in a mul-tisensory interactive environment. When you first enter the lab, you get your own **personal card,** which becomes magnetically encoded with your name and photo; as you continue through four floors of activities, every time you slide the card through the scanner on a new terminal, your name and photo are inserted into whatever program is up.

On your way out, you can print out a personalized certificate recording all the activities you tried. To prevent overcrowding, the Sony Wonder folks have set up a timed-ticket system; call 1 week to 3 months ahead to reserve your time slot, especially if you're planning to come before 2pm on a weekday September through June (this place is *very* popular with school groups). If you haven't reserved a slot, you'll be admitted on a first-come, first-served basis, which may mean you'll have to wait in line in the lobby (a comic robot, b.b. wonderbot, helps you pass the time with goofy interactive chat). *Note:* Following an upgrade, the Lab was expected to reopen its second and third floors by the end of 2008; call to get the latest updates on the openings.

550 Madison Ave. (entrance on 56th St.). ✆ **212/833-8100;** for reservations call 212/833-5414 Mon–Fri 8am–2pm. www.sonywondertechlab.com. Free admission. Tues–Sat 10am–5pm. Subway: N, R, 4, 5, 6 to 59th St.; E, V to Fifth Ave.

Sports Museum of America ★ **Ages 4 & up.** Opened in 2008, this ultra-interactive museum is the only one to celebrate all American sports under one roof. It's got 19 themed galleries, sports artifacts (Wayne Gretsky's hockey stick, Reggie Jackson's World Series bat, even Jason Kidd's first-grade basketball jersey), and 20 original movies. It's the new home of the Heisman trophy, college football's MVP, and the site of the Billie Jean King International Women's Sports Center.

28 Broadway (entrance on Beaver St. near *Charging Bull* statue). ✆ **212/747-0900** or 888/762-8587. www.sportsmuseum.com. Tickets $27 adults, $20 kids, free for children 3 and under. Daily 9am–7pm. Subway: 4, 5 to Bowling Green; R, W, 1 to Rector St.; or 2, 3 to Wall St.

The Studio Museum in Harlem **Ages 6 & up.** It all depends on what the current exhibition is, but this savvy uptown museum mounts some very interesting art in its cool, high-ceilinged white galleries and often has good Saturday-morning family workshops. It's a reasonably sized place for a dose of art viewing, and a good start to a Harlem neighborhood exploration.

144 W. 125th St. (btwn Lenox Ave. and Adam Clayton Powell Blvd.). ✆ **212/864-4500.** www.studio museuminharlem.org. Suggested donation $7 adults, $3 students and seniors, free for children 12 and under. Wed–Fri and Sun noon–6pm (Sat opens at 10am). Subway: A, B, C, D, 2, 3, 4, 5, 6 to 125th St.

4 MUSEUMS IN THE OUTER BOROUGHS

IN BROOKLYN

Brooklyn Children's Museum ★★ **All ages.** Technically the oldest children's museum in the country, founded in 1899, the Brooklyn Children's Museum is also one of the best in the country, and the big yellow building reopened in September 2008 with an array of hands-on exhibits that will interest kids up to age 14. The emphasis on technology, TV, and video will appeal to older children (witness the pair of hip New York boys, ages 10 and 12, who wandered into a *Sesame Street* exhibit, saw themselves on a monitor, and wound up happily clowning around alongside various *Sesame Street* characters they thought they'd outgrown). There's also an emphasis on nature, with exhibits exploring animals' eating habits and plants' growing habits in a hands-on greenhouse. In the Animal Outpost, staff members bring out the museum's permanent animal inhabitants, including a beautiful and enormous amber-colored python named Fantasia, to demonstrate their traits. In the MusicMix studio, kids can experiment with how various instruments produce sounds; young divas can bust a move in the Mainstage performance area; and children 5 and under can explore the bright tactile learning environment of Totally Tots in the Greenhouse and Garden. Free Friday Family Jam nights in July and August add music, theater, or dance performances at 5pm.

The museum's new daffodil-yellow expansion features a new lobby, a theater, a kids' cafe, and much more gallery space.

Getting There: By **subway,** take the no. 3 to the Kingston Avenue station, walk 6 blocks (with traffic flow) on Kingston Avenue to St. Mark's Avenue, and turn left for 1 block. Or take the no. 2 to the President Street station, walk 8 blocks on Nostrand Avenue (against traffic) to St. Mark's Avenue, turn right, and go 2 blocks. By **car,** take Atlantic Avenue east to Brooklyn Avenue, turn right, and drive 4 blocks south; or follow Eastern Parkway east from Grand Army Plaza to New York Avenue, turn left, and go 6 blocks north to St. Mark's Avenue, where you turn right and go 1 block east. Unmetered on-street parking is nearby. An alternative that's fun for kids is The Heart of Brooklyn Connection (HOB), set to begin Fall 2008, which runs Saturday and Sunday on Brooklyn's Museum Mile between 10am and 5pm, making three stops every hour—at Grand Army Plaza (at quarter past the hour), the Brooklyn Museum of Art (at 25 past the hour), and the Brooklyn Children's Museum (at a quarter to the hour). Call the museum for details.

145 Brooklyn Ave. (at St. Mark's Ave.) in Brower Park, Crown Heights. 𝄖 **718/735-4400.** www.brooklyn kids.org. Suggested admission $5 per person. Wed–Thurs 2–6pm, Fri noon–6:30pm, Sat–Sun 11am–6pm; July–Aug also open Tues 2–6pm.

Brooklyn Museum ★   **Ages 6 & up.** The superb Egyptian collection, full of over-the-top mummy cases, is the best reason to visit this big, underappreciated museum in Brooklyn, near neighbor to the Brooklyn Botanic Garden and Prospect Park; even if you're going to spend only an hour or so in the museum, there are enough other things to do nearby to justify the excursion. If your kids like history, they can wander past 27 detailed American period rooms from 1675 to 1928, including an eye-popping Moorish-style smoking room from John D. Rockefeller's own town house. If they're old enough to appreciate great art, the American and European galleries are strong, with lots of Impressionism and a load of Rodin bronzes. There's also a special gift shop just for kids, as well as lots of weekend drop-in programs for children.

200 Eastern Pkwy., at Prospect Park, Brooklyn. 𝄖 **718/638-5000.** www.brooklynart.org. Admission $8 adults, $4 students and seniors, free for children 11 and under. Wed–Fri 10am–5pm; Sat–Sun 11am–6pm (1st Sat of the month 11am–11pm). Parking $3 for 1st hour, $2 per hour after that. Subway: 2, 3 to Eastern Pkwy.

Jewish Children's Museum   **All ages.** Multimedia and hands-on are the watch-words for this museum out in Crown Heights, dedicated to explicating Judaism to youngsters of all faiths. Push buttons to trigger a multimedia "re-creation" of Creation; clamber around a large-than-life replica of a Shabbat table setting and shop in a Kosher supermarket; play Mini-Golf's Six Holes of Life; be a newscaster reporting on the miracle of the oil from the war with the Maccabees; feel the rush of the Red Sea parting on either side of you and stand atop Mount Sinai to receive the Ten Commandments alongside Moses—yep, it's all simulated here. Developed under the guidance of Rabbi Menachem M. Schneerson, otherwise known as the Lubavitcher Rebbe, this handsome facility offers a pretty persuasive reason to head out to Brooklyn.

792 Eastern Parkway (at Kingston Ave.), Brooklyn. 𝄖 **718/467-0600.** www.jcmonline.org. Admission $10, free for children 1 and under. Mon–Thurs 10am–4pm; Sun 10am–6pm. Closed Jan 1 and all Jewish holidays. Subway: 3 to Kingston Ave.

Lefferts Homestead Children's Historic House Museum   **All ages.** This Dutch colonial farmhouse has been filled with exhibits for kids—old-fashioned toys, puppets, storybook corners, art activities—and absolutely everything in it is touchable. It's a little shabby, but who cares when your kids are allowed to run up and down the stairs and jump off the porch and just enjoy themselves? On summer Sundays, come for the afternoon story hours under the big tree outside, and go on to visit the nearby Prospect Park Wildlife Center (p. 183) and take a spin on the stunning carved animals of the vintage Prospect Park Carousel.

Flatbush Ave., Brooklyn. ✆ **718/789-2822.** Free admission. Thurs–Sun noon–5pm (to 6pm July to Labor Day). Subway: B, Q, S to Prospect Park.

New York Transit Museum ★   **Ages 3 & up.** The cool thing about this museum is that it's built in a disused subway station, with exhibits sprawling down the tunnels. Kids love the pair of bus cabs they can climb into and pretend to drive and the set of vintage subway cars they can lope through, hanging on straps and swinging around poles. Beyond that, the collection dwells on antique turnstiles and fare boxes, switching apparatuses, and subway-station mosaics, all of which are of consuming interest to the adult subway fanatics who flock here (a breed unto themselves, as we met on one of the periodic Nostalgia Train expeditions where vintage cars are taken out for a spin on today's tracks). The sheer amount of stuff makes this place good for an hour, more if your kid is transportation-obsessed.

At the corner of Boerum Place and Schermerhorn St., Brooklyn. ✆ **718/694-1600.** www.mta.nyc.ny.us/ mta/museum. Admission $5 adults, $3 seniors and children 17 and under. Tues–Fri 10am–4pm; Sat–Sun noon–5pm. Subway 2, 3, 4, 5 to Borough Hall; A, C, G to Hoyt/Schermerhorn sts.; A, C, F to Jay St./Borough Hall; M, R to Court St.

IN QUEENS

American Museum of the Moving Image ★★   **Ages 8 & up.** *Note:* This museum is currently closed for a major expansion but is scheduled to reopen in late 2009; check the website for the latest updates. This superb resource for cinephiles is housed in the Kaufman Astoria Studio, where talkies were made long ago and *Sesame Street* is filmed today (unfortunately, you cannot tour the set). At interactive workstations, you can fiddle with sound effects, dub in new dialogue, call up different soundtracks, create your own digital animation, and even add your face (a la Woody Allen's *Zelig*) to classic movie scenes. Many of the historic artifacts on display (a 1910 wooden Pathé camera, a 1959 Philco TV set, Charlton Heston's chariot from *Ben-Hur*) may mean nothing to youngsters, but the extensive costume gallery should grab them (items like Robin Williams's padded housedress from *Mrs. Doubtfire*), as will the ghoulish masks in the makeup exhibition and the special effects artifacts—you'll see a character model of Yoda from 1980's *The Empire Strikes Back,* before computer animation rendered such puppetry obsolete. There's a fun display of tie-in toys and lunchboxes promoting TV shows from *Howdy Doody* to *The Simpsons*. Classic movie serials are screened every afternoon in Tut's Fever Movie Palace, an over-the-top ancient-Egypt-themed "cinema" designed by Red Grooms and Lysiane Luong. The on-site cafe is a welcome convenience, too. The new expansion will include a three-story addition, a 264-seat film theater, a 71-seat screening room, and two amphitheaters.

35th Ave. and 36th St., Astoria, Queens. ✆ **718/784-0077.** www.ammi.org. Admission (includes film and video programs) $10 adults, $7.50 students and seniors, $5 children 5–18, free for children 4 and under. Wed–Thurs 11am–5pm; Fri 11am–8pm (free admission after 4pm); Sat–Sun 11am–6:30pm. Subway: N, W to Broadway; G, R, V to Steinway St.

New York Hall of Science ★★ **Ages 3 & up.** Like the wonderful Imaginarium in San Francisco, this is a completely hands-on museum that makes learning really fun—you can pedal furiously on a bicycle to turn a huge propeller; you can watch a bank of rotating electric fans create wind; you can hunt for microbes and fungi with microscopes; you can use colored Plexiglas tiles to make your own rainbow; you can watch your brother get really huge and then really tiny as he walks across an optically distorted room. Put your ear to glass pipes, and you can hear different pitches; stand in front of a special light scope, and you can cast three different-colored shadows at once.

Best of all, no activity takes more than a minute to execute, which means that kids sprint from one to another instead of hogging a demo station—you rarely have to wait your turn to try anything. And the new **Science Playground** (additional $4; appropriate for kids 6 and older; closed Jan–Feb) is an awesome 65,000-square-foot space with loads of interactive activities indoors and out, including a gigantic teeter-totter, a light-activated kinetic sculpture, windmills, and a water-play area.

There's a limited cafe here, but you'd be better off packing a lunch—there aren't many options in the neighborhood. Definitely combine the science museum with a stop at the nearby Queens Wildlife Center and/or Queens Museum of Art (both later in this chapter).

47-01 111th St., Flushing Meadows–Corona Park, Corona, Queens. ✆ **718/699-0005.** www.nyscience. org. Admission $11 adults, $8 children 2–17 and seniors; $4 Science Playground fee; free to all Fri 2–5pm and Sun 10–11am during school year. Sept–June Tues–Thurs 9:30am–2pm, Fri 9:30am–5pm, Sat–Sun noon–5pm; July–Aug Mon–Fri 9:30am–5pm, Sat–Sun 10am–6pm. Closed major holidays. Parking $10. Subway: 7 to 111th St.

Queens County Farm Museum **All ages.** Still a working farm, this 18th-century homestead is a bucolic spot of fields and orchards and barns full of animals, with ongoing demonstrations of agricultural arts—plowing, planting, apple picking, reaping, milking cows, birthing foals, incubating chicks, and so on. Come on a weekend, when you can go inside the simple three-room frame farmhouse, built in 1772, and go on a hayride ($4). From mid-September to October, weekend visitors can try to find their way through a giant corn maze ($7 adults, $4 children 4–11).

73-50 Little Neck Pkwy., Floral Park, Queens. ✆ **718/347-3276.** www.queensfarm.org. Free admission. Mon–Fri 10am–5pm (grounds only); Sat–Sun 10am–5pm (house and grounds). Special events admission fees vary. Subway: E, F to Kew Gardens/Union Tpk., then Q46 bus to Little Neck Pkwy.

Queens Museum of Art **Ages 8 & up.** Besides the fact that it's parked next to the Unisphere, that famous stainless-steel globe from the 1964 World's Fair, the chief reason for children to visit this museum of 20th-century art is the **Panorama** ★, an awesomely huge three-dimensional re-creation of the New York skyline. Originally built in 1964, it's been faithfully updated; laser-light shafts stand in place of the World Trade Center, replicating the "Tribute in Light" that marked the towers' place for a few months after the 9/11 tragedy. The lights are timed to show the progress of a day every 9 minutes. Kids will love picking out familiar landmarks; anyone who enjoys dollhouses, Polly Pockets, and Micro Machines can marvel over the incredibly detailed small-scale rendering of a city that's often all too large-scale.

NYC Building (next to the Unisphere), Flushing Meadows–Corona Park, Queens. ✆ **718/592-9700.** www.queensmuseum.org. Admission $5 adults, $2.50 students and seniors, free for children 4 and under. Wed–Fri 10am–5pm, Sat–Sun noon–5pm; July–Aug until 6pm (and until 8pm Fri). Subway: 7 to Willett's Point/Shea Stadium, then walk south over ramp into park and head for the Unisphere.

Historic Richmond Town ★ Ages 5 & up. Somewhat off the beaten track, this 100-acre re-creation includes 27 buildings spanning the 17th to the early 20th centuries—which may create a disjointed effect for historical purists, but kids generally don't care. Three little streets are set up like a small village, and kids can run in and out of the house, shops, inns, and schoolhouses (there are even a couple of outhouses!) and basically just have a ball. Many buildings were moved here from other sites on Staten Island; they range from a neoclassical courthouse to a little schoolhouse dating from 1695, the oldest elementary school building in the country. Costumed interpreters are in action July and August, demonstrating crafts like basket weaving, spinning, weaving, tinsmithing, and printing. A good full day's expedition.

441 Clarke Ave., Staten Island. ℂ **718/351-1611.** www.historicrichmondtown.org. Admission $5 adults, $4 seniors, $3.50 children 5–17, free for children 4 and under. Wed–Sun 1–5pm; July–Aug open early (10am) Wed–Fri. From the Staten Island Ferry, take bus no. S74 to Richmond Rd./Court Place.

Staten Island Children's Museum ★ Ages 10 & under. Of all the area's children's museums, this one has the loveliest setting—on the lawns and gardens of the Snug Harbor Cultural Center, formerly a home for retired seamen. There's already plenty to do on-site, with weekend workshops and a host of interactive exhibits that help children explore the wonders of water, insects, computers, and animals (there's more of an emphasis on natural sciences here than at its more urban counterparts). *A bonus:* You get here via the Staten Island Ferry, with only a short added bus ride from the terminus.

1000 Richmond Terrace, Staten Island. ℂ **718/273-2060.** www.statenislandkids.org. Admission $5, free for children under 1 (grandparents free on Wed). Tues–Fri noon–5pm, Sat–Sun 10am–5pm; July–Aug Tues–Sun 10am–5pm (until 8pm Wed). From the Staten Island Ferry, take the S40 bus (Richmond Terrace) to the Snug Harbor center, with its black wrought-iron gate. The museum is in Building M.

IN NEW JERSEY

The Liberty Science Center ★★ All ages. This science center just across the river in Jersey City, New Jersey, reopened in July 2007 after a 2-year, $110-million expansion that doubled its size. The museum has not so much been refurbished but literally *reinvented,* shifting its mission from, in its own words: "encouraging science literacy to inspiring science activism." It has six large interactive exhibition spaces, the country's largest IMAX Dome theater, and the Joseph D. Williams 3D Science Theater. Among the permanent exhibitions: **I Explore,** where kids age 1 through 5 can play a xylophone made up of hanging rock slabs or explore beneath the street; **Eat and Be Eaten,** where you explore the food chain in imaginative ways; and **Skyscraper!,** where you can walk amid a scaled-down cityscape. There's much to do here—it's a blast. You can take public transportation to get here (see below) or ride in a Liberty Island **water taxi** from the World Financial Center to Liberty State Park—but you'll have a 20-minute walk from the ferry landing to the museum; see the website for the latest schedule (ℂ **201/985-8000;** www.libertylandingmarina.com; round-trip $14 adults, $12 seniors, $10 children 7–12, and free kids 6 and under).

Liberty State Park, 222 Jersey City Blvd. (btwn Philip and Wilson sts.). ℂ **201/200-1000.** www.lsc.org. Admission $16 adults, $12 seniors and children 7–12, free for kids 6 and under. Mon–Fri 9am–5pm; Sat–Sun 9am–6pm. Take the PATH train to Exchange Place or Pavonia/Newport, transfer to the Hudson-Bergen Light Rail to Liberty State Park. Ferry to Liberty.

5 BEST RIDES

Coney Island   All ages. Open in summer months, this cluster of small private amusement parks is on the rebound, with the spruced-up boardwalk, the new Brooklyn Cyclones ballpark, and the New York Aquarium within easy walking distance. At 10th Street, the vintage **Cyclone** roller coaster ($8), built in 1927 and now a city landmark, offers riders over 54 inches tall the thrill of an eight-story drop at one point. The Cyclone is pretty much all that remains of the 1960s-era amusement park **Astroland,** which closed its doors September 2008. **Demo's Wonder Wheel** park (www.wonderwheel.com) next door at 12th Street features the landmark **Wonder Wheel** ($6), an ingenious double Ferris wheel built in 1920 that circles high over the boardwalk. The area also has minigolf, go-carts, and even a freak show, not to mention the original Nathan's hot dog stand.

Coney Island USA, 1208 Surf Ave., Brooklyn. ✆ **718/372-5159.** www.coneyisland.com. Admission to parks free; Astroland's Pay One Price (P.O.P.) Wristbands for unlimited rides $26 except Fri and Sat nights and all day Sat, Sun, and holidays. All rides $2.50–$6. Parks open weekends only noon–8pm Apr–May and Sept–Oct; daily noon–midnight June to Labor Day. Subway: D, N to Coney Island/Stillwell Ave.; F, Q to W. 8th St.

New York Skyride (Overrated   Ages 5 & up. "Passengers" are seated on a large platform that begins to tilt and jolt and careen wildly while a big screen shows you "crashing" your way around New York landmarks, with lots of ear-splitting recorded sound effects. There's zero sightseeing information—it's just a crazed 8-minute simulation of speeding through the cityscape. Count on a long line, up to 30 minutes at times. Not worth the tourist-soaking price.

In the Empire State Building (2nd floor), Fifth Ave. at 34th St. ✆ **888/SKYRIDE** or 212/279-9777. www. skyride.com. Admission $30 adults, $23 children 12–17 and seniors, and $16 children 5–11; combination tickets with Empire State Building $40 adults, $25 seniors, $32 children 12–17, and $19 children 5–11. Daily 10am–10pm. Subway: B, D, F, N, Q, R, V, W to 34th St.

Roosevelt Island Tram (Value   All ages. A pair of big red cable cars swing over the East River alongside the 59th Street/Queensboro Bridge to Roosevelt Island. Though most of the trip is actually over an unglamorous wedge of East Side real estate, it does go over the river, and you're high up enough to get good views of Manhattan up and down (and it has been the star of several movies—including *Spider-Man* in 2002). There are few seats—only a narrow hard bench at either end of a car that holds 30 or so—so get onboard quick to grab a seat by the front windows. Once you're on Roosevelt Island, site of a former smallpox hospital, you can turn right around and ride back—or you can take a ride on the red shuttle bus to loop around this island housing development, a sprawl of modern apartment blocks with lots of riverside green space and little playgrounds tucked away everywhere. The village's main street looks like something out of the 1960s British TV series *The Prisoner*—a curved main street cutting between bland shop fronts (one of everything: post office, library, church, deli, Chinese restaurant, bank, school). Getting there on the cable car is more than half the fun.

Manhattan terminus: Second Ave. and 60th St. ✆ **212/832-4540.** www.rioc.com. Fare $4 round-trip including children 5 and older, $2 seniors with MetroCard, free for children 4 and under. Subway: 4, 5, 6 to 59th St.

Staten Island Ferry ★ (Value) **All ages.** Walk right on at the South Ferry Terminal, and you can chug across New York Harbor, past the Statue of Liberty, to Staten Island, where you walk around the barriers and get on again for the return ride. The whole round-trip should take about an hour. Most of the ferry decks are now glassed in, alas, but the views are still great. A friend of mine tells me that his mother used to herd her kids onto the ferry on hot summer nights to sleep when their un-air-conditioned apartment got too hot; that's the kind of wonderful institution the Staten Island Ferry is in the hearts of New Yorkers.

Departing from S. Ferry in Battery Park. ℰ **718/727-2508.** Free tickets. Subway: R, W to Whitehall St.; 1, 9 to South Ferry.

Toys "R" Us Ferris Wheel **All ages.** Inside the three-story atrium of this immense Times Square toy-o-rama, there's an honest-to-goodness big Ferris wheel with fun, funky cars resembling licensed characters and toy icons like Uncle Moneybags from Monopoly. For the money, it seems a fairly short ride; most kids have just as much fun riding free up and down in the store's glass-walled elevators.

1514 Broadway (at 44th St.). ℰ **800/869-7787.** Tickets $4, free for children 1 and under. Children under 40 in. must be accompanied by an adult. Mon–Thurs 10am–10pm; Fri–Sat 10am–11pm; Sun 11am–9pm. Subway: N, Q, R, S, W, 1, 2, 3, 7 to 42nd St./Times Square.

Victorian Gardens at the Wollman Rink **Ages 2 to 12.** In summer months Central Park's skating rink is overtaken by this squeaky-clean kiddie amusement park, featuring maybe a dozen rides. Don't expect any terrifying roller coasters or vintage charm, but it's a great Manhattan option for a summer afternoon, and there are rarely any lines.

Wollman Rink, Central Park (enter E. 62nd St.). ℰ **212/982-2229.** www.victoriangardensnyc.com. Admission Mon–Fri $6.50, Sat–Sun $7.50; children under 36 in. free with paid adult. Rides $2 each (climbing wall $10). Unlimited-ride wristband $12 Mon–Fri, $14 Sat–Sun. Mid-May to mid-Sept Mon–Thurs 11am–7pm; Fri 11am–8pm; Sat 10am–9pm; Sun 10am–8pm. Subway: A, B, C, D, 1 to 59th St./Columbus Circle; F to 57th St.; N, R, W to Fifth Ave./59th St.

6 HISTORIC HOUSES

Alice Austen House ★ **Ages 6 & up.** Many things about pioneer photographer Austen's house make it a great bet for kids. First, it's really just a cozy cottage, a low-slung gingerbread-trimmed bungalow with rolling lawns that offer dynamite views of New York Harbor. Second, Austen herself is such an appealing character, a spunky turn-of-the-20th-century woman who started taking pictures when she was 10 and just never stopped. Lots of her work is on display, and the garden has been replanted according to her photos of the original grounds. Third, you get to ride the Staten Island Ferry over. What more could you ask for?

2 Hylan Blvd., Staten Island. ℰ **718/816-4506.** www.aliceausten.org. Suggested admission $2 adults, free for children 12 and under. Thurs–Sun noon–5pm. From the Staten Island Ferry terminal, take the S51 bus 2 miles to Bay St./Hylan Blvd. Walk 1 block toward water; museum is on right.

Gracie Mansion **Ages 8 and up.** Dating back to the early 19th century, this yellow frame house—formerly a wealthy family's country house—has since 1942 been the official residence of the mayor of New York. The current mayor, Michael Bloomberg, chooses to live in his much tonier Upper East Side town house, so visitors can tour the residential areas for the first time in years, as well as the public rooms on the main floor. The tours last 45 minutes, and it's not much of a window into the past—many restorations have wiped away original features and furnishings—but it's a lovely home, nonetheless.

Carl Schurz Park, East End Ave. at 90th St. © **311** (within NYC) or **212/570-4751** for tour reservations. Admission $7 adults, $4 seniors, free for children. Wed 10am, 11am, 1pm, and 2pm. Subway: 4, 5, 6 to E. 86th St.

Merchant's House Museum ★   Ages 8 & up. The most interesting thing about the Tredwell family—who lived in this house continuously from 1835 to 1933—is that they weren't famous or unusual at all, just a stable, prosperous, upper-middle-class family whose house and furniture happened to survive intact, wallpaper and all, until it became a house museum in the mid–20th century. The house itself is a fairly notable example of Greek Revival, but your kids will probably be more struck by the old-fashioned furnishings and clothing (poignant details like a piece of needlework tossed onto a table, never to be finished). A nice trip back in time on a quiet side street not far from NYU and the East Village's funky St. Mark's Place.

29 E. 4th St. (btwn Bowery and Lafayette Sts.). © **212/777-1089.** http://merchantshouse.org. Admission $8 adults, $5 students and seniors, free for children 11 and under accompanied by an adult. Thurs–Mon noon–5pm. Subway: N or R to 8th St.; 6 to Astor Place or Bleecker St.

Morris-Jumel Mansion ★   Ages 10 & up. Dating back to 1765, this imposing mansion with its Georgian front columns had a major brush with history when Gen. George Washington used it as his headquarters in 1776. As they tour the house, however, your kids may become more interested in Eliza Jumel, the wealthy, brazen 19th-century woman who lived here for many years, during her marriage to, and after her divorce from, Aaron Burr. It's too bad this big, elegant mansion is off the beaten path for tourists.

65 Jumel Terrace (at 160th St.). © **212/923-8008.** www.morrisjumel.org. Admission $4 adults, $3 students and seniors, free for children 12 and under. Wed–Sun 10am–4pm. Mon and Tues by appt. only. Subway: C to 163rd St.

Mount Vernon Hotel Museum and Garden ★   Ages 6 & up. Back in the 1820s and 1830s, when this part of the Upper East Side was considered a country retreat, the Mount Vernon Hotel was a fashionable day resort for genteel travelers. What's surprising is how much this site still feels like a retreat, surrounded by city as it is: The surrounding gardens, planted in 18th-century style, offer a welcome whiff of horticulture, and eight period rooms inside this former carriage house—restored by the Colonial Dames of America—re-create what life in the old inn might've been like. Considering its convenient location, it's curious that this museum isn't better known. Guided tours, which leave on the hour from the gift shop, may be a bit slow for young children, but are worth it.

421 E. 61st St. (btwn First and York aves.). © **212/838-6878.** www.mvhm.org. Admission $8 adults, $7 students and seniors, free for children 12 and under. Tues–Sun 11am–4pm (June–July Tues until 9pm). Closed major holidays and Aug. Subway: F, N, R to Lexington Ave./59th St.; 4, 5, 6 to 59th St.

7 ZOOS & AQUARIUMS

Aside from the following, check out the **Bronx Zoo** (p. 157) and the **Central Park Zoo** (p. 158).

New York Aquarium   All ages. After an hour-long subway ride from Manhattan— an adventure in itself—you hit the ocean at Coney Island beach, skirting the amusement parks, and walk to the left down the boardwalk to the aquarium. In summer, you may need to plan a full day so you can also enjoy the beach or the rides, or even get a ticket for a Brooklyn Cyclones game (see chapter 11). We've gone in spring, which is not optimal—many of the exhibits are outdoors, and it was still too chilly to linger while watching the otters, penguins, and walruses on their rocky sea-cliff habitats—but out of season has its own charm, with the beach deserted and the ocean misty, cold, and gray. The kids still had a ball in the interactive **Explore the Shore** exhibit and the re-created salt marsh; and the sharks, of course, are creepily fascinating any time of year. Time your schedule so you can catch the sea lion demonstrations, too. The **Deep Sea 3D** simulator ride costs extra for a visit to the ocean floor. Pack a lunch if you're going in the cooler months, when the outdoor snack bar may be closed and nearby boardwalk joints are boarded up.

Surf Ave. and W. 8th St., Coney Island, Brooklyn. 📞 **718/265-3400** or 265-FISH. www.nyaquarium.com or www.wcs.org. Admission $13 adults, $10 seniors, and $9 children 2–12. Deep Sea 3D $6 ($4 members). Combo pass for both $17 adults, $14 seniors, $13 children. Mon–Fri 10am–5pm; Sat–Sun and holidays 10am–5:30pm. Parking $12. Subway: F or Q to W. 8th St./NY Aquarium.

Prospect Park Wildlife Center ★ All ages. Of all New York City's zoos, this one is right at the level of preschoolers and young grade-schoolers. The fanciful abstract sculptures arching over the walkway from the side entrance tell you right away you're in kid territory, and on it goes, to the Animals in Our Lives petting zoo and the outdoor Discovery Trail, where kids can hop like a wallaby, squat on their own lily pads, or huddle inside a giant turtle shell. There's a mini-amphitheater built in front of the glass-enclosed environment where a troop of hamadryas baboons scamper around—somebody here knows which animals kids most like to watch. It's small, clean, safe, and tons of fun. Once you're out here, make it a full day by visiting nearby Lefferts Homestead (p. 177), New York's only historic house set up just for kids, and taking a ride on the gorgeous antique Prospect Park Carousel (p. 170), only steps from the zoo entrance. The subway ride from Manhattan isn't all that long, leaving you off only a block or so from the zoo.

450 Flatbush Ave., Prospect Park, Brooklyn. 📞 **718/399-7339.** www.wcs.org. Admission $6 adults, $2.25 seniors, $2 children 3–12, free for children 2 and under. Mon–Fri 10am–5pm; Sat–Sun 10am–5:30pm. Subway: Q or S (Franklin Ave. Shuttle) to Prospect Park.

Queens Wildlife Center All ages. Though it may not rate a trip out to Queens from Manhattan on its own account, this smart little zoo is a natural add-on to a New York Hall of Science excursion (p. 178) and a good excuse for a tramp through the old World's Fair grounds. The zoo's focus is on North American species (don't expect exotics here, though my sons considered the American bison plenty exciting) arranged along a hand-somely landscaped walking trail. You feel surrounded by wilderness, yet the pathway is actually pretty short—it won't tax young legs—and the loop shouldn't take more than 15 or 20 minutes. Across the park road is a minifarm with domestic animals that'll satisfy the yen for feeding and stroking warm furry creatures.

53–51 111th St. (at 54th Ave.), in Flushing Meadows Park, Queens. 📞 **718/271-1500.** www.wcs.org. Admission $6 adults, $2.25 seniors, $2 children 3–12, free for children 2 and under. Mon–Fri 10am–5pm; Sat–Sun 10am–5:30pm. Subway: 7 to 111th St. (Queens).

Staten Island Zoo All ages. The little Staten Island Zoo isn't under the umbrella of the Wildlife Conservation Society, as are the other zoos around here, and it's definitely a poor cousin. But you may want to combine this with a visit to the Staten Island Children's Museum (p. 179), especially if you're into snakes—the reptile collection is a standout. The 8 acres are also home to a small aquarium and a fair number of birds. You won't see a lot of large animals, but several small mammal species that kids love to gaze at—the red panda, bush babies, otters, meerkats, and the colorful snout of a mandrill. Feeding times are frequent attractions, and there's a small children's zoo, for younger kids who like their nature hands-on.

614 Broadway, Barrett Park, Staten Island. ✆ **718/442-3101.** www.statenislandzoo.org. Admission $7 adults, $5 seniors, $4 children 3–14, free for children 2 and under; admission by donation Wed after 2pm. Daily 10am–4:45pm. Closed Thanksgiving, Dec 25, and Jan 1. Free parking except for special events. From the Staten Island Ferry, catch the S48 bus, get off at Broadway and Forest Ave., turn left, and go 2½ blocks up Broadway.

---

8 GARDENS

Brooklyn Botanic Garden ★★　**All ages.** Every month, something new is blooming at this 52-acre garden beside the Brooklyn Museum and across from Prospect Park. Starting in spring, Daffodil Hill dazzles the eye with a field of stunning yellow; then delicate pink cherry blossoms fringe the Japanese Pond (local Japanese families flock in for blossom viewing). A riot of roses fills the Cranford Rose Garden as summer sets in, and thickets of rhododendron bloom near the Eastern Parkway entrance. There's also a fragrance garden for the blind, coupled with a sweet little Shakespeare Garden featuring all sorts of plants mentioned in Shakespeare's plays. Year-round, you can stroll through the **Steinhardt Conservatory,** with its outstanding bonsai collection, orchids, waterlilies, and the Trail of Evolution, a pathway lined with increasingly sophisticated plant forms. You'll also find a terrace cafe, a lovely gardening gift shop, and frequent weekend programs for children and families. Kids may get a kick out of the Celebrity Path, inlaid with the names of famous Brooklynites from Mae West to Woody Allen.

1000 Washington Ave. (at Eastern Pkwy.), Brooklyn. ✆ **718/623-7200.** www.bbg.org. Admission $8 adults, $4 students and seniors, free for children 15 and under; free Tues and Sat until noon. Tues–Fri 8am–6pm; Sat–Sun and holidays 10am–6pm (Oct–Mar closes 4:30pm). Open holiday Mon; closed Thanksgiving, Dec 25, and Jan 1. Subway: 2, 3 to Eastern Pkwy.; B, Q, or S to Prospect Park; 4 to Franklin Ave. (the B train does not run to Prospect Park on weekends).

Conservatory Garden ⟨Finds⟩　**All ages.** Central Park's only patch of formal garden is a delightful 6-acre surprise in Manhattan and rarely crowded because it's so far uptown. Walk through glorious wrought-iron gates (which once fronted the Fifth Ave. mansion of Cornelius Vanderbilt II), and turn left to find the Children's Garden, with beds of flowers blooming around a wishing well with a statue of the children from Frances Hodgson Burnett's *The Secret Garden.* The central section of the garden is a long lush lawn flanked by a pair of walkways lined with flowering trees; the northern end has a circular design, with a fountain of the Three Graces surrounded by flower beds—a spectacular blaze of tulips in spring and chrysanthemums in fall. On spring and summer weekends, there's nearly always a wedding party here getting photographed. With restrooms and a fair-weather outdoor cafe, it's a welcome refuge, a perfect place to let your kids stretch their legs after a Museum Mile trek.

Central Park at 105th St. ✆ **212/360-2766.** www.centralparknyc.org. Free admission. Daily 8am–dusk. Free tours Apr–Oct Sat 11am. Subway: 6 to 96th St., then walk up Fifth Ave.

New York Botanical Garden ★★　**All ages.** This lushly planted 250-acre park— five times bigger than the Brooklyn Botanic Garden (see above)—is a real magnet for families. The stunning 8-acre **Everett Children's Adventure Garden** (separate admission

Holiday Train Show at the New York Botanical Garden

Few places celebrate the Christmas holidays with as much sheer theatricality as New York. In the Bronx, the New York Botanical Garden is the site for the wonderful **Holiday Train Show ★★★** where model trains and trolleys zip around a glittering holiday landscape comprised of architectural reproductions of well-known New York landmarks and historic buildings—all made *entirely out of plant materials*. It's an astonishing feat of artistry, with dollhouse-size versions of icons such as Yankee Stadium, Grand Central Station, and the Empire State Building crafted from twigs, pine cones, acorn caps, palm and magnolia leaves, dried moss—even walnut shells and orange slices. Kids of all ages are entranced (and I was blown away). Each year brings a new creation; in 2008 the show introduced Ellis Island and the George Washington Bridge (✆ **718/817-8700;** www.nybg.org; $20 adults, $7 children 2–12, free for children 1 and under). Take the 15-minute Metro-North Railroad from Grand Central to the Botanical Gardens stop. The train show runs from November to early January.

$3 adults, $2 seniors and students, $1 children 2–12) tempts youngsters with cunning minitrails and mazes and topiaries and fanciful sculptures, not to mention hands-on stations where they can learn about pollination, chlorophyll, root systems, and all that good stuff. Other highlights are the Wild Wetland Trail, which leads through a natural ecosystem; the Ruth Rea Howell Family Garden, where young city dwellers can plant, weed, water, and compost tidy little garden plots; the 19th-century Snuff Mill, perched on its riverside terrace; a **rock garden** (admission $1 adults; 50¢ students, seniors, and children 2–12); a huge formal rose garden; a steep rhododendron valley; and the immense Victorian-era greenhouse complex of the **Enid Haupt Conservatory** (admission $5 adults; $4 students and seniors; and $3 for children 2–12), which alone makes the garden a delightful destination year-round.

A narrated **tram** ($2 adults, $2 children 2–12) swings around the grounds to help you cover the territory. Spring is intoxicating here, what with the huge stands of azaleas, magnolias, dogwood, and lilacs, but it's a blast even in winter, when the Holiday Garden Railway exhibit is set up in the Conservatory—a large-scale model train wending its way through fanciful landscapes and cityscapes. Although the botanical garden is right next to the Bronx Zoo (p. 157), you'd have to be very ambitious (and very good walkers) to do justice to both in 1 day, since their sites are so spread out—but if you're game, it can be done.

Getting There: Metro-North trains from Grand Central Terminal make the 20-minute trip to the Botanical Garden Station; cross Southern Boulevard, and you're at the entrance. One-way fare is $5 off-peak or $6.50 peak. By **car,** take the Henry Hudson Parkway to the Mosholu Parkway; at the end of the Mosholu, turn right onto Kazimiroff Boulevard, and follow the garden perimeter to the entrance. By **subway,** take the 4 or D to Bedford Park Boulevard. Walk east 8 blocks or take the Bx26 bus to Garden.

200th St. and Kazimiroff (Southern) Blvd., the Bronx. ✆ **718/817-8700.** www.nybg.org. Admission to grounds only, $6 adults ($5 Bronx residents), $3 seniors, $3 students, $1 children 2–12, free for children 1 and under. All Gardens Pass (covers all extra charges) $20 adults, $18 students and seniors, $7 children 2–12; free to all Wed. Tues–Sun and Mon holidays 10am–6pm (Nov–Mar until 5pm). Parking $12.

Wave Hill ★   All ages. A very suburban enclave in the Bronx, Riverdale has some fine houses on its Hudson River shore, notably this 28-acre estate with two mansions and extensive gardens. Over the years many famous people lived here, as tenants or as guests (writers Mark Twain and William Makepeace Thackeray, conductor Arturo Toscanini, Theodore Roosevelt); at one time the Tudor-style house was also the official residence of Great Britain's ambassador to the U.N. But there's not much to see inside the houses—just let your kids play on the grounds, which offer one of the few unobstructed views across the Hudson to the magnificent New Jersey Palisades.

Nobody minds if youngsters run on the grass, and the formal gardens are world famous. Favorite spots include the Aquatic Garden, with a pair of pergolas enclosing a formal pool; the nook-filled Wild Garden; and a terraced series of small walled gardens showing off cactuses and alpine flowers. Below the mansions' smooth lawns sprawls a 10-acre woodland with walking trails that give kids a nice bit of a hike. Excellent children's workshops are held on weekends in the learning center; call or check the website for a current schedule.

Getting There: The **MTA** (✆ **718/330-1234**) bus no. BxM1 (from the East Side) or BxM2 (from the West Side) goes to 252nd Street; then walk west across the parkway bridge and follow the signs to the main gate. The fare is $5 one-way; a child under 45 inches may sit on a parent's lap free. Or take the **Metro-North train** (✆ **212/532-4900**) to the Riverdale stop, walk up 254th Street, turn right on Independence Avenue, and go to the main gate at 249th Street. The one-way fare is $6.50 peak and $5 off-peak. By **car,** take the Henry Hudson Parkway to the 246th Street exit and drive straight north to 252nd Street; turn left to cross the parkway overpass, turn left at the light, and drive south to 249th Street, where you turn right and follow it to the Wave Hill gate.

675 W. 252nd St., Riverdale, the Bronx (entrance at 249th St. and Independence Ave.). ✆ **718/549-3200.** www.wavehill.org. Admission $6 adults, $3 students and seniors, free for children 5 and under; free to all Tues, Sat before noon, and daily Dec–Feb. Tues–Sun 9am–5:30pm (mid-Oct to mid-May closes 4:30pm, June–Aug Wed until 9pm). Parking $8.

9 NATURE CENTERS

Note that Central Park is covered in-depth on p. 204 in chapter 9.

The Dairy   All ages. This charming 19th-century structure, with patterned roof tiles and gaily painted gingerbread trim, actually started life as a dairy, back in the days when people grazed cows on Central Park's meadows (children could stop here to buy a cool cup of milk fresh from the udder). There aren't too many Guernseys left in Manhattan, so nowadays the Dairy is the park's chief visitor information center, with a roomful of displays about the park's landscape. There are always a few hands-on activities for youngsters, and it's a pleasant short stroll from the carousel, the zoo, or Wollman Rink.

In Central Park, midpark at 65th St. ✆ **212/794-6564.** Free admission. Tues–Sun 10am–5pm. Subway: 6 to 68th St.; A, B, C, D, 1 to 59th St./Columbus Circle.

Dana Discovery Center ★   All ages. After Harlem Meer was dredged out in the early 1990s and its banks beautifully relandscaped, this pretty structure on its north shore opened as a nature-study center, bringing visitors uptown for the first time in years. If your kids are keen to catch a fish, they can head to the Meer in warm months to try their hands at catch-and-release fishing (April–Oct Tues–Sun 10am–4pm). Weekend family workshops run year-round (usually at 1pm, but call for schedules), and a room overlooking the Meer's serene waters is set up with hands-on nature exhibits. Stroll around the Meer to the neighboring Conservatory Garden (p. 184).

In Central Park at 110th St., near Fifth Ave. © 212/860-1370. www.centralpark.com. Free admission. Tues–Sun 10am–5pm (closes 4pm in winter). Subway: 2, 3 to 110th St. Bus: M2, M3, or M4 to 110th St./Fifth Ave.

Henry Luce Nature Observatory at Belvedere Castle ★ All ages.

Inside this tiny folly of a castle, built in 1872 as an optical illusion to make the lake to the south look bigger (the woods of the Ramble have since grown so high they now obscure the lake view), children enjoy interactive exhibits on Central Park's natural habitats. But the real thrill is outside, where visitors can stand on the rocky terrace hanging high over Turtle Pond and the outdoor **Delacorte Theater,** or walk onto the castle's upper-level terraces for some super views of the Upper West Side, including the American Museum of Natural History. This castle even has a U.S. Weather Service station on top—note the twirling weather vanes on the tower. Stroll down the hillside west of the castle, a neatly planted **Shakespeare Garden** (appropriate, since the neighboring Delacorte is home to the Public Theater's free Shakespeare in the Park series), or scamper down the long slope to the east, where turtles and ducks populate the adjacent pond.

In Central Park, midpark at 79th St. © 212/772-0210. Free admission. Tues–Sun 10am–5pm. Subway: B, C to 79th St.

Inwood Hill Urban Ecology Center All ages.

This Art Deco canoe house, tiled in aqua and white, holds weekend walking tours of the surrounding park, with its marsh, meadow, and steep rock cliffs. A telescope inside the center lets kids zoom in on details of the neighboring marsh and meadow; other exhibits include hands-on geology displays, an aquarium, and a flip-book of pictures of the native plants and animals. Few Manhattanites venture up to this northern tip of the island, but it's a stunning site.

Inwood Hill Park, 218th St. and Indian Rd. © 212/304-2365. Free admission. Daily 11am–4pm. Subway: 1 to 215th St., then walk several blocks to Indian Rd.

Prospect Park Audubon Center ★ All ages.

In a magnificently restored century-old terra-cotta boathouse on the shore of a 60-acre man-made lake, the Audubon Society's Brooklyn outpost offers two stories of child-friendly exhibits on the local bird population—songbirds, waders, raptors, woodpeckers, and the rest of the avian crew. Kids can pore over books, videos, feathered models, and computer simulations, all against a background of piped-in birdcalls. Nature walks and boat tours of the lake start from the boathouse as well.

Inside Lincoln Rd./Ocean Ave. park entrance, The Lake, Prospect Park, Brooklyn. © 718/287-3400. Free admission. Thurs–Sun and holidays noon–5pm (Jan–Mar weekends only). Subway: B, Q, S to Prospect Park.

---

10 KID-FRIENDLY TOURS

BUS TOURS

Gray Line Tours Double-Decker Bus Tours All ages.

Though lengthy narrated bus tours can make some younger children squirm like crazy, they're convenient for seeing a lot of sights without running your kids ragged. Hop-on/hop-off tours provide a happy medium—you get driven around and spoon-fed information, and when your kids get restless, you just jump off at the next stop, expecting to get back on again later.

Operating both red double-decker buses and bright red trolley buses, Gray Line offers so many options, it could make your head spin. Besides the 2-day **Grand Tour,** which would take 5 hours if you didn't hop on and off, there's a **Lower Manhattan loop,** an **Upper Manhattan loop,** the **Grand Tour plus Statue of Liberty 2-day option,** and the **Lower Manhattan plus Statue of Liberty 1-day option.** More traditional escorted sightseeing tours—the kind where you have to stick with the same groups of bus pals throughout—include both half-day and full-day Manhattan routes that involve a buffet lunch, as well as escorted Harlem tours (the Sun version includes a gospel church service).

Main stop at Port Authority Bus Terminal (42nd St. and Eighth Ave.). ℭ **800/669-0051** or 212/397-2600. www.graylinenewyork.com. Full city tour $50 adults, $40 children 11 and under; Upper or Lower Manhattan loop $40 adults, $30 children 11 and under, free for children 4 and under if sitting in adult lap. Daily 8am–6pm.

Magic Bus (M5 city bus) ⓥ Value   **All ages.** It's an ordinary city bus route, but it happens to rumble past a host of sights you'd like to see in its 90-minute loop, and you may even get some narration over the PA. You can board anywhere along the route, which is marked with a dotted line on the three city maps in this chapter. I recommend catching the bus at 125th Street and Riverside Drive, where you'll first wheel past **Grant's Tomb** (122nd St.) and gleaming neo-Gothic **Riverside Church** with its carillon bell tower (120th St.). You'll proceed down handsome residential **Riverside Drive** (Riverside Park and the Hudson lie out the right-side window) to 72nd Street, where the route jogs east to Broadway and then south past **Lincoln Center.** At Columbus Circle it turns east and goes across 59th Street—also called Central Park South because it borders the south side of the park (look to your left)—where it turns right at the ornate **Plaza Hotel** at 58th Street. Down Fifth Avenue you'll go, past **Tiffany & Company** (on your left on the south side of 57th St.); **St. Patrick's Cathedral** (on your left at 51st St.); **Rockefeller Center** (on your right from 51st to 48th sts.); the main research library of the **New York Public Library** with its famous stone lions (on the right from 42nd to 40th sts.); the **Empire State Building** (on the right at 34th St.); the narrow wedge-shaped **Flatiron Building** (on the left at 23rd St.); to the white arch of **Washington Square** (facing the foot of Fifth Ave.). After circling the square, you'll go back north up Sixth Avenue, which from 16th to 23rd streets takes you past **Ladies' Mile,** the late-19th-century department store district (many of the old stores have been restored for megastore tenants like Barnes & Noble and Bed Bath & Beyond); the Herald Square shopping intersection where **Macy's** department store presides at 34th Street; **Bryant Park** (on your right from 40th to 42nd sts.), which was the site of a World's Fair in 1853; more of Rockefeller Center, including **Radio City Music Hall** (on your right at 50th St.); and back to 59th Street to retrace the route back north, as far as 178th Street.

Recommended starting point: 125th St. and Riverside Dr. Fare $2, exact change or MetroCard.

BOAT TOURS

Circle Line Sightseeing Cruises ★   **Ages 3 & up.** Circle Line dominates the market on from-the-water sightseeing cruises, operating out of two locations: Pier 83, midtown at the Hudson River end of 42nd Street, and downtown at South Street Seaport's Pier 16. The experience of being out on the water with the wind in your hair is marvelous by itself, but getting a minicourse in New York history and architecture is a definite bonus. Go early in your trip to get a firm sense of Manhattan as a whole.

Starting from 42nd Street, the classic New York City experience is the **3-hour tour** ($31 adults, $26 seniors, $18 children 12 and under) that chugs around the entire Manhattan island in a low-slung steamer. Sit on the left-hand side of the boat for the best views. On the first leg, you deconstruct the Midtown skyline, get a good look at the Chelsea Piers, pass Battery Park City, and swoop past Ellis Island and the Statue of Liberty. Then the boats cut across New York Harbor and go up the east side of the island, past Wall Street and South Street Seaport, and under the East River bridges, getting a view of the other end of Midtown, with the United Nations looming over the river at 42nd Street. You'll continue north past the Upper East Side, seeing the mayor's official residence, Gracie Mansion. You get to go through Hell Gate (where the East River merges with the Harlem River), glimpse the brand-new Yankee Stadium on the Bronx bluffs to your right, and slide through Spuyten Duyvil, where the Harlem River empties into the Hudson. There's not much to see on the northern end of the island, but the guides gamely fill in with lots of trivia. (It really is the guide that makes the trip—it's great to have a narrator who is full of wonderful obscure trivia.) When you pass under the George Washington Bridge, look out for the little red lighthouse featured in Hildegarde H. Swift's classic children's book *The Little Red Lighthouse and the Great Grey Bridge.*

Also **departing from 42nd Street** are 2-hour **semicircle cruises** ($27 adults, $23 seniors, $16 children 12 and under), which go as far as the U.N. and then loop back; and 75-minute **Liberty Cruises** ($21 adults, $18 seniors, $13 children 12 and under), which steam past Liberty and Ellis islands. But if your kids are like the ones I know, they'll want to do the 3-hour circuit instead because it's cool to go *all the way around.* That's the *point,* Mom. Of course, you can always save time *and* score coolness points by taking the high-speed boat *The Beast* (daily May–Sept; weekends only Oct; $19 adults, $13 children 12 and under, must be over 40 in.), its hull painted with huge chomping shark teeth to look like it's eating the waves before it. Cruising at speeds up to 45 mph, the Beast buzzes past the New York skyline, pausing briefly at the Statue of Liberty, and then zips back to port, all within an adrenaline-pumping 30 minutes.

From the Seaport, there's a similar high-speed boat called *The Shark* (daily June to mid-Sept; $21 adults, $19 seniors, $15 children 4–12), as well as the hour-long narrated *Zephyr* harbor cruise (daily May to mid-Sept; $25 adults, $23 seniors, $15 children 4–12), which crosses the harbor to swing past Ellis Island and the Statue of Liberty and then back to the Seaport. Restrooms and a snack bar are onboard.

Ⓒ **212/563-3200.** (1) Pier 83, at the foot of W. 42nd St. at the Hudson River. www.circleline42.com. Parking $20. Bus: Westbound M42 to the Hudson River. (2) Pier 16 at South Street Seaport. www.circleline downtown.com. Subway: 2, 3, 4, 5 to Fulton St.; A, C to Broadway/Nassau St.

The Pioneer   All ages. Two-hour harbor cruises aboard a historic schooner depart a couple of times a day (schedules vary) from South Street Seaport. The time warp experience of setting sail from this old seaport is somewhat diluted by the views of very modern downtown skyscrapers and the chug of barges, tugboats, and tour boats on the water around you, but it could still be a memorable throwback to an earlier era. New York viewed from the water is quite a sight.

Departing from Pier 16 at South Street Seaport. Ⓒ **212/748-8590.** www.southstseaport.org. Admission $25–$35 adults, $20–$30 students and seniors, $15–$25 children 12 and under.

Small Journeys, Inc   All ages. These custom-designed group tours may be a tad expensive for individual families, but if you can hook up with another two or three broods, go for it, because Steven Kavee and his guides really gear their tours to kids' interests. The company also designs behind-the-scenes field trips for school groups, going on-site to meet professionals in fashion, art, theater, music, interior design, whatever. Transportation costs—whether by van, by limo, by bus, or on foot—are additional, depending on the sights involved. Arrange well in advance.

114 W. 86th St., New York, NY 10024. ✆ **212/874-7300** or ✆ 914/762-4700. www.smalljourneys.com. Tickets $290 per group for 4-hr. tour.

STUDIO TOURS

Little Airplane Productions   All ages. The popular commercial-free network for preschoolers, Noggin, has produced a number of hit kids' animated shows, among them *The Wonder Pets* (initially produced for Nick Jr.) and *Oobi*. The studio that creates and produces these two shows (and others) is actually located in the South Street Seaport. Little Airplane offers studio tours on Tuesday and Thursday (and one Sat a month), in which visitors can see where the shows' animation, voice-overs, and music are made. The on-site Little Airplane shop has toys, Wonder Pets paraphernalia, and original artwork. Tours are limited to 10 people.

207 Front St. ✆ 212/965-8999. www.littleairplane.com. Tickets $10 per person. Tues and Thurs 11am and 4pm (call about Sat times). Reservations required.

WALKING TOURS

For detailed strolls around the city and even Brooklyn, you may want to check out *Frommer's Memorable Walks in New York.* Take into account, however, that some of the walks (such as the Greenwich Village literary tours) may not be of much interest to kids.

Several organizations run a number of tours; check the schedules in *Big Apple Parent, New York Family,* or *New York ParentGuide,* available free at children's bookstores and clothing stores all over town.

ARTime (✆ 718/797-1573), as its name implies, runs walking tours oriented toward the fine arts, usually focusing on museums and galleries. Because they don't cover as much physical ground as some of the neighborhood and architectural tours (no more than 2 or 3 blocks btwn art galleries), they're quite suitable for younger kids—so long as the kids are into art. Tour guides gear their talks to children age 5 to 10. Tours last about 1¹/₂ hours and cost $25 for one adult plus a child and $5 for each additional child (an extra adult tagging along is free). You can usually book a tour in advance—they run from October to June, the first Saturday of every month at 11am.

Big Onion Walking Tours (✆ 212/439-1090; www.bigonion.com) are designed primarily for adults, but kids 8 and up will respond to many of their lively topics, which often touch on the multiethnic dimensions of New York's mosaic. Tours can last as long as 2¹/₂ hours; they cost $15 for adults, $12 for students and seniors. The **Grand Central Partnership** (✆ 212/883-2420) sponsors a free 1¹/₂-hour walking tour along East 42nd Street—an area that includes such Midtown classics as the Chrysler Building, the Daily News Building, and the old Bowery Savings Bank. With its historical/architectural emphasis, this may be a bit scholarly for kids 9 and under, but the length (and the price) makes it worth trying out. Tours depart Friday at 12:30pm from the Whitney Museum at Phillip Morris, 120 Park Ave., at 42nd Street. Kids might also enjoy the 1-hour lunchtime tour of Grand Central Station run by the **Municipal Arts Society** (© 212/935-3960 for reservations and details, 212/439-1049 to get a schedule by mail; www.mas.org), which meets every Wednesday at 12:30pm (suggested donation $10; call the society to find out where to meet). Other Municipal Arts Society tours explore the city's architecture and neighborhoods from an urban-design perspective; they may run as long as 7 hours and cost between $10 and $15, but the knowledgeable, enthusiastic guides make it worthwhile. For some of the popular weekend tours, you may need to reserve a couple of weeks in advance; call for times.

Street Smarts NY (© 212/969-8262; www.streetsmartsny.com) runs weekend walking tours that might be of interest to older children, depending on the theme, such as "Greenwich Village Past and Present" or "Manhattan Murder Mysteries." They cost $10.

Neighborhood Strolls

Manhattan is one of the greatest walking cities in the world. On this densely packed island, it seems there's something new to see every half a block—an intriguing shop, a museum, a beautiful piece of architecture, or an eccentric fellow pedestrian. Even children who normally drag their feet when forced to walk from the far end of a parking lot may cover several blocks without noticing, absorbed by the continual stream of sights. Almost every place you want to go can be reached on foot, often more quickly, and for sure more cheaply, than via taxi, subway, or bus. And along the way you'll get a great window on the way New Yorkers live.

If you're already planning to go to one of the neighborhoods described in this chapter to visit an attraction, restaurant, or shop, allow extra time to explore the immediate area. Most of these sections of the city are worth a visit simply so you can drink in the kaleidoscope of street life that is New York.

1 MIDTOWN

LOBBY HOPPING

Start at the biggie: the **Empire State Building** (p. 165), 34th Street and Fifth Avenue, whose streamlined 1931 interior includes murals of the Seven Wonders of the World. Then head up Fifth Avenue to the **New York Public Library** at 41st Street, where you can walk up the steps between the famous lions (Patience and Fortitude) and peek into the ornate lobby, eternally cool in white marble. Turn east onto 42nd Street to pop into **Grand Central Terminal** on the north side of 42nd Street at Park Avenue, which, though technically not a lobby, has a gloriously restored main room that'll knock your socks off. Gaze up at the constellations painted or electronically twinkling on the soaring azure ceiling; check out the elegant waiting room; and then descend into the marbled catacombs to find a shopping concourse and a food court, populated with commuters scurrying for their trains. Try out the whispering gallery in the large tiled vault outside the Oyster Bar—if two people face the walls in diagonal corners, they can hear each other's softest speaking voices. One block farther east on 42nd Street, on the northeast corner of 42nd and Lex, you can duck into the **Chrysler Building,** whose steel-tipped Deco spire is so notable on the skyline. The small lobby is surprisingly warm and rich looking (think luxury-car glove compartment), with black marble and inlaid wood. Continue east to the end of 42nd Street to visit the **United Nations** (p. 164); even if you don't plan to do a U.N. tour, walk around the U.N. complex's beautiful Rose Garden, with broad paved walkways overlooking the East River.

ROCKEFELLER CENTER AREA

The heart of Midtown is Rockefeller Center, a huge streamlined office/retail complex of pale limestone built in the 1930s by the famously wealthy Rockefeller family. Start on Fifth Avenue between 49th and 50th streets at the **Channel Gardens,** which lie between the British building on the north and the French building on the south (like the English

Channel lies between Britain and France—get it?). The Channel Gardens slope down to
Rockefeller Plaza, the center's heart. Beneath the colossal gilded statue of the Greek god Prometheus, there's a jewel of an ice-skating rink (in winter) or an open-air restaurant, the Rock Center Café (in summer). Behind Prometheus, where the giant Christmas tree stands every December, rises **30 Rockefeller Plaza** (aka **30 Rock**), home of the NBC TV network; if you're here between 7 and 10am, stop outside the glass pagoda on the north side of 49th Street to watch the *Today* show being broadcast live. Hosts Meredith Viera and Matt Lauer often take to the streets outside to film various segments.

Head across 50th Street toward Sixth Avenue (excuse me, the Avenue of the Americas) to find the entrance for the **Top of the Rock** observation deck (p. 165) atop 30 Rockefeller Center; from here you'll get a dynamite view of the entire city. Once you've come back down to earth, roam inside 30 Rock's lobby, studying the monumental murals by José Maria Sert. Take the escalators down from the lobby and you can prowl the maze of concourses and tunnels connecting the Rockefeller Center buildings in an underground world of shops and restaurants (good to know about on rainy days). Leaving 30 Rock through the Sixth Avenue entrance, turn around to see the glittering mosaics decorating the portico. On 50th Street are massive stone bas-relief figures framing the doors, jauntily dressed in nothing but attitude and a little city soot. My sons are convinced the one on the left is intentionally mooning. Across 50th Street is **Radio City Music Hall.** Go west to Sixth Avenue for the best views of Radio City's neon-jazzed streamlined facade. This landmark Art Deco theater still hosts live stage shows as well as a continual lineup of pop concerts; see chapter 11 for details.

Return to Fifth Avenue along 50th Street and turn left to pass the **International Building,** with its famous bronze statue of Atlas carrying the world. Across the street is Rockefeller Center's famous neighbor, **St. Patrick's Cathedral,** seat of the Archdiocese of New York. Step inside for a look at this graceful circa-1879 neo-Gothic church—if you're lucky, there'll be a wedding to watch.

TIMES SQUARE

There was a time, not so long ago, when New York families strenuously avoided the Times Square area when out on the town with their kids. Those days are gone: The old Forty Deuce of two-bit porn shops and poor-man's peep shows has given way to the über-G-rated 42nd Street, a family-friendly theme park with neon razzle-dazzle to spare. It's a sight, alright, with giant animated billboards and illuminated jumbotrons.

The neighborhood's revival has been a boon to the glorious old Broadway theaters pocketed along the side streets of Times Square. (*Note:* Try to avoid this stroll before or after theater times; the crowds can be dense and the going slow as molasses.) If you start at the intersection of 42nd Street and Seventh Avenue and head west on 42nd Street, you'll pass two gloriously restored theaters—Disney's ornate **New Amsterdam Theater** on the south side of the street and the **New Victory Theater** on the north—both of which specialize in family entertainment; farther west on the south side, you'll find a bustling theater-themed 24-hour McDonald's and the New York branch of **Madame Tussauds** (p. 160). Toward the end of the block, two megamultiplex cinemas face off across 42nd Street closer to Eighth Avenue—the 13-screen **Loews** (with an homage-to-Broadway lobby and a great retro neon sign flashing on the facade) and the 25-screen **AMC Empire,** which boasts the gilded moldings and frescoed dome of an old Broadway theater as its lobby. Flanking them are two new chain hotels: a Hilton on the south side and a Westin across the street. Take a moment at the Hilton's street entrance to admire the adorable little bronze figures by Tom Otterness scampering about the doorway.

If you head north up Broadway from 42nd Street, your kids may not allow you to cruise past the **Toys "R" Us** flagship store at the northeast corner of Broadway and 47th Street without stopping in. Older kids may ask to stop between 44th and 45th streets to peer up into the floor-to-ceiling windows of the **MTV studio** on the mezzanine level of 1515 Broadway; a line forms on the sidewalk every afternoon to join the studio audience for *TRL*. Note: As this book went to press, *TRL* had been cancelled, but it was unclear whether a new show might use the popular studio. (Early mornings, ABC's *Good Morning America* gang holds court on the southeast corner of 44th and Broadway, and later in the afternoon *Late Night with David Letterman* may be filming segments on the street outside the **Ed Sullivan Theater,** up at 53rd and Broadway.) Tourists flock into the bright and busy restored theater lobby that now features the **Times Square Visitors Center** on Seventh Avenue between 46th and 47th streets, and hopeful theatergoers line up for half-price tickets at the **TKTS** booth on the mid-Broadway island.

You don't need to pay any entrance fee just to marvel at the intersection's immense high-definition advertising signs, designed to be as bright and as gimmicky as possible. Despite the changes in display technology, one advertiser has remained constant: For decades there's been a **Coca-Cola** sign facing south at 47th Street. Just plant yourselves on one of the mid-Broadway islands and crane your neck. Don't be ashamed to gawk; we all do.

2 DOWNTOWN

WALL STREET LOBBY HOPPING

The narrow urban canyons of this skyscraper crammed neighborhood are another iconic Manhattan sight, familiar even to youngsters—they're the prototype of many a futuristic movie and video game landscape.

Begin at the corner of Broad and Pearl streets, where the modern **85 Broad St.** building pays tribute to the archaeological past: The curved lobby shows where old Stone Street used to run, and the Pearl Street sidewalks outside contain glassed-over pits revealing foundations of the old **Stadt Huys,** the town hall of 17th-century Nieuw Amsterdam. Follow Pearl Street down to State Street, and turn left. Even if you're not visiting the **National Museum of the American Indian** (p. 173), go inside the **Alexander Hamilton Customs House** on Bowling Green, Broadway, and State Street, across from Battery Park. Just past the museum's front desk (admission is free) is the glorious Grand Rotunda, with a huge circular ceiling mural celebrating New York history. Outside, Bowling Green may be a simple patch of concrete today, but in the Revolutionary era there was a famous riot here, in which outraged colonists toppled a statue of the English king; you can still see the broken spikes on the iron fence, which originally were topped by little crowns.

Heading up Broadway, you'll pass the venerable Gothic-style **Trinity Church,** tucked among the skyscrapers at the head of Wall Street (Alexander Hamilton and Robert Fulton are among the famous New Yorkers buried in its graveyard). Wall Street marks the limits of the original Dutch settlement, where a wooden wall was built in 1653 to protect the settlers. Turn right down Wall Street to see, on the north side, the Greek Revival **Federal Hall,** with its statue of George Washington marking the spot where our first President took his oath of office in 1789; turn right down Broad Street to see the **New York Stock Exchange** (8 Broad St.), with mythological figures crowding its triangular pediment.

> ⓕ**Fun** Facts   **The Big, Big Apple**
>
> From 1913 to 1974, New York City could boast of the tallest building in the world. The **Woolworth Building** was the tallest from 1913 to 1930, when it was supplanted by the **Chrysler Building** on 42nd Street. The Chrysler Building didn't hold its title very long—it was taken over a few months later, in 1931, by the **Empire State Building,** which ruled until the **World Trade Towers** arrived in 1972. New York lost the crown soon, however, when the Twin Towers were edged out by Chicago's Sears Tower in 1974.

Return to Broadway and turn right (north); between Dey and Fulton streets, **195 Broadway**—built from 1915 to 1922 as AT&T headquarters—looks like a wedding cake stacked with several levels of classical columns (in fact it has more exterior columns than any other building in the world). Go in the lobby to see even more columns. Then proceed uptown to the **Woolworth Building** at Park Place and Broadway, the world's tallest building from 1913 to 1930. The Woolworth Building is a splendid example of neo-Gothic skyscraper design, and the lobby's sculptured ceiling is worth several minutes' study. Ask your kids to look for the self-portrait of the architect hugging his building in his arms and a Scrooge-like caricature of Mr. Woolworth hoarding his wealth.

GREENWICH VILLAGE

Start in the heart of the Village, **Washington Square,** with its white triumphal arch at the foot of Fifth Avenue. The handsome red-brick houses on the north side of the square date from a time when Greenwich Village really was a separate country village. Much of the rest of Washington Square is now surrounded by the modern buildings of **New York University,** but the park's crowd is an eclectic swirl of all sorts of New Yorkers, not just college students. Weekends usually attract street performers, and on many afternoons there are informal speed-chess competitions going on beneath the shade trees at the southwest corner of the park. The park is currently undergoing a top-to-bottom renovation, which is expected to be completed by late 2009.

For a taste of the bohemian Village, go south from the park (down Thompson, Sullivan, or MacDougal) to **Bleecker Street,** lined with inexpensive restaurants, cafes, and long-established music clubs. Turn right to go west on Bleecker Street. A couple of vintage coffeehouses remain just off Bleecker on MacDougal: **Cafe Dante** (83 MacDougal St.) and **Caffe Reggio** (119 MacDougal St.), holdouts from the Village's beatnik days (Dante has been here since 1915; Reggio since 1927). One longtime Bleecker Street stalwart, **Café Figaro,** shut down in June 2008. At Sixth Avenue, Bleecker takes an unpredictable angle north, like many West Village streets, and changes into a foodie neighborhood, with some great food shops selling bread, pastries, sausage, pizza, and seafood. You can get some great homemade Parmesan cheese sticks and cheese puffs at **Murray's Cheese Shop,** at 254 Bleecker Street.

Return to Sixth Avenue, and go north to West 9th Street; the castlelike red-brick building on your left is **Jefferson Market,** originally a courthouse and now a branch of the public library. Its lovely outdoor garden is sometimes open to the public in the afternoon. Turn right (east) onto West 11th Street. The brick wall on your right surrounds a tiny cemetery, one of several belonging to **Shearith Israel,** the oldest Jewish congregation in the country. Continue down the block, lined with classic brick townhouses, until you see one that's startlingly modern: **18 W. 11th St.** Inside the large picture window, the owner's stuffed Paddington bear is usually dressed in a timely fashion, with a yellow slicker on if it's raining or a Yankees or Mets cap in baseball season, depending on which team is winning. The modern structure replaced the original Greek Revival home, which was accidentally destroyed in 1970 by members of the radical Weathermen group, who were making bombs in the basement.

Follow 11th Street to Fifth Avenue—turn right to get back to Washington Square or left to make a stop at the **Forbes Magazine Galleries** (p. 170), with its collections of toy soldiers and toy boats.

THE EAST VILLAGE

The funky East Village is a magnet for preteens and teenagers determined to score high on the hipness scale. Start on **Astor Place,** the busy intersection of Fourth Avenue, Lafayette Street, and East 8th Street, where sidewalk peddlers usually hawk everything from hammered silver jewelry to vinyl LPs to well-thumbed paperbacks to secondhand lamps and furniture. The hulking brownstone building to the south is **Cooper Union,** a progressive school of architecture, art, and engineering founded in 1859. Head east on what should be 8th Street, here called **St. Mark's Place;** busy day and night, the block of St. Mark's between Third and Second avenues is lined with vintage-clothing stores, food shops and cheap restaurants, and bars. Beatniks hung out here in the 1950s, hippies in the 1960s, and punks in the 1970s. Interestingly, this neighborhood also has long-established enclaves of Ukrainian immigrants, centered on 7th Street, and Russian immigrants, on 9th and 10th streets, as you can see if you stroll around farther. The city's "Little Tokyo"—a conglomeration of Japanese restaurants, noodle shops, sake bars, and grocery and snack shops—is centered on 9th Street between Second and Third avenues.

At Second Avenue, you may want to turn left and go 2 blocks north to the fieldstone **St. Mark's-in-the-Bowery Church,** the city's oldest continually used church building— Peter Stuyvesant, the famous governor of the Dutch colony of Nieuw Amsterdam, used to worship here. In fact, this area used to be his farm, and **Stuyvesant Street,** which angles south back to Astor Place, is named for him. Stroll past the early-19th-century town houses on Stuyvesant Street and try to imagine what the Village looked like back then—before the beatniks, hippies, and punks took over.

If you're looking for club-kid coolness, follow St. Mark's Place until it ends at Avenue A. (Manhattan widens here, requiring a set of lettered avenues to be added east of the numbered ones—hence the neighborhood's nickname, Alphabet City.) You'll be at **Tompkins Square** (bounded by Ave. A, E. 7th St., Ave. B, and E. 10th St.), much spruced up (and with a spiffy children's park) since the late 1980s, when it held a resident camp of homeless people. Nowadays much of this neighborhood, long the low-rent-or-no-rent domain of squatters, struggling artists, and anarchists, has been gentrified, and Avenue A is lined with restaurants, shops, and cafes.

CHINATOWN

Begin on **Canal Street,** the major thoroughfare cutting across Manhattan at this point; Canal Street used to be the northern boundary of Chinatown before its population spilled over into Little Italy and the Lower East Side. Walk east from Centre Street to the Bowery on the south side of Canal Street, where produce and fish stores pile their wares on the sidewalks. Point out to your kids the Chinese lettering on every sign and the pagoda-shaped pay phone stations. Turn right (south) at the Bowery. On the Bowery's east side, a gargantuan statue of the Chinese philosopher Confucius dominates the little plaza in front of **Confucius Plaza,** a modern red-brick residential development.

Continue south on the Bowery 2 blocks to the frantic intersection called **Chatham Square,** with its big Chinese arch in the middle. Then backtrack on the Bowery a few steps to narrow sloping Pell Street, where you turn left. A Hong Kong–like jumble of restaurants and neon signs, Pell leads you west 1 block to busy Mott Street, filled with Chinese restaurants and shops selling souvenirs, colorful Chinese slippers and hats, and lots of fun, dirt-cheap tchotchkes (Chinese dragons, back scratchers, little Buddhas, plastic swimming frogs) that little kids find irresistible. Barbecued ducks hang in glass storefronts, and dim sum shops draw big lunchtime crowds. Turn right on Mott and go 1 block to Bayard Street, where you should turn left and go a block to Mulberry. **Columbus Park** is on your left, where Chinatown residents old and young congregate.

LITTLE ITALY

There's not much left to this classic tenement neighborhood, what with Chinatown encroaching on the south and SoHo on the west; you and your kids can easily do the whole bit in half an hour, even if you stop along the way to eat lunch. On weekends Mulberry Street becomes a pedestrian mall, which makes it even easier to traverse with young ones. From Canal Street, walk up **Mulberry Street** to Houston Street, past several Italian restaurants that thrive on the tourist trade; what used to be **Umberto's Clam House** (which moved 2 blocks away, to 86 Broome St.), at 129 Mulberry St., was the site of a famous 1972 Mafia hit when a wiseguy named Joey Gallo was rubbed out while reportedly dining on scungilli with clam sauce.

Along Mulberry and the streets branching off it, look for stores selling religious medals and figures and others selling glorious foodstuffs—fresh pastas and raviolis, imported olive oil and vinegars. At the intersection of Mulberry and Broome streets, **Caffé Roma,** 385 Broome St., is a great old-fashioned tin-ceiling pastry shop where you can stop for cannoli and espresso. Look above the shop signs to see the tracery of iron fire escapes hanging out over the street, a distinguishing feature of these turn-of-the-20th-century tenement buildings, which slumlords designed to cram in as many small rooms as possible onto the narrow lots.

LOWER EAST SIDE

Once a teeming slum for waves of new immigrants, the Lower East Side has been transformed of late into a hipster hangout. The main shopping drag, **Orchard Street,** though still full of discount-clothing and dry goods stores (many of them still Jewish-owned and shut up tight on Sat), now also has renovated storefronts and trendy boutiques. While you'll admire the changing retail mix and classic tenement architecture, lure your kids to walk with the promise of a good nosh. Start out at **Kossar's** (367 Grand St., btwn Essex and Norfolk sts.), a glorious time warp of a bagel factory where customers can watch the bakers slide trays full of ring-shaped dough into a vintage oven. The bialys are incredibly dense and flavorful, especially when you get them warm. Return to Orchard Street, turn right, and head north to Broome Street for the fascinating **Lower East Side Tenement Museum** (p. 171), which explores the district's immigrant past. Pickle lovers (you know who you are), don't miss **Guss' Pickles** (85 Orchard St., btwn Grand and Broome sts.). Window-shop your way north 4 more blocks to East Houston Street, where you can take care of whatever appetite you may have: **Katz's Delicatessen** (E. Houston St. at Ludlow

St., 1 block east of Orchard) has sit-down service for such deli favorites as pastrami (best in town), corned beef, and luscious brisket sandwiches; the long-established family deli **Russ and Daughters** (179 E. Houston St., btwn Orchard and Allen sts.) specializes in lox, whitefish, and herring; and **Yonah Schimmel Knishes** (137 E. Houston St., at Forsyth St.) offers an amazing selection of Yiddish knishes—pockets of thin dough stuffed with everything from kasha to blueberries to sweet potatoes.

3 UPTOWN

MORNINGSIDE HEIGHTS

The upper end of the Upper West Side, this neighborhood is Manhattan's college town. The place to start, however, is at 112th Street and Amsterdam Avenue, on the front steps of the Episcopal **Cathedral of St. John the Divine.** This will be the largest cathedral in the world if they ever finish building it; they've been at it for over a century, since 1892, but if your kids have studied medieval history at all, they'll know that most of the great European cathedrals took a couple of centuries to complete, too. St. John the Divine is so huge that the Statue of Liberty could fit under the central dome, and the tiny-looking figure of Christ you see in the rose window over the front doors is actually life-size.

New York Top 10 Movie & TV Sites

If New York didn't exist, Hollywood would've had to invent it to get the perfect movie set. Film companies shoot on location here so often, my kids learned from an early age what it means when we run into a phalanx of trailers, lighting equipment, and headset-wearing production assistants: *They're making a movie!* Here are 10 of the most famous sites around town, with an emphasis on those flicks and television shows that kids have seen:

1. **Columbia University Low Library steps** (Upper West Side, 117th St. btwn Broadway and Amsterdam Ave.)—where *Spider-Man* recovers after his fateful spider bite, where Mary-Kate Olsen tries to save Ashley's scholarship in *New York Minute,* and where three fired Columbia professors decide to go into business as *Ghostbusters.*

2. **Tom's Diner** (Upper West Side, 112th St. and Broadway)—where Jerry and his pals from Seinfeld hold their endless discussions, while Jerry eats cornflakes, Elaine devours big salads, and George tries to avoid the bill.

3. **Grove and Bedford streets** (Greenwich Village)—where TV's *Friends* live, in the apartment building on the southeast corner. Go a little farther west to where Grove crooks north and peer through a gate to see the fountain where they splash around in the credits.

4. **14 Moore St.** (TriBeCa)—where the *Ghostbusters* set up office in an old firehouse (it's still a working firehouse).

5. **The Plaza Hotel** (Midtown, 59th St. and Fifth Ave.)—where Eloise scampers in the many Eloise TV movies, and Macaulay Culkin rings up a whale of a room service bill in *Home Alone 2.*

Notice how only two of the arches over the front doors have statues in them; empty niches in the other arches await future stone carvers' work. Go inside and stroll around, stopping on the north aisle at Poet's Corner, where paving stones honor selected American poets. Go out to the garden just south of the cathedral to see the Children's Fountain, a fanciful huge sculpture surrounded by peewee sculptures created by local schoolchildren. On the lawns of the surrounding cathedral close, you can sometimes spot a pair of peacocks strutting and preening.

Go north on Amsterdam Avenue to 117th Street, where you can pass through wrought-iron gates into **Columbia University,** New York's Ivy League college. As you cross the campus, notice the broad steps of Low Memorial Library on your right; kids will recognize it as the place Peter Parker visited for a fateful high-school field trip in *Spider-Man*. Exit the campus through the matching set of gates onto Broadway and cross the street to enter the gates of **Barnard College,** Columbia's all-women sister college. Or head north on Broadway to 120th Street: Columbia's **Teachers College** is the big, dark, red-brick building on the northeast corner (read the roll call of history's greatest teachers inscribed around the roofline). The **Union Theological Seminary** is the medieval-looking gray stone complex on the northwest corner of 120th Street, complemented by the red-brick **Jewish Theological Seminary** on the northeast corner of Broadway and 122nd Street. Turn left on 120th Street and go west to Riverside Drive, where **Riverside**

6. **The Empire State Building** (Midtown, 34th St. and Fifth Ave.)—where Tom Hanks and Meg Ryan meet in *Sleepless in Seattle,* just like the reuniting lovers did in the many versions of *An Affair to Remember.* And who could forget what *King Kong* did to this place?

7. **55 Central Park West** (Upper West Side)—where the ancient spirit Gozar must be driven out of Sigourney Weaver in *Ghostbusters* (the top of this vari-colored Art Deco building looks significantly different in the movie, though—an elaborate rooftop was matted in). Later in the movie, the nerdy accountant played by Rick Moranis roams glassy-eyed outside Tavern on the Green, the festively lit restaurant across the street in Central Park.

8. **The American Museum of Natural History** (Upper West Side, Central Park West at 79th St.)—where the mermaid in *Splash* escapes, where Cary Grant works on his dinosaur in *Bringing Up Baby,* and where the Macy's parade begins in *Miracle on 34th Street.* And don't forget that *Friends'* Ross Geller works here as a paleontologist.

9. **The front steps of the New York Public Library** (Midtown, Fifth Ave. at 41st St.)—where Holly Golightly researches eligible millionaires in *Breakfast at Tiffany's,* an apparition flips open card catalogs in the opening of *Ghostbusters,* and Peter Parker sees his beloved uncle slain in *Spider-Man.*

10. **The central fountain in Lincoln Center Plaza** (Upper West Side, 64th St. and Broadway)—where Bialystock and Bloom dance in *The Producers.*

Church stands on the right. If its pale limestone reminds you of a Gothic version of Rockefeller Center, it's no coincidence, since John J. Rockefeller was one of its founders in 1930. Across Riverside Drive and several yards north sits the columned neoclassical **Grant National Memorial Monument,** where President Ulysses S. Grant and his wife, Julia, are buried. (Ask your kids the corny old joke: "Who's buried in Grant's Tomb?") Admission is free—step inside and peer down into the sunken chamber where the couple's dark marble tombs are laid. The high-ceilinged memorial offers excellent exhibits about Grant's life and the Civil War he won for the Union, but my kids' favorite part is outside, in the plaza around the tomb, with its nutty mosaic benches designed by New York public school students.

4 BROOKLYN

CROSSING THE BROOKLYN BRIDGE

As thrilling a sight as this beautiful brown-hued East River bridge is from afar, with its Gothic-style towers and lacy mesh of cables, the view from the bridge is even more thrilling. A **boardwalklike pedestrian walkway** goes all the way across, raised slightly above the car traffic. One mile long, it should take about half an hour to traverse—except you'll be tempted to stop more than once to ooh and ahh at the vision of Manhattan's skyscrapers thrusting upward, with the great harbor and Verrazano Bridge beyond.

Why has the Brooklyn Bridge captured the popular imagination so much more than its neighbors to the north, the Manhattan and Williamsburg bridges? Well, for one thing, it was the very first steel-wire suspension bridge in the world when it opened in 1883. Until then, the only way to get from Manhattan to Brooklyn, at that time separate cities, had been via ferry (crossing from Manhattan's Fulton St. to Brooklyn's Fulton St., both named after steamship inventor Robert Fulton, who operated the ferry company).

Since then, however, the Brooklyn Bridge has become a byword in New York lore. The standard old joke defines a con artist as a guy trying to sell rubes the deed to the Brooklyn Bridge ("Brother, have I got a bridge to sell you . . ."). Cocky teenage hoodlums have proved their bravado by shinnying up its cables, and suicides with a flair for the dramatic have plummeted to their deaths from those same cables into the tidal currents below. The bridge has appeared in countless movies and TV shows, its outline practically synonymous with New York City.

ⓕ Fun Facts   The Curse of the Brooklyn Bridge

The Brooklyn Bridge took 16 years to build, from 1867 to 1883, and it seemed to have a bit of a curse on it—the original designer, John A. Roebling, died from tetanus contracted when his foot was crushed while surveying the site, and his son, Washington, who took over the job, fell ill with the bends after diving in the river to supervise the workmen laying the pilings. A virtual invalid afterward, Washington Roebling watched the bridge going up through a telescope from his house in nearby Brooklyn Heights, while his wife actually supervised much of the completion of the project.

The Manhattan entrance ramps to the bridge begin by the plaza in front of the city's **Municipal Building,** along Centre Street just south of Chambers Street; pedestrian ramps on the other side empty out into Brooklyn's downtown, which is a bit of a wasteland on weekends, but it isn't a far walk from here to **Brooklyn Heights,** one of the loveliest brownstone neighborhoods you'll ever see. Go armed with a map. If your kids aren't hardy urban trekkers, walk halfway to get the view and then double back to Manhattan. Be aware that it can get awfully windy once you're over the water!

For the Active Family

Don't make the mistake of assuming that New Yorkers are soft, flabby city folk—on the contrary, we end up walking much more than car-dependent suburbanites do, and the city's huge complement of parks makes it easy to ride bikes, play tennis, jog or stroll, toss a Frisbee, fly a kite, skate, or skateboard. And what do you do when you have a dog in New York City? Well, you don't just open a door and put him out in the back yard. You *walk* the dog, sometimes several times a day.

Yes, New York is also a perfect spot for sitting on a park bench and watching the passing parade go by. New York parents as a breed tend to be too compulsive to just laze around in the parks, however—at the drop of a hat, they'll enlist their children in classes for anything from chess and computers to horseback riding and fencing. Staying active in New York is a year-round proposition, and neither the dog days of summer nor the ice days of winter slow down kids' activities. Though many classes and workshops require full-series enrollment, I've listed below a number of drop-in classes that are available for visiting families, or for local kids who want to do something on the spur of the moment.

1 GREEN NEW YORK: THE TOP PARKS

Though New York is studded with squares where you can find a patch of grass and some benches, it has only a handful of parks large enough for a real exploration. Some of these are somewhat off the beaten track: **Flushing Meadows–Corona Park** in Queens (take the no. 7 train to 111th St. or Willets Point/Shea Stadium) and **Van Cortlandt Park** in the Bronx (take the no. 1 train to 242nd St.) are both loaded with recreational facilities, but they're so big and spread out, you can't just ramble around aimlessly. **Fort Tryon Park,** at the northern end of Manhattan (take the A train to 190th St.), a wooded strip of park on high ground overlooking the Hudson River, is lovely but off the beaten path—it's not worth a special trip unless you're already coming to visit **The Cloisters** (which you definitely should do—p. 169). Then there's compact **Riverbank State Park,** perched over the Hudson River at the western end of 145th Street, which offers a slew of top-notch recreational facilities (see "Sports & Games," later in this chapter) but hardly any untrammeled grass. For other green pleasures in the city, see "Gardens" and "Nature Centers" in chapter 7.

New Yorkers, however, more than make do with the five great parks listed below. The larger three—Central Park, Riverside Park, and Prospect Park—were laid out in the 19th century by the team of Frederick Law Olmsted and Calvert Vaux, a pair of inspired amateurs who virtually invented the art of urban landscape design. These guys really knew how to maximize space, with twisting paths and artful hills and dales that make you feel as though you've left the city as soon as you're 10 paces inside the park. Later, park commissioners slapped on recreational amenities like tennis courts and playgrounds

American Museum
  of Natural History **14**
The Bandshell **25**
Belvedere Castle **16**
Bethesda Fountain **24**
Bow Bridge **21**
The Carousel **30**
Central Park Zoo **35**
Cherry Hill Fountain **23**
Chess & Checkers House **31**
Conservatory Garden **5**
Conservatory Water
  (Sailboat Pond) **19**
The Dairy **32**
Dana Discovery Center **6**
Delacorte Arch **33**
Delacorte Theater **11**
Duke Ellington Circle **7**
Great Hill **1**
Great Lawn **9**
Harlem Meer **6**
Heckscher Playground **37**
Henry Luce Nature Observatory **16**
Information booth **36**
Jacqueline Kennedy Onassis
  Reservoir **4**
The Lake **20**
Lasker Rink/Lasker Pool **5**
Loeb Boathouse **18**
The Mall **27**
Metropolitan Museum of Art **8**
Mineral Springs Pavilion **26**
North Meadow
  Recreation Center **3**
The Obelisk (Cleopatra's Needle) **10**
The Pool **5**
The Pond **39**
The Ramble **17**
Shakespeare Garden **12**
Sheep Meadow **29**
Strawberry Fields **22**
Swedish Cottage **15**
Tavern on the Green **28**
Tennis House **2**
Tisch Children's Zoo **34**
Turtle Pond **13**
Wollman Rink/Victorian Gardens **38**

ⓘ Information
Ⓜ Subway stop
--- Bridle path
⋯⋯ Path of Animal
  Statue Walk

0   1/5 mi
0   0.2 km

FOR THE ACTIVE FAMILY

9

GREEN NEW YORK: THE TOP PARKS

Stalking the Animal Statues in Central Park

In the course of half an hour's walk, you and your kids can bag a couple dozen animals in the wilds of Central Park—statue animals, that is.

Start on the northwest corner of East 79th Street and Fifth Avenue. A few steps into the park, on your right are **(1–3) three bronze bears,** a copy of a Paul Manship statue that's in the Metropolitan Museum directly north. Continue on the path into the park, going through a vaulted tunnel under the East Drive and veering to your left (south) to reach the east end of Turtle Pond. There you'll find King Jagiello of Poland astride a **(4) magnificent horse.** Stroll uphill to your left to the drive and walk downtown (south) on the road, keeping to the right-hand jogging path if there's car traffic in the park. About halfway down the hill, atop a massive rock outcropping on your right, crouches a **(5) bronze panther,** peering out of the foliage ready to pounce on unsuspecting joggers.

Cross the East Drive at the pedestrian crossing near the Loeb Boathouse and walk down a short, steep, grassy slope to a path leading south to the Conservatory Water. The Alice in Wonderland statue at the pond's north end has not only the **(6) White Rabbit** but also the **(7) Cheshire Cat,** Alice's **(8) kitten Dinah,** and **(9) assorted mice,** along with the usual number of children climbing all over the giant mushrooms. Swing around to the west side of the pond to find the **(10) Ugly Duckling** waddling past the statue of Danish storyteller Hans Christian Andersen.

Take either path leading south from the Conservatory Water up the hill to the 72nd Street Transverse; cross 72nd Street, turn right to cross the circular drive, and then veer left to follow the drive southward. On your right, the ground rises to the Rumsey Playground (less a playground these days than a plaza for special events). Set amid the steps rising to Rumsey's entrance gate is a big **(11) stone goose,** with who else but Mother Goose riding on its back. (Walk around to identify carved scenes from various nursery rhymes.) Go west, away from the

that may not strictly have been what Olmsted and Vaux envisioned, but nothing has seriously marred the beauty of these detailed landscapes.

Central Park ★★★   At 840 acres, this park—one of the world's greatest—is a vital resource for the city. Set right in the middle of things, with frequent entrances cut into its low brownstone wall, it separates the Upper West Side from the Upper East Side, lying between Midtown at the south end and Harlem at the north end. It's big enough to give you a real sense of escape, and when you're walking around the park, the only roads you have to deal with are the circular park drive and one cross-cut at 72nd Street; both are closed to car traffic weekdays 10am to 3pm and 7 to 10pm, as well as 7pm Friday to 6am Monday (holidays are traffic-free, too). Four other east-west streets cross the park—66th, 79th, 86th, and 96th—but because they're cunningly hidden beneath overpasses, you'll never notice them.

The section of the park below 72nd Street is somewhat formal. Starting at 59th Street and Fifth Avenue—where **horse-drawn carriages** line up to give tourists a ridiculously drive, past Rumsey downhill to the plaza in front of the Bandshell (watch for roller skaters on weekends!). At the western edge of the plaza, you'll find a **(12–13) pair of eagles** devouring a hapless **(14) mountain goat.** Bear right to return to the 72nd Street transverse, where a left turn will take you west. On your left, just before 72nd Street meets the West Drive, look up on another big outcropping to find the **(15) falcon** lighting on the glove of the falconer.

Retrace your steps a short distance east on 72nd Street to the Dead Road, a broad asphalt lane bordering the Sheep Meadow, where skaters and volleyball games proliferate on warm-weather weekends. Turn right and follow the Dead Road south to find the Indian hunter with his faithful **(16) dog.** Turn left, following the circular drive past the foot of the Mall; cross under the drive via a brick-vaulted tunnel (try out the echoes). The path swings uphill on the east side of the drive to reach one of the most famous animal statues in the park, **(17) Balto the sled dog,** hero of a 1995 animated film.

From here the path leads south through another underpass past the gates of the Children's Zoo; look for a **(18–19) pair of goats** prancing atop the zoo's wrought-iron entrance arch. On through a second underpass, you'll come up to the red-brick Delacorte Arch. In a niche to the right of the arch is a bronze **(20) dancing bear,** and the glockenspiel on top of the arch features **(21–26) a hippo, a goat, a penguin, a kangaroo, an elephant, and a bear**—plus a **(27–28) pair of monkeys** squatting on top, hammering the bells. The musical clock performs on the hour and half-hour; stick around to watch if possible. Then proceed south on the walkway past the Central Park Zoo; at the southern end of the zoo's red-brick structures, turn to your right to see another niche with a **(29) dancing goat** inside.

After stalking all this sculpted prey, your kids may well feel as mine did: "Mom, can we see some live animals now?" And here you are, right near the gates of the zoo, ready to grant their wish.

overpriced (about $34 for 20 min.) ride through the park—you'll find the **Pond,** a picturesque small body of water reflecting Midtown skyscrapers. Just northwest of this you'll find the **Wollman Rink** (p. 224), where you can ice-skate in winter and roller-skate in summer, and **the Dairy** visitor center (p. 186). From the Dairy, follow a path west under an arch to the **Central Park Carousel** (p. 170). The **ball fields** west and south of here are fun even for spectators on summer weekday evenings, when some very competitive after-work leagues (including Broadway actors) slug it out. As you walk up the West Drive past the **Tavern on the Green** restaurant (p. 107), your kids may be interested to know that it was originally built as a sheepfold in 1870 when the **Sheep Meadow,** the broad fenced-in green lawn on your right, was still used for grazing sheep. The **Mineral Springs Pavilion,** just north of the Sheep Meadow, has a snack bar and restrooms.

Go north across 72nd Street to **Strawberry Fields,** a gem of a bit of landscape laid out in memory of Beatle John Lennon, who lived across Central Park West from here in the Dakota apartment building. It seems there are always flowers laid in tribute to Lennon on the black-and-white mosaic medallion that reads IMAGINE. Across the drive to the northeast lies the **Lake,** a body of water larger than the Pond—large enough, in fact, for boating. To rent rowboats, cross the park along the 72nd Street Transverse. Along the way, though, stop off at two postcard views that your kids may recognize from scores of movies and TV shows: Turn left at **Cherry Hill Fountain** and walk over lovely **Bow Bridge,** or take either the lakeside path or 72nd Street to **Bethesda Terrace,** a grand lakeshore plaza featuring the **Bethesda Fountain.** The lakeside path continues, winding north to the **Loeb Boathouse** (© 212/517-2233; www.thecentralparkboathouse.com), where you can rent boats and also get something to eat (in clement weather) with great views of the lake. The fast-food **Boathouse Café** specializes in burgers, soups, salads, and snacks and serves breakfast, lunch, and dinner (daily 8am–8pm). The casual **Boathouse Bar & Grill** (Apr–Oct 11am–11pm) is a sit-down alfresco cafe where you can dine on grilled chicken, crab cakes, and shrimp cocktail; it's a bit of a singles hang at happy hour—lunch may be the ideal time to come. The more upscale **Boathouse Restaurant** here serves lunch and dinner Monday through Friday, brunch and dinner on weekends (Mon–Fri noon–4pm and 5:30–9:30pm; Sat–Sun 9:30am–4pm and 6–9:30pm). The boathouse is open March through October daily from 10am to dusk, depending on the weather; rowboat rental is $12 per hour (cash only, $30 cash deposit required; maximum five people per boat).

Across East Drive and just above 72nd Street, the **Conservatory Water** (also known as the Sailboat Pond) is a fun area even for the littlest ones, with its large, serene formal pool. The *Alice in Wonderland* statue at the north end features a giant mushroom that just begs to be clambered on. From April to October you can rent one-quarter-scale radio-controlled model sailboats ($10 per hr.) from a stand beside the boathouse (shades of *Stuart Little*). There's a cafe on the pond's east side, which also has restrooms. Stroll back south through a shady green strip with winding paths, passing a couple of good playgrounds (see "The Playground Lowdown," below). As you head downhill toward a rugged stone arch, expect to see a gaggle of sidewalk performers on weekends, some of whom are delightful to watch—allow for a little dawdling time. Passing through the arch brings you to the **Tisch Children's Zoo,** then south to the **Delacorte Arch,** with its delightful glockenspiel chiming every hour, and finally to the **Central Park Zoo** (p. 158).

North of the Lake, the **Ramble** is a compact wilderness that's easier than you'd think to get lost in; navigate with care, and stick to daylight hours when there are plenty of other folks around (it's known as the best place in the park for a mugging, rare as that may be). Situated on a major North American flyway, this is, against all odds, a bird-watcher's paradise right in the middle of the big city; the **Henry Luce Nature Observatory** (p. 187) at the nearby Belvedere Castle can provide you with equipment to find and identify several species. Look overhead for nests and along the lake's marshy northern shore for frogs.

Above 79th Street, two museums dominate the park: the **Metropolitan Museum of Art** (p. 160), inside the park at East 82nd Street, and the **American Museum of Natural History** (p. 152), facing the park at West 79th Street and Central Park West. Midpark, between them, lies the **Great Lawn,** a huge stretch of grass and ball fields where crowds happily congregate in summer for gatherings ranging from Metropolitan Opera concerts to special events like Disney premieres and major rock concerts. At the south end of the Great Lawn, **Turtle Pond** protects a habitat for turtles, ducks, and dragonflies. To the west of it lie the **Delacorte Theater,** home of summer's free Shakespeare in the Park (and another essential set of restrooms); the picturesque wooden **Swedish Cottage Marionette Theatre** (p. 167), where daily marionette shows are held; and, up on the hill, the **Shakespeare Garden** and **Belvedere Castle** with its nature center.

Between 86th and 96th streets, the major feature of the park is the **Jacqueline Kennedy Onassis Reservoir,** named in 1995 in honor of the former First Lady who lived for years nearby at 1040 Fifth Ave. (at 85th St.). A cinder track makes a 1¹/₂-mile loop around the reservoir, much of it lined with cherry trees that are breathtaking in spring; you may prefer to walk along the bridle path circling the reservoir, where not so long ago experienced riders brought their mounts from the old **Claremont Stables,** which closed its doors in 2007. You'll still see horseback riders trotting down the bridle path, but don't worry: It's spacious enough for you and the horses. North of the reservoir is the tan stucco **Tennis Center** (see "Tennis" under "Sports & Games," later in this chapter), which also has restrooms.

Above 96th Street the east side of the park has two big attractions: the **Conservatory Garden** (p. 184), at 105th Street and Fifth Avenue, which has restrooms, and **Harlem Meer,** the graceful pond at the northeast corner of the park, where the **Dana Discovery Center** (p. 186) runs nature workshops and hands out fishing poles so even youngsters can try their hand at angling in the meer. Midpark, right off of the 97th Street Transverse, the **North Meadow Recreation Center,** undiscovered by many Manhattanites, has lots of sports facilities, including well-groomed ball fields, handball courts, basketball courts, and climbing walls. See "Sports & Games," later in this chapter, for more details; the staff here will even lend you equipment free (call ℂ **212/348-4867** to reserve equipment, and be sure to bring a valid photo ID).

On the west side of the park, a stroll above 96th Street will take you to a picturesque and little-known area at West 100th Street: the **Pool,** a willow-fringed pond with a lively waterfall at the east end; my kids love to hang over the railing on the bridge and watch the cascading waters beneath. North of here, the **Great Hill** has a high, broad lawn perfectly suited to picnics. At the top of the park, at 110th Street, is the **Lasker Rink,** which converts in summer into the **Lasker Pool.**

Be wary about going too deep into the park this far north, however, because it's less populated and the surrounding neighborhoods include some risky elements. Kids flock to the pool and Harlem Meer on weekend days, and lots of families skate at Lasker Rink; but the social scene is rougher in summer, when the rink turns into a pool.

From 59th to 110th sts., btwn Central Park West (Eighth Ave.) and Fifth Ave. ℂ **212/310-6600;** visitor center 212/794-6564; event hot line 888/NY-PARKS or 212/360-3456. www.centralparknyc.org. Subway: 1 to 59th St./Columbus Circle; N, Q, R, W to 57th St./Seventh Ave.; N, R, W to Fifth Ave./59th St.; B, C to any stop from 59th St./Columbus Circle to 110th St.; 4, 5, 6 to any stop from 59th St. to 103rd St.

Riverside Park ★★   Long, narrow Riverside Park really shows off designer Frederick Law Olmsted's ingenuity: Beneath it lie miles of underground railroad tracks, while the Henry Hudson Parkway, a major thoroughfare out of the city, bisects it lengthwise (you can't always get to the river shore as a result). But between West 83rd and West 96th streets, Riverside Park features a broad paved **promenade** with stone railings where you can lean over and gaze west over the Hudson; the pavement here makes it super for leisurely biking and skating, though you'll have to weave through strolling crowds on summer Sundays. The **dog run** near 86th Street always manages to entertain children even if they don't have a pooch to exercise, and the **community garden** along the median strip at 91st Street is simply glorious.

The southern end of Riverside Park, from 72nd to 83rd streets, is flatter and more open than the rest of the park, and it is unbelievably beautiful in spring, when all the flowering trees unfurl. If you want to fly a kite, this can be a good place for it, with breezes blowing in from the river. Above 96th Street, the park gets more rustic and less crowded, with some very steep paths plummeting down the slope from Riverside Drive.

At 72nd Street, 79th Street, and 86th Street, paths dip under the West Side Highway to the park's lower section, which hugs the banks of the Hudson River. At the southern end, the **72nd Street recreational pier** offers a wonderful view up and down the Hudson; a wide riverside path leads north from there to the **79th Street Boat Basin**—a marina full of bobbing houseboats, not all necessarily seaworthy. The grassy shade behind the esplanade makes a good place for a picnic, or you can stop for a good, casual meal at the **Boat Basin Café** (p. 112). Follow the bike path on north, past a platoon of ball fields and tennis courts and a sister cafe at 105th Street; the bike path meanders along the river more or less all the way to the George Washington Bridge.

Btwn the Hudson River and Riverside Dr., from 72nd to 153rd sts. © **212/496-2103.** Subway: 2, 3 to 72nd St. or 96th St.; 1 to any stop from 72nd St. to 125th St.

Prospect Park ★★　Designers Frederick Law Olmsted and Calvert Vaux considered this park their crowning achievement. The main draws for kids are the super trio of attractions on the park's east side, along Flatbush Avenue: the **Prospect Park Audubon Center** (p. 187), the **Lefferts Homestead Children's Historic House Museum** (p. 177), and the **Prospect Park Carousel** (p. 170). Across Flatbush Avenue, you'll find the **Brooklyn Museum** (p. 176) and the **Brooklyn Botanic Garden** (p. 184), which aren't part of the park proper but were always considered part of the overall scheme. On weekends and holidays from noon to 5pm, a free hourly trolley runs continually among all these attractions (call © **718/965-8999** for schedule).

The focus for nature lovers in Prospect Park is in the park's southern end at the **Boathouse,** a glorious Italianate tiled structure dating from 1905, where the **Audubon Center** (© **718/287-3400;** admission free; Apr 5–Nov 23 Thurs–Sun and holidays noon–5pm; Nov 29–Mar 29 weekends and school holidays noon–4pm) offers two floors of exhibits, nature workshops for kids, and nature walks, both ranger-led and self-guided, along the Lullwater and through the wooded Ravine. **Electric-boat tours** leave from the landing in front of the boathouse for $6 per ride for ages 13 and up, $3 for children 3 to 12. Prospect Park's own **Wollman Rink** sits on the northern shore of the 60-acre lake.

If outdoor play is on your agenda, head for the **Long Meadow,** 90 acres of rolling greensward just inside the park's ornate entrance on Grand Army Plaza. Warm-weather weekends always see plenty of picnic action on the meadow, with lots of families tossing Frisbees and working on little sluggers' pitching arms; it's not so great for kite flying, since the meadow is set down in one huge gentle hollow. Brooklyn's sizable Middle Eastern and Caribbean populations give cookout hours here a special spicy aroma. In winter the slopes along the edges of the meadow are just the ticket for trying out that new sled or pair of cross-country skis. The park's circular drive follows a 3.5-mile loop that's great for biking or in-line skating.

Bounded by Prospect Park W. (Ninth Ave.), Eastern Pkwy., Flatbush Ave., Parkside Ave., and Prospect Park S., Brooklyn. © **718/965-8951,** events hot line 718/965-8999. www.prospectpark.org. Subway: 2, 3 to Grand Army Plaza or Eastern Pkwy.; Q to Prospect Park or Parkside Ave.; F to 15th St./Prospect Park.

Carl Schurz Park ★　Though not as extensive as its West Side counterpart, Riverside Park, Carl Schurz Park—named after a prominent 19th-century German immigrant who was a newspaper editor, senator, and cabinet member—offers some very good East River views, and behind them, a few delicious green landscaped dells to wander through. Along the river, **John Finley Walk** (which actually continues south for several blocks past the park) is a paved promenade with wide-open views of the Triborough Bridge to the northeast, the railroad bridge spanning the rough waters of Hell Gate, and, across the river, the small lighthouse on the northern tip of Roosevelt Island; otherwise, it's just warehouses and boxy modern apartment complexes across the water.

No bikes or skating are allowed, but there's an enclosed **dog run** just inside the park about halfway up; come right before dinnertime, and watch the dogs romp. Walk to the north end of the promenade, where it loops around **Gracie Mansion,** the mayor's yellow clapboard residence (built as a country house in 1799, when this still was country); stand by the railing and face south to see how this tranquil park is built over four lanes of car traffic, on the busy FDR Drive—another good example of New York City maximizing its real estate.

Along the East River from E. 84th to E. 90th sts. Subway: 4, 5, 6 to 86th St.

Hudson River Park ★★   The long-term plan is to create a nearly continuous strip of park along Manhattan's Hudson shore from Battery Park to West 59th Street. Don't expect to find big lawns and woods; this is a narrow strip of landfill, much of it devoted to a paved riverside esplanade. But it's Manhattan's best-developed strip of riverside, and its determined reopening after the 9/11 tragedy sent a strong signal to New York (and the world) that downtown Manhattan would prevail.

The oldest section, city-run **Battery Park,** is southernmost, occupying the tip of Manhattan Island. An expanse of grass with some fine old trees, it's crisscrossed by paved paths and dotted with statues; round brownstone **Castle Clinton National Monument** stands here, where you can purchase ferry tickets to the Statue of Liberty and Ellis Island—the ferries embark from Battery Park's waterfront pilings. Hot dog carts, T-shirt vendors, and street musicians are allowed in Battery Park.

Battery Park City comes next, a large office/retail/residential development built in the early 1980s, with a beautiful **Esplanade** serving as its spine. The heart of the complex—the World Financial Center's tony retail mall, the **Winter Garden Atrium**—features a cascade of marble steps leading to a huge glass window, outdoor plaza, and yacht basin. At the southern end, the **Museum of Jewish Heritage** presides over a terrace with great harbor views; the garden area around **South Cove** is fun for kids, where they can scamper over a small bridge and up into a postmodern gazebo echoing the Statue of Liberty's crown.

North of Battery Park City, the park traces the Hudson shore north to 59th Street, with a bike path, recreational piers (including a wonderful toddlers' water park at Pier 51 and Jane St.), and loads of athletic facilities tucked between busy West Street and the river, with strips of fiercely green lawn and flower-filled planters wherever possible. These riverside swaths of green are a perfect spot to get away from it all—and on a sunny afternoon, when the wide sky arches overhead and the broad Hudson sparkles a stone's throw away, it's an exhilarating place to be.

West of West St., from W. 59th St. to the bottom tip of Manhattan. ✆ 212/627-2020. www.hudsonriver park.org. Subway: 1, 2, 3 to Chambers St. and stations north; E to Chambers St./World Trade Center; 4, 5 to Bowling Green.

2 THE PLAYGROUND LOWDOWN

CENTRAL PARK

Central Park's "adventure playgrounds," most built in the 1980s, feature imaginative designs incorporating lots of places to climb, jump, slide, and hide out, as well as lots of sand to dig in or safely land on. In the 1990s, a new generation of playground arrived,

CENTRAL PARK PLAYGROUNDS

West Side

Abraham and Joseph Spector
  Playground **16**
Diana Ross Playground **21**
Heckscher Playground **31**
Mariners Playground **18**
Ross Pinetum Playground **17**
Rudin Playground **6**
Safari Playground **13**
West 67th Street Playground **28**
West 99th Street Playground **5**
Wild West Playground **12**

East Side

Ancient Playground
  (closed for renovations) **19**
Bernard Family Playground **3**
Billy Johnson Playground
  (aka Rustic Playground) **29**
East 72nd Street Playground **27**
East 96th Street Playground **8**
East 100th Street Playground **7**
James Michael Levin
  Playground **25**
Pat Hoffman Friedman
  Playground **22**

RIVERSIDE PARK PLAYGROUNDS

Claremont Playground **1**
Dinosaur Park **4**
Henry Neufeld Playground
  (Elephant Park) **23**
Hippo Park **10**
River Run Playground **15**
West 110th Street
  Playground **2**

OTHER MANHATTAN PLAYGROUNDS

The Upper West Side

Sol Bloom Playground **11**
Tecumseh Playground **24**

The Upper East Side

Carl Schurz Park Playground **20**
Hunter School Playground **9**
John Jay Park **26**
Ruppert Park **14**
St. Catherine's Playground **30**

Midtown

DeWitt Clinton Park **32**
Sutton Place Park **33**
Tudor City Playground **34**

Chelsea & the Flatiron District

Augustus Saint-Gaudens Park **37**
Chelsea Waterside Park **35**
Clement Clarke Moore Park **36**
Union Square Playgrounds **38**

Greenwich Village & the East Village

Downing Street Playground **43**
Bleecker Street Playground **40**
Mercer Playground **44**
Pier 51 Water Park **39**
Tompkins Square Park **41**
Washington Square Park
  Playgrounds **42**

SoHo, Little Italy & Chinatown

Columbus Park **48**
De Salvio Playground **47**
First Street Playground **45**
Vesuvio Playground **46**

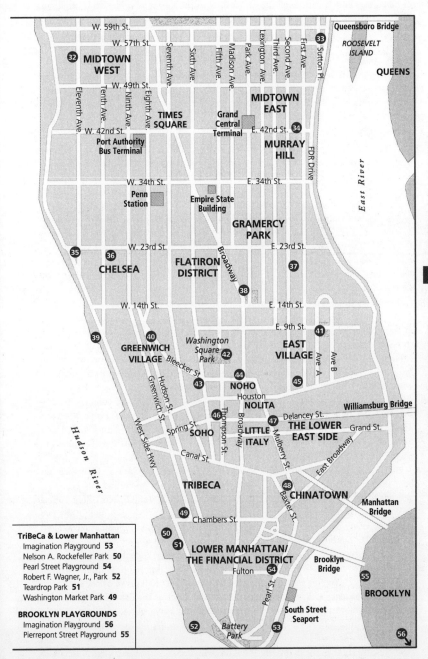

TriBeCa & Lower Manhattan
Imagination Playground **53**
Nelson A. Rockefeller Park **50**
Pearl Street Playground **54**
Robert F. Wagner, Jr., Park **52**
Teardrop Park **51**
Washington Market Park **49**

BROOKLYN PLAYGROUNDS
Imagination Playground **56**
Pierrepont Street Playground **55**

with rubber-mat ground surfaces (as opposed to asphalt) and large, complex structures of metal bars coated with tough plastic, usually in primary colors. The playgrounds are surrounded by iron palings so kids don't wander away unsupervised; they all have drinking fountains, operational from Memorial Day to Labor Day, though none has restrooms; and many have sprinklers to make summertime play a whole lot cooler (which makes up somewhat for the city's appalling lack of decent public pools).

The playgrounds listed below have bucket swings for toddlers and babies and either tire swings or flat swings for older kids. The Parks Department keeps playground equipment decently well maintained, often with the help of neighborhood parents who join in for monthly cleanup days.

THE WEST SIDE   The largest playground in Central Park, **Heckscher Playground,** midpark at 62nd Street, has emerged from a $10-million renovation with a brand-new moat and upgraded equipment. Its most appealing feature is the wide-open center space, covered in patches of artificial turf and soft springy asphalt—perfect for tag and Red Rover and Capture the Flag games. Though very little of the playground is shaded by trees, there are cooling jets of spray in summer.

Just north of Tavern on the Green, the **West 67th Street Playground** has two sections: a renovated 1970s playground atop a small hill, and a smaller fenced playground across the path with primary-colored pipe-frame climbing structures and bucket swings. The hilltop is deliciously shady, with a nice bi-level brown timber treehouse, and sprinklers set in a little concrete amphitheater that spills running water into a long raised basin. The sightlines aren't too bad.

The well-shaded **Diana Ross Playground** at West 81st Street—so named because the singer donated money to the park after violent incidents marred her Central Park concert in the early 1980s—was one of the first adventure playgrounds, and now it could use some refurbishment. The weathered wood structures, set in sandpits, are complex enough to inspire some really fun games, with webs of chains to climb on, suspension bridges to bounce on, and fireman's poles to slide down. But the design isn't geared to younger kids, who may have some trouble climbing where they want to go (which means you'll have to climb up after them to give them a boost). There are two hulking climbing structures set right in the middle; the sightlines can be a problem. Two giant pluses: There are public restrooms nearby (next to the Delacorte Theater—usually dirty but infinitely preferable to soiled undies), and you're only a block north of the American Museum of Natural History.

A nautical theme prevails at the **Mariners Playground,** on 85th Street, which has boat-shaped climbing structures, rowboats to rock in, fish designs around the sprinklers, and lots of shade. A stone's throw away, the **Abraham and Joseph Spector Playground** at West 86th Street sits on a rise of land with lots of picnickable grass around it. Its two best features are the nice fenced-off toddler area (baby swings, sandbox, sprinklers) and an irresistible rambling wooden treehouse with a giant rope to swing on, Tarzan-style. Many of the playground's structures are set in sand, however, and a long wooden bridge arches over the middle of the immense sandpit, which makes sightlines problematic if you're in the toddler area and trying to keep an eye on older kids down by the treehouse. The paved sprinkler area gets very active in summer. Across the drive are some bucket swings midpark in the shady cool of the **Ross Pinetum Playground.**

The delightful **Safari Playground** at West 91st Street is an imaginative playscape where children scramble over a herd of hippo sculptures and hop in and out of a green rowboat embedded in the pavement. It has no swings or slides and only two rudimentary climbing structures, but kids hardly notice—they're so busy with jump-ropes and hop-scotch and sidewalk chalk and running in and out of the sprinklers. With picnic tables and lots of shade, it attracts swarms of preschoolers. At West 93rd Street, the **Wild West Playground** is extremely popular with uptown families, especially in summer, when sprinklers send water rushing down the long central gully into a circular wading pool at the far end. Four square fortlike wood towers at the center make this a great spot for playing all sorts of war games; three of the towers anchor big sandpits surrounded by low wooden palisades, with tire swings, slides, a bouncy suspension bridge, and weathered wood climbing structures (the fourth has a rubber-mat surface that's good for playing ball). The towers in the center make the sightlines a bit of a problem, and the combination of water gully and sandpit means lots of wet, gravelly muck in your kids' shoes when you get home.

At West 96th Street, the newer **Rudin Playground** is set on an island between two busy transverse roads, meaning a bit more noise and exhaust than at other playgrounds; the gate leads straight out to Central Park West, which can also be a problem. But in other respects it's a pleasant place, with a central paved sprinkler area, a vine-hung pergola shading a set of benches, and a trio of brightly colored pipe-rail climbing gyms that modulate from low toddler-friendly structures to a fairly demanding set of parallel bars and swinging rings. There's only one small concrete-edged sandbox, but there are lots of well-shaded bucket swings for babies.

The **West 110th Street Playground** recently got its first reconstruction in more than 70 years, with a spongy new rubber surface (poured in place), with one section devoted to school-age kids and the other, with a sandbox and climbing sets, to toddlers. There are good lawns nearby for picnicking, and right across the drive are the North Meadow playing fields.

THE EAST SIDE   At East 67th Street, the **Billy Johnson Playground ★** (also known as the **Rustic Playground**) is one of the park's most imaginative play spaces. You enter through a leafy wooden arbor; straight ahead is an arched stone bridge that looks very much like the famous Bow Bridge over the Lake to the north, connecting a pair of lushly planted islands. On your left is a midsize sandpit with a slide; on your right, a terrace with picnic tables. Best of all, behind the stone bridge, steps lead up a steep rock outcropping to the top of a 45-foot-long curved metal slide actually set into the face of the rock; daredevil kids in the know bring a square of corrugated cardboard to sit on to make the slide superfast, sort of like a waterless log-flume ride. The big problem with the Rustic Playground is that you can't see past the bridges and islands in the center; if one of your children is doing repeat trips down that slide—it can be addictive—you can't monitor the rest of the playground if your other children are elsewhere. Still, it's a wonderful place for a pre- or post-zoo frolic.

The **East 72nd Street Playground** is another dinosaur from the era of brown timber, brick pyramids, metal slides, and concrete. These hulking shapes make the sightlines pretty bad, and the ground surface, mostly sand, looks a bit dirty. It's quite shady, though, and the entrance is set safely inside the park. Kids in this neighborhood prefer to go to the **James Michael Levin Playground,** set well inside the park near East 76th Street, with a small iron entrance gate everyone conscientiously keeps latched. The centerpiece of this graceful wide-open playground is a fountain featuring scenes from classic fairy tales; kids swarm between the climbing structure near the gate and a decent-size concrete sandbox at the other end, with plenty of open pavement in between for skating, hopscotch, and the like. Sightlines are super, and the people here are pretty well behaved;

but the place gets crowded after school. On the north side of East 79th Street, the **Pat Hoffman Friedman Playground** is a well-sheltered small area behind a replica of the Metropolitan Museum's American Wing's statue *Three Bears* by Paul Manship; there's not much here except bucket swings, a tiny concrete sandbox, a metal slide, and a few climbing bars. It's a handy place for a quick stop right after a visit to the Metropolitan, though only the 4-and-under set will be satisfied.

Undergoing a complete overhaul and expected to reopen in 2009, the **Ancient Playground** at East 84th Street pays homage to the neighboring Metropolitan Museum's Egyptian Temple of Dendur, visible through the glass wall right across the road.

The popular **East 96th Street Playground** sits at the top of a short, steep rise from Fifth Avenue. A good-size toddler area is set off by iron palings in the center; other separately defined areas include a rubber-matted zone with tire swings and wooden pilings to climb on; a large modern metal-bar structure with all sorts of bridges, ladders, towers, and plastic slides; a cool little treehouse platform in a shady back corner; and a paved expanse surrounding a big water sprinkler. Sightlines are very good.

The well-shaded **East 100th Street Playground** has a coil of red steel that becomes a run-through tunnel of spraying water in summer; the climbing structure is particularly imaginative, with lots of inspiring nooks for all sorts of make-believe. Best of all, this playground is wheelchair accessible. It's adjacent to an extensive lawn that sees lots of ball playing and picnic action on weekends. On the east shore of Harlem Meer, at 108th Street, the **Bernard Family Playground** features a large steel-bar climbing apparatus, painted maroon and forest green, mounted on black rubber matting. It also has a small, clean sandbox; a paved sprinkler section; and a few bucket swings. Only a few yards away, there's a marvelous tiny sand beach where small children can happily dig, sift, and mold sand beside the lapping meer water.

RIVERSIDE PARK

The **Henry Neufeld Playground** at West 76th Street is commonly known as the **Elephant Park,** after a set of five plump little stone pachyderms set around an open expanse of asphalt. This pleasant playground also has two modern climbing structures, a fenced swing area, a small fenced sandbox with very clean sand, and restrooms (hallelujah!) actually kept decently clean. There's an active set of basketball courts next to it. The only drawback is that traffic roars on the West Side Highway right past the bushes on the other side of the back fence. At the **River Run Playground** at West 83rd Street, a sprinkler feeds into a sculpted replica of the Hudson River; this, in turn, flows into a whimsical 35-foot sandbox, with sculptural forms of castles, classical gods, and woodland animals frolicking around it. Parents appreciate another form of running water here—the working restrooms.

The **Hippo Park** (down a steep hill from Riverside Dr., at W. 91st St.) derives its nickname from the wonderful hippopotamus sculptures in the middle, which children can climb on. It has swings for both tots and big kids, smallish sandboxes, and sprinklers in summer. An energetic group of neighborhood parents has organized drop-in arts and crafts classes in summer, as well as regular attendants to keep the restrooms clean and safe.

A few blocks north at 97th Street and Riverside Drive, the **Dinosaur Park** also has sculptures (dinosaurs, naturally) and a huge sprinkler area, great for cooling off in summer, though it gets crowded after school. There are restrooms here as well. Set alongside the Riverside Drive promenade on the park's upper level, the **West 110th Street Playground** has small climbing structures, bucket swings, and little sandboxes that make it best for toddlers. The farthest north, the shady **Claremont Playground,** at West 124th Street (right behind Grant's Tomb), has spouting porpoise sprinklers, a sandbox shaped like a huge rowboat, and—ta-da!—more restrooms.

THE UPPER WEST SIDE

Sandwiched between Riverside and Central parks, the West Side has plenty of access to playgrounds, though few between the parks. If you're at the American Museum of Natural History, it may be handy to stop on Amsterdam Avenue at 77th Street (northeast corner) at the **Tecumseh Playground,** which features a rootin' tootin' Western theme, with climbing structures shaped like Conestoga wagons and longhorn cattle. On West 92nd Street between Central Park West and Columbus Avenue, the **Sol Bloom Playground** not only has two great climbing structures (one toddler-scaled) on a soft red-and-black checkerboard surface, but also is the focus of lots of neighborhood athletics, with basketball hoops, a paved softball diamond, and a handball court.

THE UPPER EAST SIDE

The **Carl Schurz Park Playground ★**, at 84th Street and East End Avenue, is my top choice on the East Side. This large, well-shaded playground was recently renovated and has several multilevel climbing structures of red-and-green plastic-coated steel and weathered wood—ladders, slides, bridges, steering wheels, climbing chains, and sliding poles provide plenty of playtime interest. It also has a separate sprinkler area and lots of open pavement in the middle that just cries out for a rousing game of Red Rover or Prisoners All. You'll see lots of little girls in uniforms in the afternoons, after nearby Chapin and Brearley schools let out. Adjacent **Carl Schurz Park** (p. 208) has a superb riverside promenade.

St. Catherine's Playground, on the west side of First Avenue between 67th and 68th streets, is undeniably urban—iron palings, asphalt paving, traffic churning past on three sides—but it's definitely a welcome spot in this near-Midtown neighborhood, roomy and fairly shady with a couple of terraced levels. The park is designed after the floor pattern of the Santa Maria sopra Minerva church in Rome—and the play areas represent the church pews. There's a set of happening basketball and handball courts on the other side of a chain-link fence. **John Jay Park,** on 76th Street east of York Avenue, has some nice up-to-date climbing structures for toddlers in the shady outer area and some for older kids inside the chain-link fence. There are also wide-open asphalt surfaces to run (and fall) on, a small East River lookout, and an outdoor pool open in summer (see "Swimming" under "Sports & Games," later in this chapter).

Ruppert Park (89th to 90th sts., along Second Ave.) has limited playground equipment, but smaller children have fun frolicking on the landscaped series of terraces, with lots of curved paths, flower beds, and benches for play-date tête-à-têtes. The **Hunter School Playground,** on Madison Avenue between 94th and 95th streets, is notable for its Madison Avenue entrance, which incorporates a red-brick castlelike facade, the remnant of a demolished turn-of-the-20th-century National Guard armory. (A similar armory, still intact, is down Park Ave. btwn 66th and 67th sts.) Though this playground is open to the public only after school hours, it may be worth a special detour to let your kids scamper up and down the steps between the stout brick towers, through a wide arch that just cries out for a moat and drawbridge.

x

At the east end of 42nd Street, the **Tudor City** residential complex is set on a terrace above First Avenue; halfway up the stairs that rise on the south side of 42nd Street just past Second Avenue is a small fenced playground with a rubberized surface and primary-colored climbing structures. Overlooking the river, **Sutton Place Park** is set in a quiet cul-de-sac where East 57th Street dead-ends just past Sutton Place. This tiny brick-paved play area—a few steps down from street level, on a terrace above the FDR Drive, with lots of shade and some great views of the 59th Street Bridge arching over the East River—is best for infants and toddlers, since there's no playground equipment to speak of, just wooden benches, one absurdly small iron-fenced sandbox, and a large bronze wart hog (Pumbaa!) on a pedestal.

Over on the far West Side, in a grimy neighborhood once called Hell's Kitchen (nowadays more gentrified and relabeled Clinton), the **DeWitt Clinton Park** playground (btwn 52nd and 53rd sts. on Eleventh Ave.) is set behind a balding set of ball fields, with the West Side Highway rumbling beyond a fence. Still, the playground equipment is excellent, set in pleasant shade, with a nicely executed Erie Canal theme (DeWitt Clinton was the politician who got the Erie Canal built a couple centuries ago—but you already knew that, right?).

CHELSEA, THE FLATIRON DISTRICT & GRAMERCY PARK

Chelsea Waterside Park, right across 11th Avenue from the Chelsea Piers recreational complex at 23rd Street, has a cheery little playground nestled beside the turf athletic fields. It's got some nice water jets and a sand play area, and best of all, it's designed to be wheelchair accessible. Named for the clergyman who wrote *A Visit from St. Nicholas* (better known as *The Night Before Christmas*), **Clement Clarke Moore Park** (southeast corner of Tenth Ave. and 22nd St.) is a pleasant, shady, paved corner lot with benches, concrete sculptures, and one rubberized-steel climbing structure.

In the Flatiron District, the most centrally located are two playgrounds in **Union Square,** side by side near Broadway and 16th Street. The large, fenced-in playground is currently closed and undergoing a major $14-million renovation along with the restoration of the park's historic pavilion and plaza—it's expected to reopen in spring 2009. Outside the fence is a small, sand-filled playground with a few swings and little else. The Union Square Greenmarket, operating Monday, Wednesday, Friday, and Saturday, is only a few steps away, which makes playground picnics very handy. Somewhat off the beaten track in the Gramercy Park area is **Augustus Saint-Gaudens Park** (19th St. and Second Ave.), which has shade; good climbing structures; and lots of open pavement, some with basketball hoops.

GREENWICH VILLAGE & THE EAST VILLAGE

The focal point of the Village, **Washington Square Park,** at the foot of Fifth Avenue (btwn 4th and 6th sts., though the names are changed here for a couple of blocks), has on the north side a bustling playground with lots of climbing structures, set off by a fence from the rest of the park. A pair of greenish tortoises spouts water from their beaks in summer. A smaller, fenced playground on the north side of the park is just right for smaller tots. The park is currently undergoing a major multimillion-dollar redesign and renovation, and the two playgrounds were being closed at press time—the park is expected to fully reopen in late 2009.

Older kids may be attracted to the **Mercer Playground,** a long, narrow strip on the west side of Mercer Street between Bleecker and West 3rd streets; instead of climbing equipment, it features a long skating path and a spray shower, but it feels pretty desultory to me. Farther west, at Sixth Avenue and Bleecker Street, the **Downing Street Playground** is buffered by a red-brick wall from the surrounding traffic; go through the iron gate, and you'll find swings and wooden climbing structures in an asphalt-paved yard. Or follow Bleecker Street west to the point where it dead-ends at Hudson Street to find the always-hopping **Bleecker Street Playground,** fenced off with iron palings. It's got swings, a sandbox, picnic tables, sprinklers, and a stretch of asphalt just big enough for hopscotch or a round of double-dutch jump-roping.

Way over west on the banks of the Hudson, the wonderful **Pier 51 Water Park** ★ in the Hudson River Park (west of West St. btwn Jane and Horatio sts.) not only has a shallow lazy river for foot wading, water sprinklers, and cool things to climb, but is literally built on the pier, with sparkling riverside views. It's got a spongy surface and is remarkably clean—a perfect spot for the under-6 set.

Once-derelict **Tompkins Square Park** ★ has become a leafy haven in the increasingly gentrified East Village, and it has no fewer than three good-size fenced-off playgrounds with black rubberized ground surfaces and rubber-coated metal play structures in bold primary colors; it's even got a small 3-foot pool for a cool summertime soak. The biggest and busiest playground is along Avenue A at East 9th Street; the other two are along East 7th Street. After a vigorous play session, head down the avenue for pizza at **Two Boots** (p. 135).

SOHO, LOWER EAST SIDE & CHINATOWN

The **Vesuvio Playground** (formerly known as the Thompson Street Playground) ★, on the east side of Thompson Street between Prince and Spring streets, is a welcome romping spot for young children in SoHo. A 2008 renovation has only made it better, with climbing structures on a forgiving surface, a sparkling 3-foot minipool, and flowering cherry trees. Good for stretching limbs in fair weather, it's about halfway between the New York Fire Museum and the Children's Museum for the Arts, both on Spring Street. At the corner of Mulberry and Spring streets in Little Italy, the **De Salvio Playground** has a couple of bright modern climbers set in a paved, fenced-in corner lot, with a few benches under the trees.

Tucked between First Street and Houston Street just west of First Avenue, the neatly enclosed **First Street Playground** is the pleasantest Lower East Side playground for younger kids, with shade trees and colorful coated-steel climbing structures. In the tree-shaded **Columbus Park,** at Worth Street between Baxter and Mulberry streets in Chinatown, hordes of Asian and Asian-American children scramble over the climbing structures and dangle on the swings, while elderly men play chess nearby. This is one of the city's oldest urban parks. A 2007 renovation added a state-of-the-art playing field, spiffy new landscaping, and a restored historic pavilion. It's hard to fathom that throughout much of the 19th century this park was the center of one of the city's most notorious and dangerous slums.

TRIBECA & LOWER MANHATTAN

Washington Market Park ★, on Greenwich Street between Chambers and Duane streets, is one of the nicest small greenswards in the city, a $2^{1}/_{2}$-acre lawn sprouting up where the city's rough-and-tumble wholesale food markets used to be. The gentle rises of the grassy area, punctuated with a delightful gazebo, are perfect for picnics and Frisbee

Imagination Playground: A Playscape of Loose Parts

By the time you read this, one of the most unusual and exciting playgrounds in New York City should be ready for some heavy-duty play. The **Imagination Playground** at Burling Slip in the South Street Seaport forgoes typically static playground equipment—slides, swings, climbing sets—for an unstructured, constantly changing environment of sand, water, and "loose parts" where kids are invited to play in unique and creative ways. The playground is the brainchild of David Rockwell, the award-winning architect of Broadway stage sets, restaurant spaces, and theaters. Go to www.imaginationplayground.org for the latest details.

games, and there's a fanciful maritime-themed wrought-iron fence at the south end, where PS 234 sits. A pleasant fenced **playground** is enclosed along the park's eastern wall, with lots of wooden climbing sets and shade. Nearby is the little **Teardrop Park,** between Murray and Warren streets, which basically consists of a long (two-story) tubular slide built over rock boulders and delivers sliders into a big sandpit. It's an awesome ride.

The **Nelson A. Rockefeller Park ★**, at the west end of Chambers and Warren streets, is a thriving swath of green along the river esplanade. The super climbing structures, made of weathered wood and royal-blue steel, provide bridges and platforms where kids can scamper aboveground; on ground level are three good-size sand areas, one wheelchair accessible. The northern section is set aside for toddlers, with a delicious bronze dodo bird set in a tiny splashing area; there's another sprinkler area for older kids, with a stone elephant and hippo. At the southern end is one of the coolest pieces of playground equipment in the city: a red steel whirligig seating eight, powered by pedals mounted beneath every other seat. Though most of the playground is unshaded, several wooden arbors along the sides allow parents and sleeping babies to duck out of the sun. Go up the esplanade to the fanciful sculpture park with its wade-in fountain, too.

Across the street from South Street Seaport, iron fences surround a triangular lot at Fulton and Pearl streets, where the **Pearl Street Playground** has a delightfully complicated climbing structure where kids can let off steam.

BROOKLYN

At the south end of the Promenade in Brooklyn Heights, the excellent **Pierrepont Street Playground** has restrooms (not always clean, however), a separate yard for the very young, lots of shade trees, and loads of slides. Add to that plenty of neighborhood buzz and a peerless view across the East River to Manhattan. The **Imagination Playground ★** in Prospect Park (east side of the park, near the Lincoln Rd. entrance) is as fanciful as its name promises: a bronze dragon spouts water, a black-and-white-striped bridge twists like a helix, child-size masks are mounted for children to peek through, and a central sculpture features the little boy Peter and his dog Willie from Ezra Jack Keats's beloved children's books. (It is not, however, connected to David Rockwell's playground of the same name; see box above.)

3 SPORTS & GAMES

BASEBALL

Organized Little League games around the city in spring snap up most of the groomed baseball fields on spring weekends; after work, grown-up leagues fill the parks on weekday evenings. Central Park has some very nice fields: at the **Great Lawn** (midpark btwn 81st and 86th sts.), **Heckscher Ballfields** (midpark btwn 63rd and 66th sts.), and the **North Meadow** (midpark btwn 97th and 100th sts.). Anyone can reserve a ball field for use; call the Parks & Recreation department at ℂ **212/408-0226**) and find out what's available for the time you want. The cost is $10 per 2-hour session (after 5:30pm, $8 gets you a 1¹/₂-hr. session). If you don't want to get that formal, try the North Meadow facilities, which are sometimes free on a walk-in basis, provided no one has reserved them; a handful of other Manhattan parks, including **DeWitt Clinton Park** (btwn 52nd and 53rd sts. on Eleventh Ave.) and **Riverside Park** (west of Riverside Dr., in the section north of 103rd St.; take stairs down from the promenade level), have baseball diamonds with chain-link backstops that are usually free for pickup games.

If your slugger just wants to work on batting form, check out **batting cages** at The **Baseball Center NYC,** 202 W. 74th St., between Broadway and Amsterdam Avenue (ℂ **212/362-0344;** www.thebaseballcenter.com; $50 per half-hour, $80 per hr., for one to five players); at the **Chelsea Piers Field House,** 23rd Street and the West Side Highway, Pier 62 (ℂ **212/336-6500;** www.chelseapiers.com; $2 per 10 balls); in **Hudson River Park** on West Street, just north of Chambers Street (ℂ **212/627-2020;** www.hudsonriverpark.org; $2 per 15 balls); or at **Randall's Island Family Golf Center,** across the Triborough Bridge on Randall's Island (ℂ **212/427-5689;** $2 for 15 balls).

BASKETBALL

Several city-run playgrounds have asphalt half courts where some pretty aggressive games of one-on-one take place. The famous courts at **Sixth Avenue and West 4th Street**—known as "The Cage"—are a breeding ground for serious hoop-dreamers; the action (not to mention the trash talk) is so fast and furious, kids are better off watching than playing. *Insider tip:* The McDonald's across 4th Street has an upstairs seating area with picture windows overlooking the courts, practically as good as a skybox. Intrepid kids may be able to get a pickup game at **St. Catherine's Playground** (First Ave. btwn 67th and 68th sts.); **Central Park**'s courts just northeast of the Great Lawn (midpark at 85th St.); **Riverside Park** courts at West 76th Street; the **Sol Bloom Playground** (W. 92nd St. btwn Central Park West and Columbus Ave.); or **Goat Park** (Amsterdam Ave. and 99th St.), named after Earl "the Goat" Manigault, a high-jumping, high-scoring street player who watched his peers win NBA offers while his own life unraveled in disappointment and drug addiction. Manigault redeemed himself by running athletic programs for kids in this very park, for which he will be forever remembered.

If you didn't bring your own ball, head to the paved outdoor courts at Central Park's **North Meadow Recreation Center** (midpark, just north of the 97th St. transverse road); at the recreation center's offices right next to the courts, you can borrow a basketball, along with a whole bag full of other sports equipment. If pickup games aren't your style, organize a group of kids and book a basketball court at the **Chelsea Piers Field House,** Pier 62 at Chelsea Piers, 23rd Street and the West Side Highway (ℂ **212/336-6500;**

www.chelseapiers.com; $155 per hour to reserve a court, $10 to walk in and play; call for availability).

BICYCLING

The circular drive in **Central Park** is probably the city's most popular biking road, a 6-mile-long circuit that includes a couple of fairly grueling hills; younger kids may want to stick to the relatively flat lower loop, which shortcuts across at 72nd Street, or even the footpath looping around the Great Lawn, midpark from 81st to 86th streets; it's off-limits to bikes, but trikes are usually tolerated. The wide sidewalk bordering the park walls is also good for young riders, with few cross streets to negotiate; follow it up either Fifth Avenue or Central Park West. Park drives are closed to traffic weekdays 10am to 3pm and all weekend long, from 7pm Friday to 7am Monday. Bike traffic circles the park clockwise.

For more ambitious cyclists, the marked **Hudson River bike path** runs all the way from the Battery Park at the southern tip of the island to the George Washington Bridge, which crosses the Hudson at 181st Street. One section, around 125th Street, is still hard to navigate; you may have to turn to city streets for a few blocks at this point. But otherwise, it's smooth, level, and clear sailing all the way, with some amazing river views. The trail begins with the **Battery Park Promenade,** then runs north along West Street, past Greenwich Village and then Chelsea Piers. Things get pretty urban as you follow the bike lane beside the West Side Highway through Midtown (keep an eye out for turning traffic), but at 72nd Street you'll enter **Riverside Park.** The path cruises along through Riverside's lower section and continues north of 125th Street as a strip of green tucked between the river and the West Side Highway, neatly paved and landscaped.

Riverside Park also offers a flat, wide promenade from 83rd to 96th streets, perhaps better for younger bikers. And like Central Park, Riverside is bordered by wide sidewalks, either of asphalt or of distinctive hexagonal paving stones, so you can cruise along the west side of Riverside Drive from 79th Street up to 125th Street with very few cross streets to worry about.

On weekends, there's little traffic in **Lower Manhattan,** and it's great fun circling the deserted skyscrapers along Wall Street. Just south of City Hall, broad entrance ramps lead onto the Brooklyn Bridge, with broad bike/pedestrian lanes leading you over the river (see "Crossing the Brooklyn Bridge," on p. 200).

The circular road in Brooklyn's **Prospect Park** is another great traffic-free place to ride on weekends; it's only 3¹/₂ miles long and has just one really tough hill.

Now here's the catch: Very few of Manhattan's many bicycle rental shops stock bikes for kids; apparently, the insurance costs are too prohibitive. The ones that do are **Larry & Jeff's Bicycles Plus,** 1690 Second Ave., between 87th and 88th streets (✆ 212/722-2201), charging $8 per hour, $30 for a full day (daily 10am–8pm); and **Pedal Pusher,** 1306 Second Ave., at 69th Street (✆ 212/288-5592; Wed–Mon 10am–6pm), charging $6 per hour, $25 per day. If you're downtown, check out the **Hub Station,** at 73 Morton St., at Hudson Street (✆ 212/965-9334; daily 10am–8pm), charging $7 per hour, $35 per day; it's just 2 blocks from the Hudson River.

BOWLING

Bowlmor Lanes Down in the Village, 42-lane Bowlmor survives as a sort of hip throwback, with a long, sleek bar, a restaurant, a VIP lounge, and lots of postmodern date bowling (DJs, glow-in-the-dark pins, nude bowling parties, and so on), alongside some ferocious league action at night. Daytimes, though, are relatively uncrowded, which is good for families, because no one under 21 is allowed after 5pm. There's automatic scoring, and gutter bumpers are available to keep kids' balls in the alley. *Trivia fans take note:* The first *Bowling for Dollars* TV game show was shot here, and Nixon bowled here regularly in the 1950s.

110 University Place (btwn 12th and 13th sts.). ☎ 212/255-8188. www.bowlmor.com. Bowling for children 11am–5pm daily. Mon–Thurs $7.95 per person per game; Fri–Sun $11. Shoe rental $6. Subway: N, Q, R, W, 4, 5, 6 to 14th St.; L to Union Square.

Chelsea Piers AMF Bowling ★   This sparkling 40-lane facility at Chelsea Piers (it's in the next building south from the Field House) sees lots of family action on weekends. There's also a games arcade, and waiters from the on-site restaurant will bring food right to your lane. Gutter bumpers are much in demand here.

Pier 60 at Chelsea Piers, 23rd St. and the West Side Hwy. at the Hudson River. ☎ 212/835-2695. www.chelseapiers.com. Bowling for children Mon–Wed and Sun 9am–11pm; Thurs–Sat 9am–9pm. Mon–Fri 9am–5pm $8 per person per game; Sat–Sun 9am–5pm $9; Sun–Thurs after 5pm $10; Fri–Sat after 5pm $11. Shoe rental $6. Subway: C, E, F, N, R, V, W, 1 to 23rd St. station. Bus: M23 across 23rd St.

Harlem Lanes   Gospel Bowling on Monday nights? Let me guess: This must be Harlem. Just off the 125th Street strip, this sleek new 24-lane facility occupies two floors of the same building as the Alhambra Ballroom; the third floor is best for families, while more of a lounge atmosphere prevails on the fourth floor. Ask about the Family Four Pack special bowling package, available Sunday through Wednesday 11am to 8pm. The cafe has some tempting food, from Jamaican meat patties and jerk chicken to Cajun BBQ shrimp.

2116 Adam Clayton Powell Blvd. at 126th St., 3rd and 4th floors. ☎ 212/678-2695. www.harlemlanes.com. Mon–Thurs 11am–11pm; Fri–Sat 11am–2am (no children allowed after 6pm on Fri and Sat); Sun 11am–9pm. $6.50 per person per game Mon–Fri before 6pm; $7.50 all day Sat–Sun. Shoe rental $4.50 adults, $2.50 children. Subway: A, B, C, D, 2, 3 to 125th St.

Leisure Time Bowling   Budding bowlers used to have to brave the unattractive bus terminal to find a surprisingly clean and modern 30-lane Port Authority complex, with its main entrance on Ninth Avenue.

550 Ninth Ave., in the Port Authority Bus Terminal, 2nd level (enter at 40th St. and Eighth Ave.). ☎ 212/268-6906. www.leisuretimebowl.com. Mon–Wed 10am–midnight; Thurs 10am–2am; Fri 10am–3am; Sat 11am–3am; Sun 11am–11pm. $6 per person per game; $9 after 5pm Fri–Sat. Shoe rental $5. Subway: A, C, E to 42nd St./Port Authority.

CHESS

It's possible to play at the outdoor chessboards beside the **Central Park Chess and Checkers House,** midpark at 67th Street, just west of the Dairy; the boards are built into the stone tables and you can pick up chess pieces at the Dairy. The real scene for kids, however, is in Greenwich Village, where two chess stores sit a few doors away from each other on Thompson Street between 3rd and Bleecker streets: **Chess Forum,** 219 Thompson St. (☎ 212/475-2369), and the **Chess Shop,** 230 Thompson St. (☎ 212/475-9580). Loads of kids stream in to play, especially on Saturday, and the charges are minimal—children play free at the Chess Forum. Either store can also arrange lessons at $30 per hour.

CLIMBING

Three venues in Manhattan cater to young climbers with walls scaled to their size: the **Chelsea Piers Field House,** Pier 62, 23rd Street and the West Side Highway (☎ 212/336-6500; www.chelseapiers.com; $27 per 1¹/₂-hr. session; Mon–Thurs 4–5:30pm for children

5–16); the **Extra Vertical Climbing Center,** 61 W. 62nd St. between Broadway and Columbus Ave. (© **212/586-5718;** www.extravertical.com; $9 first climb, $5 additional climbs; child lesson $65, parent plus child $130; ages 5 and up; open weekdays 3–10pm, weekends noon–8pm, summers daily noon–10pm); and the **North Meadow Recreation Center,** Central Park, midpark at 97th Street (© **212/348-4867,** ext. 14; Sun 11am–1pm and Tues 5:30–7:30pm), which offers open climb sessions at no charge for kids ages 8 to 17.

FISHING

Believe it or not, you actually can fish in Manhattan. At the north end of Central Park, the **Harlem Meer** has been stocked with fish; April to October, take your kids before 3pm to the Dana Discovery Center on the north shore (near E. 110th St.; © **212/860-1370**) and the staff will give them simple fishing poles and some bait. The Hudson River Park Trust sponsors **Big City Fishing,** catch-and-release fishing off piers 46 and 84 on summer weekends (www.hudsonriverpark.org; 10:30am–5pm); fishing poles, gear, bait, and even instructions are provided free.

GOLF

Golf Club at Chelsea Piers This is truly an amazing facility: a four-level driving range, where 52 golfers at a time can slam balls out into a huge open space bounded by high-tech mesh, all the while enjoying incredible Hudson River views. Stalls are heated for year-round play, and you don't have to lug around buckets of balls—a computerized system in the floor slides a new ball up on your tee as soon as you've hit the previous one. You pay for as many balls as you wish and get a magnetized card to swipe in a slot at the tee; the computer subtracts how many you hit and you can come back whenever you want to hit the rest. There's also a 1,000-square-foot practice putting green, and pros are available for lessons at the attached Jim McLean Golf Academy.

Pier 59 at Chelsea Piers, 23rd St. and the West Side Hwy., at the Hudson River. © **212/336-6400.** www.chelseapiers.com. Minimum charge $25, which gets you 90 balls at peak times, 147 other times. Apr–Sept daily 6:30am–midnight; Oct–Mar daily 6:30am–11pm. Subway: C, E, F, N, R, V, W, 1, 9 to 23rd St. station. Bus: M23 across 23rd St.

Randall's Island Golf Center Randall's Island is one of the city's best-kept sports secrets; with lots of ball fields, it's a haven for amateur athletes and a quick drive across the Triborough Bridge from Manhattan. Along with a driving range, batting cages, a golf shop, and a snack bar, there's a nifty minigolf course at this golf complex on the island. If you don't have a car, you can take a shuttle bus ($10), leaving from the northeast corner of Third Avenue and 72nd, 77th, 86th, and 96th streets every hour on the hour (11am–11pm weekdays; 9am–11pm weekends, on the half-hour 11am–6pm).

1 Randall's Island. © **212/427-5689.** www.randallsislandgolfcenter.com. Driving range $12 for bucket of 160 balls (112 balls after 2pm), $8 for 85 balls (68 balls after 2pm). Minigolf $6 adults, $4 children 15 and under. Batting cages $2 for 15 pitches. Mon 11am–11pm; Tues–Sun 6am–11pm. Free parking; shuttle available (see above).

GYMNASTICS

Chelsea Piers Field House The city has many gymnastics facilities, but most are available only for those taking scheduled classes. The Field House is your best option for drop-in sessions, but what a fabulous resource this is. It boasts an indoor climbing wall scaled perfectly for young climbers and a gymnastics area you have to see to believe—spring floors, in-ground trampolines, deep foam pits for practicing dismounts, and loads

of bars, beams, rings, horses, and vaults. Kids 4 and older can check out the Field **223**
House at an Open Gym session, while children 6 months to 3 years old can occupy
themselves happily in the Toddler Adventure Center, a separate playroom with soft
climbing structures.

Pier 62 at Chelsea Piers, 23rd St. and the West Side Hwy., at the Hudson River. ✆ **212/336-6500.** Admission $11 to Toddler Adventure Center, $27 to Open Gym & Climb. Call for schedule. Subway: C, E, F, N, R, V, W, 1, 9 to 23rd St. station. Bus: M23 across 23rd St.

HORSEBACK RIDING

Note: The 115-year-old **Claremont Stables,** the only riding stables close to Central Park, shuttered the doors of its charming 1892 stables in 2007.

Bronx Equestrian Center   Right off the Hutchinson Parkway on City Island, this small stable offers not only lessons and ring riding, but also trail rides in quiet woodlands. Pony rides are available for younger riders.

Shore Rd. S., City Island, the Bronx. ✆ **718/885-0551.** www.bronxequestriancenter.com. Trail rides $35 per hour; private lesson $40 per half-hour, $65 per hour. Pony rides $5. Daily 9am–7pm.

Kensington Stables Value   To me, this is one of the best horseback deals in New York City, provided the schlep to Brooklyn doesn't daunt you. For $37 per hour, you can join a guided trail ride through leafy Prospect Park, riding either English or Western saddle; because there's a guide along, even inexperienced riders can join in. Lessons at the stable can be English or Western saddle. Call ahead if you want to book a lesson; drop-ins are welcome for the trail rides.

51 Caton Place, Brooklyn. ✆ **718/972-4588.** www.kensingtonstables.com. $57 per hour private lesson, $34 per half-hour private lesson; $47 per hour group lesson for 3 or more. Daily 10am–sundown. Subway: F to Fort Hamilton Pkwy.

New York City Riding Academy   Yet another of the many sports options on Randall's Island is this up-and-coming riding stable in a quiet area on the East River shore, a good bet for beginners. Riding is all Western saddles and in a ring; there are ponies for smaller riders.

Wards Island Park (take E. 102nd St. footbridge from Manhattan; by car, go over Triborough Bridge, follow road past golf center and psychiatric hospital, continue past baseball fields and turn right). ✆ **212/860-2986.** Lesson $30 per half-hour. Daily 9am–6pm.

Riverdale Equestrian Centre   Founded by former Olympians Rusty Holzer and Ashley Nicoll Holzer, this 21-acre stable in spacious Van Cortlandt Park offers quality instruction and well-cared-for mounts, with some spacious outdoor rings and jumping instruction. Ask about its Young Rider program. It also now offers guided trail rides for experienced riders in Central Park (through Nov). All saddles are English; riders must be over 6. Call a few days in advance to book lesson time.

In Van Cortlandt Park at W. 254th St. and Broadway, Riverdale, the Bronx. ✆ **718/548-4848.** www.riverdale riding.com. $85 per hour private lesson, $45 per half-hour private lesson; $65 per hour semiprivate lesson (for advanced riders only), $40 per half-hour semiprivate lesson. Mon–Fri 11am–9:30pm; Sat–Sun 11am–5pm. Subway: 1 to 242nd St. Bus: Liberty Lines BxM3.

ICE-SKATING

Lasker Rink   Cheaper and less crowded than its Central Park cousin the Wollman Rink, uptown's Lasker is well populated by families on weekends. The ice here doesn't get as chewed up as Wollman's, but the rental skates are not of great quality.

FOR THE ACTIVE FAMILY

In Central Park at 110th St. and Lenox Ave. ☏ **212/534-7639.** Admission $4 adults, $2 children. Skate rental $3.75. Nov–Mar daily 11am–3pm and 4–7pm. Subway: 2, 3 to 110th St.

Riverbank State Park This roomy, open-air rink on Riverbank's topmost level is very much in demand with school hockey teams, but public skating sessions are leisurely and pleasant—a boon for tentative young skaters. It's rarely crowded, though some fast and furious teenage skaters here don't always watch out for little ones. In summer it converts to a roller rink.

145th St. and Riverside Dr. ☏ **212/694-3642.** Admission $4.50 adults, $2.50 children 12 and under. Skate rental $3.50. Late Oct to Mar Fri 6–9pm; Sat–Sun noon–3pm and 4–7pm. Subway: 1 to 145th St. Bus: M11, Bx19.

Rockefeller Plaza Rink No doubt the most famous rink in town—and the easiest to find if you're a first-time visitor staying in a Midtown hotel—the Rockefeller Plaza Rink does have undeniable charm, especially in December, when you get to skate under the gargantuan Christmas tree. The golden statue of Prometheus reclines at rinkside, and tourists crowd around the railings above, staring down as you pirouette around (though the ice is sunken far enough below street level that you're hardly aware of your audience). It's expensive (particularly around the holidays), you have to pay again if you want to skate for more than 45 minutes, and the rink is so small you can't get up much speed; there's usually a crowd, which means a wait in line to get in as well as a bit of jostling once you're on the ice. But do it once for the glamour of it.

Lower Plaza, Rockefeller Plaza (off Fifth Ave. btwn 49th and 50th sts.). ☏ **212/332-7654.** Admission Jan–Apr Mon–Thurs $10 adults, $7.50 children 11 and under; weekends and holidays $14 adults, $8.50 children 11 and under; skate rental $8. Admission in high season (Nov to New Year's) weekdays $13–$14 adults, $9–$10 children 11 and under; weekends and holidays $15–$17 adults, $12 children 11 and under; skate rental $8. Skating sessions daily Oct–Apr; call for exact schedule. Subway: B, D, F, V to 47th–50th sts./Rockefeller Center.

Sky Rink ★ Open 7 days a week year-round, this facility offers not one but two permanent ice rinks—the benefit of permanent ice being that the skating surface has more give than ice rinks laid down on top of other surfaces. (This is how Sky Rink justifies its relatively high prices.) The East Rink is booked up pretty solid with figure skating classes and hockey programs, but the West Rink is open for general skating sessions every afternoon, somewhere between noon and 6:30pm, and some evenings to 9pm (call for the current schedule). If you're a good enough skater to look around, you can gaze out the windows to a wide-open Hudson view. It's a special treat to skate here in summer, wearing a T-shirt and shorts.

Pier 61 at Chelsea Piers, 23rd St. at the Hudson River. ☏ **212/336-6100.** www.chelseapiers.com. Admission $13 adults, $10 children 12 and under. Skate rental $7; helmet rental $3.75; coin-operated lockers 75¢ (bring 3 quarters). Call for schedule of public skating sessions. Subway: C, E, F, N, R, V, W, 1 to 23rd St. Bus: M23 across 23rd St.

Wollman Rink Central Park's chief skating rink, at the southern end of the park nearest to Midtown, makes a super place to spin around the ice outdoors, with a rock-music soundtrack piped in and a skyscraper skyline rising right beyond the trees. After school and on weekends, the ice can be thronged, but since skaters aren't limited to set session times, you can still get your money's worth if you hang out at the rink for a while, maybe refortifying yourself with food and hot chocolate from the snack bar while the Zamboni reslicks the ice surface.

IN-LINE SKATING & ROLLER-SKATING

In **Central Park,** the top place for skating on weekends is the plaza by the Bandshell (just south of 72nd St., at the end of the Mall). The entire 6-mile loop of the circular drive is generally popular with skaters on weekends, though it includes some challenging hills that may be too much for young skaters; they should stick to the so-called Inner Loop, from 72nd Street down to 60th Street, which is mostly level. **New York Skate Out** (✆ 212/486-1919 or 917/257-7648; www.nyskate.com) organizes skating lessons and tours for kids ($40 per session) weekend mornings and Tuesday through Thursday after school, meeting at the Fifth Avenue entrance at 72nd Street; it runs a free kids' skate Saturday from 3 to 4pm.

Other **favorite skating pavements** around the city are the promenade in Riverside Park, West 83rd to 96th streets; the Upper East Side's walkway on the bank of the East River from 60th Street on north; the riverside Promenade in Battery Park City; and the skate path of Hudson River Park from Chambers Street up to 59th Street.

Skate-rental outlets have proliferated in Manhattan, but not all rent skates in children's sizes. Try **Blades Board & Skate** at one of its Manhattan locations; the branch at 120 W. 72nd St., between Columbus Avenue and Broadway (✆ **212/787-3911**), is closest to Central Park. If you don't have your own wheels, you'll have to go to the following rinks, where skates are available for use at the rink only.

Riverbank State Park Perched above the banks of the Hudson, this sizable roofed rink catches lots of cooling breezes in summer, though it's an uptown trek.

145th St. and Riverside Dr. ✆ **212/694-3642.** Admission $1. Skate rental $4. May–Sept Mon–Thurs 3–6pm; Fri–Sun 2–5pm and 6–9pm. Subway: 1 to 145th St. Bus: M11.

Roller Rink A pair of open-air roller-skating rinks is set out on the northernmost of Chelsea's recreational piers. Though roller-hockey leagues keep the rinks busy, at least one or the other is open for general skating Saturday 1 to 5pm. In-line-skating instruction is offered as well. Between the rinks, the Skate Pit has been set up for those who want to do stunt skating or skateboarding (see "Skateboarding," below).

Pier 62 at Chelsea Piers, 23rd St. and the West Side Hwy., at the Hudson River. ✆ **212/336-6200.** www. chelseapiers.com. Admission $8 adults, $7 children 12 and under. Skate rental (including protective gear) $19 adults, $14 children. Credit card deposit required. Subway: C, E, F, N, R, V, W, 1, 9 to 23rd St. Bus: M23 across 23rd St.

KAYAKING

During the summer months, the volunteer-run **Downtown Boathouse** (✆ **646/613-0740;** www.downtownboathouse.org; no reservations; check website for updated schedules) organizes free walk-up kayaking Saturday and Sunday on the Hudson River at **Pier 40** (West St. near Houston St.); they also have Hudson River locations at 56th and 72nd streets. Children 15 and under must be accompanied by an adult in the same boat; young children must go in a double kayak with one or two adults. Life jackets, kayaks, and paddles are provided; you can take a kayak out onto the water for 20 minutes. Come wearing a bathing suit, or a T-shirt and shorts that you don't mind getting wet.

Primo sites in Manhattan for trick skateboarders include Midtown's **Penn Plaza** (next to Penn Station), the **Seagram Building** on Park Avenue and 52nd Street, and the **Grace Building** plaza at 43rd Street and Sixth Avenue; in and around **Union Square** (14th to 17th sts., Broadway to Park Avenue South) and the island around the cube sculpture at **Astor Place** (E. 8th and Lafayette sts., in the East Village); and, downtown, spots near City Hall, including the **Police Plaza** and the **Brooklyn Banks,** those swerving concrete ramps around the entrance to the Brooklyn Bridge. But the party's always moving: visit www.5050skateboarding.com for more suggestions.

Ramps have been set up for aggressive skateboarding in **Riverside Park,** at about 108th Street, west of the promenade (© **212/408-0239;** May–Oct; admission $3); at the **Hudson River Skate Park** (West St. just north of 30th St.; free); and at **Chelsea Piers,** Pier 62, 23rd Street and the West Side Highway (© **212/336-6200;** admission $14; open Mon–Thurs 4–7pm, Sat–Sun 11am–5pm). The primo sources for boards, either sale or rental, is **Blades Board & Skate;** of its several locations all over town, the handiest for these skateboarding sites are at 120 W. 72nd St., between Broadway and Columbus Avenue (© **212/787-3911**).

SWIMMING

The city parks' public pools range from the big, noisy, and overrun to small oases in busy urban parks. Still, they have improved by leaps and bounds in the past few years in regard to cleanliness, upkeep, and orderliness—and a number are simply stunning. **Hamilton Fish,** on the Lower East Side (128 Pitt St., btwn Houston and Stanton sts.; © 212/387-7687), is an Olympic-size pool with a smaller kids' pool. **Lasker Pool** (© 212/534-7639), in a beautiful north Central Park location overlooking the Harlem Meer, is an ice rink in winter and a swimming pool in summer. I also like the 3-foot-deep minipools at **Tompkins Square Park** in the East Village and **Vesuvio Park** (formerly the Thompson Street Park) in SoHo—both perfect for kids 7 and under (see "Playgrounds," earlier in this chapter). The city's outdoor pools are open July and August; go to **www.nycgov parks.org** for the details on all of the city's 54 public pools.

An option worth knowing about is the drop-in swim pass at the Upper East Side's **Asphalt Green,** York Avenue between 90th and 91st streets (© 212/369-8890; www. asphaltgreen.org). A family of four can buy a day pass for $48 ($5 each additional child); call for family swim hours. Asphalt Green has two marvelous, clean pools: one 25-yard-long heated outdoor pool, and an Olympic-size 50m indoor pool, with a raised lower section ideal for young swimmers. The city's only other Olympic-size pool is at **Riverbank State Park,** 145th Street and Riverside Drive (© 212/694-3665), which also offers a smaller outdoor pool in summer; use of the Riverbank pools is far cheaper than Asphalt Green, at $2 for adults and $1 for kids 15 and under, free for children 4 and under, and it's available daily from 9am to 6pm.

TENNIS

Very few public tennis courts are available in Manhattan, where most serious tennis players belong to private clubs. **Riverside Park** offers two sets, one at 116th Street and Riverside Drive, the other a well-maintained set of 10 clay courts at 96th Street in the lower section of the park. Play is first-come, first-served, but there's not usually much of a wait. At the city's premier public facility, the **Central Park Tennis Center,** midpark at West 93rd Street, matters are somewhat more complicated. Players who have bought an annual tennis permit ($100 adults, $20 seniors, $10 juniors) can make advance reservations by phone for $7 by calling weekdays from 10am to 2pm or 4 to 7pm (© **212/316-0800** for information and reservations). Anyone else can get a single-play ticket for $7 at the Tennis Center on the day of play, entitling you to an hour of court time (2 hr. for doubles players). You can sign up for a specific court time—in person only—or put your name on the no-show list to take the next available court; players who don't show up 15 minutes before their booked court time get bumped, so plenty of folks from that standby list do get to play. When the hourly bell rings, there's a mass exodus from the courts—26 Har-Tru and 4 hard courts. If you don't have your own racket, you can rent one at the pro shop ($5 for 1 hr.), and they do have kid-size rackets. The Tennis Center is open daily from 6:30am to dusk, April to November. Staff pros also offer lessons; call for prices and availability.

It may be worth an excursion into Queens just to play on the site of the U.S. Open, the **U.S.T.A. Billie Jean King National Tennis Center** in Flushing Meadows–Corona Park (take the no. 7 subway to the Shea Stadium stop). Call the center at © **718/760-6200** to reserve a court, no more than 2 days in advance. Per-hour fees for outdoor courts are $18 to $56. The center is open Monday to Friday from 6am to midnight, Saturday 8am to midnight, and Sunday 8am to 11pm.

TRAPEZE

Yes, that's right—in New York City your child can take a trapeze lesson, in a special trapeze arena right beside the West Side Highway in Hudson River Park, run by **Trapeze School New York** (West St. btwn Vestry and Desbrosses sts.; © **917/797-1872;** www. trapezeschool.com). Classes are offered even for total novices, so long as they are 6 years or older (accompanied by a parent or guardian, of course); don't worry, Mom, all sorts of reassuring nets and harnesses are provided. As you might expect, it'll cost you plenty—classes last 2 hours and cost $47 to $75, depending on the skill level and time of day, and that's on top of an initial $22 registration fee. Still, it's an exhilarating experience, and those I know who've done it thought it was worth every penny. Take lots of videos.

4 CLASSES & WORKSHOPS

ART & SCIENCE WORKSHOPS

Dana Discovery Center   Summer weekends usually see free entertainment out on the plaza here, and arts-and-crafts workshops, science displays, puppet shows, and the like are regularly held inside this beautiful pondside facility, a short walk north of the Conservatory Garden.

In Central Park at the Harlem Meer, 110th St. at Lenox Ave. © 212/860-1370. Tues–Sun 10am–5pm. Subway: 2, 3 to 110th St. Bus: M2, M3, M4 to 110th St./Fifth Ave.

Metropolitan Museum of Art   Indisputably one of the world's great museums, the Met scores big points with families for its frequent programs—they require no reservations and are free with museum admission, which means you can drop in on the spur of the moment and have a transforming experience. Hello Met!, an introduction to the museum, is held daily at 2pm for kids 5 to 12 and their parents; kids zero in on a few specific artworks via sketching and conversation in daily workshops (called Start With Art for ages 3–7, Art Mornings for ages 5–12, Look Again on weekends), and there are occasional 6pm Art Evenings as well for ages 6 to 12 and their families. My children and

New York Kids' Top Five Cheap Thrills

1. Ride in the front car of the subway train, standing at the front window to watch the train hurtle down the tunnel.
2. Stand on the street gratings above a subway line when the train comes thundering along underneath.
3. Run into the middle of a flock of pigeons, and make them all fly up at once.
4. In a skyscraper elevator, stand on tiptoe when the elevator starts to go up, and lower to a squat as you speed upward.
5. On the double-long accordion-style city buses, sit in the seats right in the hinge so you can swivel when the bus turns a corner.

I did workshops at least once a week one summer, and they never failed to be fascinating. Check in at the information desk in the entrance hall to find out what's happening when.

Uris Auditorium, Metropolitan Museum of Art, 1000 Fifth Ave. (at 82nd St.). ℂ **212/535-7710;** for program schedules, call ℂ **212/570-3930.** www.metmuseum.org. Suggested museum admission $20 adults, $10 students and seniors, free for children 12 and under. Tues–Thurs and Sun 9:30am–5:30pm; Fri–Sat 9:30am–9pm. Subway: 4, 5, 6 to 86th St.

92nd Street Y Affiliated with the YMHA (Young Men's Hebrew Association), this is one of the city's greatest cultural resources, with loads of evening programs in music and the arts, and a vast roster of sign-up classes for adults and children. Call to ask what is currently available on a drop-in basis.

1395 Lexington Ave. (at 92nd St.). ℂ **212/996-1100.** www.92y.org. Subway: 4, 5, 6 to 86th St.

DROP-IN CRAFTS

The Craft Studio Plasterwork painting is a big draw here—superheroes, harlequin masks, rainbows, cars, picture frames, puppies, kittens, dinosaurs, you name it, you can paint it (with a little help from the friendly staff). You pay according to the price of the piece you choose. Terra-cotta pots are available for painting (think Mother's Day presents), as are other assorted ceramic items. The space is roomy and well lit, with a rainforest decor, and the shop carries a good number of excellent crafts and toys.

1657 Third Ave. (btwn 92nd and 93rd sts.). ℂ **212/831-6626.** www.craftstudionyc.com. Mon–Sat 10am–6pm; Sun 11am–6pm. Subway: 4, 5, 6 to 86th St.; 6 to 96th St.

Little Shop of Crafts Pick a piece of precast plaster from wall racks—there are more than 1,000 pieces to choose from—and you can paint it whatever colors you choose, daub on designs in finger wax, sprinkle glitter all over, and just generally make it your own masterpiece. There's no charge except the price of the plaster pieces, which are $13 and up. The staff helps out as much as you need; teenagers labor intently for hours over incredibly detailed curlicues, while little kids are allowed to happily slap on paint as they please. They also carry a full line of functional pottery pieces to decorate; you can't take them home for about a week, but shipping is available for out-of-towners. Bead crafts and T-shirt painting are also on the menu, or you can stuff your own cuddly cloth animal to take home.

Make The ceramic items that customers paint here must be glazed and fired in a kiln,
which means you pick them up a week after you've painted them—not as good on the
instant-gratification score as the plaster-painting shops described above. On the other
hand, you'll end up with a real piece of pottery, from a mug to a piggy bank to a pitcher
to a platter, a keepsake that's also functional.

(1) 1566 Second Ave. (btwn 81st and 82nd sts.). © **212/570-6868.** Subway: 4, 5, 6 to 86th St. (2) 506
Amsterdam Ave. (btwn 84th and 85th sts.). © **212/579-5575.** Subway: 1 to 86th St. www.makemeaning.
com. Mon–Wed 10am–7pm; Thurs–Sat 10am–10pm; Sun 10am–6pm; after 5pm, adults only. Cost is base
charge for item ($3–$60), plus $6 per half-hour work time.

MUSEUM WEEKEND WORKSHOPS

On weekends, a number of major Manhattan museums seek to attract families by offering children's workshops, usually free with museum admission. Times vary, so be sure to
call ahead.

The **Children's Museum of Manhattan,** 212 W. 83rd St., between Amsterdam Avenue and Broadway (© **212/721-1223;** www.cmom.org; admission $10, free for children
under 1), always has a lineup of fun workshops, often themed to holidays. The **Children's Museum of the Arts,** 182 Lafayette St., between Broome and Grand streets
(© **212/274-0986;** www.cmany.org; admission $9, free for children under 1), sets up
hands-on art projects every day, providing materials for kids to create anything from
papier-mâché masks to found-art collages to giant mobiles; weekend projects are even
more ambitious. Midtown's **Museum of Television and Radio,** 25 W. 52nd St., between
Fifth and Sixth avenues (© **212/621-6600;** www.mtr.org; admission $10 adults, $8
students, $5 kids 13 and under), has fun Saturday workshops, including a series in which
kids can re-create old radio scripts. The magnificent **Cathedral of St. John the Divine,**
1047 Amsterdam Ave., at 114th Street (© **212/662-2133;** www.stjohndivine.org),
offers family medieval art workshops Saturday mornings at 10am for a $5 fee (cathedral
admission is free). Up in Riverdale, **Wave Hill,** 675 W. 252nd St., the Bronx (© **718/
549-3200;** www.wavehill.org; admission $6 adults, $3 students, $2 for kids 6–18), orga-
nizes superb hands-on children's workshops combining arts and crafts with nature study,
helping children appreciate the estate's magnificent gardens and Hudson River landscape.

Sunday is workshop day at these two excellent Judaic museums, which are closed for
the Sabbath on Friday and Saturday: The **Jewish Museum,** 1109 Fifth Ave., at 92nd
Street (© **212/423-3200;** www.thejewishmuseum.org; admission $12 adults, $7.50
students, free for kids 11 and under); and down in Battery Park City, the **Museum of
Jewish Heritage—A Living Memorial to the Holocaust,** 18 First Place, at Battery Place
(© **646/437-4200;** www.mjhnyc.org; admission $10 adults, $5 students, free for kids
12 and under).

At least once a month, the **Asia Society,** 725 Park Ave., at 70th Street (© **212/288-
6400;** www.asiasociety.org; admission $10 adults, $5 students, free for kids 15 and
under), comes up with really super workshops exploring various facets of different Asian
cultures—Chinese storytellers, Indonesian puppets. And less frequently, the **China Institute,** 125 E. 65th St., between Park and Lexington avenues (© **212/744-8181;** www.
chinainstitute.org; admission $7 for adults, $4 students, free for children 12 and under),

offers similar workshops usually around the Chinese New Year or connected with current rotating shows in its galleries.

If art is your child's special interest, don't miss the workshops offered by the **Museum of Modern Art,** 11 W. 53rd St., between Fifth and Sixth avenues (✆ **212/708-9400;** www.moma.org; admission $20 adults, $16 seniors, $12 students, free for children 15 and under), which organizes Saturday tours for 4-year-olds, gallery talks for children ages 5 to 10, hands-on classes for the entire family, and family-oriented programs of classic short films. The **Whitney Museum of American Art,** 945 Madison Ave., at 75th Street (✆ **212/570-3600;** www.whitney.org; admission $15 adults, $10 students, free for kids 11 and under); the **American Folk Art Museum,** 45 W. 53rd St., between Fifth and Sixth avenues (✆ **212/265-1040;** www.folkartmuseum.org; admission $9 adults, $7 students, free for kids 11 and under; $1 materials fee for workshops); and the **Studio Museum in Harlem,** 144 W. 125th St., between Lenox Avenue and Adam Clayton Powell Boulevard (✆ **212/864-4500;** www.studiomuseum.org; admission free for workshop participants), present frequent art workshops highlighting aspects of their collections or current exhibitions.

10

Shopping with Your Kids

As any serious grown-up shopper knows, the world capital of finance is also a world capital of conspicuous consumption. The children's market is no different. New York City offers a staggeringly wide range of ways for you to spend money on your kids—whether in boutiques selling state-of-the-art children's frocks, toy stores crammed with imported marvels, wondrous hobby shops stocked with rarities, or bookstores piled high with a mind-boggling selection of books. Some of these stores are destinations in themselves (think the Times Square Toys "R" Us store, with its giant animatronic dinosaur, or fabled FAO Schwarz, its doormen dressed splendiferously as toy soldiers); others are small, serendipitous gems you stumble upon as you round a corner. Still others showcase goods with price tags that may have you whistling a happy tune *out* the door. Luckily, you'll have little trouble getting your hands on fun, goofy souvenirs and cool New York–abilia that doesn't cost a pretty penny.

Without a doubt, some of the best children's stores in the city are museum stores, many with delightful, innovative offerings you won't find anywhere else. So that means you can get in some quality museum time *and* do some serious shopping, all in one fell swoop.

1 THE SHOPPING SCENE

SHOPPING HOURS & SALES TAX

Neighborhood stores are generally open daily from 10am to 7pm; stores may not open until noon on Sunday. Street fairs and flea markets are generally weekends-only operations.

New York City has an **8.375% sales tax,** although on clothing and shoe purchases, you don't have to pay sales tax at all. Takeout food, groceries, and services are exempt from sales tax.

TOP SHOPPING DISTRICTS

CHELSEA   The best of the city's two baby megastores, **buybuy BABY,** is located here, on 7th Avenue and 25th Street. Don't miss **Books of Wonder,** one of Manhattan's best children's bookstores.

CHINATOWN   This is cheap tchotchkes central, with oodles of irresistible MADE IN CHINA toys for sale on the sidewalks. You can also get colorful paper umbrellas, Chinese dragons and lanterns, kids' Chinese slippers and cheongsams, and other inexpensive exotica.

THE EAST VILLAGE   The shops here have a funky edge, but you'll find lots of adorable clothes and unique toys. The toy-filled **Dinosaur Hill** is a good place to start; you can find chic clothing with a downtown sensibility at the boutiques **Crembebè** and **Sons + Daughters.** Have any aspiring punksters head to St. Marks Place to **Trash & Vaudeville** (4 St. Marks Place; ✆ 212/982-3590) or **Andy's Chee-Pees** (St. Marks Place; ✆ 212/253-8404; www.andyscheepees.com) for rock-star duds, vintage leather jackets, and faded Levis.

GREENWICH VILLAGE   This neighborhood has an increasing number of notable shops, including **Kid O,** with its brilliant selection of toys and books; **Doodle Doo's,** a toy store/haircutting salon; and **Ibiza Kidz,** with its racks of Splendid Little, Cotton Caboodle, and other incredibly soft, deliciously fashionable clothes. For older kids who are into comics, trading cards, vintage records, and sci-fi/fantasy stuff, there's **Forbidden Planet.** Greenwich Village is also chess central: On Thompson Street just south of Washington Square, the **Chess Shop** and the **Chess Forum** sell beautiful chess sets and let kids play for hours.

MIDTOWN   This is where you'll find the big boys of retailing, as well as those stores designed as much for tourist gawping as for actual shopping. FAO Schwarz is a must-see attraction for kids of all ages. **American Girl Place** is without question an essential stop for girls between the ages of 6 and 12, with the flagship store of **Build-A-Bear Workshop** just down Fifth Avenue a huge draw for younger boys and girls as well. The truly impressive **Toys "R" Us** flagship store in the Times Square area is worlds away from the chain's usual strip mall outlets. The cleverly designed **Niketown** and **NBA Store** are magnets for sports-loving older kids. A number of big department stores reign over Midtown, including **Saks Fifth Avenue, Bloomingdales,** and **Macy's**—all with choice children's departments. Don't miss the jewel box of a baby boutique inside the serene interiors of **Takashimaya,** the elegant Japanese department store on Fifth Avenue.

NOHO   Back in the 1970s and 1980s, the large cast-iron buildings (formerly manufacturing businesses) along Broadway below Astor Place were where teens and preteens flocked for jeans and vintage clothes, army surplus, and Doc Martens. Alas, these funky businesses have been largely displaced by big retailers like **Old Navy, H&M, UNIQLO**—all of which have a good selection of kids' clothes, by the way—and even a downtown **Bloomingdales,** which replaced the much-lamented old Canal Jeans store.

NOLITA/LITTLE ITALY   Nolita, a small grid of streets east of Broadway and south of Houston (and once part of Little Italy), is packed with hip boutiques and cafes; the original St. Patrick's Cathedral occupies a central, shaded spot. It has a number of good children's boutiques along Elizabeth and Prince streets, including **Character, Daily 2.3.5,** and **Soho Baby.** If you're looking for **cheesy souvenirs**—catnip to kids, of course—Little Italy has a smattering of tourist-oriented souvenir emporiums.

SOHO   Not so long ago this fabled neighborhood, with its cobblestoned streets and landmark cast-iron architecture, was the domain of pioneering loft-dwelling artists and cutting-edge art galleries. It's now shopping central, with designer boutiques cozying up to retailers like J. Crew (and **Crewcuts**) and cosmetics stores—the art galleries have largely gone on to funkier pastures. The charming, all-purpose **Giggle** opened its first New York store here, with übermodern, high-end furniture, clothes, and toys. For sophisticated French imports, head to **Julian and Sara** or **Les Petits Chapelais.** Older kids go for the aggressively ironic boutique **Kidrobot.**

SOUTH STREET SEAPORT/WALL STREET   This historic neighborhood along the East River has seen a spurt of family gentrification since the departure of the Fulton Fish

Market. The piers at **South Street Seaport** feature a characterless mix of midrange chain stores and odd boutiques, but the area just north has developed into a small but appealing neighborhood of cobblestoned streets, renovated landmark buildings, boutiques, and restaurants, with a couple of good kids' stores in the mix. The **World Financial Center** has few shops kids will be interested in, but the Winter Garden Atrium is a stunning space with a long cascade of marble steps that kids seem to find irresistible. You can also stroll along the Battery Park City waterfront and watch boats skim the water and have a good view of the Statue of Liberty.

TRIBECA This is the city's new Gold Coast, with big media money filling huge loft apartments and a baby boom filling an army of Bugaboos. I also think it's the most kid-friendly neighborhood in town, with an almost small-town vibe: uncrowded sidewalks great for strolling, minimal traffic, spacious kid-friendly restaurants, and a beautiful children's park. Oh, and a growing concentration of terrific kids' stores (among them: **Blue Bench, Shoofly, Babylicious,** and **Babesta**).

UNION SQUARE The city's other baby megastore, **Babies "R" Us,** is here, on the east side of the park. A large **Barnes & Noble,** with a very good children's department (and scheduled story times), is located in a beautiful landmark building on the north side of Union Square.

THE UPPER EAST SIDE This neighborhood has the largest concentration of children's clothing stores in the city. And, as befitting its demographics, it also has some of the priciest (and preppy-est) kids' shops in town. If you're shopping without kids in tow, a serious Madison Avenue expedition could take all day—many designer kids' boutiques are located between 62nd and 96th streets (**Jacadi** and **Bonpoint** even have two Madison Ave. locations). Shops along Lexington and Third avenues are a little more reasonable, especially in the toy realm: **Mary Arnold Toys** and the **New York Doll Hospital** (and **Homboms** is worth the extra walk over to First Ave.). Older boys can augment their card collections at **Alex's MVP Cards & Comics** or get into model-making and RPG games at **Games Workshop.**

THE UPPER WEST SIDE This has long been a down-to-earth, family-centric neighborhood, with lots of toy and clothing shops (although UWS fixture Morris Brothers—clothing neighborhood children since 1940—shuttered its doors in 2007, a victim of rising rents). Don't miss the outstanding stores in the American Museum of Natural History and the Children's Museum of Manhattan. A number of good toy stores are located on Amsterdam Avenue between 79th and 86th streets, including the generic but stocked-to-the-gills **West Side Kids.**

DEPARTMENT STORES

Bergdorf Goodman Some people are intimidated by this fabled store's exclusive reputation and the intimate, gallery-like departments. But don't be: Once you get past the frosty first floor, you'll find a memorable, even welcoming shopping experience, with some excellent sales. The children's department (on the seventh floor) is small but choice, with brands such as Splendid, Ella Moss, and Noodle and Boo and a good assortment of fine layette. 754 Fifth Ave. (at 57th St.). ✆ **800/558-1855.** www.bergdorfgoodman.com. Subway: N, R to Fifth Ave.

Bloomingdale's Bloomie's layette department is extravagant, geared toward pregnant shopaholics going on a final binge before the demands of motherhood put their shopping days to an end. Like the rest of the store, the kids' clothing departments can be

claustrophobic, and there's no toy department to speak of. 1000 Third Ave. (at 59th St.).
© 212/705-2000. www.bloomingdales.com. Subway: 4, 5, 6 to 59th St.

Lord & Taylor   This slightly dowdy Midtown matron has gotten a spiffy makeover, but it's still blessedly free of crowds most of the time. It stocks traditional layette items and children's clothes. Its Christmas window displays are among the best in town—with meticulously detailed historic scenes featuring tiny costumed moving figures. 424 Fifth Ave. (at 39th St.). © 212/391-3344. www.lordandtaylor.com. Subway: B, D, F, V to 42nd St.

Macy's Herald Square   Macy's flagship in Midtown is one of the world's biggest department stores, with a solidly middle-class orientation and a reputation for moving the merchandise with ongoing (often deeply discounted) sales. It's within crawling distance of a number of subway stations and usually packed to the gills with people chasing the markdowns. However, the children's departments are huge and carry a broad range of merchandise, including lots of sturdy playwear for boys and girls. This is the only Manhattan department store with a significant toy department, though the selection is fairly run-of-the-mill. At Christmastime, Macy's still mounts a free Santaland on its eighth floor, a state-of-the-art extravaganza with long lines and Santa himself taking requests. 151 W. 34th St. (from Broadway to Seventh Ave.). © 212/695-4400. www.macys.com. Subway: B, D, F, N, Q, R, V, W to 34th St.

Saks Fifth Avenue   Sleek and chic, Saks does best for the very young, with a fairly good infant-wear department, but its departments for older kids often have special themed characters and fun events. It's worth including in your Rockefeller Center expeditions, especially since the store's restaurant, **Café SFA,** is such a winner. 611 Fifth Ave. (at 50th St.). © 212/753-4000. www.saksfifthavenue.com. Subway: B, D, F, V to 47th–50th sts./ Rockefeller Center.

Takashimaya   The baby and toddler department in this elegant zone of Zen is small but delightful, with animal rocking chairs to amuse the kids and lovely (and, yes, pricey) clothes; the department plans to expand with larger sizes for slightly older kids. It's a peaceful respite from the Fifth Avenue crowds. 611 Fifth Ave. (at 50th St.). © 212/753-4000. www.saksfifthavenue.com. Subway: B, D, F, V to 47th–50th sts./Rockefeller Center.

BABY MEGASTORES

Babies "R" Us   This three-story Union Square baby emporium has all the basics you need to keep your little one well fed, bathed, rested, and properly clothed—and the competition from buybuy BABY (see below) has prodded them to offer better (and trendier) brands. Don't expect much help from the staff, though. It's the franchise's only location in Manhattan. 754 Fifth Ave. (at 57th St.). © 800/558-1855. www.bergdorfgoodman. com. Subway: N, R to Fifth Ave.

buybuy BABY ★   This is the best baby department store in the city when it comes to toys and games, feeding and bathing items, linens, strollers, car seats, and furniture; the clothing line is fairly pedestrian but reasonably priced. It's a Bugaboo specialist, with all the latest models and accouterments. 1000 Third Ave. (at 59th St.). © 212/705-2000. www.buy buybaby.com. Subway: 4, 5, 6 to 59th St.

GREENMARKETS/STREET FAIRS

The city's largest greenmarket, **Union Square Greenmarket,** 16th Street between Broadway and Park Avenue South, runs Monday, Wednesday, Friday, and Saturday and has some truly glorious produce from rural New York State, New Jersey, and Pennsylvania.

There's a newly renovated playground directly south of the greenmarket, so pick up lunch (crisp apples, apple cider, fresh cheddar cheese, muffins, or hearty seven-grain bread in fall; fresh berries, heirloom cherry tomatoes, just-squeezed juices in summer) and eat on a bench while the kids clamber away.

From May to October various stretches of Manhattan streets are closed to traffic for **street fairs,** featuring booths selling everything from T-shirts to audiotapes to potted palms and hand-knit Peruvian sweaters. The food booths are even more fun—sizzling-hot stir-fries, heaping tacos, or foot-long hot dogs. Sometimes, there'll be a petting zoo or one of those inflated bouncing castles. You tend to see the same vendors weekend after weekend, and little that's for sale is really special. But the main things are the crowd, the sunshine, and the car-free strolling. To find out where street fairs will be held throughout the city, look under "Events" in the "Spare Times" section of the Friday *New York Times.*

2 SHOPPING A TO Z

My listings are mainly for kid-specific stores and merchandise. If you want to check out what New York offers adult shoppers, see *Frommer's New York City.*

BOOKS

Note that many of these bookstores offer story hours and appearances by children's book authors—for details see "Story Hours," in Chapter 11.

Bank Street College Book Store This narrow, bright uptown store has a wonderful selection of more than 40,000 titles and an extremely knowledgeable staff. It's connected to an outstanding education college, so there's also a great section for parents and teachers. 610 W. 112th St. (at Broadway). ℭ 212/678-1654. www.bankstreetbooks.com. Subway: 1 to 110th St.

Barnes & Noble Far from being bland mall outlets, the Manhattan branches of this megastore have great children's sections (especially the 86th St., 21st St., and Union Square locations), with informed salespeople, frequent story hours, and plenty of room for kids to frolic, where the salespeople never complain if your toddler pulls every board book off the shelf and leaves it on the floor. The store's cafes are a good option for a midday snack, too, and there are big, clean restrooms available. A giant new Barnes & Noble has just opened in TriBeCa next door to a Whole Foods supermarket (97 Warren St., at Greenwich St.; ℭ 212/587-5389). (1) 240 E. 86th St. (btwn Second and Third aves.). ℭ 212/794-1962. Subway: 4, 5, 6 to 86th St. (2) 2289 Broadway (at 82nd St.). ℭ 212/362-8835. Subway: 1 to 79th St. (3) 1972 Broadway (at 66th St.). ℭ 212/595-6859. Subway: 1 to 66th St./Lincoln Center. (4) Citicorp Building (at Third Ave. and 54th St.). ℭ 212/750-8033. Subway: E, V to Lexington Ave./53rd St. (5) Rockefeller Center, 600 Fifth Ave. (at 48th St.). ℭ 212/765-0590. Subway: B, D, F, V to 47th–57th sts./Rockefeller Center. (6) Union Square, 33 E. 17th St. (btwn Broadway and Park Ave.). ℭ 212/253-0810. Subway: N, Q, R, W, 4, 5, 6 to 14th St.; L to Union Square. (7) 396 Sixth Ave. (at 8th St.). ℭ 212/674-8780. Subway: A, B, C, D, E, F, V to W. 4th St.

Bookberries A cozy little carpeted nook has been partitioned off for kids in this small East Side store. The selection is fairly good, though the picture books may be haphazardly alphabetized—probably because so many little hands have pulled them out—a good sign. 983 Lexington Ave. (at 71st St.). ℭ 212/794-9400. Subway: 6 to 68th St.

Books of Wonder ★   One of the few specialty children's bookstores left in town, this great Chelsea shop has a lot of hard-to-find titles, as well as collectors' items (the Oz books, original Nancy Drews, illustrators' original art). The staff is friendly, helpful, and knowledgeable. Plus, it's got an outpost of the **Cupcake Cafe** (p. 117) right in the store, with cupcakes to eat on-site or gorgeously decorated cakes for celebrations later. 18 W. 18th St. (btwn Fifth and Sixth aves.). © 212/989-3270. www.booksofwonder.net. Subway: 1 to 18th St.

Borders   This chain megastore has a large and welcoming children's section, with plenty for older kids as well as picture books for the younger set. The atmosphere is very conducive to browsing. www.borders.com. (1) 10 Columbus Circle (at Eighth Ave.). © 212/823-9775. Subway: A, B, C, D, 1 to 59th St./Columbus Circle. (2) 461 Park Ave. (at 57th St.). © 212/980-6785. Subway: 4, 5, 6 to 59th St. (3) 550 Second Ave. (at 31st St.) in Kips Bay Plaza. © 212/685-3938. Subway: 6 to 33rd St. (4) 2 Penn Plaza (7th Ave. and 31st St.). © 212/244-1814. Subway: 1, 2, 3 to 34th St. (5) 100 Broadway (at Pine St.). © 212/964-1988. Subway: 2, 3, 4, 5 to Wall St.

Logos Bookstore (Finds)   Near Carl Schurz Park, this pleasant shop has a good children's corner at the back, near the small but leafy outdoor garden, a delightful place for reading in fair weather. While the store's specialty is religious books, this isn't heavily emphasized in the kids' selection, which does include some interesting titles from smaller publishers. 1575 York Ave. (btwn 83rd and 84th sts.). © 212/517-7292. http://logosbookstore nyc.com. Subway: 4, 5, 6 to 86th St.

Scholastic Store ★   Big, bright, and glossy, this outlet of the big children's publisher has an obvious motive for selling Scholastic books, activities, and tie-in toys, but considering how many of the titles your kids love are published by Scholastic—from Clifford the Big Red Dog to Harry Potter—it's a worthwhile SoHo stop. 557 Broadway (btwn Prince and Spring). © 212/343-6166. www.scholasticstore.com. Subway: R, W to Prince St.

Shakespeare & Co.   The uptown branch of this local chain offers a decent children's section, with pint-size chairs and a carpet for in-store reading. The selection is intelligent, if skewed toward "worthy" picture books and classics. 939 Lexington Ave. (btwn 68th and 69th sts.). © 212/570-0201. www.shakeandco.com. Subway: 6 to 68th St.

The Strand   The venerated used-bookseller touting "18 Miles of Books" actually has a great children's section, where you can get new bestsellers and classics at substantial discounts. 828 Broadway (at 12th St.). © 212/472-1452. www.strandbooks.com. Subway: N, R, 4, 5, 6 to 14th St.

Westsider Books   This excellent little used-book store—narrow and dusky, with books to the ceiling—has a small children's section with some real finds. 2246 Broadway (btwn 80th and 81st sts.). © 212/362-0706. Subway: 1 to 79th St.

CANDY, CHOCOLATE & SWEETS

Chocolate Bar   Cashing in on the designer chocolate vogue, this boutique in the East Village will intrigue older kids who've outgrown stuffing their faces with Hershey's Kisses. You can sit down and sip a cocoa or latte while you're browsing. You can also visit the Chocolate Bar in its new third-floor location in Henri Bendel at 712 Fifth Avenue. 127 7th St. (btwn First Ave. and Ave. A). © 212/366-1541. www.chocolatebarnyc.com. Subway: N, R to 8th St.; 6 to Astor Place.

Dylan's Candy Bar   The creation of Ralph Lauren's daughter, Dylan's is a candy-colored, sweet-shoppe-themed bi-level boutique full of specialty candy, from imported sweets to store-brand designer chocolates. There's some hard-to-find stuff here, though

SHOPPING WITH YOUR KIDS

10

SHOPPING A TO Z

Baby Mega Stores
Babies "R" Us **35**
buybuy BABY **32**

CLOTHES SHOPPING BY NEIGHBORHOOD
Chelsea
Baby Depot at Burlington Coat Factory **33**

East Village
Crembebé **40**
Sons + Daughters **41**

Flatiron
Space Kiddets **34**

Greenwich Village
Ibiza Kidz **37**
Lucky Wang **38**
Yoya **36**

NoHo
Calypso Enfants **48**

NoLiTa
Soho Baby **45**

SoHo
Julian & Sara **43**
Les Petits Chapelais **46**
Lilliput **44**
Patagonia SoHo **42**

TriBeCa
Babesta **51**
Babylicious **49**
Koh's Kids **50**

Upper East Side
All Dressed Up **14**
Bambini **11**
Bonpoint **8, 27, 39**
Catimimi **10**
Flora and Henri **20**
Infinity **10**
Jacadi **6, 7, 25, 28**
La Layette **30**

Lester's **16**
Lily Pulitzer **12**
Magic Windows/ Magic Windows for Teens **9**
Petit Bateau **11**
Prince & Princess **18**
San Francisco Clothing **26**
Small Change **15**
Spring Flowers Children's Boutique **21, 29, 31**
Talbots Kids **17, 31**
Tutti Bambini **22**
Zittles (Zitomer Department Store) **19**

Upper West Side
Berkley Girl **3, 23**
Bonne Nuit **5**
Greenstones **2, 19**
Karin Alexis **1**
Z'Baby Company **4, 24, 47**

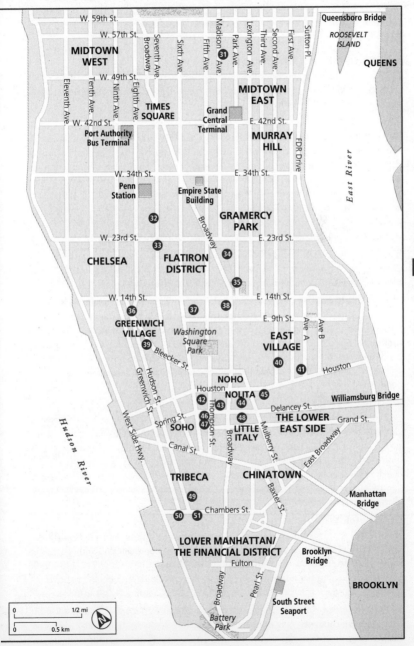

UNIQLO This Japanese export specializes in quality, well-made casual wear. It has a small children's section, but your teens and 'tweens will love the soft cotton tees of all shapes and colors, cargo pants, and simple knit dresses—building blocks for a stylin' wardrobe at very reasonable prices. Go to **www.uniqlo.com/us** for the latest locations in Manhattan.

Clothing by neighborhood

Keep in mind that a number of the following stores have more than one location, often in other neighborhoods altogether. That's why we've included listing information for all the stores' locations in Manhattan.

Chelsea

Baby Depot at Burlington Coat Factory Clothing up to size 16, boys' and girls', can be found on the third floor of this big discount store in the megastore shopping district wedged between Chelsea and the Flatiron District. The brands are quite respectable—Carter's, Buster Brown, Guess—but not very appealingly displayed, jammed onto racks under fluorescent lighting. 707 Seventh Ave. (btwn 22nd and 23rd sts.). © 212/229-1300. www.coat.com. Subway: F, V to 23rd St.

East Village

Crembebè This little shop has a real sense of style; it carries sophisticated European brands, popular American labels (Splendid), and cool downtown clothing from local designers in sizes newborn to 12 years. 68 Second Ave. (btwn 3rd and 4th sts.). © 212/979-6848. www.crembebe.com. Subway: 6 to Astor Place, F to Second Ave.

Sons + Daughters ★ This shop is nicely stocked with excellent brands—check out the sturdy cotton knitwear from the Dutch company Imps & Elfs or the adorable antique flower dresses from Room Seven—and if you love the soft cotton separates from C&C California, you can get them here. The store also has a smart collection of toys, games, and books, arts and crafts, and nursery and mealtime necessities. 35 Ave. A (btwn 1st and 2nd sts.). © 212/253-7797. www.sonsanddaughtersinc.com. Subway: 6 to Astor Place, F to Second Ave.

Flatiron District

Space Kiddets ★ I admit it: I love this store for its great selection of adorable, trendy clothing for wee ones (up to teens)—it can be pricey, but the sales are terrific and the staff is always helpful. Look for name brands like Splendid and Petit Bateau as well as hipster and little-known brands you won't find anywhere else in New York City—my daughter loves her green furry spotted coat made by the Japanese company Boohomes. Closed Sunday. 26 E. 22nd St. (btwn Broadway and Park Avenue South). © 212/420-9878. www.spacekiddets.com. Subway: N, R, W, 6 to 23rd St.

Greenwich Village

Ibiza Kidz ★ This Village shop sells dreamy children's clothes with a bohemian sensibility (Splendid, Cotton Caboodle). The look is stylish and colorful, with a sense of whimsy. Its **sister store** at 61 Fourth Ave. (btwn 9th and 10th sts.; © 212/228-7990; www.ibizakidz.com) has a superb collection of shoes, socks, layette books, and toys. 42 University Place. (at 9th St.). © 212/228-7990 or 212/375-9984. Subway: N, R, W to 8th St.

Lucky Wang ★ Adorable children's kimonos, colorful kimono tops, and flower-print wrap dresses: This store sells hip, charming ensembles you won't find anywhere else. Lucky Wang also sells of-the-moment brands like Splendid, as well as the latest Jellycat

CENTRAL PARK

Central Park South

Grand
Army
Plaza

59th St.

Bloomingdale's

58th St.

Bergdorf
Goodman

57th St.

57th St.

56th St.

56th St.

Seventh Ave.

55th St.

54th St.

Fifth Ave.

Madison Ave.

Takashimaya

53rd St.

52nd St.

(Ave. of the Americas)

Park Ave.

Lexington Ave.

Third Ave.

51st St.

St. Patrick's
Cathedral

50th St.

ROCKEFELLER
CENTER

Saks

49th St.

Sixth Ave.

48th St.

47th St.

46th St.

Fifth Ave.

45th St.

Duffy
Square

44th St.

43rd St.

Vanderbilt Ave.

Grand
Central
Terminal

TIMES
SQUARE

42nd St.

Bryant
Park

New York
Public Library

41st St.

Madison Ave.

40th St.

Broadway

39th St.

Lord &
Taylor

38th St.

Lexington Ave.

Third Ave.

37th St.

Seventh Ave.

36th St.

Park Ave. South

Fifth Ave.

35th St.

Macy's

HERALD
SQUARE

34th St.

M Subway

Penn
Station

Empire State
Building

0   1/5 mi

0   0.2 km

33rd St.

stuffed toys. 799 Broadway (at 10th St.). ✆ 212/353-2850. www.luckywang.com. Subway: N, R, W to 14th St.

Yoya　Gosh, the stuff in this baby and toddler boutique is beautiful, from the dresses (Judith Lacroix, Marie Chantal, Tocca, Splendid, Tzawa) to the furniture (Netto, Bloom) to the sleek silver and gold rattles. And gosh, it is pricey (good sales, though). It's got an up-to-the-minute selection of Jellycat stuffed toys—priced reasonably and the perfect baby gift. The staff could benefit from dialing down the attitude a notch or two, however. 636 Hudson St. (at Horatio St.). ✆ 646/336-6844. www.yoyashop.com. Subway: A, E to 14th St.

NoHo

Calypso Enfants　St. Barts–inspired French designer ensembles for newborns to size 10 draw fashion-conscious downtown parents to this NoHo shop. While you're in the neighborhood, check out the **Calypso Outlet** store across the street at 424 Broome St., which often has deeply discounted children's clothes. 407 Broome St. (btwn Crosby and Lafayette sts.). ✆ 212/966-3234. www.calypso-celle.com. Subway: B, D, F, V to Broadway/Lafayette St.

Nolita

Soho Baby　This pleasant shop has a good selection of stylish clothing for sizes newborn to 6 years. It also has bedding, stuffed animals, and toys. 251 Elizabeth St. (btwn Prince and Houston sts.). ✆ 212/625-8538. Subway: R, W to Prince St.; B, D, F, V to Broadway/Lafayette St.

SoHo

Julian & Sara　For 15 years, this tiny SoHo shop has been selling lovely, upscale things in sizes for newborns to 16 years, for girls and boys. 103 Mercer St. (btwn Prince and Spring sts.). ✆ 212/226-1989. www.julianandsara.com. Subway: R, W to Prince St.

Les Petits Chapelais ★　The Brittany-inspired fashions by French designer Nathalie Simonneaux in this darling SoHo boutique are refreshingly child-appropriate, sturdy looking, and colorful. The classic Sailor Collection is delightful. Sizes 0 to 10. 86 Thompson St. (at Spring St.). ✆ 212/625-1023. www.lespetitschapelais.com. Subway: C, E to Spring St.

Lilliput ★　A fashion-conscious, European boho sensibility rules in these crammed-full shops (in two locations on the same street) carrying play and dressy clothes in sizes up to 18; expect such quality international labels as Petit Bateau, Repetto, and Lili Gaufrette. A battery of windup toys and a good-size selection of tulle skirts for dress-up fun give you a clue to the spirit of the place. (1) 265 Lafayette St. (btwn Prince and Spring sts.). ✆ 212/965-9567. (2) 240 Lafayette St. (btwn Prince and Spring sts.). ✆ 212/965-9201. www.lilliput soho.com. Subway: 6 to Spring St.; B, D, F, V to Broadway/Lafayette St.

Patagonia SoHo　This outdoor specialist has a small but excellent selection of solid kids' clothes—specializing, as you might guess, in winter fleece and down outerwear from toddler sizes on up. It's a big, handsome store, with wood floors and a warm, friendly staff. 101 Wooster St. (btwn Prince and Spring sts.). ✆ 212/343-1176. www.patagonia.com. Subway: 6 to Spring St.; R to Prince St.

TriBeCa

Babesta ★　If it's "plain vanilla" you're after, head elsewhere. This small clothing store makes no bones about its fun, contemporary rock-'n'-roll sensibility. That doesn't mean the cool kids' clothes aren't supremely wearable and good quality, because they are. Yes, you can get your Ramones T-shirts and psychedelic rompers here, but you can also get perfectly darling Kit+Lilli sundresses. By the time you read this, **Babesta Cribs** (56 Warren St.) will have opened across the street, selling modern furniture, strollers, highchairs, and home decor. 66 W. Broadway (btwn Murray and Warren sts.). © **212/608-4522**. www. **243** babesta.com. Subway: A, C, E, 1, 2, 3 to Chambers St.

Babylicious ★ Although this TriBeCa boutique also stocks fun and educational toys, accessories, and gifts for kids from birth to 5 years old, it's the stylish play clothes, in sizes from newborn to 4T, that stand out. It also specializes in cool party favors. 51 Hudson St. (btwn Duane and Jay sts.). © **212/406-7440**. www.babyliciousnyc.com. Subway: A, C, E, 1, 2, 3 to Chambers St.

Koh's Kids ★ This TriBeCa shop is crammed to the rafters with a good assortment of quality casual clothes and shoes for the newborn to size 14 set, as well as plenty of nifty toys and gifts. 311 Greenwich St. (btwn Chambers and Reade sts.). © **212/791-6915**. Subway: A, C, E, 1, 2, 3 to Chambers St.

Upper East Side
All Dressed Up ★ Filling a strategic important market niche in Manhattan, this Upper East Side boutique provides drop-dead party gowns for preteens—just the thing for getting through the stream of bar/bat mitzvahs that inevitably occupy one's seventh-grade social calendar. Lovely, appropriate dresses, with just the right hint of sophistication. Closed Sunday and Monday in summer. 1201 Lexington Ave. (btwn 82nd and 83rd sts.). © **212/452-3181**. Subway: 4, 5, 6 to 86th St.

Bambini This beautiful, humorless, blond-wood store stocks European children's clothes (brand names like Simonetta and Cacharel) and shoes. The clothes are indeed handsome, but at princess prices—$50 for a dead-plain polo shirt or $375 for a smocked party frock. 1088 Madison Ave. (btwn 81st and 82nd sts.). © **212/717-6742**. Subway: 6 to 77th St.; 4, 5, 6 to 86th St.

Bonpoint ★ This boutique takes the cake—it has some of the most expensive children's clothes in town (up to size 16 girls and 12 boys)—and the selection is beautiful. Everything sold is the store's private label, and the fabrics are gorgeous, no question about it; the styles are classic, understated, and perfectly cut. Bonpoint has two Upper East Side locations and a downtown store on newly fashionable Bleecker Street. www.bonpoint. com. (1) 1269 Madison Ave. (at 91st St.). © **212/722-7720**. Subway: 4, 5, 6 to 86th St. (2) 811 Madison Ave. (at 68th St.). © **212/879-0900**. Subway: 6 to 68th St. (3) 392 Bleecker St. (btwn W. 11th and Perry sts.). © **212/647-1700**. Subway: 1, 9 to Christopher St.

Catimini ★ These colorful French kids' clothes (mostly size 8 and under) show an ineffable sense of style, with sassy prints and deep-colored solids cut into simple, roomy clothes with real flair. The store has a bold, clean look and friendly staff. The clothes aren't cheap, but they're casual and sturdy enough that you'll get lots of wear out of them. Closed Sunday July to August. 1125 Madison Ave. (at 84th St.). © **212/987-0688**. www.catimini. com. Subway: 6 to 96th St.

Flora and Henri ★ This shop showcases a delightful designer line of drapey European knits in sizes newborn to 12. 1023 Lexington Ave. (btwn 73rd and 74th sts.). © **212/249-1695**. www.florahenri.com. Subway: 6 to 77th St.

Infinity As a friend of mine says, "At a certain age, all girls want to look like either a construction worker or a tramp." This is the store for both sensibilities. T-shirts and jeans and skimpy knit dresses rule, along with lots of the dumpy backpacks every school kid has to have. Infinity doesn't necessarily try to be hip; it just stocks what kids like to wear, damn the parents. Bring your preteen here to prove you do indeed get it. 1116 Madison Ave. (at 83rd St.). © **212/517-4232**. www.infinitynyc.com. Subway: 4, 5, 6 to 86th St.

Jacadi A French chain, Jacadi sells expensive, sturdy, stylish clothes, cut for comfort, for boys and girls from babies up to age 12. Each season's line is color-coordinated, handy for mixing and matching, and the store looks tidy and very put together as a result. Jacadi has three locations on the Upper East Side and one store near Columbus Circle on the west side. www.jacadiusa.com. (1) 1296 Madison Ave. (at 92nd St.). ℂ 212/369-1616. Subway: 4, 5, 6 to 86th St. (2) 787 Madison Ave. (btwn 66th and 67th sts.). ℂ 212/535-3200. Subway: 6 to 68th St. (3) 1841 Broadway (at 60th St.). ℂ 212/246-2753. Subway: 1 to 59th St./Columbus Circle. (4) 1260 Third Ave. (at 72nd St.). ℂ 212/717/9292. Subway: 6 to 68th St.

La Layette You can't go wrong with these classic, tastefully understated infant clothes (to size 2) and gifts. Nothing over-the-top here: soft cotton take-home sets, christening gowns, embroidered sweaters, engraved silver picture frames, hand-painted plates, elegant bassinets, personalized pillows, and ruffley crib bedding. Closed Sunday and Saturday July to August. 170 E. 61st St. (btwn Lexington and Third aves.). ℂ 212/688-7072. www.lalayette.com. Subway: 4, 5, 6 to 59th St.

Lester's ★ This roomy shop is an East Side staple for clothing and shoes, ages newborn to 12—most of the stock is imported, and designer styles abound, but the prices aren't too out of whack. The girls' clothes trend toward more daring looks. This is the place for boys to buy a real suit, with knowledgeable fitters and tailors available and a wide range of styles to choose from (more casual clothes are stocked, too). The layette department features imported and designer styles at fairly reasonable prices. 1534 Second Ave. (at 80th St.). ℂ 212/734-9292. www.lestersnyc.com. Subway: 6 to 77th St.

Lilly Pulitzer It's preppie heaven at the brand's new flagship store, appropriately ensconced on a tony Madison Avenue block. The bright colors and eye-catching prints are hard to resist in a city where black is perpetually the new black. The store has a selection of girls' clothes in sizes 3 months to 14. 1020 Madison Ave. (at 79th St.). ℂ 212/744-4620. www.lillypulitzer.com. Subway: 6 to 77th St.

Magic Windows Here you'll find East Side–conservative, traditional baby clothes (sizes up to 6X), all in pastel blues and pinks, as well as a collection of preteen clothing (up to 16). The tiny white cotton sweaters are adorable. Brands include Lilly Pulitzer and Ralph Lauren. When you graduate from Magic Windows, you get to buy precociously chic party dresses from **Magic Windows for Teens** next door. The clothes really are pretty, if a trifle adult. www.magicwindowskids.com. (1) 1186 Madison Ave. (at 87th St.). ℂ 212/289-0181. Subway: 4, 5, 6 to 86th St. (2) 1186 Madison Ave. (at 87th St.). ℂ 212/289-0028. Subway: 4, 5, 6 to 86th St.

Petit Bateau ★ As the flagship store for this upscale clothing label, this is a good source for classic, understated French style (meaning country-club-ish clothes of which *Maman* would approve). The baby clothes are meltingly soft and lovely, but keep in mind when sizing that the Petit Bateau baby is long and lean. Carries clothing for boys and girls up to size 18. 1094 Madison Ave. (at 82nd St.). ℂ 212/988-8884. www.petit-bateau.us. Subway: 4, 5, 6 to 86th St.; 6 to 77th St.

Prince & Princess The name tells you all you need to know about the fabulous (taffeta, silk, velvet) imported clothes for boys and girls at this haughty, tiny shop. You don't have to have aristocratic connections to shop here, but it can't hurt. Closed Sunday. 41 E. 78th (btwn Park and Madison aves.). ℂ 212/879-8989. www.princeandprincess.com. Subway: 6 to 77th St.

San Francisco Clothing   This East Side women's clothing store has a surprisingly darling line of little girls' clothing, in well-cut minipreppie styles and top-quality fabrics. Don't let the wood-paneled decor and snooty staff put you off—with play clothes under $50 and dresses under $75, this is an upscale shop worth checking out. Closed Sunday. 975 Lexington Ave. (btwn 70th and 71st sts.). ✆ 212/472-8740. Subway: 6 to 68th St.

Small Change   As expensive children's clothing shops go, this isn't a bad choice for that special party dress. The store buyers clearly have a sense of style. The prices can be high ($280 for a boy's navy blazer!), but this East Side store understands its upscale customers and their private-school needs. Closed Sunday in summer. 1196 Lexington Ave. (at 83rd St.). ✆ 212/772-6455. Subway: 6 to 79th St.

Spring Flowers Children's Boutique ★   The clothes here are achingly beautiful and correspondingly pricey. But oh—those Italian bronze slip-ons with the grosgrain bow! That Audrey Dress in blue silk taffeta! You *can* buy big-skirt party gowns for only $100—but you can also pay $450 for that irresistible Audrey Dress. Don't come here for rock-star trendy: This stuff is conservatively styled, with creamy linen shorts and vests for little boys and tea dresses and classic cardigans for little girls. Spring Flowers has casual wear and shoes, but it's the classic dress-up stuff that catches the eye, round racks bulging with petticoats and crisp pinafores, many with lovely floral prints. Closed Sunday. www.springflowerschildren.com. (1) 1050 Third Ave. (at 62nd St.). ✆ 212/758-2669. Subway: 4, 5, 6 to 59th St. (2) 907 Madison Ave. (at 72nd St.). ✆ 212/717-8182. Subway: 6 to 68th St. (3) 538 Madison Ave. (at 55th St.). ✆ 212/207-4606. Subway: 6 to 51st St.

Talbots Kids   Yes, the adult Talbots store can suffer from matronly clothes, but this junior version (for newborns to teens) is surprisingly bright and casual and cool. Clothes are tailored but stylish, with a coherent mix-and-match look. For classic-cut winter coats, sweaters, and other wardrobe staples, it can't be beat. For khaki pants and polos and sweaters in solid colors and traditional stripes, this place has the advantage of one-stop shopping. When my sons finally agree to wear a navy blazer and rep tie, this is where we buy them—they fit, they look great, and I don't have to pay through the nose for something they'll wear only a dozen times. Button-down Oxford-cloth shirts, too—go all the way. www.talbots.com. (1) 1523 Second Ave. (at 79th St.). ✆ 212/570-1630. Subway: 6 to 77th St. (2) 527 Madison Ave. (at 54th St.). ✆ 212/758-4152. Subway: 6 to 51st St.

Tutti Bambini ★   Carrying a wide range of labels—imported, made in the U.S.A., whatever—this busy little East Side shop knows its look: funky and fun. It carries sizes up to 10, with brand names like Lili Gaufrette, Victoria Kids, JKKS, and Charlie Rockets, and tends toward designs adults wouldn't mind wearing. Most of the other shoppers I saw had kids in tow, which means they were picking out clothes the kids themselves like to wear—always a good sign. 1480 First Ave. (btwn 77th and 78th sts.). ✆ 212/472-4238. Subway: 6 to 77th St.

Zittles (Zitomer Department Store)   Bursting at the seams, this drugstore's upstairs children's clothing department, Zittles, has some very upscale imported clothes (dresses in the $50–$500 range) that manage to look cheesy in the fluorescent light, jammed together on chrome racks as they are. But don't be put off by that; it's worth a stop if you're on a quest for something special. 969 Madison Ave. (btwn 75th and 76th sts.). ✆ 212/737-5560. www.zitomer.com. Subway: 6 to 77th St.

Upper West Side

Berkley Girl ★   Fashion-conscious West Side girls from toddlers to size 16 can outfit themselves in the latest styles in this busy boutique across from the Natural History

Museum. They'll know the labels, from Missoni to Juicy Couture. It now has a second location on the Upper East Side. www.berkleygirl.com. (1) 410 Columbus (btwn 79th and 80th sts.). ℭ **212/877-4770.** Subway: B, C to 81st St. (2) 1418 Second Ave. (at 74th St.). ℭ **212/744-9507.** Subway: 6 to 77th St.

Bonne Nuit Does your daughter dream of a pink taffeta party frock? Here's where you can find just the right one. This lingerie shop carries elegant clothes for both girls and boys, adult and children's loungewear, and some beautiful layette items. 30 Lincoln Plaza (at 63rd St.). ℭ **212/489-9730.** Subway: 1 to 66th St./Lincoln Center.

Greenstones ★ Upscale imported kids' clothes, in cuts and fabrics that kids can actually play in. Sizes run from newborn to 12 years (the East Side shops carry up to size 8 only). On the boys' end, it's big on sweaters and corduroys, embracing a kind of yacht-club look (every sweater has a design, it seems)—good for boys who wouldn't be caught dead in the Poindexter outfits sold elsewhere on Madison Avenue. Lots of items are well-nigh irresistible. Greenstones also has two locations on the Upper East Side. (1) 442 Columbus Ave. (at 81st St.). ℭ **212/580-4322.** Subway: B, C to 79th St. (2) 1184 Madison Ave. (btwn 86th and 87th sts.). ℭ **212/427-1665.** Subway: 4, 5, 6 to 86th St. (3) 1410 Second Ave. (at 73rd St.). ℭ **212/794-0530.** Subway: 6 to 68th St./Hunter College.

Karin Alexis ★ Every item in this charming Upper West side boutique is designed by the shop's owner and made right in New York. Sturdily constructed and cut roomy for toddler play, the clothes have a funky, sunny charm. 2587 Broadway (btwn 97th and 98th sts.). ℭ **212/769-9550.** www.karinalexis.com. Subway: 1, 2, 3 to 96th St.

Z'Baby Company ★ Handily located both uptown and down, Z'Baby features hip and casual French and Italian clothes (boys' sizes newborn to 10, girls up to 14) with upscale labels. The dresses have an airy boho flair in styles I'd love to wear myself. (1) 100 W. 72nd St. (at Columbus Ave.). ℭ **212/579-BABY** (579-2229). Subway: B, C, 1, 2, 3 to 72nd St. (2) 996 Lexington Ave. (at 72nd St.). ℭ **212/472-2229.** Subway: 6 to 68th St. (3) 196 Spring St. (btwn Thompson and Sullivan sts.). ℭ **212/431-5436.** Subway: 6 to 68th St.

COMIC BOOKS, TRADING CARDS & COLLECTIBLE FIGURES

All these stores have a wide stock of cards and/or comics, but whether they've got that rare item you're looking for is always a question. If you're really on a quest for something special, call the whole lot until you strike gold. Otherwise, drop in for a browse at which-ever shop you're nearest.

Alex's MVP Cards This friendly neighborhood store specializes in comics and sports cards and wax packs, as well as a decent supply of nonsports toys and supplies. 256 E. 89th St. (at Second Ave.). ℭ **212/831-2273.** Subway: 4, 5, 6 to 86th St.

Chameleon Comics Here you'll find Marvel and DC comics, a wide range of sports cards, and action-figure toys and statues. Closed Sunday. 3 Maiden Lane (btwn Nassau St. and Broadway). ℭ **212/587-1603.** www.chameleoncomics.com. Subway: A, C to Broadway/Nassau St.; 2, 3, 4, 5 to Fulton St.

Cosmic Comics This is a good source for comics, in addition to action figures, non-sports trading cards, T-shirts, models, trade paperbacks, and videos. 10 E. 23rd St. ℭ **212/460-5322.** www.cosmiccomics.com. Subway: 6 to 23rd St.

Forbidden Planet   This store is a valuable source for comics and assorted sci-fi and
fantasy paraphernalia. 840 Broadway (at 13th St.). ℂ 212/473-1576. www.fpnyc.com. Subway:
N, Q, R, W, 4, 5, 6 to 14th St.; L to Union Square.

Gotham City Comics   A wide-ranging stock of comics, sports cards, action figures,
and T-shirts, with some rarities—it's one of those places where collectors could browse
happily for a long time. 796 Lexington Ave. (at 62nd St.), 2nd Floor. ℂ 212/980-0009. Subway:
4, 5, 6 to 59th St.

Gotta Have It   The trove of sports collectibles in the gallery here includes a good stock
of sports cards, including plenty of rarities. It also has rock-'n'-roll and other entertainment memorabilia. Closed Sunday except during Thanksgiving and Christmas holidays.
153 E. 57th St. (btwn Lexington and Third aves.). ℂ 212/750-7900. www.gottahaveit.com. Subway: 6 to 59th St.

Jim Hanley's Universe   Comic books old and new, plus fantasy role-playing games,
can be found here. 4 W. 33rd St. (btwn Fifth Ave. and Broadway). ℂ 212/268-7088. www.jh
universe.com. Subway: B, D, F, N, Q, R, V, W to 34th St./Herald Square.

Kidrobot   Purveying what the store itself describes as "urban vinyl action figures," this
tiny SoHo shop is often packed with kids and slacker hipsters. You'll know your kid will
dig this place if he or she recognizes these product lines: Homies, Kubriks, Dunnys, and
Stifkas. 126 Prince St. (btwn Greene and Wooster sts.). ℂ 212/966-6688. www.kidrobot.com.
Subway: R, W to Prince St.

St. Mark's Comics   Anything comic-related can be bought here, including books,
magazines, action figures, and toys; the shop has its own subculture buzz. www.stmarks
comics.com. (1) 11 St. Mark's Place (btwn Second and Third aves.). ℂ 212/598-9439. Subway: 6
to Astor Place (2) 148 Montague St., Brooklyn. ℂ 718/935-0911. Subway: M, R, 2, 3, 4, 5 to Court
St./Borough Hall.

Toy Tokyo Showroom NYC (Finds)   Amid the grungy hipness of St. Mark's Place, this
fascinating little store specializes in Japanese imports of vinyl figures, sought by connois-
seurs (of which your own progeny may be one). 121 Second Ave. (at 9th St.). ℂ 212/673-5424.
www.toytokyo.com. Subway: 6 to Astor Place.

CRAFTS, MODELS & TRAINS

Bruce Frank (Finds)   For the child who wants to go beyond stringing plastic beads to
attempt some more advanced jewelry making, this snug little shop selling Indonesian art
and antiques carries an absolutely amazing selection of handmade and ethnographic
beads. 215 W. 83rd St. (btwn Broadway and Amsterdam Ave.). ℂ 212/595-3746. www.bruce
frankbeads.com. Subway: 1 to 86th St.

The Craft Studio   The rainforest-themed site for parties has an excellent front section
with lots of crafts kits, art materials, puzzles, and other toys. Walk in and paint on plaster,
wood, or terra-cotta pots. Their private parties (for kids ages 3 and up) have 16 different
craft themes, from doll making to chocolate to PJs and puppets. Closed Sunday July to
August. 1657 Third Ave. (btwn 92nd and 93rd sts.). ℂ 212/831-6626. www.craftstudionyc.com.
Subway: 6 to 96th St.

Games Workshop   Manhattan has three branches of this U.K.-based chain of stores,
selling its own line of character models and hosting elaborate fantasy-game tournaments.
For certain boys, it's a sort of clubhouse. www.gamesworkshop.com. (1) 1457 Third Ave.
(at 83rd St.). ℂ 212/744-1390. Subway: 4, 5, 6 to 86th St. (2) 269 72nd St. (at Amsterdam Ave.).

ℂ 212/362-0726. Subway: 1, 2, 3 to 72nd St. (3) 54 E. 8th St. (at University Place). ℂ 212/982-6314. Subway: A, B, C, D, E, F, V to W. 4th St.

Jan's Hobby Shop ★   This stocked-to-the-rafters shop is a wondrous source for all kinds of wooden boat models—in everything from balsa wood to mahogany—as well as plastic model kits (loads of Revell planes and race cars) and die-cast metal items for collectors. The display cases of military models are awesome. 1435 Lexington Ave. (btwn 93rd and 94th sts.). ℂ 212/861-5075. Subway: 4, 5, 6 to 96th St.

Red Caboose ★   New York's most intense model-railroad shop, the Red Caboose has been selling all gauges and scales of trains since 1942, as well as equipment and supplies desired by modelers. The stock of train and automobile kits is growing all the time, too. Closed Sunday (except during the holiday season). 23 W. 45th St. (btwn Fifth and Sixth aves.); enter the lobby and go downstairs at the back. ℂ 212/575-0155. www.theredcaboose. com. Subway: B, D, F, V to 47th–50th sts./Rockefeller Center.

Trainworld ★   True electric-train fanatics may want to venture out to this huge store for train sets. Note to *Sopranos* fans: The scene where model-train aficionado Bobby Bacala gets whacked was filmed here. Closed Sunday. 751 McDonald Ave., Brooklyn. ℂ 718/436-7072. www.trainworld.com. Subway: F to Ditmas Ave.

DOLLS & DOLLHOUSES

American Girl Place ★   Buying an American Girl doll may be the first serious investment of a girl's life, and it's a sizable expenditure, not to be taken lightly. Whom to choose? Molly, the spunky World War II–era girl with the glasses and pigtails? Victorian Samantha, the rich, lonely orphan in her fur-trimmed cloak? Addy, the runaway black slave? Each of these beautifully made 18-inch dolls has her own story; a series of books written about her; and a dozen or so detailed, historically accurate outfits. American Girl Place—one of only five stores (the others are in Atlanta, Chicago, Dallas, and Los Angeles) where you can buy these dolls in person, rather than by catalog or online—is like a shrine for young doll owners, and many bring their dolls with them to worship here. Besides the historical dolls, other doll lines such as Bitty Babies, Hopscotch School, Angelina Ballerina, and American Girls of Today are displayed, along with books, accessories, and a fair number of clothes for the doll owners themselves. The store also boasts a doll hair salon, a theater, and a usually booked-up **cafe** (p. 118). 609 Fifth Ave. (at 49th St.). ℂ 877/AG-PLACE. www.americangirl.com. Subway: E, V to Fifth Ave./53rd St.; B, D, F, V to 47th–50th sts./Rockefeller Center.

Manhattan Doll House Shop ★   Newly located as a dollhouse boutique in FAO Schwarz, this wonderful shop not only has a truly awesome selection of kits and finished dollhouses, but carries all the furnishings, right down to electrical fixtures. Full-size dolls are also repaired and sold. FAO Schwarz, 767 Fifth Ave. (btwn E. 58th and 59th sts.). ℂ 212/644-9400. www.manhattandollhouse.com. Subway: 6 to 23rd St.

Mary Arnold Toys ★   This top-notch East Side toyshop includes an outstanding doll section—Madame Alexander, Corolle, Götz, and the like. Closed Sunday. 1010 Lexington Ave. (btwn 72nd and 73rd sts.). ℂ 212/744-8510. Subway: 6 to 77th St.

New York Doll Hospital ★   Since 1900, young New Yorkers have climbed the stairs to this musty space bearing their precious dolls and stuffed animals in need of repairs. You can also buy antique and discontinued dolls and kitschy collectibles like a Charlie McCarthy doll, a Howdy Doody, a Daddy Warbucks tie-in from the movie *Annie,* or a

Pee-wee Herman doll. A wonderful jumble of dolls' heads, arms, and legs on the floor
gives the place a slightly Twilight Zone–ish atmosphere. No credit cards are accepted.
Closed Sunday. 787 Lexington Ave. (btwn 61st and 62nd sts.), 2nd Floor. ✆ **212/838-7527.**
Subway: 4, 5, 6 to 59th St.

Tiny Doll House ★   In this small, well-organized shop, rows of perfectly put-together
miniature rooms flank the side walls, while a few empty doll mansions preside regally
over the center of the room. Wallpaper, carpeting, lamps, cutlery—a tasteful selection of
all the tiny furnishings you'll ever need. Before you go inside, warn little would-be customers not to touch, as the staff is somewhat gun-shy about kids breaking the delicate
miniatures. Closed Saturday July to August. 314 E. 78th St. (btwn First and Second aves.).
✆ **212/744-3719.** Subway: 6 to 77th St.

FURNITURE, CRIBS & STROLLERS

ABC Carpet & Home ★   You may not know that this fabulous home-furnishings
store has a children's department, but it does, and it's a doozy. Just don't expect to go
poking around in a bargain bin, because you won't find one here (although it does have
occasional sales). Yes, like much of the rest of ABC's inventory, the kids' stuff is pricey,
but choice. The shop sells hand-painted furniture as well as beautifully crafted wooden
and iron cribs, bed canopies fashioned of vintage saris, sumptuous organic bedding,
whimsical lamps. And toys. 888 Broadway (at 19th St.). ✆ **212/473-5000.** www.abchome.com.
Subway: N, R, 4, 5, 6 to 14th St.

Albee Baby Carriage Co.   This store may be crowded and a little disorganized, but
what these folks don't know about nursery equipment ain't worth knowing. There's
always an unwieldy mother-to-be collapsed in a glider rocker, looking glassy-eyed as she
(and her mother and/or husband) orders a couple thousand dollars' worth of baby
stuff—I wonder how many labors have started here over the years. Closed Sunday. 715
Amsterdam Ave. (at 95th St.). ✆ **212/662-7337.** www.albeebaby.com. Subway: 1, 2, 3 to 96th St.

Baby Depot at Burlington Coat Factory (Value)   Toil up to the third floor of this
discount emporium to find a Toys "R" Us–ish collection of layettes, cribs, strollers, car
seats, and clothing. The prices are fairly low—just don't expect top-of-the-line furnishings for your nursery. 707 Sixth Ave. (btwn 22nd and 23rd sts.). ✆ **212/229-1300.** www.burlington
coatfactory.com. Subway: F, V to 23rd St.

Bellini   If you want to start your infant off with upscale tastes, this pricey baby-furniture
boutique is where to do it. The service can be offhand (unless, of course, you're spending a
bundle), but the look is pretty with an edge of fun, nothing way-out. 1305 Second Ave.
(btwn 68th and 69th sts.). ✆ **212/517-9233.** www.bellini.com. Subway: 6 to 68th St.

Blue Bench ★ (Finds)   This sweet store has an urban/country vibe. Its hand-painted,
antiqued furniture (Little Folk Art and the Jane Keltner Collection), arranged to give the
store a real nursery feel, sets the mood. The store also sells bedding, artwork, and toys,
including a great selection of Jellycat stuffed animals. I always find something here I've
never seen elsewhere. They will also help you conceptualize the design of your kids'
rooms, from floor plan layout to window and door treatments to artwork. 159 Duane St.
(btwn W. Broadway and Hudson sts.). ✆ **212/267-1500.** www.bluebenchnyc.com. Subway: A, C,
E, 1, 2, 3 to Chambers St.

Giggle ★   This complete baby and toddler lifestyle store in SoHo has become an
essential all-purpose stop for hip and happening New York parents ever since it opened

its flagship store in SoHo, with the latest hip and happening brands on display in colorful designer stores (complete with a stroller parking lot). The stores are so stylish and smartly laid out, it's a pleasure to shop here. Look for high-end furniture brands like Oeuf, Stokke, Peg Perego, Cabine—as well as organic cotton clothing and eco-friendly wares. It now has an Upper East Side location as well. www.giggle.com. (1) 120 Wooster St. (btwn Prince and Spring sts.). ✆ 212/334-5817. Subway: R to Prince St. (2) 1033 Lexington Ave. (at 74th St.). ✆ 212/24904249. Subway: 6 to 77th St.

Kids Supply Co. This boutique sells some intriguing children's furniture, featuring warm woods and bold colors and a sophisticated sense of style. Quality stuff, built to withstand children. Closed Sunday July through August. 1343 Madison Ave. (at 94th St.). ✆ 212/426-1200. www.kidssupply.com. Subway: 6 to 96th St.

Little Folks Shop Little Folks sells a solid range of nursery outfittings and strollers—with such stylin' brands as Bugaboo, BOB Strollers, Mutsy, and Quinny—plus layettes and clothes up to size 7. Closed Saturday. 123 E. 23rd St. (btwn Park and Lexington aves.). ✆ 212/982-9669. www.littlefolksnyc.com. Subway: 6 to 23rd St.

Planet Kids ★ Big, bright, and bustling, this Upper East Side source has a wide range of furnishing and paraphernalia for babies and toddlers. It has an Upper West Side location (see contact info below) and is opening a new store near Lincoln Center (193–194 Amsterdam Ave., btwn 68th and 69th sts.). www.planetkidsny.com. (1) 247 E. 86th St. (btwn Third and Second aves.). ✆ 212/426-2040. Subway: 4, 5, 6 to 86th St. (2) 2688 Broadway (at 104th St.). ✆ 212/864-8705. Subway: 1 to 103rd St.

Schneider's ★ This downtown source offers not only nursery essentials but also furniture for kids' and even teenagers' bedrooms, as well as strollers, car seats, and layette must-haves—all at competitive prices. Closed Sunday. 41 W. 25th St. (btwn Sixth Ave. and Broadway). ✆ 212/228-3540. www.schneidersbaby.com. Subway: F, N, R, V, W to 23rd St.

GAMES

Chess Forum ★ Competing head-to-head with the Village Chess Shop right up the street, the Chess Forum is big on chess lessons for kids, along with selling a large variety of exquisite sets for chess, backgammon, cribbage, and dominoes. Celebrity customers include David Lee Roth, Sean Lennon, Yoko Ono, and Harvey Keitel. 219 Thompson St. (btwn 3rd and Bleecker sts.). ✆ 212/475-2369. www.chessforum.com. Subway: A, B, C, D, E, F, V to W. 4th St.

Compleat Strategist ★ This specialist shop stocks a fairly mind-boggling array of games, from chess and backgammon to military simulations and role-playing games, but doesn't neglect board games for the younger set, including some noncompetitive games for nonreaders. Fun for browsing. Closed Sunday. 11 E. 33rd St. (btwn Fifth and Madison aves.). ✆ 212/685-3880. www.compleatstrategist.com. Subway: 6 to 33rd St.

Neutral Ground Along with selling an eclectic array of games, especially role-playing games, this store sponsors Magic the Gathering tournaments, role-playing campaigns, and miniature battles. It's in a new location about 10 blocks farther uptown. 15 W. 37th St. (btwn Fifth and Sixth aves.). ✆ 212/633-1288. www.neutralground.com. Subway: N, R, W, 1 to 28th St.

Village Chess Shop ★ Come to this 36-year-old shop to play or stock up on exotic chess sets, esoteric chess manuals, and a slew of related computer software, as well as clocks for speed chess. In the summer it has chess events in Bryant Park. 230 Thompson St. (btwn 3rd and Bleecker sts.). ✆ 212/475-9580. www.chess-shop.com. Subway: A, B, C, D, E, F, V to W. 4th St.

HAIRCUTS

Cozy's Cuts for Kids   Spanking clean and bright, Cozy's plays videos to keep kids happy in the chair—which may be a regular barber chair or a yellow Jeep. Après-cut, the little ones are rewarded with lollipops, balloons, and favors—all the usual bribes. Cozy's has enough quality toys to double as a toy store, which unfortunately means you've got to ward off toy requests when you come in only for a haircut, but what the hey, at least you have no trouble getting the kids in the door. Closed Sunday in summer. www.cozys cutsforkids.com. (1) 1125 Madison Ave. (at 84th St.). ⓒ **212/744-1716.** Subway: 4, 5, 6 to 86th St. (2) 1416 Second Ave. (at 74th St.). ⓒ **212/585-2699.** Subway: 6 to 77th St. (3) 448 Amsterdam Ave. (btwn 81st and 82nd sts.). ⓒ **212/579-2600.** Subway: 1 to 79th St.

Doodle Doo's   This pleasant downtown store is both a kids' haircutting salon and a toy store. The little ones can sit in a race car or a boat (or a regular barber's chair) and watch their favorite videos while the expert cutters work fast and keep the mood upbeat. 543 Hudson St. (near Perry St.). ⓒ **212/627-3667.** www.doodledoos.com. Subway: 1 to Christopher St.

Kids Cuts   In its new location inside Homefront Kids, this salon still cuts hair well at reasonable prices. Closed Monday. 202 E. 29th St. (at Third Ave.). ⓒ **212/684-5252.** www.kids cutsny.com. Subway: 6 to 33rd St.

Kidville   There's a multitude of classes and activities for little kids at this Upper West Side hangout, but even if you haven't registered in a class, you can still drop by for a haircut. Kidville also has a salon at its Upper East Side location (163 E. 84th St. btwn Third and Lex aves.; ⓒ **212/772-8435**). 466 Columbus Ave. (btwn 82nd and 83rd sts.). ⓒ **212/362-7792.** www.kidville.com. Subway: 1 to 79th St.

Whipper Snippers   Patient, cheerful haircutters ply their scissors downtown at this bright and busy salon/toyshop, run by savvy neighborhood parents. 106 Reade St. (btwn W. Broadway and Church St.). ⓒ **212/227-2600.** www.whippersnippers.com. Subway: A, C, E, 1, 2, 3 to Chambers St.

JEWELRY & ACCESSORIES

Claire's   Costume jewelry, hair doodads, and a grab bag of slumber-party-worthy gift items make these bouncy chain shops a hit with 'tweens. www.claires.com. (1) 2267 Broadway (btwn 81st and 82nd sts.). ⓒ **212/877-2655.** Subway: 1 to 79th St. (2) 1385 Broadway (btwn 37th and 38th sts.). ⓒ **212/302-6616.** Subway: B, D, F, N, Q, R, V, W to 34th St. (3) 89 South Street Seaport (2nd Floor). ⓒ **212/566-0193.** Subway: 2, 3, 4, 5 to Fulton St.; A, C to Broadway/ Nassau St.

GirlProps (Value)   This groovy costume jewelry shop in SoHo is where you can pick up tons of plastic adornments for a buck or two. www.girlprops.com. 153 Prince St. (btwn W. Broadway and Thompson St.). ⓒ **212/505-7615.** Subway: R, W to Prince St.

Ricky's (Value)   For hair ornaments, youthful makeup, and great Halloween costumes, Ricky's has a definite cool quotient, especially with teens and 'tweens. Ricky's has 17 locations in Manhattan; the following are just a sampling. Check the website to see if there's one near you. www.rickysnyc.com. (1) 144 E. 8th St. (btwn Mercer and Greene sts.). ⓒ **212/254-5247.** Subway: N, R, W to 8th St. (2) 375 Broadway (btwn Franklin and White sts.). ⓒ **212/ 925-5490.** Subway: 1 to Franklin St. (3) 590 Broadway (btwn Houston and Prince sts.). ⓒ **212/226- 5552.** Subway: R, W to Prince St.; 6 to Spring St. (4) 466 Sixth Ave. (btwn 11th and 12th sts.). ⓒ **212/ 924-3401.** Subway: 1,2 3 to 14th St. (5) 383 Fifth Ave. (btwn 35th and 36th sts.). ⓒ **212/481-6701.** Subway: B, D, F, N, Q, R, V, W to 34th St. (6) 1189 First Ave. (at 64th St.). ⓒ **212/879-8361.** Subway:

6 to 68th St. (7) 112 W. 72nd St. (btwn Broadway and Columbus Ave.). © **212/769-3678.** Subway: 1, 2, 3 to 72nd St. (8) 1380 Third Ave. (btwn 78th and 79th sts.). © **212/737-7724.** Subway: 6 to 77th St. (9) 472 Columbus Ave. (at 83rd St.). © **212/724-4590.** Subway: 1 to 86th St.

MAGIC & GAGS

Abracadabra ★   Harry Potter fans can indulge some serious fantasies at this ever-growing magic superstore, so large it even has a stage and a cafe on-site. Its several thousand feet of space are stocked with every magic trick, costume, and gag under the sun. Warning to parents of skittish youngsters: Some of the masks on display are extremely lifelike and gruesome as all get-out. Closed Monday. 19 W. 21st St. (btwn Fifth and Sixth aves.). © **212/627-5194.** www.abracadabrasuperstore.com. Subway: F, V to 23rd St.

Tannen's Magic ★   Amateur or professional, magicians shop here, and the array of equipment is impressive. In the interests of developing future magicians, Tannen's also hosts ongoing lectures and classes in New York and runs a Magic Camp (for ages 12–20) in Pennsylvania (David Blaine is a former grad). Magic is serious business here. Closed Sunday. 45 W. 34th St., Suite 608 (btwn Fifth and Sixth aves.). © **212/929-4500.** www.tannens.com. Subway: B, D, F, N, Q, R, V, W to 34th St.

MUSIC

Bleecker Bob's Golden Oldies ★ (Finds   Like a scene out of the movie *High Fidelity,* this famous Village hangout still has bins full of vinyl, with some very obscure albums, and staff who really know their arcane music trivia. Older kids who are into esoterica and nostalgia might dig it. 118 W. 3rd St. (btwn Sixth Ave. and MacDougal St.). © **212/475-9677.** www.bleeckerbobs.com. Subway: A, B, C, D, E, F, V to W. 4th St.

Colony Music Center ★ (Finds   Nobody ever sells sheet music anymore—well, nobody except for Colony, which has a mind-blowing assortment of song sheets and scores for your budding musician, including jazz, rock, and every Broadway show tune ever written. Even better, you'll be rubbing shoulders with real professional musicians as you browse the narrow aisles. The huge selection of easy piano books is great for beginners, and—who knew?—it's also the world's largest karaoke dealer. 1619 Broadway (at 49th St.). © **212/265-2050.** www.colonymusic.com. Subway: 1 to 50th St.

Guitar Center   Manhattan's only location of this national music chain is a two-story emporium selling guitars, drums, organs, the works. It's very user-friendly and a very cool place to be when a serious musician stops in to sample the wares. 25 W. 14th St. (btwn Fifth and Sixth aves.). © **212/463-7500.** www.guitarcenter.com. Subway: F, V to W. 14th St.

House of Oldies (Finds   Like Bleecker Bob's (see above), the House of Oldies prides itself on hard-to-find vintage recordings, especially 45s and LPs. If your kids don't know what a "record" is, bring them here for a history lesson. Closed Sunday and Monday. 35 Carmine St. (btwn Bleecker and Bedford sts.). © **212/243-0500.** www.houseofoldies.com. Subway: A, B, C, D, E, F, V to W. 4th St.

Manny's Music ★   In business since 1935 and located on Midtown's Music Row, Manny's is one store that welcomes kids to fiddle around on the instruments for sale. 156 W. 48th St. (btwn Sixth and Seventh aves.). © **212/819-0576.** www.mannysmusic.com. Subway: B, D, F, V to 47th–50th sts./Rockefeller Center.

Matt Umanov Guitars ★   Unlike what it calls the "supermarket-style music stores," this intimate shop has been selling guitars—and only guitars (oh, and a few mandolins, banjos, and ukuleles)—in the Village since 1965. Check out its selection of gorgeous

vintage guitars. 273 Bleecker St. (btwn Sixth and Seventh aves.). ✆ 212/675-2157. www.umanov
guitars.com. Subway: A, B, C, D, E, F, V to W. 4th St.

Virgin Megastore   Everybody's favorite hip Brit tycoon Richard Branson moved into Times Square in a big way with this three-story megamart for recorded music—along with a bookstore, cafe, and movieplex. The music selection is good and deep, and there are lots of listening posts around so you can sample the sounds before you buy. Dig the weird smoke-blowing bronze facade of the Union Square branch. www.virginmegastore. com. (1) 1540 Broadway (at 45th St.). ✆ 212/921-1020. Subway: N, Q, R, S, W, 1, 2, 3, 7 to 42nd St./ Times Square. (2) 52 E. 14th St. (at Park Ave.). ✆ 212/598-4666. Subway: N, Q, R, W, 4, 5, 6 to 14th St.; L to Union Square.

SHOES

East Side Kids   Free popcorn is dispensed to shoe-shopping kids, which means the place looks like a pigsty by the end of the day. But the range of shoes is wide, from chic to totally playground-friendly. Closed Sunday. 1298 Madison Ave. (btwn 92nd and 93rd sts.). ✆ 212/360-5000. www.eastsidekidsshoes.com. Subway: 6 to 96th St.

Harry's Shoes for Kids ★   The bustling West Side shoe store finally spun off its children's shoe operation into a separate store up the street. It's a sweet place, with a great selection of quality shoes. Broadway (btwn 83rd and 84th sts.). ✆ 212/874-2034. www.harrys- shoes.com. Subway: 1 to 86th St.

Ibiza Kidz   This Village kids' boutique sells a terrific collection of shoes from newborn through women's sizes, as well as books and stuffed animals. The stock shows real flair, with top brands like Primigi, Naturino, Geox, Umi, and Saucony. 61 Fourth Ave. (btwn 9th and 10th sts.). ✆ 212/228-7990 or 212/375-9984. www.ibizakidz.com. Subway: N, R, W to 8th St.

Lester's ★   This all-purpose children's clothing store provides one-stop shopping with a full-service shoe department in the back. 1534 Second Ave. (at 80th St.). ✆ 212/734-9292. www.lestersnyc.com. Subway: 6 to 77th St.

Little Eric Shoes ★   High style is the watchword here—get your 4-year-old shod here if you want to wow the admissions officer at your kindergarten interview. Yes, they've got plain patent leather Mary Janes and classic penny loafers in peewee sizes, but also cowboy boots, beautiful Italian brands, and other trendy styles. 1118 Madison Ave. (at 83rd St.). ✆ 212/717-1513. Subway: 4, 5, 6 to 86th St.

Naturino   This spare, chic boutique is the prime source for imported children's shoes by Naturino, Moschino, and Oilily. Closed Sunday July to August. 1184 Madison Ave. (btwn 86th and 87th sts.). ✆ 212/427-0679. Subway: 4, 5, 6 to 86th St.

The Shoe Garden ★ Finds   This charming little store has great styles, with brands from Naturino and Primigi to Geox, Merrell, and Ecco, and a helpful staff. 152 W. 10th St. (btwn Sixth and Seventh aves.). ✆ 212/427-0679. www.shoegardennyc.com. Subway: 1, 9 to Christopher St.

Shoofly ★   A whimsical collection of designer hats for kids hangs from tree branches poking out of one wall; low shelves, bins, and steamer trunks overflow with an assort- ment of shoes, sandals, socks, mittens, hair bows, belts, and ties, running the gamut from goofy to glam. It's always fun shopping here, even if you don't buy. The prices aren't outlandish, but the sense of style is—just what little New Yorkers need to look really cool. 42 Hudson St. (btwn Duane and Thomas sts.). ✆ 212/406-3270. www.shooflynyc.com. Subway: 1, 2, 3 to Chambers St.

A World of Museum Shops

New York City museums have really excellent gift shops, often selling items for children that you can't find anywhere else. Some are so good, we shop there without visiting the museum at all (and you don't have to pay admission to hit the shops). So when you're out and about in New York City, don't forget the following wonderful museum boutiques (see chapter 6 for more details about these and other NYC museums). Note that most make sure to stock lots of inexpensive impulse-buy items, knowing full well how the gift-shop bribe works for families.

The renowned gift shop at the **Metropolitan Museum of Art** (1000 Fifth Ave. at 82nd St.; ☎ 212/535-7710; closed Mon) is filled with great gifts, books, toys, and games. The large children's department on the upper level includes beautiful books, craft kits, coloring books, art materials, dolls, puzzles, and games. Echoing the Met's great arms and armor galleries, there are loads of toy knights here, as well as toy Roman legionnaires and charioteers (in tribute to the vast classical art galleries) and Egyptian trinkets (tying into the mummies on display).

Farther north along the Upper East Side's Museum Mile, three other excellent choices are the **Cooper-Hewitt National Design Museum** (2 E. 91st St. at Fifth Ave.; ☎ 212/849-8300; closed Mon), which offers some very clever toys and books in a gorgeous stately home setting; the **Jewish Museum** (1109 Fifth Ave. at 92nd St.; ☎ 212/423-3200; closed Sat), a super source for children's books about Judaism as well as toys, games, and puzzles (plus the best dreidel selection in town); and **The Museum of the City of New York** (1220 Fifth Ave. at 103rd St.; ☎ 212/534-1672; www.mcny.org; closed Mon), which has a pleasant selection of toys and books, in line with its excellent toy galleries inside.

On the Upper West Side, the intelligent toys and books sold at the **Children's Museum of Manhattan** (212 W. 83rd St. btwn Broadway and Amsterdam Ave.; ☎ 212/721-1234; www.cmom.org; closed Mon in summer, Mon–Tues during the school year) never fail to delight. Some of the stock features tie-ins to special exhibits, but there's always a wide range of wholesome, educational-yet-fun items for kids 10 and under. At the nearby **American Museum of Natural History** (Central Park West at 79th St.; ☎ 212/769-5100; www. amnh.org; open daily), you'll have to pay admission to visit most of the gift

Tip Top Kids ★ Ⓥalue   Bright, cheerful, and relaxed, this children's annex to Tip Top Shoes has a vibe similar to Harry's Shoes (see above). Here the staff handles children with good humor, and the selection offers quality shoes at fair prices. Brands like Elefanten, Aster, Timberland, Sperry, and Bass, as well as Stride Rite and Adidas are popular here. 149 W. 72nd St. (btwn Broadway and Columbus Ave.). ☎ 212/874-1004. www.tiptopshoes.com. Subway: 1, 2, 3 to 72nd St.

Trust Fund Babies   If you can get past the obnoxious name, step into this handsome Nolita store, with its ultrasoft knitwear for babies and toddlers. Nice indeed, but it's the shops, with the exception of the Planetarium Shop near the West 81st Street entrance. If you're inside the museum anyway, though, you'll find an impressive array of educational toys, games, stuffed animals, and nature books in the main shop near the Central Park West entrance; smaller boutiques tucked around the museum may be geared to special exhibitions or particular interests.

If you're in Midtown, a trio of museums along West 53rd Street between Fifth and Sixth avenues offer a fun shopping diversion for kids: the **Museum of Modern Art** (11 W. 53rd St.; ✆ **212/708-9400;** www.moma.org; closed Tues) and the **American Folk Art Museum** (45 W. 53rd St.; ✆ **212/265-1040;** www. folkartmuseum.org; open daily). The MoMA shop is famous for its art books, cool games and puzzles, and visually appealing *objets,* and the narrow little gallery at the folk-art museum has a small but brilliant selection of things that will strike kids' fancy. The **Museum of Arts and Design** (2 Columbus Circle; ✆ **212/956-3535;** www.madmuseum.org; open daily) will be ensconced in its new Columbus Circle location by the time you read this, but should continue to sell such nifty gifts as handmade baseballs imprinted with NYC street maps or the *New York Times* crossword puzzle.

Downtown, head to the **Rubin Museum of Art** (150 W. 17th St.; ✆ **212/620-5000;** www.rmanyc.org; closed Tues), which has a wonderful gift shop specializing in items from the Himalayas, from a fantastic Nepalese wool tiger rug ($750)—every kid's room needs one—to unique toys, books, and games.

Up in the Bronx, the **New York Botanical Garden** (Bronx River Pkwy., at Fordham Rd.; ✆ **718/817-8700;** www.nybg.org) has a fabulous store with a worthy kids' section, where you can find a good assortment of Thomas the Tank Engine toys, kids' gardening sets, Indonesian crocheted hats, games, books, and musical instruments.

Finally, some of the city's best places for stuffed animals are the gift shops at the various zoos. While you might not go to the Bronx or Prospect Park just to visit the zoos' boutiques, the one at the **Central Park Zoo** (in Central Park, near the park entrance at Fifth Ave. and 64th St.; ✆ **212/439-6500;** open daily) is incredibly handy, displaying even more plush species than the zoo's live ones. Again, it's outside the admission barriers, so anyone can walk in.

children's shoes you've come for—tiny beaded Moroccan-inspired shoes of green or burnt orange, embedded with jewels—some even with genie-style pointed toes! 239 Elizabeth St. (btwn Houston and Prince sts.). ✆ **212/219-3600.** B, D, F, V to Broadway-Lafayette.

SHOWER & BABY GIFTS

Tiffany & Co. ★ Wanna score points? A silver spoon, rattle, teething ring, or baby cup from Tiffany's is still the classy way to celebrate a new arrival, and no new parent minds duplicates of these classics. Get the spoon or cup engraved for an extra touch; you can do it all by phone or online, though visiting this fabled store is usually a pleasure. All except the cup are under $100, so why not go for it? A child is born only once. 727 Fifth Ave. (at 56th St.). ☏ 212/755-8000. www.tiffany.com. Subway: N, R, W to Fifth Ave./59th St.

SOFTWARE & ELECTRONIC GAMES

Electronics Boutique/Game Stop   Racks full of computer software and accessories, as well as those Game Boy, PlayStation 2, and Xbox games kids think they can't live without. The staff make it their business to know about the latest hot games, even if it means steering you away from a rip-off. Our family makes a supply stop here at least once a month. www.ebgames.com. (1) 30 Rockefeller Center, concourse level. ☏ 212/765-3857. Subway: B, D, F, V to 47th–50th sts./Rockefeller Center. (2) 901 Sixth Ave. (at 33rd St.). ☏ 212/564-4156. Subway: B, D, F, N, R, V to 33rd St. (3) 1282 Broadway (at 33rd St.). ☏ 212/967-9070. Subway: B, D, F, N, Q, R, V, W to 34th St. (4) 1470 Third Ave. (at 83rd St.). ☏ 212/288-5370. Subway: 4, 5, 6 to 86th St. (5) 128 E. 86th St. (btwn Park and Lexington aves.). ☏ 212/423-1844. Subway: 4, 5, 6 to 86th St. (6) 2330 Broadway (btwn 84th and 85th sts.). ☏ 917/441-4160. Subway: 1, 2, 3 to 86th St. (7) 2764 Broadway (at 106th St.). ☏ 212/864-4292. Subway: 1 to 103rd St. (8) 251 W. 125th St. (btwn Seventh and Eighth aves.). ☏ 212/749-7434. Subway: 1 to 125th St. (9) 324 First Ave. (at 19th St.). ☏ 212/995-0085. Subway: L, N, Q, R, W, 4, 5, 6 to 14th St./Union Square. (10) 107 E. 14th St. ☏ 646/602-1483. Subway: N, Q, R, W, 4, 5, 6 to 14th St.; L to Union Square. (11) 743 Broadway (btwn 7th and 8th sts.). ☏ 212/979-7678. Subway: 6 to Astor Place; N, R, W to 8th St. (12) 687 Broadway (btwn W. 3rd and W. 4th sts.). ☏ 212/473-6571. Subway: N, R, W to 8th St. (13) Pier 17 at South Street Seaport, 2nd Floor. ☏ 212/227-1945. Subway: 2, 3, 4, 5 to Fulton St.; A, C to Broadway/Nassau St.

SPORTS STUFF

Blades Board & Skate   In-line skaters and skateboarders gear up at this chain of specialty stores, where you can have your own board custom-built for $500 or so. Get your helmets and kneepads here as well. Rentals are available. See chapter 8 for skateboarding info. www.blades.com. (1) 120 W. 72nd St. (btwn Broadway and Columbus Ave.). ☏ 212/787-3911. Subway: B, C, 1, 2, 3 to 72nd St. (2) 659 Broadway (at Bleecker St.). ☏ 212/477-7350. Subway: B, D, F, V to Broadway/Lafayette St.

Eastern Mountain Sports   This place is big on camping gear and outdoor wear, along with equipment for climbing walls—the ideal place to buy a sleeping bag that doesn't have Mickey Mouse or Batman all over the lining. 591 Broadway (at Houston St.). ☏ 212/966-8730. www.ems.com. Subway: B, D, F, V to Broadway/Lafayette St.

Mets Official Clubhouse Shop   Mets fans stock up on blue-and-orange team paraphernalia and memorabilia here. You can buy game tickets, too. Let's go, Mets! 11 W. 42nd St. (btwn Fifth and Sixth aves.). ☏ 212/768-9534. Subway: B, D to 42nd St.

NBA Store   This three-story player in the Fifth Avenue Parade of Theme Stores celebrates hoop dreams in a big way, with lots of gleaming blond hardwood floors, high ceilings, and fun b-ball–themed merchandise. The jerseys in stock show a decided preference for New York–area teams (Knicks, Nets, Liberty), but there's plenty for fans of all stripes. The on-site cafe is reasonably priced and offers burgers, chicken fingers, and shakes—your usual arena food. 666 Fifth Ave. (btwn 52nd and 53rd sts.). ☏ 212/515-6221. www.nba.com/nycstore. Subway: E, V to Fifth Ave./53rd St.

Niketown   This glitzy temple to sports and sneakers is more of a museum/attraction than a place to buy shoes, with several interactive stations where kids can measure their feet, test their reach and reflexes, and generally try to be like Mike (or Tiger these days). **257**

6 E. 57th St. (btwn Fifth and Madison aves.). ℭ **212/891-6453.** Subway: N, R, W to Fifth Ave./59th St.

Paragon Sports Paragon is good for sports clothing and total gear, including lots of camping equipment, ski stuff, and a golf department with a tiny putting green. It has a good shoe selection on the bottom floor. 867 Broadway (at 18th St.). ℭ **212/255-8036.** www. paragonsports.com. Subway: N, Q, R, W, 4, 5, 6 to 14th St.; L to Union Square.

Princeton Ski Shop Large, bright, and modern, this ski-equipment shop has a great selection of gear for all members of the family. Some price tags run high, but this is *skiing*, after all—you'll pay a lot more if you wait until you get to the resort to buy those goggles, gloves, and parkas. 21 E. 22nd St. (btwn Broadway and Park Avenue South). ℭ **212/228-4400.** Subway: N, R, W, 6 to 23rd St.

Scandinavian Ski and Sports Shop (Finds) The array of quality ski equipment and clothing here is huge, and the ladies really know the meaning of service. There's a decent stock of cycling, camping, and tennis gear, too. Look for good end-of-season sales. Closed Sunday. 16 E. 55th St. (btwn Fifth and Madison aves.). ℭ **212/757-8524.** Subway: F to 57th St.

Yankees Official Clubhouse Shop Bronx Bomber fans can indulge their mer-chandise-buying addictions here. Also a good source for tickets. (1) 393 Fifth Ave. (btwn 36th and 37th sts.). ℭ **212/685-4693.** Subway: 6 to 33rd St. (2) 110 E. 59th St. (btwn Park and Lexington aves.). ℭ **212/758-7844.** Subway: 4, 5, 6 to 59th St. (3) 745 Seventh Ave. (at 49th St.). ℭ **212/391-0360.** Subway: T to 50th St. (4) 294 W. 42nd St. (Times Square). ℭ **212/768-9555.** Sub-way: N, Q, R, S, W, 1, 2, 3, 7, 9 to 42nd St./Times Square; A, C, E to 42nd St./Port Authority. (5) 8 Fulton St., South Street Seaport. ℭ **212/514-7182.** Subway: 2, 3, 4, 5 to Fulton St.

TOYS, GIFTS & GADGETS

Note: The Upper West Side institution **Penny Whistle Toys,** opened by Meredith Brokaw (Tom's wife) in 1978, closed for good in June 2008.

A Time for Children ★ This Upper West Side store has lots of good reasons to stop in, among them the top selection of toys, including giant *Good Night Moon* puzzles and Paddington Bear dolls, as well as Hanna Anderson baby and toddler clothes. But the best reason to shop here is because 100% of the profits go to the Children's Aid Society, a charitable organization that has helped out underprivileged city kids for more than 150 years. 506 Amsterdam Ave. (btwn 84th and 85th sts.). ℭ **212/580-8202.** www.atimeforchildren. org. Subway: 1, 9 to 86th St.

Alphabets The East Village sensibility of this wacky gift-a-torium translates well to more mainstream neighborhoods; central to the concept is lots of campy kids' stuff—Etch A Sketch and Mr. Potato Head, yes, but also some truly goofball stuff like a chess set with the Simpson family (Homer and Bart, that is)—which is probably bought by as many adults as children. Loads of one-of-a-kind T-shirts abound. www.alphabetsnyc.com. (1) 115 Ave. A (at 7th St.). ℭ **212/475-7250.** Subway: 6 to Astor Place. (2) 47 Greenwich Ave. (btwn Sixth and Seventh aves.). ℭ **212/229-2966.** Subway: 1, 2, 3 to 14th St. (3) 2284 Broadway (btwn 82nd and 83rd sts.). ℭ **212/579-5702.** Subway: 1 to 79th St.

Balloon Saloon All your balloon needs can be met in this store—which does a brisk business supplying balloons and party decor to Manhattan's movers and shakers—but it's also crammed with winning toys, from retro Bozo Bopper punching bags to games, puzzles, and gag gifts like fake moustaches. 133 W. Broadway (near Duane St.). ℭ **800/540-0749.** www.balloonsaloon.com. Subway: A, C, E, 1, 2, 3 to Chambers St.

SHOPPING WITH YOUR KIDS

10

SHOPPING A TO Z

Boomerang Toys ★ This award-winning TriBeCa toy store is a wonder, its shelves crammed with the latest and greatest stuff for kids from baby to 'tweens. It's the official flagship store for Bruder Trucks and has a good selection of toy trains, including Thomas and Brio. It has quality dollhouses, castles, tricycles, stuffed toys—the works. A second location is inside the World Financial Center in Battery Park City. www.boomerangtoys. com. (1) 173 W. Broadway (at Worth St.). ✆ **212/226-7650.** Subway: 1, 9 to Franklin St. (2) 2 World Financial Center, 225 Liberty St. ✆ **212/786-3011.** Subway: A, C, E, 1, 2, 3 to Chambers St.

Build-A-Bear Workshop The two-story flagship location of this mall-based chain is quite impressive—in fact, it's the biggest Build-A-Bear Workshop in the whole world. It has a number of only-in-New-York items as well as a full line of international bear outfits and accessories. Both boys and girls have a blast choosing a limp bear form and seeing it stuffed right before their eyes (not to mention getting to put a red satin heart inside, or even a voice box with their own recorded message on it). Downstairs offers a party room and the cheery **Eat with Your Bear Hands Café**—not a bad bet if you've been shopping for hours and couldn't get a reservation at American Girl Place just up the street. 565 Fifth Ave. (at 46th St.). ✆ **212/871-7080.** www.buildabearworkshop.com. Subway: S, 4, 5, 6, 7 to 42nd St./Grand Central.

Character Don't be confused by the front of this store, which looks more like a sleek design studio than a children's toy store. Head to the back for the real treasures. If you love Tintin, Babar, and Elmer the elephant, you'll find a trove of goodies, from a full collection of books to toys, figurines, and classic Tintin posters. 19 Prince St. (near Elizabeth St.). ✆ **212/274-1566.** Subway: R to Prince St.

Children's General Store This charming toy boutique is a welcome addition to the shopping at Grand Central Terminal, offering some unusual handmade and imported toys you won't see in most other stores. The emphasis is on well-made toys with a certain imagination-sparking value. (1) Grand Central Station, Lexington Passage. ✆ **212/682-0004.** Subway: S, 4, 5, 6, 7 to 42nd St./Grand Central. (2) 168 E. 91st St. (btwn Lexington and Third aves.). ✆ **212/426-4479.** Subway: 4, 5, 6 to 86th St.

The Conran Shop ★ ⒻFindsⒻ I had no idea that the midtown furniture and design store of British designer Terence Conran even had a children's section, but it does, and it's fabulous. The selection of toys here is simply first-rate, with impeccable sourcing. You can buy giant whale and fish mobiles from Belgian stylist Miriam de Loor; 3-D puzzles designed by sculptor Alexander Caldor for his grandchildren in the 1920s; retro toys such as windup robots or mailbox banks; toys and puzzles from venerated French toy maker Vilac; darling crocheted toadstools by Anne-Claire Petit; real foosball tables; and even a mint-green mini-Vespa ($325). Bridgemarket, 407 E. 59th St. (at First Ave.). ✆ **866/755-9079.** www.conranusa.com. Subway: 4, 5, 6 to 59th St.

Daily 2.3.5 ★ This is where you find the kind of "where'd you get *that?*" toys and goofy gifts that convince the folks back home that you have traveled somewhere truly cool and wondrous. The collection at this delightful Nolita shop is eclectic, to say the least, with lots of post-retro windup toys, gag gifts (spy glasses and fake noses), light-up tops, and teeny-tiny Horner harmonicas—even freeze-dried astronaut ice-cream sandwiches. Wow! 235 Elizabeth St. (btwn Prince and Houston sts.). ✆ **212/334-9728.** Subway: N, R to Prince St.; B, D to Broadway/Lafayette.

Didis Children's Boutique On cool, spare, back-lit white shelves, you'll find beautiful, almost museum-quality imported toys. Closed Sunday in summer. 1196 Madison Ave. (btwn 88th and 89th sts.). ✆ **212/860-4001.** www.didis.com. Subway: 4, 5, 6 to 86th St.

Dinosaur Hill ★   Selling imported toys, mobiles, dollhouses, wooden blocks, art supplies, and puppets—notably an extensive line of handmade marionettes—this airy East
Village shop also has a battery of under-$2 stuff so no child will have to leave empty-
handed. 306 E. 9th St. (near Second Ave.). ℂ 212/473-5850. www.dinosaurhill.com. Subway: 6
to Astor Place.

Doodle Doo's   This downtown store is both a kids' haircutting salon and a toy store.
The toy collection is rich, with lots of the current usual suspects: Melissa & Doug toys
and puzzles, Kettler tricycles, and books galore. 543 Hudson St. (near Perry St.). ℂ 212/627-
3667. www.doodledoos.com. Subway: 1 to Christopher St.

E.A.T. Gifts   Next door to the absurdly overpriced E.A.T. cafe, this gift store isn't really
designed for kids—it's crowded and there's an annoying "don't touch" factor—but somehow, every time we wander in, there's something we find we can't live without. Little gift
books, bath toys, tiny shaped soaps and crayons, chocolate novelties—it's like quicksand
for the reluctant shopper. 1062 Madison Ave. (btwn 80th and 81st sts.). ℂ 212/861-2544. Subway: 6 to 77th St.

FAO Schwarz ★   Risen like a phoenix from the ashes of corporate bankruptcy, this
Manhattan toy mecca has reemerged as a sleek, streamlined multistory temple of conspicuous consumption. The focus is on larger-than-life stuffed animals, collectible Bar-
bies and other dolls, antique toys, elegant dress-up clothes, top-of-the-line art kits,
high-end electronic cars and robots (what kid doesn't want his or her own mini-Mer-
cedes?), and a panoply of other toys you won't find at any mall. Downstairs is a spacious
baby and toddler section, with some yummy clothes and children's books. Costumed
characters, doormen dressed as toy soldiers, story hours, and a soda shoppe add to the
fairy-dust ambience. Even if you don't intend to buy, stroll around and gawk to
your heart's content; it's one of those only-in-Manhattan experiences your kids will
remember. 767 Fifth Ave. (at 58th St.). ℂ 212/644-9400. www.faoschwarz.com. Subway: N, R, W
to Fifth Ave.

Giggle ★   This bright and colorful baby and toddler lifestyle store hits all the hot
buttons of the modern urban parent. The designer furniture is clean-lined and thoroughly 21st century; the clothes are smart and fashioned of natural materials (not a stitch
of spandex); toys are eco-friendly and educational; and bedding, feeding, bathing, and
changing supplies represent the latest in functional chic. All of which, of course, comes
at a price. But you can find some nifty toys here, including cool minimalist dollhouses,
Manhattan Toy infant playthings, organic cotton plushies, Kettler trikes, and environmentally friendly wooden toys. www.giggle.com. (1) 120 Wooster St. (btwn Prince and
Spring sts.). ℂ 212/334-5817. Subway: R to Prince St. (2) 1033 Lexington Ave. (at 74th St.). ℂ 212/
24904249. Subway: 6 to 77th St.

Hammacher Schlemmer ★   You want gadgets? They've got gadgets—high-quality
gadgets to do everything under the sun, including some things you've never thought of
doing before. Older kids and adults get a kick out of the unique and ingenious products,
and don't worry if most items are way out of your price range—the ratio of browsers to
buyers is usually pretty high. Closed Sunday. 147 E. 57th St. (btwn Lexington and Third
aves.). ℂ 212/421-9000. www.hammacher.com. Subway: 4, 5, 6 to 59th St.

Homboms (Finds)   Crowded into this storefront is a deep selection of stuff to play
with, best for its arts-and-crafts materials, puzzles, board games, PLAYMOBILs, and
other small-motor activities. It's definitely a place that rewards a long, slow browse. 1500
First Ave. (btwn 78th and 79th sts.). ℂ 212/717-5300. Subway: 6 to 77th St.

Ibiza Kidz ★   This Village kids boutique has a tip-top selection of toys, as well as books and stuffed animals. You can find Manhattan Toy products for the under-1 set, as well as charming items from Folkmanis puppets, Melissa & Doug, and Radio Flyer. 61 Fourth Ave. (btwn 9th and 10th sts.). ℂ **212/228-7990** or 212/375-9984. www.ibizakidz.com. Subway: N, R, W to 8th St.

Kidding Around ★   This shop carries top imports and creative toys in a stuffed-to-the-gills space. If you can't find that special something anywhere else, odds are you'll find it here, in spades. 60 W. 15th St. (btwn Fifth and Sixth aves.). ℂ **212/645-6337.** www.kidding aroundnyc.com. Subway: N, Q, R, W, 4, 5, 6 to 14th St.; L to Union Square.

Kid O ★   This superb shop has a wonderful selection of creative preschool toys, blocks, puzzles, and books chosen with great care and ecological sensitivity; it's become a downtown fixture in no time. 123 W. 10th St. (btwn Sixth and Greenwich aves.). ℂ **212/366-KIDO** (366-5436). www.kidonyc.com. Subway: 1, 2, 3, 9 to 14th St.

Little Airplane ★   The studio of Little Airplane Productions, home of *The Wonder Pets* and other hot kiddie shows, has a charming shop on-site that sells toys, Wonder Pets paraphernalia, and collectibles in a historic South Street Seaport structure. Be sure to ask about the studio tours, held twice daily on Tuesdays and Thursdays ($10 per person). 207 Front St. (btwn Beekman and Fulton sts.), 2nd Floor. ℂ **212/965-8999.** Subway: 2, 3, 4, 5 to Fulton St.

Mary Arnold Toys ★   Mary Arnold's is intelligently laid out with nooks where children can fiddle and browse without clogging the aisles. Quality toys—LEGOs, BRIOs, PLAYMOBILs—many shelves of board games, lots of dress-up costumes, and a very impressive doll department make this a never-fail destination to satisfy kids of any age or interest. Closed Sunday. 1010 Lexington Ave. (btwn 72nd and 73rd sts.). ℂ **212/744-8510.** Subway: 6 to 77th St.

Robot Village ★   This interactive little store tucked away on an Upper West Side side street makes a great play date or party destination; kids can gather around worktables and create their own robots, from a number of age-appropriate materials, or stage battles with the robots they have already created. Everything from books to windup toys to robot kits to collectible robots to batteries—it's pretty much the robot capital of Manhattan. Closed Monday. 252 W. 81st St. (btwn Broadway and West End Ave.). ℂ **212/799-7626.** www.robot village.com. Subway: 1 to 79th St.

The Scholastic Store ★   Lots of quality educational toys as well as book tie-ins can be found in this airy, bright store downstairs from the publisher's SoHo offices. There's even room to play with them, and lots of in-store events to keep things hopping. Intelligently stocked and refreshingly free of blatant self-promotion. 557 Broadway (btwn Prince and Spring sts.). ℂ **212/343-6166.** www.scholasticstore.com. Subway: R, W to Prince St.

Shoofly ★   If you're looking for party favors, stocking stuffers, or just inexpensive gewgaws to keep your wee one amused, this store has a genius selection of small toys. How about teeny-tiny Slinkys? Or miniature windup toys? Or light-up rubber hammers? The store also has a small but excellent selection of larger toys, puzzles, and games. 42 Hudson St. (btwn Duane and Thomas sts.). ℂ **212/406-3270.** www.shooflynyc.com. Subway: A, C, E, 1, 2, 3 to Chambers St.

Soho Baby   This store has an interesting assortment of toys and gifts, including hand-made felt books, top-quality kid-size pianos, and stuffed animals. 251 Elizabeth St. (btwn Prince and Houston sts.). ☎ 212/625-8538. Subway: R, W to Prince St.; B, D, F, V to Broadway/ Lafayette St.

Sons + Daughters ★   I'm crazy about this store's collection of toys, games, books, arts and crafts, and fun stuff. It has everything from Radio Flyer scooters to Bruder trucks to a great assortment of games and puzzles you won't find anywhere else. If you're looking for a special something for someone, check out the Sons + Daughters website, which lists the staff's favorite stuff by age. 35 Ave. A (btwn 1st and 2nd sts.). ☎ 212/253-7797. www.sons anddaughtersinc.com. Subway: 6 to Astor Place; F to Second Ave.

Space Kiddets   This is the clothing store's toy-store offshoot, with lots of classic toys, games, and books. The lighting is a little dim, but the selection is good. Closed Sunday. 46 E. 21st St. (btwn Broadway and Park Avenue South). ☎ 212/420-9878. www.spacekiddets. com. Subway: N, R, W, 6 to 23rd St.

Stationery & Toy World ⓕ**inds**   There's a delightfully unpretentious clutter of mass-market toys amid the spiral notebooks and ballpoint pens at this friendly West Side storefront. It's a good place for reward and bribe toys and fun little surprises. Closed Sunday July to August. 125 W. 72nd St. (btwn Columbus Ave. and Broadway). ☎ 212/580-3922. Subway: 1, 2, 3 to 72nd St.

Toys "R" Us   The space is huge, bright, sparkling clean, and full of fun, from the amazing scale models of New York landmarks in the LEGO section to the pink Barbie clubhouse to the adorable Candyland-themed sweet shop upstairs. Though the stock is fairly mass market, it has everything on hand, and the prices are (surprise!) not jacked up to pay Manhattan rents. *One warning:* There's a menacing animatronic dinosaur out of *Jurassic Park* in the back corner of the second floor, in case you've got a skittish younger child. Oh, and another warning: It can be excruciatingly crowded in high season. 1514 Broadway at 44th St. ☎ 800/869-7787. www.toysrus.com. Subway: N, Q, R, S, W, 1, 2, 3, 7, 9 to 42nd St./Times Square.

West Side Kids ★   This generic-looking West Side store has lotsa LEGOS, T.C. Timber, PLAYMOBILs, some truly elegant dolls and stuffed animals, every crafts kit known to youth, an impressive board game selection, and a whole wall of superb imported infant and toddler items. The staff is knowledgeable, the selection intelligent and responsible. It's great for one-stop shopping. 498 Amsterdam Ave. (at 84th St.). ☎ 212/496-7282. Subway: 1 to 86th St.

Whipper Snippers   This upbeat haircut salon is also a super toy store, with all the quality toys like LEGO, PLAYMOBIL, and Groovy Girls that you won't mind buying. 106 Reade St. (btwn W. Broadway and Church St.). ☎ 212/227-2600. www.whippersnippers.com. Subway: A, C, E, 1, 2, 3 to Chambers St.

The World of Disney   The Disney Corporation's three-story Fifth Avenue flagship store borrows liberally from Disney theme parks to present a big, glossy stage set of an emporium. You'll find not only tons of Disney-themed merchandise, but also lots of interactive areas: Shoppers can visit the Princess Castle Court for glittery costume jewelry and crafts, Goofy's Candy Company sweets boutique (similar to Candy Land at the Times Square Toys "R" Us), a make-your-own Mr. Potato Head room, a Friendship

Room where Disney characters provide several daily photo ops, and a MultiMedia Zone with listening stations and gaming stations for trying out the latest Disney products. 711 Fifth Ave. (at 55th St.). © 212/702-0702. www.worldofdisney.com. Subway: E, V to Fifth Ave.

Zittles The Zitomer drugstore's toy department just kept expanding and crowded out the second floor; now it's got its own name and a floor all to itself. Finally, this overflowing selection of toys has room to be properly displayed, even with a little flair. For a good mix of quality items and unsnobby mainstream toys, it's a source worth knowing about. 969 Madison Ave. (btwn 75th and 76th sts.). © 212/737-2040. www.zitomer.com. Subway: 6 to 68th St.

Entertainment for the Whole Family

Being the theater capital of the United States doesn't necessarily make New York City the children's theater capital—most of those struggling actors and playwrights and directors are too intent on breaking into the Big Time to pay much mind to kid stuff. On the other hand, the major classical-music venues—Lincoln Center and Carnegie Hall—have in the past few years seen the wisdom of introducing children to music *early*, perhaps because impresarios realize (with panic) that their core audience is rapidly aging and needs to be replaced. In any case, there's a lot of talent hanging around this city, and when enterprising organizers decide to put on a show for young audiences, the production values are generally high.

New York parents tend to be culture hounds, so plays and concerts for children are usually well attended—which means that, as for adult productions, you've got to reserve in advance. Compared to the $100 you can pay for orchestra seats in the big Broadway theaters, ticket prices for kids' events aren't usually outrageous, though a few major annual events—like the Big Apple Circus and *The Nutcracker*—get away with higher prices.

FINDING OUT WHAT'S ON Both the weekly *Time Out New York* (www. timeout.com/newyork) and its offspring **Time Out Kids** (www.timeout.com/new york/kids) have up-to-date, detailed listings of cultural events kids would enjoy, as does the website **gocitykids.com**. The local parents' monthly *Big Apple Parent* (www.parentsknow.com), which carries a calendar of upcoming kids events, can usually be picked up free at public libraries, toy stores, and kids' clothing stores.

The **Theatre Development Fund** lists current theater offerings online at www.tdf. org. You can get event listings for **Lincoln Center** by calling ✆ 212/546-2656 or visiting www.lincolncenter.org. For events in **city parks,** which are plentiful in summer (and often free!), call ✆ **311;** outside NYC call **212/New York** or go online to www.nycgovparks.org.

Every Friday the *New York Times* (www.nytimes.com) runs a "Family Fare" column in its "Weekend" arts section, and you may also find useful listings in *New York* magazine (http://nymag.com) and the *Village Voice* (www.villagevoice.com).

For a complete listing of current Broadway and Off-Broadway shows, visit **www. playbill.com**. Not only do they give you all the basic information, but you also can sign up to receive a regular update via e-mail, informing you which shows offer discounted tickets of anywhere from 10% to 50%.

GETTING TICKETS The Radio City Christmas show and seasonal runs like *The Nutcracker,* the Big Apple Circus, and the Ringling Bros. and Barnum & Bailey Circus should be reserved weeks or even months in advance, as should Broadway plays and popular long-running shows. For pro-sports events, ticket availability is a matter of how well the team's been doing lately, though even rotten season records haven't freed up Knicks or Jets tickets, whose venues are long sold out to season ticket holders. You can usually find scalpers hovering around Madison Square Garden, but you'll pay through the nose and might be sold bogus tickets; using a ticket agent would be a safer bet if your youngster desperately wants to see a game.

Madison Square Garden events and major theater productions offer their tickets through **Ticketmaster** (© **800/755-4000,** 212/307-4100, or 212/307-7171; www.ticketmaster.com) or through **Tele-Charge** (© **800/432-7250** or 212/239-6200; www.telecharge.com). **Madison Square Garden** events also have their own box office (© **212/465-MSG1;** www.thegarden.com). For smaller children's theater companies and puppet shows, contact the box office numbers in separate listings below (some are simply answering machines where you leave your number so the organizer can call you back).

Same-day tickets for many Broadway, Off-Broadway, and Lincoln Center events can be bought in person at the **TKTS booths** (© **212/912-9770;** www.tdf.org) in Midtown on the pedestrian island called Duffy Square at 47th Street and Broadway (open Mon–Sat 3–8pm for evening performances, Wed and Sat 10am–2pm for matinees, Sun 11am–3pm for matinees and 3pm until a half-hour before curtain time for evening shows). Remember, no evening tickets are sold from 10am to 2pm at Times Square. (Temporarily during renovation,

the Midtown TKTS booth is located at the Marriott Marquis Hotel, W. 46th St. btwn Broadway and 8th Ave.) The **South Street Seaport TKTS** booth, 199 Water St., is located at the corner of Front and John streets, near the Resnick/Prudential building (daily Mon–Sat 11am–6pm, Sun 11am–4pm). At TKTS Seaport, matinee tickets are sold only on the day before the performance. A new TKTS booth has opened in **Downtown Brooklyn** (1 MetroTech Center, Jay St. and Myrtle Ave.; Mon–Fri 11am–6pm).

The earlier you line up, the more options you will have. Most tickets are sold at half-price, though some are discounted only 25%, but you'll have to have cash or traveler's checks—no plastic. A $4 TKTS service charge is added. TKTS often has long lines, which move fairly fast but not fast enough for restless small kids. (*Tip:* Window 6, the "PLAY ONLY" window, often has a shorter wait.) The surrounding assemblage of wild lit-up signs can provide some distraction while you're waiting, and sometimes mimes and jugglers and street musicians work the crowd. But if you can swing it, one parent should take the youngsters for a walk while the other hangs out in line.

Another option: BroadwayBox.com, where tickets can be found online for 50% less (and without the headaches associated with waiting and standing at the TKTS booth).

1 THE BIG VENUES

Brooklyn Academy of Music (BAM) Theater, dance, music, puppetry—an impressively international selection of productions rolls through BAM in the course of a year, with a tendency toward the avant-garde. A handful of reasonably priced performances are suited to youngsters, especially the 2-day BAM Kids Film Festival at BAM Rose Cinemas in the spring. Age levels are specified for each performance. 30 Lafayette Ave., Brooklyn. © **718/636-4100.** www.bam.org. Subway: B, Q, 2, 3, 4, 5 to Atlantic Ave.; C to Lafayette Ave.; G to Fulton St.; D, M, N, R to Pacific St. BAM is within walking distance from the B, C, D, G, M, N, Q, R, 2, 3, 4, and 5 trains.

Lincoln Center   With resident companies including the Metropolitan Opera, New York City Ballet, New York City Opera, New York Philharmonic, Film Society, Jazz at Lincoln Center, and the Lincoln Center Theater (all covered in various sections below), something exciting is always brewing at this world-class arts center—with an increasing amount geared for families. 65th and Broadway. 🕾 **212/875-5456.** www.lincolncenter.org. Subway: 1 to 66th St./Lincoln Center.

Madison Square Garden   B-ball, hockey, WWE wrestling, the circus, ice shows, and rock concerts occupy this large arena in a grubby part of Midtown. It can be an intimidating space for a small child, but older kids will recognize it for what it is: a big-league venue with lots of urban electricity. Tickets for most events here are also handled through Ticketmaster. The **WaMu Theater at Madison Square Garden** (www.wamuat msg.com), part of the Garden complex, hosts concerts and live touring stage shows like *Sesame Street Live.*

New Victory Theater   This lovely, renovated century-old theater on 42nd Street has an impressive lineup of entertainment totally for kids. In 2008, Americans for the Arts awarded the New Vic with their prestigious National Award for helping change public education through the arts. You'll find high-profile talent such as London's Young Vic Theatre Company, Theater for a New Audience, Circus Oz, Mabou Mines, and the Peking Acrobats, as well as idiosyncratic acts like the Flying Karamazov Brothers, the Flaming Idiots, and Thwack. Target age groups vary, but there are significant offerings for that tricky age group of 8- to 12-year-olds—too old for puppet shows but still too young for many Broadway shows. There are many special workshops and meet-the-cast events as well, especially through the VicTeens program. New York parents have learned to book tickets far in advance, even if they've never heard of the artists; the runs are generally only 3 weeks long and often sell out. The season is September through June, with extra showtimes during holidays and spring vacation. 209 W. 42nd St. (btwn Seventh and Eighth aves.). 🕾 **646/223-3020** or 212/239-6200 (Telecharge). www.newvictory.org. Tickets $10–$35. Subway: N, Q, R, S, W, 1, 2, 3, 7 to 42nd St./Times Square; A, C, E to 42nd St./Port Authority.

Radio City Music Hall   The Art Deco interior of this Rockefeller Center showcase is a marvel in itself, but kids probably won't notice—they'll be too busy gaping at the vast proscenium of the stage. Besides mounting its own live stage shows twice a year (see "Seasonal Events," below), Radio City hosts concerts, including the occasional family show. For most events children who are 2 years old and older require a ticket. However, a child who has not reached his or her second birthday does not require a ticket but must sit on a parent or guardian's lap. For certain children's events such as *Barney,* all children who have reached their first birthday require a ticket. Please check the specific event before purchasing tickets. For more information, contact Guest Relations at 212/465-6225. 1260 Sixth Ave. (at 50th St.). 🕾 **212/307-7171** (Ticketmaster). www.radiocity.com. Subway: B, D, F to 47th–50th sts./Rockefeller Center.

Symphony Space   Besides the Just Kidding series (see the listing for Symphony Space under "Weekend Shows," below), this recently renovated Upper West Side theater hosts an eclectic variety of events: international dance troupes, and, in spring, a really great series of short-story readings by famous actors and writers. 2537 Broadway (at 95th St.). 🕾 **212/864-5400.** www.symphonyspace.org. Subway: 1, 2, 3 to 96th St.

2 SEASONAL EVENTS

Big Apple Circus   **All ages.** This beloved one-ring circus performs in a tent (heated, of course) at Lincoln Center from October to January. In 2¼ hours, the Big Apple Circus manages to pack in clowns, elephants, trapeze artists, bareback riders, and something for everyone. Skilled circus artists and a sophisticated sense of humor make this a good show for adults who'd rather be charmed than stunned. A splendid time is guaranteed for all. In Damrosch Park behind Lincoln Center, Broadway and 64th St. ✆ **212/307-4100.** (Mailing address: 505 Eighth Ave., 19th Floor, New York, NY 10018.) www.bigapplecircus.org. Tickets $38–$125, free for children 1 and under. Subway: 1 to 66th St./Lincoln Center.

Cirque du Soleil   **Ages 10 & up.** Not your ordinary big-top show by any means, Cirque du Soleil productions change from year to year, but they're always sophisticated visual spectacles, a creative blend of acrobatics, dance, music, and traditional clowning with an edgy twist. Shows tend to run 2½ hours long. WaMu Theater at MSG is home to the holiday-season production of *Wintuk,* running from October 8, 2008, to January 2009; *KOOZA* will arrive in spring 2009. On Randall's Island. ✆ **800/678-5440** or 514/790-1245. www.cirquedusoleil.com. Tickets $42–$95. Buses: X80 event buses leave from Lexington Ave. and East 125th St. Ferry: NY Waterway ferries run to Randall's Island from E. 34th St. (✆ 800/53-FERRY; www.nywaterway.com). Parking $10.

The Nutcracker ★★★   **Ages 10 & up.** The city's best *Nutcracker* is staged every December by the New York City Ballet in Lincoln Center, with several stunning effects (like a Christmas tree that grows up out of the stage to gi-normous proportions). Although the newly named David H. Koch Theater is undergoing renovations, it will not affect the New York City Ballet schedule. At the David H. Koch Theater (formerly the New York State Theater) in Lincoln Center, Broadway and 63rd St. ✆ **212/870-5570.** www.nycballet.com. Tickets $29–$215. Subway: 1 to 66th St./Lincoln Center.

Nutcracker Ⓕinds   **Ages 3 & up.** The New York Theatre Ballet's abbreviated version of Tchaikovsky's holiday classic ballet lasts about 1 hour, cutting out a lot of the first act to focus on the magical elements of the story. Alongside the classical ballet elements, bits of juggling have been thrown in, and Herr Drosselmeyer has some speaking parts to set up the story. Children are allowed—even expected—to make noises and jump out of their seats. A nice introduction to the ballet for younger audiences. Florence Gould Hall, 55 E. 59th St. (btwn Park and Madison aves.). ✆ **212/355-6160** or 212/307-4100 (Ticketmaster). www.nytb.org. Tickets $31 adults, $26 children 12 and under. Subway: 4, 5, 6 to 59th St.

Radio City Music Hall Christmas Spectacular   **Ages 3 & up.** The Rockettes gotta perform somewhere, and this is it. Radio City's elegant Art Deco interior, with its immense stage, cries out for a stage extravaganza like this—lots of music, lavish effects, corny holiday motifs, and that classic precision kick line. The Christmas Show runs early November to the first week in January, usually one show a day until the holidays loom close, when up to five shows a day are performed. It's an annual tradition, and the magic still works, dazzling the Nickelodeon (and now Noggin) generation. 1260 Sixth Ave. (at 50th St.). ✆ **212/307-1000** (Ticketmaster). Tickets $40–$140. Subway: B, D, F to 47th–50th sts./Rockefeller Center.

Ringling Bros. and Barnum & Bailey Circus   **Ages 6 & up.** This glitzy, humongous circus takes up residence at the Garden for 6 weeks every spring, beginning in late March, starring death-defying aerialists, wild animal acts, lumbering elephants, snarling

Street Performers

When former Mayor Giuliani cleared away the vagrants and the squeegee men from New York City streets, the crime rate plummeted, but the number of street performers also dwindled. They're still around, however—keep on the lookout. Top spots for catching jugglers, acrobats, break dancers, and magicians are at South Street Seaport, by the Statue of Liberty ferry line in Battery Park, by the TKTS line in Duffy Square, on the Central Park pathways just north of the children's zoo around 65th Street, at Bethesda Terrace just north of 72nd Street in Central Park, on the steps leading up to the Metropolitan Museum of Art, and by the fountain in Washington Square Park.

The subways see their fair share of entertainers—there's actually a great space set up for them in the Times Square and Grand Central stations, near the Times Square shuttle platform. The 34th Street station for the B, D, F, N, Q, R, V, and W trains often attracts good musicians as well, including an Andean pipe band that's really primo.

There's no guarantee these people will be any good, of course. Standouts in my mind include the guy who plays electric harmonica on the Times Square platforms in Midtown; the Crowtations Motown-singing hand puppets near 72nd Street in Central Park; the magician with the 1960s political agenda who works under the trees near the children's zoo; and a man who tangos very romantically with a dummy of a woman. Remember, you're under no obligation to give these people money, but if you think they're good, you should. Unlike panhandlers, these people are at least doing something for their money.

bears, hordes of clowns, the whole shebang. Smaller kids may be overwhelmed by the sheer size of the Garden, not to mention the flashing lights and eardrum-blasting music. Adults may be overwhelmed by the barrage of vendors selling junk food and junky souvenirs at wildly inflated prices. Still, it's the Greatest Show on Earth and pretty darn impressive. At Madison Square Garden, Seventh Ave. btwn 31st and 33rd sts. (✆ **800/755-4000**, 212/465-MSG1, or 212/307-7171 (Ticketmaster). www.ringling.com. Tickets $10–$50. Subway: A, C, E, 1, 2, 3 to 34th St.

Shakespeare in the Park Ages 10 & up. From June to August of each summer, The New York Public Theater produces two free shows at the outdoor Delacorte Theater in Central Park, at least one of them by Shakespeare. Recent years have included the much-loved *A Midsummer Night's Dream,* a musical of *Two Gentlemen of Verona,* and *Macbeth.* The line to get tickets forms early each day (9 or 10am), snaking around the Great Lawn; but once the box office opens it moves quickly, and all tickets are soon distributed. The wait can be tedious, but it's a small price for free theater in a beautiful setting. *Note:* A limited number of tickets are available online the day of the performance. Register at www.publictheater.org. Log on between midnight and 1pm the day of the performance and again from 1 to 6pm to see if you have been selected for a pair of tickets. At the Delacorte Theater, Central Park. (✆ **212/260/2400**. www.publictheater.org. Tickets free (limit 2 per person in line). Subway: B, C to 81st St.

3 WEEKEND SHOWS

Henry Street Settlement Abrons Arts Center   Ages 4 to 12. On weekends this Lower East Side cultural center—a longtime mainstay of the neighborhood—runs a series for kids and their parents at 2pm, with performances twice a month. The company does a wide variety of shows, including dance performances, plays based on updated fairy tales, improv sessions, and puppet shows, all nicely multicultural and very professional. Call for reservations a week in advance. Check the website—the schedule is continually subject to change. 466 Grand St. (at Pitt St.). ⓒ 212/598-0400. www.henrystreet.org. Tickets $10 adults, $5 children 4–12. Subway: F to Delancey St.; B, D to Grand St.; J, M to Essex St.

Symphony Space   Ages 5 & up. October through April, the Just Kidding series presents weekend performances for kids—often concerts with stars like Tom Chapin or the a cappella group the Persuasions, or film and storytelling. Eclectic, multicultural, and fun. 2537 Broadway (at 95th St.). ⓒ 212/864-5400. www.symphonyspace.org. Tickets generally $18–$23 ($20–$25 day of show) adults, $13 children 11 and under. Subway: 1, 2, 3 to 96th St.

4 THEATER

LONG-RUNNING SHOWS

It's always hard to predict which Broadway and Off-Broadway shows will still be running by the time you read this (much less by the time you get to New York), but these shows are a pretty safe bet—many have been running for a long time with no sign of letting up. Most of them (except *The Lion King*) are usually available for half-price at the TKTS booth at 47th Street and Broadway.

The Little Mermaid ★   Ages 5 & up. The beloved Disney film has been turned into a surprisingly affecting Broadway musical (2¹/₂ hr. long) that keeps regular Broadway hours—8pm shows Wednesday through Saturday, 2pm matinees Wednesday and Saturday, a 1pm Sunday matinee, and an early-bird 6:30pm Sunday-night show. At the Lunt-Fontanne Theatre, 205 W. 46th St. (at Broadway). ⓒ 212/575-9200. www.disneyonbroadway.com. Tickets $52–$122. Subway: 1 to 50th St.

Blue Man Group   Ages 8 & up. Faces painted blue, this trio has been committing weird mayhem onstage since 1992, with lots of flashing strobes and percussion effects. The hip performance-art elements are directed to adults, but preteens dig the show, too. It runs slightly under 2 hours. At the Astor Place Theater, 434 Lafayette St. (btwn E. 4th St. and Astor Place). ⓒ 212/254-4370 or 212/307-4100 (Ticketmaster). www.blueman.com. Tickets $68 and $78. Subway: 6 to Astor Place.

Legally Blonde: The Musical   Ages 5 & up. In this "girl empowerment" musical based on the popular movie, Elle Woods proves that, as the billboards say, "being true to yourself never goes out of style." The special "Elle's Lounge VIP Experience," held during two matinees twice a month, is popular with girls 9 to 15 and their moms; the $200 VIP ticket includes a tote bag with goodies and an orchestra seat "in the pink." At the Palace Theatre, 1564 Broadway (btwn 46th and 47th sts.). ⓒ 212/307-4100. www.legallyblondethemusical.com. Tickets $45–$120. Subway: C, E, 1 to 50th St.

Al Hirschfeld **19**
Ambassador **11**
American Airlines **45**
American Place **34**
Barrymore **26**
Belasco **36**
Booth **30**
Broadhurst **23**
Broadway **4**
Brooks Atkinson **16**
Circle in the Square **10**
City Center Stage **2**
Cort **33**
Douglas Fairbanks **49**
Duffy **27**
Ethel Barrymore **14**
Eugene O'Neill **12**

Ford Center for the
  Performing Arts **44**
Gershwin **7**
Helen Hayes **40**
Imperial **18**
John Golden **20**
Longacre **15**
Lunt-Fontanne **28**
Lyceum **35**
Majestic **21**
Marquis **31**
Minskoff **38**
Mitzi E. Newhouse **1**
Music Box **25**
Nederlander **43**
Neil Simon **6**
New Amsterdam **42**

New Victory **41**
Palace **32**
Playwright's Horizons **48**
Plymouth **29**
Richard Rogers **17**
Royale **24**
Samuel Beckett **47**
St. James **22**
Shubert **39**
Stardust **8**
Studio 54 **3**
Town Hall **37**
Virginia **5**
Vivian Beaumont **1**
Walter Kerr **13**
WestSide **46**
Winter Garden **9**

The Lion King ★★★ **All ages.** Still a hot ticket, this adaptation of a Disney animated movie is worth planning your trip around. Tony-award-winning director Julie Taymor discarded glitzy special effects and made stage magic instead with puppets, dancers, masks, billowing cloths, and imagination, drawing strongly on African folk traditions. This show is genuinely moving, even—dare I say it?—better than the movie. Call for tickets many months in advance, line up outside for same-day returns, or splurge on a ticket agent, but somehow get your children to see this play. At the Minskoff Theatre, 1515 Broadway at 45th St. ☎ 212/307-4747 or 212/307-4100 (Ticketmaster). www.disneyon broadway.com. Tickets $51–$121. Subway: N, Q, R, S, W, 1, 2, 3 to 42nd St./Times Square.

Shrek, The Musical **All ages.** The lovable ogre comes to life on stage in this 21st-century fairy tale based on the blockbuster movie. At the Broadway Theatre, 1681 Broadway (at 53rd St.). ☎ 212/307-4747. www.shrekthemusical.com. Tickets $52–$112. Subway: N, R, W to 49th St.

Stomp **Ages 8 & up.** What kid hasn't made music by tapping a broom handle on the floor or crashing two pot lids together? This troupe of eight athletic-looking dancers does the same sort of rhythmic stuff with everyday objects for an hour and a half, and it's undeniably captivating. Early evening performances Saturday and Sunday make it possible to see this without being out too late. At the Orpheum Theater, 126 Second Ave. (btwn 7th and 8th sts.). ☎ 212/477-2477 or 212/307-4100 (Ticketmaster). Tickets $40–$69. Subway: 6 to Astor Place.

CHILDREN'S THEATER COMPANIES

Galli's Fairytale Theater **Ages 3 and up.** Modern interpretations of classic fairy tales, with plenty of audience interaction. At the Galli Theater NY, 38 W. 38th St., 3rd Floor (btwn Fifth and Sixth aves.). ☎ 212/352-3101. www.galli-group.com. Tickets $12–$17. Subway: N, Q, R, S, W, 1, 2, 3 to 42nd St./Times Square.

IMPROV 4 Kids **Ages 4 and up.** Ever dreamed of raising a little stand-up comedian? Here's your chance to see if he or she's got the goods. The official outreach program of the former Laugh Factory comedy group now known as *Eight Is Never Enough* teaches children comedy arts and shows kids a deliciously good time in the process. Shows are Saturdays at 3pm, and you can buy half-price tickets online. Times Square Arts Center, 300 W. 43rd St. (at Eighth Ave.). ☎ 212/352-3101 or 212/568-6560. www.improv4kids.com. Tickets $20. Subway A, C, E to Port Authority Terminal.

Literally Alive **Ages 3 to 10.** This company performs two to three shows a year showcasing classic children's stories with original music. Past shows include *The Velveteen Rabbit* and Oscar Wilde's *The Selfish Giant*. It also provides preshow arts-and-crafts workshops on Saturday and Sunday beginning at noon before a 1pm show. Check the website for weekday performances during school vacations as well. Currently in residence at the Players Theatre, 115 MacDougal St. (btwn Bleecker and W. 3rd sts.). ☎ 212/866-5170. www.literallyalive.com. Tickets $25 (www.theatermania.com). Subway; A, C, E, D, F, V to W. 4th St.

Manhattan Theater Source **Ages 5 & up.** This bustling Greenwich Village theater organization works a few hour-long productions for kids—both musicals and straight plays—into their yearly schedule. 177 MacDougal St. (btwn 8th St. and Waverly Place). ☎ 212/260-4698. www.theatersource.org. Tickets $18. Subway: A, B, C, D, E, F, V to W. 4th St.

New Perspectives Theatre **Ages 4 & up.** New Perspectives' World Voices series comprises eight different productions a year, Saturdays and Sundays at 11am and 1pm, many of them adaptations of various ethnic fables. Shows run about an hour, including a preshow activity. Middle-school and high-school students can also enjoy two Shakespearean plays performed throughout the year. Performing at the Pelican Studio Theatre, 750 Eighth Ave. ℂ 212/730-2030. www.newperspectivestheatre.org. Tickets $8 ($6 per person for families of 4 or more). Shakespeare shows $15 adults, $12 students. Subway: A, C, E to 34th St.

Paper Bag Players   Ages 4 to 9. January to March, this veteran troupe presents original 1-hour plays with a pleasant edge of nuttiness, on Saturday at 2pm and Sunday at 1 and 3pm. The company's trademark is using everyday materials like paper bags and corrugated cardboard for all the costumes, sets, and props, giving the productions a homegrown look that somehow makes them very appealing to kids. Each year they perform in various locations throughout the city. ℂ 212/663-0390. www.thepaperbagplayers. org. Tickets $10–$25.

Shadow Box Theatre   Ages 4 & up. The children's theater-in-residence at the Brooklyn Music School Playhouse specializes in original musicals with multicultural themes, featuring singing, dancing, and puppetry. November to May they present four or five productions, each running about a month, with weekday and weekend performances. They also do various performances in Manhattan as well as Brooklyn. Call ahead for a schedule. At the Brooklyn Music School Playhouse, 126 St. Felix St., Brooklyn, NY 11217. ℂ 212/724-0677. (Mailing address 325 West End Ave., New York, NY 10023.) www.shadowboxtheatre.org.

Theater for a New Audience   Ages 8 & up. This top-notch Off-Broadway company devotes itself to the classics, mostly Shakespeare. By no means for children only, its vigorous productions do attract lots of school groups because they're a great way to introduce youngsters to the Bard. From January to April there are two or three productions, playing Tuesday to Saturday nights, with a Saturday matinee. Performing at the Duke, 229 W. 42nd St. (btwn Seventh and Eighth aves.). ℂ 466/223-3010. www.tfana.org.

TheatreworksUSA   Ages 4 & up. One of the city's top choices for kids, this long-running troupe presents witty, vivid musical versions of classic books like *The Lion, the Witch, and the Wardrobe; Charlotte's Web;* or *The Plant That Ate Dirty Socks,* as well as some original story scripts. They put on a dozen or so plays each year, with several performances of each, so you can count on something every weekend at 2pm from September to March. Children under age 4 are not admitted. The family series musicals are held at the Lucille Lortel Theatre, 1212 Christopher St. (ℂ 212/647-1100 or 800/497-5007). At the Auditorium at Equitable Tower, 787 Seventh Ave. (at 51st St.). ℂ 800/497-5007 or 212/647-1100. Subway: 1 to 50th St.; N, R, W to 49th St.; B, D, E to Seventh Ave.

Thirteenth Street Repertory Theater   Ages 4 & up. Alongside its grown-up productions, this Greenwich Village company puts on two original children's shows on Saturday and Sunday at 1 and 3pm year-round. With recorded music and special effects, shows like *Wiseacre Farm* and *Rumple Who?* are perfectly calibrated for a young audience, with healthy doses of humor. Reservations are recommended a couple of days in advance of the performance. 50 W. 13th St. ℂ 212/675-6677. www.13thstreetrep.org. Tickets to children's shows $10. Subway: F, V, 1, 2, 3 to 14th St.; A, C, E to W. 4th St.; N, Q, R, W, 4, 5, 6 to Union Square; L to Sixth Ave.

Tribeca Performing Arts   Ages 3 & up. Offering a mixed bag of events—some starring kids, others with adult performers, others with puppets or dancers or actors performing in sign language—this downtown arts center brings to town a full season of children's entertainment with its Family, Folk, and Fairy Tale series (Oct–June Sat or Sun at 1:30pm). Past productions have included musical versions of classics like *Hans Brinker* and *The Reluctant Dragon,* as well as retellings of children's books such as *The House at*

272 *Pooh Corner.* 199 Chambers St. (btwn Greenwich St. and the West Side Hwy.). ✆ **212/220 1460.** www.tribecapac.org. All tickets $25.

KIDS ONSTAGE

City Lights   Ages 4 & up. Several times a year, students 7 to 18 who've taken classes at the City Lights school perform—an original play in the winter and a musical (like *Pippin*) in the spring. A junior musical for younger children is performed in May as well as part of the spring performance festival. Other events include stage readings for family audiences. Check the website for directions to current venues. Most performances are held at 630 Ninth Ave. (btwn 44th and 45th sts.). ✆ **212/262-0200.** www.clyouththeatre. org.

New Media Repertory Company   Ages 4 to 18. The nonprofit New Media Children's Theater Company performances are by and for kids, with lots of participation from the youthful audience. A new original play is presented every February and March on Saturday at 3pm. The young performers are students at the program's acting workshops. Reservations are essential. 512 E. 80th St. (btwn York and East End aves.). ✆ **212/734-5195.** www.newmediarep.org. Tickets $10. Subway: 6 to 77th St.

TADA!   Ages 3 & up. The most energetic and successful of NYC's theater schools for kids, TADA! has even performed at the White House. A diverse group of professional kid performers, ages 8 to 17, stars in TADA!'s sprightly original musicals. They play weekends in January, March, and December (including one Fri-night show, unusual for children's companies; two Sat matinees; and two Sun matinees). In July—when most other children's entertainment dries up—TADA! comes to the rescue with weekday shows as well as a summer musical in Madison Square Park (Broadway at 23rd St.). Even adults without children have been known to see TADA!'s shows, which tells you something about how lively they are. 15 W. 28th St. (btwn Broadway and Fifth aves.). ✆ **212/252-1619.** www.tadatheater.com. Tickets $25 adults, $10 children. Subway: N, R, W, 1 to 28th St.; A, B, C, D, E, F, Q, 2, 3 to 34th St.

5 CONCERTS

The Amato Opera Theatre (Finds)   Ages 5 & up. One of the oldest arts organizations in the United States, the delightfully intimate Opera Amato in the East Village offers, from October to May, a special children's series, "Opera in Brief"—90-minute shows on Saturday mornings at 11:30am, usually condensed versions of kid pleasers like *Hansel and Gretel* and *The Mikado.* This is a wonderful opportunity to introduce your children to the beauty of opera. 319 Bowery (near 2nd St.). ✆ **212/228-8200.** www.amato.org. Tickets $20 adults; $15 children, seniors, and students. Subway: 6 to Bleecker St.; B, D, F, V to Broadway/Lafayette.

Brooklyn Center for the Performing Arts   Ages 3 & up. The center's FamilyFun Series presents six productions a year, plus an annual December *Nutcracker* ballet ($35 adults, $18 children 12 and under). It's a multicultural grab bag of cultural events appealing to kids—circuses, puppet shows, jugglers, classical-music concerts, plays, and ballet. Performances in 2008 included productions of *Sleeping Beauty.* ✆ **718/951-4500.** www. brooklyncenter.com. Tickets $15–$35. Subway: 2 to Flatbush Ave.

Carnegie Hall Family Concerts (Value) **Ages 5 to 12.** Six or seven Saturdays a year, October through May, Carnegie Hall presents hour-long concerts at 2pm, preceded by 1pm activities like demonstrations, craft workshops, and storytelling. Performers might include anyone from the Chicago Youth Symphony Orchestra to classical-music stars such as cellist Yo-Yo Ma and clarinetist Richard Stoltzman. Advance reservations recommended. At Carnegie Hall, 881 Seventh Ave. (at 57th St.). © 212/247-7800. www.carnegiehall. org. Tickets $9. Subway: N, Q, R, W to 57th St./Seventh Ave.

CarnegieKids (Value) **Ages 3 to 6.** These 45-minute weekday-morning concerts are designed especially for preschoolers and kindergartners, using storytellers and musicians who interact with the children in the audience, letting them sing and move around to the music. The program occurs in November and again in March, Monday through Friday, with shows at 10 and 11:30am. Held in the intimate Kaplan Space at Carnegie Hall, corner of 57th St. and Seventh Ave. © 212/247-7800. www.carnegiehall.org. Tickets from $6, by mail order or reservation only. Subway: N, Q, R, W to 57th St./Seventh Ave.

Jazz for Young People **Ages 5 & up.** Under the aegis of superstar trumpeter Wynton Marsalis, this series consists of two shows (noon and 2pm) on Saturdays at Lincoln Center's new Rose Theater in the Time-Warner Center on Columbus Circle. 33 W. 60th St. (at Broadway). © 212/721-6500 for tickets; 212/258-9800 for information. www.jazzatlincoln center.org. Tickets $12–$32 ($35 for 3-performance series). Subway: A, B, C, D, 1 to 59th St./ Columbus Circle.

Jazz Standard **Ages 5 & up.** The Jazz Standard Youth Orchestra, an ensemble of about 20 gifted high-school musicians, entertains during a jazz brunch for children, Sunday from 1 to 3pm (shows start at 2pm) from September to June. Delicious food is catered from the acclaimed barbecue restaurant **Blue Smoke** downstairs (see chapter 6). Reservations recommended. 116 E. 27th St. (btwn Park and Lexington aves.). © 212/576-2232. www.jazzstandard.com. $5 donation. Subway: 6 to 28th St.

Little Orchestra Society **Ages 3 to 12.** Two series—Happy Concerts for Young People (ages 6–12) and Lolli-Pop Concerts (ages 3–5)—are designed to introduce kids to classical music, using first-class professional artists (moonlighting Philharmonic members, New York City Ballet stars, and the like). This organization has been around since the 1950s, and the quality is top-notch. The Lolli-Pop series, held at the **Kaye Playhouse** at Hunter College (68th St. btwn Park and Lexington aves.), uses cutesy costumed figures to help teach wee ones about music; it is a three-concert series with four performance times for each, two on Saturday and two on Sunday, and it's so popular that you pretty much have to buy a whole series (series $60–$150; $40 for single tickets, if there are any seats left) to get in. It's easier to score tickets for Happy Concerts; there are two Saturday performances for each of the three concerts per year, but they are held in a much larger space, Lincoln Center's **Avery Fisher Hall** (Broadway at 65th St.). Happy Concert subscription prices range from $24 to $126, with individual tickets ranging from $10 to $50. There are also some nonsubscription events every year, like *Peter and the Wolf* and the annual Menotti's *Amahl and the Night Visitors,* a fully staged opera with live animals—the works. Mailing address: 330 W. 42nd, 12th Floor, New York, NY 10036-6902. © 212/971-9500. www.littleorchestra.org.

Meet the Music **Ages 6 to 12.** The Chamber Music Society of Lincoln Center puts in its bid for young audiences with this upbeat Sunday-afternoon series. Even modern pieces by Aaron Copland or Andrew Lloyd Webber might be performed, so long as they're played by a small group of musicians, one player to a part. With narrators, props, and audience participation, the concerts engage fidgety youngsters admirably. Merkin Concert Hall, 129 W. 67th St. (btwn Broadway and Amsterdam Ave.). (✆ 212/875-5788. www. chambermusicsociety.org. Series tickets $40. Subway: 1 to 66th St./Lincoln Center.

Young People's Concerts **Ages 6 to 12.** Want to turn your kid into a hard-core classical-music fan? Four Saturdays a year the New York Philharmonic trots out musicians like violin prodigy Sarah Chang and conductors Kurt Mazur and Leonard Slatkin to introduce kids to major selections from the classical repertory—not just the chestnuts like *Eine kleine Nachtmusik,* but also pieces by moderns like George Gershwin and Charles Ives. Topping it off, free 12:45pm interactive Kid Zone Live sessions precede the 2pm concerts. Older kids (12–17) can graduate to Philharmonic Teens, which gives them discount seats to the orchestra's weekday Rush Hour Concerts (at 6:45pm). Often rush tickets can be purchased for select concerts up to 10 days before. There are often free pre- and post-concert meet-the-artist events. Avery Fisher Hall, Lincoln Center, Broadway and 64th St. (✆ 212/721-6500 or 212/875-5656. www.nyphil.org. Tickets $5–$25. Subway: 1 to 66th St./Lincoln Center.

---

6 FILMS

11

If it's standard feature-film fare you want, Manhattan is packed with cinema screens, including the busy 13-screen **AMC Loews Lincoln Square complex** at 68th and Broadway, where each theater entrance evokes a different classic New York movie palace; and the multiplex **Regal E-Walk Stadium 13** and **AMC Empire** cinemas, both located on West 42nd Street between Broadway and Eighth Avenue. For more unusual films geared to a young audience, here are your choices:

AMC Loews IMAX Theater **Ages 3 & up.** Not just IMAX but 3-D IMAX—awesome. The screen is eight stories high, and a cool headset puts you in the extraspatial dimension. Needless to say, there isn't a lot of film material for this format and some of the offerings aren't 3-D. But Loews has managed to get movies that go beyond documentaries into actual storytelling features—like *Across the Sea of Time,* which tells of a young Russian immigrant boy searching for relatives in Manhattan (think of it as a live-action *An American Tale*). Most shows run about 45 minutes to an hour. Target ages for the scheduled films vary, so check ahead—and as always with IMAX, consider whether your youngster is suited to the medium's heightened sensory impact. At AMC Loews Lincoln Square, Broadway and 68th St. (✆ 212/336-5000. Tickets $15 adults, $12 children 12 and under. Subway: 1 to 66th St./Lincoln Center.

American Museum of Natural History IMAX Theater Ages 3 & up. The screen at the Natural History Museum isn't quite as huge as the one at the AMC Loews Lincoln Square IMAX (see above), but unless you get out your measuring tape, you'd never know. The main thing is that your whole field of vision is occupied, which somehow doubles the sensory impact of a movie—something to consider before you take young, skittish children inside. You have a choice of dazzling 3-D IMAX movies every day, some more intense than others, though all have an educational bent. Whether you're in outer space, underwater with prehistoric sea monsters, or deep in the rainforest, the sights and sounds tend to include a speeding camera taking you on a visual thrill ride that swoops over rising and falling terrain, the hallmark of the IMAX experience.

Buy the combination ticket when you enter, or stop by the ticket counter near the museum's 77th Street entrance. There's a movie every 45 minutes or so, though school groups get first dibs on seats weekday mornings (the public is then admitted on a first-come, first-served basis). The museum is open daily year-round, except on Thanksgiving and Christmas. At the American Museum of Natural History, Central Park West at 79th St. ℂ 212/769-5200. www.amnh.org. Tickets (includes museum admission) $15 adults, $11 seniors and students over 12, $8.50 ages 2–12. Subway: B, C to 81st St./Museum of Natural History; 1 to 79th St.

BAMKids Film Festival **Ages 2 to 13.** For 2 days each spring (generally a weekend in Feb or Mar), BAMKids treats its young audience to an array of international feature-length films and shorts. Selections have ranged from animated favorites like *Babar: King of Elephants* to quality classics like *The Red Balloon*. Guest appearances by featured animators and directors make the experience for youngsters even more meaningful. Call for a schedule. At the Brooklyn Academy of Music (BAM) Rose Cinemas, 30 Lafayette Ave., Brooklyn. ℂ 718/636-4100. www.bam.org. Tickets $10 adults, $6 kids. Subway: B, Q, 2, 3, 4, 5 to Atlantic Ave.; C to Lafayette Ave.; G to Fulton St.; or D, M, N, R to Pacific St.

Children's International Film Festival (Finds) **Ages 3 & up.** Held in March, this excellent festival brings a wide range of films and videos, from commercial features to animation to shorts and documentaries from around the world, screened at venues around town. And how's this for interactive: Young viewers get to vote to award festival prizes for certain portions of the program. Way cool. 295 Greenwich St. (at Chambers). ℂ 212/349-0330. www.gkids.com. Ticket prices for individual films vary.

Fresh Air Flicks Ages 5 & up. This is the pedestrian New Yorker's version of a drive-in movie: outdoor movies, screened in New York City parks on summer evenings and under the Brooklyn Bridge. The *Movies Under the Stars* series may not be first-run (try classics like *Annie Hall, Bee Movie,* or *West Side Story*), but admission is free; and you can spread out a blanket and have a picnic while you're claiming your spot. Locations include Bryant Park, the Bandshell at 72nd St. Central Park, and Riverside Park (at both 70th and 103rd sts.). ℂ 212/NEW-YORK (639-9675). www.nycgovparks.org or ℂ 877/215-5500 (www.freshair flicks.com).

New York Public Library Ages 3 to 8. Along with story hours, children's rooms at several Manhattan branch libraries may run an hour-long program of short films once a month, many of them made from children's books—*Madeline, Curious George, Doctor DeSoto,* and so on. Various branches around Manhattan. For a monthly schedule, contact the NYPL at 8 W. 40th St., New York, NY 10018 (ℂ 212/221-7676 or 212/869-8089; www.nypl.org), or stop by any branch to pick up schedule brochure.

7 DANCE

American Ballet Theatre Ages 8 & up. On this enormous stage, the spring season (May–June) features both modern works and some classic story ballets like *Swan Lake, Giselle,* and *Sleeping Beauty*—just the thing for budding ballerinas. Check the website for hands-on workshops for youngsters, occasionally held in conjunction with performances. Metropolitan Opera House, Lincoln Center, Broadway and 64th St. ℂ 212/362-6000. www.abt. org. Tickets $28–$145. Subway: 1 to 66th St./Lincoln Center.

Dance Theater Workshop   **Ages 4 & up.** One of the city's leading promoters of modern dance, the workshop presents, among other things, a Family Matters series, Sunday matinee events appropriate for parents and kids of all ages (not necessarily purely dance). The season usually runs September to June. 219 W. 19th St. (btwn Seventh and Eighth aves.). *C* 212/924-0077. www.dtw.org. Tickets $15–$25. Subway: C, E to 23rd St.; 1 to 18th St.

Ice Theatre of New York (Value   **Ages 5 & up.** Unlike typical ice-show companies, Ice Theatre leads figure skating strongly in the direction of dance, even commissioning noted nonskating choreographers to create new pieces for their lyrical, intriguing performances. With guest artists like Nancy Kerrigan and David Liu, the skaters take to the ice in free lunchtime shows January through March at **Rockefeller Center** (last Wed of the month) and the New Works and Artists Series at **Riverbank State Park** (145th St. and Riverside Dr.; last Thurs of the month); other performances (not free) are at the **Sky Rink** at Chelsea Piers (23rd St. at the Hudson River) in October. *C* 212/929-5811 or 212/307-7171 (Ticketmaster). www.icetheatre.org.

Joyce Theater   **Ages 6 & up.** This Chelsea theater devoted to modern dance does an admirable job of bringing in young audiences. Touring dance companies booked into the Joyce are asked to design special Saturday family matinees, with dancers showing up in the lower lobby afterward, still in costume, to meet audience members and give autographs. Two performances are held in Chelsea; a third, the "Special Family Matinee Event," is held at the Joyce SoHo Theater, a converted firehouse (155 Mercer St.; *C* 212/431-9233). 175 Eighth Ave. (at 19th St.). *C* 212/242-0800 or 212/691-9740. www.joyce.org. Tickets $32–$42 adults, $10–$20 kids. Subway: C, E to 23rd St.; 1 to 18th St.

New York City Ballet   **Ages 10 & up.** For technique, many critics feel this troupe surpasses its Lincoln Center cousin, the ABT (see above), but young balletomanes may not get the point of NYCB's more abstract pieces, following the tastes of founder George Balanchine. However, this is where the city's best *Nutcracker* is staged every December (see "Seasonal Events," earlier in this chapter). The ballet offers two seasons—April through June and Thanksgiving through February—with nightly performances (except Mon) and weekend matinees. New York State Theater, Lincoln Center, Broadway and 64th St. *C* 212/870-5570. www.nycballet.com. Tickets $35–$100. Subway: 1 to 66th St./Lincoln Center.

New York Theater Ballet   **Ages 5 & up.** Besides its splendid condensed *Nutcracker* (see "Seasonal Events," earlier in this chapter), this classical dance troupe presents three other fairy tale–based ballets each season, in the "Once Upon A Ballet" series. The quality of the dancing is excellent, and costumes are lovely, though sets are minimal on this relatively small stage. Geared for young audiences, these productions stress the storytelling elements of dance and don't run too long—which makes them a great introduction to traditional ballet. At Florence Gould Hall, 55 E. 59th St. (btwn Park and Madison aves.). *C* 212/355-6160 (theater box office), or 212/307-4100 (Ticketmaster). www.nytb.org. Tickets $10–$30. Subway: 4, 5, 6 to 59th St.; N, R, W to Lexington Ave./59th St.

8 MAGIC SHOWS

Monday Night Magic   **Ages 10 & up.** A fabulous showcase for serious magicians, Monday Night Magic varies from week to week; some performances are less appropriate for children than others (they won't admit anyone age 7 and under), so go on the website to see what this week's program offers. Acts range from hilarious to eerie to borderline raunchy, with card tricks, knife throwing, balloon tricks, and all the sleight of hand you could want. Performances run year-round, every Monday night at 8pm. The Bleecker Street Theater, 45 Bleecker St. (east of Lafayette St.). © 212/615-6432 or www.telecharge.com for tickets. www.mondaynightmagic.com. Tickets $34–$39. Subway: B, D, F, V to Broadway/Lafayette; R, W to Prince St.; 6 to Bleecker St.

9 PUPPET SHOWS

Los Kabayitos Puppet & Children's Theater   **Ages 4 and up.** Well-known tales are presented in Spanish and English simultaneously and performed with giant life-size puppets. 107 Suffolk St., 2nd Floor. © 212/260-4080, ext. 14. Subway: F, J, M, Z to Delancey St.

Puppetworks—Park Slope   **Ages 3 to 7.** Using both hand puppets and marionettes, these puppeteers retell classic children's stories. The season runs year-round, with performances on weekends at 12:30 and 2:30pm. Reservations are required. 338 6th Ave., Brooklyn. © 718/965-3391. www.puppetworks.org. Tickets $8 adults, $7 children. Subway: F to 7th Ave.

Swedish Cottage Marionette Theatre (Value)   **Ages 3 to 10.** This alpine-looking cottage holds a small stage where near-life-size marionettes prance and caper in hour-long productions of classic fairy tales—recorded soundtrack, spotlighting, full scenery, the works. A puppeteer prefaces performances with a helpful mini-seminar on puppetry. The pace is leisurely, and the sense of humor is gentle. Call 3 or 4 weeks in advance for a reservation—there are usually one or two shows a day, but they fill up fast with school groups and birthday parties. Closed Mondays in the school year, closed Sundays in summer. In Central Park (West Dr. at 81st St.). © 212/988-9093. www.cityparksfoundation.org or www.centralpark.com. Tickets $8 adults, $5 children; reservations required. Closed mid-Aug through Sept. Subway: B, C to 79th St.

10 SPECTATOR SPORTS

MUSEUM

Sports Museum of America ★   **Ages 4 & up.** Opened in 2008, this interactive museum is the only one to celebrate all American sports under one roof. It's got 19 themed galleries, sports artifacts (we're talking superstar jerseys and the like), and 20 original movies. It's the new home of the Heisman trophy, college football's MVP, and the site of the Billie Jean King International Women's Sports Center. 28 Broadway (entrance on Beaver St. near Charging Bull statue). © 212/747-0900 or 888/762-8587. Tickets $27 adults, $20 kids, free for kids 3 and under. Daily 9am–7pm. Subway: 4, 5 to Bowling Green; R, W, 1 to Rector St.; or 2, 3 to Wall St.

SPECTATOR SPORTS

Brooklyn Cyclones (Value)   **Ages 6 & up.** The hardest-to-get sports ticket in town just may be for this Mets-affiliated Class A minor-league franchise out in Brooklyn, which debuted in Coney Island in 2001. Folks line up before dawn the day season tickets go on sale, and individual tickets often sell out within an hour after online ticketing opens. However, in keeping with the Cyclones' populist profile, there are always a limited

Milestones in New York Sports History

In all the major pro sports, the lucrative New York area market sustains at least two teams, and at some periods (baseball in the 1950s, hockey today), three teams. New Yorkers, spoiled by years of sports success, aren't big on rooting for underdogs (with the exception of the 1969 Mets). Then again, we aren't used to having underdogs, maybe because New York money enables team owners to buy the best talent available, from Babe Ruth to Wayne Gretzky to Alex Rodriguez. New York fans, hooked on those championship titles, still can't get enough. Here's the sort of thing we're talking about:

- **1921–23:** Two New York baseball teams—the Giants and the Yankees—meet in the World Series for 3 consecutive years. The Giants win the first 2 years; the Yankees finally take the title in 1923, establishing a taste for victory they'll never shake.
- **1927–28:** Two consecutive World Series victories for the Yankees, both of them four-game sweeps. Babe Ruth sets his home run record at Yankee Stadium in 1927.
- **1928:** New York Rangers win hockey's Stanley Cup for the first (but not the last) time.
- **1936–37:** Two more Yankees-Giants World Series matchups—the Yankees win both times.
- **1938–39:** The Yankees continue their streak, sweeping the Cubs and then the Reds to make four World Series titles in a row.
- **1941:** The Yankees beat the Brooklyn Dodgers in the World Series.
- **1947:** Another Dodgers vs. Yankees Series; the Yankees win.
- **1949–56:** New York dominates baseball, with one of its teams winning the World Series every year—the Yankees for 5 years straight, and then the

number of general admission tickets offered at the box office at 10am on home game days. KeySpan Park strives for the way-back-when feel of the Brooklyn Dodgers' old Ebbets Field, with only 7,500 seats, alcohol-free sections, billboards advertising local small companies, and a view of Coney Island's parachute jump and boardwalk. A great place to spot good young players on their way up, and to recapture the charm that made baseball America's Game. KeySpan Park, 1904 Surf Ave. (btwn W. 17th and 19th sts.), Coney Island. ✆ 718/449-8497. www.brooklyncyclones.com. Tickets $8–$15. Subway: D, F, Q to Coney Island/Stillwell Ave.

New Jersey Devils　**Ages 8 & up.** Winners of the 1995 and 2000 Stanley Cups, the Devils have stolen the thunder from the New York area's older hockey teams, the Rangers and the Islanders. The season runs from October to mid-April, and though much of the arena gets sold out with season tickets, individual tickets for cheaper seats may be available. It's always worth checking the day of a game to see if some seats have been released. Prudential Center, Newark. ✆ 201/507-8900, 212/307-7171 (for single-game tickets), or 212/307-7171 (Ticketmaster). www.newjerseydevils.com. Tickets $20–$90. Parking $8. For game-time bus service from Manhattan's Port Authority Bus Terminal, call New Jersey Transit at ✆ 800/772-2222.

Giants in 1954 and the Dodgers in 1955 (finally beating the Yankees!), only to have the Yankees vanquish the Dodgers again in 1956. Six World Series in this 8-year period are "Subway Series"—the Yankees face the Dodgers five times and the Giants once.

- **1961:** Yankee Roger Maris breaks Babe Ruth's home run record.
- **1969:** The New York Jets win the Super Bowl; the "Miracle" Mets win the World Series.
- **1970:** The New York Knicks take the NBA championship (and again in 1973).
- **1980–83:** The New York Islanders dominate hockey, winning the Stanley Cup 4 years in a row.
- **1986:** The Mets win another World Series.
- **1987:** The Giants win the Super Bowl (and again in 1991).
- **1994:** The Rangers win another Stanley Cup.
- **1995:** This year, it's the New Jersey Devils' turn to win the Stanley Cup.
- **1998–2000:** The Yankees make regular World Series visits, winning three in a row, including the first-ever Subway Series against the Mets in 2000.
- **2000:** The New Jersey Devils win another Stanley Cup.
- **2001:** In a highly emotional post–September 11 end of season, the Yankees win their fourth consecutive World Series berth—only to lose in the seventh game to the Arizona Diamondbacks.
- **2003:** The New Jersey Devils win the Stanley Cup once more.
- **2008:** The New York Giants, with Eli Manning at the helm, win the Super Bowl.

New Jersey Nets   Ages 8 & up. The 2001–02 season was a magical one for the Nets, who won the Eastern Conference championship and battled the L.A. Lakers for the national title. With the woe-is-me Knicks in a losing holding pattern, the Nets are the metropolitan area's current b-ball darlings. The regular season runs from November to mid-April. Izod Center, East Rutherford, NJ. © **800/7NJ-NETS** (765-6387), 201/935-3900 (for single-game tickets), or 201/507-8900 (Ticketmaster). www.nba.com/nets. Tickets $18–$500. Parking $8.

New York Giants   Ages 8 & up. With their spectacular win over the undefeated New England Patriots in Super Bowl 2008, Eli and company made a lot of New Yorkers Giants fans overnight. Because football teams play only once a week, there are few home games in the course of their September-to-December season, and just about the whole stadium goes with season ticket holders—to get tickets you have to know somebody, *be* somebody, or spring for a scalper. On game days, there's a New Jersey Transit bus from Port Authority Terminal, Eighth Avenue between 40th and 42nd streets—call © **212/ 564-1114** for information. *Warning:* It's an open-air stadium, so it gets bitterly cold by the end of the season. At Giants Stadium in the Meadowlands, East Rutherford, NJ. © **201/935-8222** or 201/935-3900 for single-game tickets. www.giants.com. Tickets $40 and $50. Parking $10.

New York Islanders   **Ages 8 & up.** A lively force in recent NHL seasons, the Islanders skate on their home ice out on Long Island (hence the name) from October to mid-April. Take the Long Island Rail Road from Penn Station, Seventh Avenue between 31st and 33rd streets, to Hempstead (bus service nearby) or Westbury (take a taxi to the Nassau Coliseum). To reach the coliseum by car, take the M4 exit off the Meadowbrook Parkway. At Nassau Veterans Memorial Coliseum, Hempstead Tpk., Uniondale, NY. ✆ 800/882-ISLES (882-47537), or 631/888-9000 (Ticketmaster). www.newyorkislanders.com. Tickets $17–$262.

New York Jets   **Ages 8 & up.** Playing in the same stadium as the Giants, the Jets have had some loser seasons in the recent past; but Jets fans are die-hards, and both individual and season tickets are totally sold out—you'll need connections, ticket agents, or a scalper to attend a game, and rest assured that they will take their profits off the top. On game days there's a New Jersey Transit bus from Port Authority Terminal, Eighth Avenue between 40th and 42nd streets—call ✆ 212/564-1114 for information. The regular season runs September through December. At Giants Stadium in the Meadowlands, East Rutherford, NJ. ✆ 516/560-8200. www.newyorkjets.com. Tickets $55 and $70. Parking $10.

New York Knicks   **Ages 8 & up.** The Knicks play 41 regular-season home games a year from November to mid-April. Though the team has suffered from injuries and whirlwind managerial changes the past few volatile seasons, getting tickets is still tough, unless you're Spike Lee. There's still hope: On the day of the game, the box office sometimes releases a small number of tickets (call ✆ 212/465-6040), and there are always scalpers who'll be happy to let you pay top dollar for tickets. At Madison Square Garden, Seventh Ave. btwn 31st and 33rd sts. ✆ 212/465-MSG1 (465-6741), 212/465-JUMP (465-5867), 800/4NBA-TIX (462-2849), or 212/307-7171 (Ticketmaster). www.nyknicks.com. Tickets $40–$285. Subway: A, C, E to 34th St./Penn Station; 1, 2, 3 to 34th St.

New York Liberty   **Ages 5 & up.** The success of professional women's basketball surprised all the pundits, who never expected the public to respond so immediately to its brand of clean, fast, non-trash-talking basketball. Kids, especially girls, have been an important part of the Liberty's audience all along (it helps that its June–Aug season coincides with school vacation); plenty of on-court activities during the breaks, along with a lively dog mascot who patrols the stands looking for kids to shake paws with, boosts the entertainment quotient for younger ones. At Madison Square Garden, Seventh Ave. btwn 31st and 33rd sts. ✆ 212/465-MSG1 (465-6741) or 877/WNBA-TIX (962-2849) (Ticketmaster), 212/564-WNBA (564-9622) for info. www.nyliberty.com. Tickets $10–$260. Subway: A, C, E to 34th St./Penn Station; 1, 2, 3 to 34th St.

New York Mets   **All ages.** With the 2005 hiring of Omar Minaya as general manager, the Mets have become National League contenders in a big way. The regular season runs mid-April through early October; throughout this stretch, 81 home games will be played at the brand-new home of the Mets, **Citi Field.** Tickets are best purchased in advance, but you may still be able to get tickets at the stadium on game day if you don't care about sitting close. The food is served in multiple sit-down, climate-controlled restaurants, a majority with field views and a wide range of menu choices. The family-friendly environment includes a Fan Fest family entertainment area on the Concourse level. **NY Waterway** runs a Mets Express ferry to the ballpark ($18 adults, $12 children 11 and under); call ✆ 800/533-3779 or order from www.nywaterway.com. Ferries depart from Weehawken, New Jersey; South Street Seaport; 34th Street at the East River; and 90th Street at the East River. At Citi Field, located at the north end of Flushing Meadows Corona Park in

Queens on Flushing Bay. ✆ **718/507-METS** (507-6387) or 718/507-TIXX (507-8499). www.mets. com. Tickets $5–$117. Free for children under 32 in. Subway: 7 to Citi Field.

New York Rangers **Ages 8 & up.** The Rangers play 41 hockey games, mostly at night, at Madison Square Garden during their season, from October to mid-April. Celebrities and CEOs pay as much as $500 for prized behind-the-bench seats, but in "Blue Heaven"—the cheap seats high above the ice—true hockey fans make Rangers games an audience-participation sport. Rangers tickets usually sell out a couple of months before the season starts, so buy in advance. At Madison Square Garden, Seventh Ave. btwn 31st and 33rd sts. ✆ **212/465-MSG1** or 212/307-7171 (Ticketmaster), 212/465-4459 for info. www.newyorkrangers.com. Tickets $25–$150. Subway: A, C, E to 34th St./Penn Station; 1, 2, 3 to 34th St.

New York Red Bulls **Ages 6 & up.** Playing from March to October, the Red Bulls have built an audience among all those kids and parents who've been bitten by the soccer bug through youth leagues. Games are generally Wednesday nights or weekend days or evenings. For game-time bus service from Manhattan's Port Authority Bus Terminal, call **New Jersey Transit** (✆ **800/772-2222**). **NY Waterway** (✆ **800/533-3779**) also offers a service for $35. At Giants Stadium in the Meadowlands, East Rutherford, NJ. ✆ **201/935-3900;** for tickets **888/4-METROTIX,** or 212/307-7171 and 201/507-8900 (Ticketmaster). www.redbulls. com. Tickets $10–$146. Parking $10.

New York Yankees **All ages.** Yankees fans have never minded watching their team roll effortlessly over all the competition. Only Derek Jeter is left from the halcyon days of the team that won consistently from 1996. Owner George Steinbrenner spent megabucks to acquire a whole new team of stars such as Alex Rodriguez, Hideki Matsui, and Johnny Damon (late of the rival Boston Red Sox). And guess what? They're all Yankees now and we love them! New York's American League team plays 81 home games at the brand-new Yankee Stadium, designed by HOK Sport. The new diamond has a replica of the beautiful copper frieze that once lined the old stadium's inner wall, and at a new Monument Park beyond the center field wall, kids can gaze at the retired jersey numbers and plaques of the Yankee heroes of yesteryear. The new ballpark has indoor and outdoor food courts. From mid-April to early October; order tickets in advance or buy them at the stadium ticket office on game day (when they're playing well, ticket availability gets tight toward fall). Show up a couple of hours early and you may be able to watch batting practice. To make it a really special outing, take the **NY Waterway** *Yankee Clipper* ferry to the stadium ($22 adults, $18 children 11 and under); call ✆ **800/533-3779** or order from www.nywaterway.com. Ferries depart from Weehawken, New Jersey; South Street Seaport; 34th Street at the East River; and 90th Street at the East River. At E. 161 St. and River Ave. ✆ **718/293-6000** or 212/307-1212 (Ticketmaster). www.yankees.com. Tickets $15–$65. Subway: B, D, 4 to 161st St.

Staten Island Yankees ⟨Value⟩ **Ages 6 & up.** The Yankees' Class A minor-league team hasn't quite achieved the retro glamour of their local rivals, the Brooklyn Cyclones; but the quality of play is high, and their ballpark is a pleasantly low-key place to watch the major-league stars of tomorrow show off their goods. Best of all, it's easy to get to, being within walking distance from the Staten Island Ferry terminal (all this and a cool boat ride, too!). Richmond County Bank Ballpark at St. George, 75 Richmond Terrace, Staten Island. ✆ **718/720-9200.** www.siyanks.com. Tickets $5–$13. Parking $5.

11 STORY HOURS

Babylicious   The weekly Thursday-morning story hour at this cozy TriBeCa children's boutique is geared for youngsters age 3 months to 4 years, so expect the picture books to be short and sweet—and expect everyone to be tolerant of wee ones' natural behavior. Face painting replaces story hour during the summer months. 51 Hudson St. ℂ 212/406-7440. Subway: 1 to Franklin St.

Barnes & Noble   **Ages 2 to 7.** Many of these bookstores hold lively, well-attended weekend story hours. Call ahead, or check www.bn.com to make sure of dates and times, but in general the East 86th Street branch holds Saturday and Sunday story hours at 11am, Union Square Sunday at 2:30pm, and TriBeCa Wednesday and Thursday at 11am and 4pm. (1) 240 E. 86th St. (btwn Second and Third aves.). ℂ 212/794-1962. Subway: 4, 5, 6 to 86th St. (2) 2289 Broadway (at 82nd St.). ℂ 212/362-8835. Subway: 1 to 79th St. (3) 1972 Broadway (at 66th St.). ℂ 212/595-6859. Subway: 1 to 66th St./Lincoln Center. (4) 675 Sixth Ave. (at 21st St.). ℂ 212/727-1227. Subway: F, V to 23rd St. (5) Union Square, 33 E. 17th St. (btwn Broadway and Park Ave.). ℂ 212/253-0810. Subway: N, Q, R, W, 4, 5, 6 to 14th St.; L to Union Square. (6) 396 Sixth Ave. (at 8th St.), Subway: B, C, D, E, F, V to W. 4th St.

Books of Wonder   **Ages 3 to 7.** This great Chelsea shop runs friendly story hours on Sunday at noon. 18 W. 18th St. (btwn Fifth and Sixth aves.). ℂ 212/989-3270. www.booksofwonder.net. Subway: 1 to 18th St.

Borders Books   At these large, welcoming chain stores, well-stocked children's departments usually hold weekly story hours for preschoolers: Columbus Circle holds two on Wednesdays at 10am and 2pm, and the Second Avenue store has them at 3:30pm on Thursdays. Check www.borders.com for updates. (1) 10 Columbus Circle (at Eighth Ave.). ℂ 212/823-9775. Subway A, B, C, D, 1 to 59th St./Columbus Circle. (2) 550 Second Ave. (at 31st St.) in Kips Bay Plaza. ℂ 212/685-3938. Subway: 6 to 33rd St. (3) 2 Penn Plaza (7th Ave. and 31st St.). ℂ 212/244-1814. Subway: 1, 2, 3 to 34th St. (4) 100 Broadway (at Pine St.). ℂ 212/964-1988. Subway: 2, 3, 4, 5 to Wall St.

Central Park   **Ages 2 to 8.** June through September, there are story hours here every Saturday at 11am, rain or shine. At the Hans Christian Andersen Statue, on the west side of Conservatory Water (at 74th St.). www.centralparknyc.org. Subway: 6 to 77th St.

Logos Bookstore   This pleasant Upper East Side shop holds story time every Monday at 3pm led by Lily Nass. During warm weather, story time is held outside in the garden. There is a 20% discount on books if you are a story-time participant. 1575 York Ave. (btwn 83rd and 84th sts.). ℂ 212/517-7292. Subway: 4, 5, 6 to 86th St.

Story Time in the MoMA Sculpture Garden   **Ages 4 to 7.** Listen to stories read by well-known authors and illustrators every Thursday except in June and August. Tickets are free and distributed on a first-come, first-served basis at the Cullman Education and Research building located at 4 West 54th St., beginning at 10:30am. Also worth checking out: the **Ford Family Programs** at MoMA, designed to teach kids about the rich and varied world of modern art. 11 W. 53rd St. (btwn Fifth and Sixth aves.). ℂ 212/708/9400. www.moma.org. Subway: E, V to Fifth Ave./53rd St.; B, D, F to 47th St./50th St./Rockefeller Center.

New York Public Library Ⓥalue   **Ages 2 to 8.** Nearly every weekday, some Manhattan branch library holds a story hour or shows short films about children's books or holds some kind of cool workshop—and it's all free. You can contact the NYPL at 8 W. 40th St., New York, NY 10018 (℃ **212/221-7676**), for a monthly brochure of events for children, or visit its website at www.nypl.org/events. Better yet, stop by the **Humanities and Social Science Library** at Fifth Avenue and 42nd Street, 20 W. 53rd St. (℃ **212/ 930-0830**), to see the original Winnie-the-Pooh animals on display. Various branches around Manhattan.

Scholastic Store Weekly story hours are held Tuesdays and Thursdays at 11am at the big, bright SoHo flagship of the Scholastic publishing house. On Wednesdays at 11am there's story hour in Spanish. Saturdays often feature interactive events planned around Scholastic titles—which luckily include such winners as the Harry Potter books, the adventures of Captain Underpants, and the 39 Steps interactive series. Check events at www.scholasticstore.com. 557 Broadway (btwn Prince and Spring). ℃ **212/343-6166.** Subway: N, R, W to Prince St.

---

12 ARCADES

ESPN Zone **Ages 8 & up.** Games here, on an upper floor of this clean and glossy theme restaurant (thus less walk-in street trade, which is a plus), tend to be sports-oriented—baseball, hockey, soccer, driving simulators, that sort of thing—rather than sci-fi–based shoot 'em-ups. Recommended for 1 to 2 hours of play. Children 17 and under are not admitted without an accompanying adult, which lessens the teen hangout factor. 1472 Broadway (at 42nd St.). ℃ **212/921-3776.** www.espnzone.com. Subway: N, Q, R, S, W, 1, 2, 3, 7 to 42nd St./Times Square.

12

Side Trips from New York City

Though New York City has enough attractions to keep even the most active child busy and interested, sometimes it's a relief to get away from the jangle of honking horns and crowded streets for a little while. When the weather's nice, a day trip from Manhattan can be just the ticket.

The following places are all within an hour of the city. A car would be the most convenient way to travel, but all are also reachable by train (or even, in the case of Philipsburg Manor, boat).

If you're interested in exploring farther afield, you might want to check out *Frommer's Wonderful Weekends from New York City* or *Frommer's Great Escapes from NYC Without Wheels.*

---

1 EDISON NATIONAL HISTORIC SITE

45 min. W. of Manhattan

"I always invented to obtain money to go on inventing," Thomas Edison once said. Yes, he was a gifted chemist and visionary, but he was also a shrewd businessman who amassed a fortune. The **Edison Laboratories** in West Orange, New Jersey, will reopen in January 2009 after extensive renovations. Just a mile from the labs is **Glenmont,** Edison's imposing mansion, which gives you a personal glimpse into the life of this man whose very name became synonymous with "genius."

ESSENTIALS

If you're driving, take either the Lincoln or Holland tunnels and take either the Garden State Parkway or the New Jersey Turnpike to I-280 westbound (exit 145 from the Garden State, exit 15-W from the NJ Turnpike). Follow I-280 west to exit 10; turn right at the end of the exit ramp, go to the end of the street, and make a left onto Main Street. At the second light, Park Way, you can turn left to reach the Edison home, Glenmont (pass through a gatehouse, follow Park Way to Glen Ave., turn right, then left onto Honeysuckle Ave.). If you continue on Main Street 2 more blocks, you will reach Lakeside Avenue and the Edison Laboratories.

New Jersey Transit (✆ 800/772-2222; www.njtransit.com) bus no. 21 takes you to the Mississippi Loop in West Orange; it's a pleasant quarter-mile stroll through a private gated community from there to Glenmont; or you can take a cab to Glenmont from the bus station.

WHAT TO SEE & DO

Glenmont Already a successful inventor and businessman, Edison bought this grand 29-room red Queen Anne–style mansion in Llewellyn Park for his second wife, Mina. All the original furnishings are here. Downstairs rooms reflect the formal Victorian style

of the era, with lots of ornate carved wood, damask wallcoverings, and stained-glass
windows; things get comfier upstairs in the family living room, where Edison's children
sometimes helped him look up scientific references in shelves full of books. In the master
bedroom, you can see the imposing bed where all three Edison children were born, and
where Edison himself died. An heiress in her own right, Mina presided over the elegant
mansion, raising their children and throwing lavish dinner parties, which workaholic
Thomas did his best to avoid. As a businessman, Edison saw the benefits of putting on
a high-class social front, but he didn't enjoy socializing. One thing's for sure: This was
probably the first house in the neighborhood with a phonograph, let alone the Home
Projecting Kinetoscope—the Edison children must have been very popular for play dates.

Honeysuckle Ave., Llewellyn Park, West Orange, NJ. © 973/324-9973. www.nps.gov/edis. Free admission. Wed–Sun 9am–5pm; tours on the hour 10am–4pm. Closed Dec 25 and Jan 1.

The Edison Laboratories *Note:* At press time, the lab was scheduled to reopen in
January 2009 after extensive renovations; please call ahead to check on the latest news.
Though Edison's first lab was in Menlo Park, New Jersey, this larger West Orange complex was in operation for over 40 years and accounted for over half of his patents. Notice
how closely the ivy-covered red-brick buildings are set together—Edison designed it this
way so he wouldn't waste too much time scurrying from chemistry lab to machine shop
to drafting room. Kids may be surprised to learn that, of the 1,093 patents credited to
Edison—the most any American has ever obtained—many were actually invented by
other scientists who worked for him. Walking around the restored lab complex, you can
visualize his team of some 200 researchers, hired to refine and improve existing inventions. There were light bulbs before Edison's, but his was more reliable, long-lasting, and
easy to manufacture; the telegraph, the phonograph, the stock ticker, the movie camera
and projector were all devices that other scientists pursued at the same time, but Edison's
versions *worked better.* Another 10,000 workers in the attached factory (not part of the
historic site) then mass-produced these inventions for commercial sale—he controlled
the entire cycle. Accessories, too—there's a music recording studio you can peek into,
where Edison engineers made sure phonograph customers would have something to play
on their new machines.

11 Main St. and Lakeside Ave., West Orange, NJ. © 973/736-0550. www.nps.gov/edis. Free admission. Hours to be announced upon reopening.

---

2 GARDEN CITY, LONG ISLAND

50 min. E of Manhattan

Across the road from the Nassau Coliseum, one of the New York area's best-kept secrets
is quietly growing into a museum powerhouse. Eventually, this Mitchel Field complex—
referred to as "Museum Row"—will include a science-and-technology museum and even
a vintage carousel. If your kids are enamored with fireman and fire trucks, the newly
opened **Nassau County Firefighters Museum** (© 516/572-4177; www.ncfiremuseum.
org; Tues–Sun 10am–5pm; $4 adults, $3.50 kids 2–12) has interactive exhibits in a
10,000-square-foot facility. But the complex's two major museums—**The Long Island
Children's Museum (LICM)** and **the Cradle of Aviation Museum**—definitely make
this worth the hour's drive from Manhattan. You could spend a day here—the morning
at the children's museum, the afternoon at the aviation museum—and it still wouldn't be
enough time to see and do everything.

If you're driving, take the Long Island Expressway to exit 38 for the Northern Parkway. You'll quickly see signs for the Meadowbrook Parkway South (exit 31A). From the Meadowbrook, take exit M4 West, which will take you onto Charles Lindbergh Boulevard. The museums are on the right side after the traffic light.

Long Island Rail Road (© 718/217-5477; www.mta.nyc.ny.us/lirr) trains from Penn Station will take you to the Garden City station or the Mineola station. One-way adult fares are $6 to $8.50 (onboard fares higher), depending on time of travel. A cab ride from either station to the museum costs about $6.

WHAT TO SEE & DO

The Long Island Children's Museum (LICM)
The two-story LICM echoes with children's excitement. The ground floor is geared for the younger set, with a special **TotSpot** play area for under-5s, the ever-popular **bubble room,** and a mazelike climbing structure called **ClimbIt@LICM** (which cleverly has a ramp, so it's wheelchair accessible). The **ToolBox** area attracts young tinkerers to its carpentry worktables, where kids can discover the principles of simple machines, and **Sandy Island** is much more of a science lab than you might think—various stations demonstrate wave motions, sediment patterns, and erosion, with plenty of sand samples to peer at under microscopes.

Older kids will gravitate upstairs. In the **Communication Station,** kids explore various modes of communication, from speaking tubes to Morse Code telegraphs to telephones. The **mock TV station** is a big hit—your kids may want to see themselves projected on a giant TV screen as big-time news broadcasters—and the adjacent radio station lets them practice being DJs and putter around with sound effects. We had a ball in the **mUSic Gallery,** testing different drums and xylophones; in the **Bubbles** gallery you can not only step inside a giant bubble but also make a huge bubble honeycomb. **It's Alive!** focuses on animal habitats (including human ones), and **Bricks & Sticks** is full of young block-builders. Children 6 and up enjoy an exhibit called **Changes & Challenges,** which aims to sensitize kids to disabilities: There are wheelchairs and crutches to experiment with, Braille to touch, lenses showing what the world looks like to people with diminished sight, a phone that plays only muted conversation, and writing as it might appear to a dyslexic child. The **Pattern Studio** sounds simple—computer monitors and wooden blocks where you can fiddle around with recurrent visual images—but it's a favorite among kids and parents alike.

Like all children's museums, this one can get noisy and chaotic at times, depending on the ages of the school groups milling around. The ticket policy is set up to prevent overcrowding, though, so call in advance to get a time slot.

11 Davis Ave., Garden City, NY (museum entrance on Charles Lindbergh Blvd.). © **516/224-5800.** www. licm.org. Admission $10, free for children under 1 and members. Tickets are sold for specific time slots when crowded; in inclement weather, call ahead for schedule. Sept–June Tues–Sun 10am–5pm; July–Aug daily 10am–5pm.

Cradle of Aviation Museum ★ (Finds)
Right next door to the Long Island Children's Museum, this is like a miniversion of Washington's Air and Space Museum, fascinating but not overwhelmingly big. It's focused on Long Island's aviation history—this site is, after all, where Lindbergh took off on his historic flight to Paris. Famed aviatrix Harriet Quimby trained here, and major companies like Curtiss and Grumman were located a stone's throw away. The local-history hook really means something.

Walk into the glass atrium and there's a supersonic F-11 Tiger suspended overhead; from the gallery's catwalk entrance, you can gaze straight ahead at an authentic 1909 Bleriot monoplane, a *Spirit of St. Louis* sister plane, and Grumman Wildcats, Hellcats, and Tomcats; around the corner, in the space exploration section, there's an original 1972 lunar landing module displayed in a rugged mock moonscape. Inside a hangar you can see even more of the collection's really big aircraft, including an F-14 and the nose of a speed-record-setting El Al 707. There are plenty of hands-on activities—a hot-air balloon you can inflate, cockpits you can climb into, and a mesmerizing monitor displaying current air traffic across the U.S. For an additional $2 you can spend 20 minutes executing a simulated mission to Mars, an activity that includes 4 minutes on a better-than-average motion simulator. There's also an IMAX show every hour. Loads of volunteers, many of them retired engineers and pilots, mill about, eager to share their knowledge; a number of them personally helped to restore the planes on display.

1 Davis Ave., Garden City, NY (museum entrance on Charles Lindbergh Blvd.). ℂ **516/572-4111.** www. cradleofaviation.org. Admission $9 adults, $8 kids 2–12; IMAX tickets $8.50 adults, $6.50 kids 2–12. Tues– Sun 9:30am–5pm; IMAX open daily. Closed Dec 25 and Jan 1.

WHERE TO EAT

The Long Island Children's Museum has a cafeteria space, but you'll have to bring your own food or buy snacks at the vending machines. The Cradle of Aviation is better equipped foodwise, with the **Red Planet Cafe** selling sandwiches, packaged salads, and drinks. Otherwise, you can drive to the end of Charles Lindbergh Boulevard, keeping right at the fork, and turn left onto Stewart Avenue for the usual mix of chain restaurants in strip malls.

3 PLAYLAND

50 min. N of Manhattan

Remember the movie *Big,* when Tom Hanks's younger self made his fateful wish to be big after missing the height requirement for a roller coaster? That was shot at Playland. A pleasant antidote to the big, overhyped mega theme parks that proliferate all over the country, this old-timey collection of rides and games in a conveniently close seaside suburb is like a window into a kinder, gentler past.

ESSENTIALS

By **car,** take I-95 north to exit 19 in Rye (Playland Pkwy.) and then follow the signs to Playland. Parking costs $5 Tuesday to Friday, $7 Saturday and Sunday, and $10 holidays. Senior citizens with a valid ID only pay $1 except for holidays.

Metro-North Railroad trains take about 45 minutes from Grand Central Terminal to the Rye station. Adult one-way fares are $9.25 peak and $6.75 off-peak; children travel $4.50 peak and $3.50 off-peak. From the Rye station, take bus no. 75 to Playland. Metro-North also organizes seasonal Playland packages, which include train and bus fare and a book of Playland tickets. These packages are likely to be cheaper than buying train tickets and Playland tickets separately; call Metro-North (ℂ **800/METRO-INFO** [638-7646] or 212/532-4900; www.mta.nyc.ny.us/mnr, or www.mta.info.com) for details.

No mere rinky-dink midway, Playland is actually listed on the National Register of Historic Places. In 1923, the Westchester County Park Commission decided to create an "unequaled seaside public park to provide clean, wholesome recreation for the people of Westchester County"; Playland opened in 1928, right on Long Island Sound, and has lived up to its promise ever since. It's been kept up beautifully, with neat landscaping, landmark Art Deco buildings, and old-fashioned charm: striped awnings, painted wooden fences enclosing the rides, and festive-looking ticket booths.

Playland features so many rides, food stalls, games, and other amusements, I can't list them all. Kids 5 and under should be steered straight to **Kiddyland,** which has rides tailored to their size like the Kiddy Whip, Kiddyland Bumper Cars, and the Demolition Derby. For older kids, the most thrilling rides are probably the vintage wooden **Dragon Coaster** (tame by Busch Gardens standards, but enough to make me lose my lunch), the **Super Flight,** the **Crazy Mouse,** and **Double Shot.** Great fun are retro rides like the **Ferris wheel,** the **Whip,** and the **Grand Carousel.** A new ride, the **Playland Yo-Yo,** spins riders in swings around and around. Plan on several hours here; your kids will insist on it.

In addition to the rides, Playland has a beach, a pool, an ice rink, minigolf, and a lake for boating, which are open seasonally.

Playland Pkwy., Rye, NY. ✆ **914/813-7010.** www.ryeplayland.org. Free admission, but rides each require 2–4 points from a point card: $20 for a 20-point card, $30 for a 30-point card, $35 for a 6-hr. unlimited ride card. May–Sept noon–midnight; days of operation vary (check website for details).

WHERE TO EAT

Playland offers many types of food in **concession stands**—such as Burger King, Nathan's Hot Dogs, Caliente Express, David's Cookies, and Captain Hook. There are also attractive picnic areas.

4 PHILIPSBURG MANOR

45–50 min. N of Manhattan

Leafy, suburban Tarrytown is one of those Hudson Valley towns that has been around since colonial days and still maintains pockets of quiet charm. It's a great place to visit the past, since there are four historic homes in relative proximity: Philipsburg Manor, Sunnyside (Washington Irving's home), Van Cortlandt Manor in Croton-on-Hudson, and the Rockefeller estate, Kykuit. Of the four, Philipsburg offers the most for children, but you could easily visit two homes in 1 day if your crew has the stamina.

ESSENTIALS

By **car,** take I-95 or the Henry Hudson Parkway/Saw Mill River Parkway north to the New York State Thruway (I-87), and go west toward the Tappan Zee Bridge. Get off I-87 at exit 9, Tarrytown, the last exit before the Tappan Zee Bridge. Go left on NY 119 and then take a quick right onto U.S. 9 north. Philipsburg Manor is 2 miles north on the left.

Metro-North (✆ **800/METRO-INFO** [638-7646] or 212/532-4900; www.mta.nyc. ny.us/mnr) offers local train service from Grand Central Terminal directly to Philipsburg Manor (a 50-min. ride) or express train service to Tarrytown (a 40-min. ride). One-way adult fares are $7.50 to $10, depending on when you travel; children's fares are $3.75 to

$4 (ages 5–11 with an adult). If you get off at the Philipse Manor station, you can walk to your destination (¹/₃ mile). From the Tarrytown station, you'll need to take a cab, which costs about $6. Call for details.

For information on children's workshops and special events at any of the four historic homes in the area, check out **Historic Hudson Valley's** website at **www.hudsonvalley.org**.

VISITING THE MANOR

An 18th-century colonial farm with a working gristmill, a yard full of animals, a farmhouse, and a tenant house, Philipsburg Manor fascinates school-age children. A long wooden bridge crosses the millpond near the entrance, leading on to the main house; long and close to the water, the bridge is fun to run across, sweeping you straight into the 18th century once you reach the other side.

Guides decked out in 18th-century dress demonstrate various farm activities of that era: milling, sheep shearing, plowing, and dairying. Every half-hour a guide gives a **tour of the farmhouse,** where the wealthy Philipse family once lived. The **stone manor house,** built between 1682 and 1720, includes interesting details of colonial life, including a night box to guard candles from rat attacks and a big white mound in the kitchen you later learn is sugar (the guide allows kids several guesses on that one). However, it was African slaves who actually worked the property for the Philipse family, laboriously threshing their wheat and grinding it into flour (there was indeed slavery outside of the South, folks), and their lives centered more on the **barnyard.** Children under 8, who may have started to weary during the house tour, will perk up when they see the sheep, chickens, cows, and cats wandering about the barnyard, though they won't be allowed to pet the animals. Just be aware that with the pond and the stream so close, parental supervision is necessary at all times.

U.S. 9, Sleepy Hollow, NY. ✆ **914/631-3992** or 914/631-8200. www.hudsonvalley.org. Admission $12 adults, $10 seniors, $6 children 5–17, free for children 5 and under. April–Oct Wed–Mon 10am–5pm; Nov–Dec Wed–Mon 10am–4pm; Mar weekends only 10am–4pm. Closed Thanksgiving, Dec 25, and Jan–Feb.

WHERE TO EAT

The new **Mint Cafe** (open seasonally) offers panini-style sandwiches, salads, and ice cream with views of historic Philipsburg Manor.

---

5 MARITIME AQUARIUM AT NORWALK

---

1 hr. NE of Manhattan

Focusing on the marine ecology of Long Island Sound, the **Maritime Aquarium** is just as pleasant a place to view marine life as the New York Aquarium in Coney Island (p. 182), and if you've got a car, it's perhaps easier to get here; it's certainly easier to get here from Manhattan than it is to visit the superb Mystic Aquarium at the other end of Connecticut.

ESSENTIALS

By car, take I-95 heading east/north to the South Norwalk exit (exit 14) off I-95 and follow the signs to the Maritime Center; it's about a 6-minute drive from the highway. Or take the Hutchinson River Parkway north, which becomes the Merritt Parkway in Connecticut; take exit 39A, and follow the signs on U.S. 7 to the Maritime Center. Parking at the center costs up to $5.

Metro-North trains (© **800/METRO-INFO** [638-7646] or 212/532-4900; www. mta.nyc.ny.us/mnr) to South Norwalk cost $9.75 to $13 for adults, $5 o $6.50 for children 5 to 11, and free for children 4 and under. Travel time is about 60 minutes. From the South Norwalk station, take a short taxi ride or walk—it's only about 3 blocks. When you get off the train, turn left, and go down the stairs at the end of the platform; turn right at the bottom of the stairs, walk under the bridge, and go 1¹/₂ blocks to the first traffic light, at the intersection of Main and Monroe streets. Turn left onto Main Street, and go to the next traffic light; then turn right onto Washington Street. Go under another bridge, and continue past shops and restaurants to the next traffic light, at the corner of Washington and Water streets. You'll see the large red-brick Maritime Aquarium on your left.

EXPLORING THE AQUARIUM

Go up free-standing stairs in the lobby and across a midair bridge to the second-floor entrance, where carpeted walkways lead through a softly lit series of **20 marine habitats,** progressing from salt marsh to the ocean depths. You'll see a thousand or so marine creatures of more than 125 species, all native to Long Island Sound, including sleek speckled harbor seals that flop around an indoor/outdoor pool in the lobby (watch them being fed at 11:45am, 1:45pm, and 3:45pm) and bright-eyed otters in the woodland shoreline habitat. Sand tiger sharks circle and glare at you through the glass in enormous ocean tanks; immense, primeval-looking loggerhead turtles paddle like wise old grandpas in another tank; and jellyfish shimmer seductively in the Jellyfish Encounter. Kids who want to get really close to sea creatures—sea stars, horseshoe crabs, whelks—can linger at the **Touch Tank** or, if they're bold enough, pet a live ray at the **Ray Touch Pool.**

Two-story **Maritime Hall** has loads of interactive educational displays on fish, as well as displays on navigation and a wooden-boat workshop. The second-floor **Ocean Playscape** is a colorful marine-themed play area for children 4 and under. Aside from regular exhibits, the aquarium always has on tap some intriguing traveling exhibit or other, as well as an **IMAX theater** with a rotation of megascreen natural-history films. An excellent gift shop lies in wait at the end of your day.

N. Water St., Norwalk, CT. © **203/852-0700.** www.maritimeaquarium.org. Admission $12 adults, $11 seniors, $9.75 children 2–12; IMAX tickets $9–$12 adults, $8–$11 seniors, $6.50–$9.50 children 2–12. Daily 10am–5pm (to 6pm July to Labor Day). Closed Thanksgiving and Dec 25.

WHERE TO EAT

The **Cascade Café** on the second floor offers clam chowder, burgers, chicken fingers, pizza, sandwiches, and salads at reasonable prices. It's open daily from 10am to 4pm.

Appendix:
Fast Facts, Useful Toll-Free
Numbers & Websites

1 FAST FACTS: NEW YORK CITY

AREA CODES The area codes for New York City are 212, 646, 718, 917, and 347. Make sure to dial the area code before your call, even if you are in the same area.

ATM NETWORKS See "Money & Costs," p. 38.

BABYSITTING Many New York hotels provide babysitting services or keep a list of reliable sitters. If your hotel doesn't, call the **Baby Sitters Guild** (© 212/682-0227; www.babysittersguild.com). It provides in-room child-care, as well as on-request trips to the playground, the Central Park Zoo, and so on, for children of all ages, with licensed, bonded, insured sitters (baby nurses are trained in CPR) who speak a range of languages.

BUSINESS HOURS The city that never sleeps truly doesn't. Although Midtown **stores** tend to close at 6pm, shops in residential areas often stay open to 7pm or so, with drugstores and groceries usually going strong until 9pm or later, and delis and corner produce markets lasting on into the wee hours. Most stores (except for Midtown and Upper East Side boutiques) are open on Sunday, though they may not open until noon. **Restaurants** stay open late, usually at least until 11pm, and most are open 7 days a week. Many **museums** are closed on Monday, but several have

late hours—until 9 or 10pm—on Thursday, Friday, or Saturday. **Banks** tend to keep more standard hours—Monday to Friday 9am to 3pm, although **Commerce Bank** branches (go to www.commerce online.com for Manhattan locations) are open 7 days a week.

CAR RENTALS See "Getting Around," p. 57.

CURRENCY The most common bills are the $1 (a "buck"), $5, $10, and $20 denominations. There are also $2 bills (seldom encountered), $50 bills, and $100 bills (the last two are usually not welcome as payment for small purchases).

Coins come in seven denominations: 1¢ (1 cent, or a penny); 5¢ (5 cents, or a nickel); 10¢ (10 cents, or a dime); 25¢ (25 cents, or a quarter); 50¢ (50 cents, or a half dollar); the gold-colored Sacagawea and nearly identical Presidential coin, worth $1; and the rare silver dollar.

For additional information see "Money & Costs," p. 38.

DOCTORS The **NYU Downtown Hospital** offers physician referrals at © 888/698-3362.

DRINKING LAWS The legal age in New York for purchase and consumption of alcoholic beverages is 21; proof of age is required and often requested at bars, nightclubs, and restaurants, so it's always a good idea to bring ID when you go out. You can also be fined for drinking publicly from an open container—which means if you do want to enjoy a bottle of beer or wine during a picnic in Central Park, be certain it's covered in a brown paper bag.

DRIVING RULES See "Getting Around," p. 57.

DRUGSTORES Several **Duane Reade** stores are open 24 hours a day; **www. duanereade.com** lists them all. Some centrally located ones are at Broadway and 57th Street (✆ 212/541-9708), Broadway and 94th Street (✆ 212/663-1580), Third Avenue and 74th Street (✆ 212/744-2668), Columbus Circle at 58th Street (✆ 212/265-2302; pharmacy closes 9pm weekdays, 7pm weekends), Lexington and 47th Street (✆ 212/682-5338; pharmacy closes 8:30pm weekdays, 5pm weekends), and Third Avenue at 14th Street (✆ 212/529-7140; pharmacy closes 9pm). For **Rite-Aid** 24-hour locations, consult **www. riteaid.com**; these include the Lower East Side location at Grand and Clinton streets (✆ 212/529-7115) and Second Avenue between 30th and 31st streets (✆ 212/213-9887).

ELECTRICITY Like Canada, the United States uses 110 to 120 volts AC (60 cycles), compared to 220 to 240 volts AC (50 cycles) in most of Europe, Australia, and New Zealand. Downward converters that change 220–240 volts to 110–120 volts are difficult to find in the United States, so bring one with you.

EMBASSIES & CONSULATES All embassies are located in the nation's capital, Washington, D.C. Some consulates are located in major U.S. cities, and most nations have a mission to the United Nations in New York City. If your country isn't listed below, call for directory information in Washington, D.C. (✆ 202/555-1212) or log on to **www.embassy.org/embassies**.

The embassy of **Australia** is at 1601 Massachusetts Ave. NW, Washington, DC 20036 (✆ 202/797-3000; www.austemb. org). There are consulates in New York, Honolulu, Houston, Los Angeles, and San Francisco.

The embassy of **Canada** is at 501 Pennsylvania Ave. NW, Washington, DC 20001 (✆ 202/682-1740; www.canadianembassy. org). Other Canadian consulates are in Buffalo (New York), Detroit, Los Angeles, New York, and Seattle.

The embassy of **Ireland** is at 2234 Massachusetts Ave. NW, Washington, DC 20008 (✆ 202/462-3939; www.ireland emb.org). Irish consulates are in Boston, Chicago, New York, San Francisco, and other cities. See website for complete listing.

The embassy of **New Zealand** is at 37 Observatory Circle NW, Washington, DC 20008 (✆ 202/328-4800; www.nz embassy.com). New Zealand consulates are in Los Angeles, Salt Lake City, San Francisco, and Seattle.

The embassy of the **United Kingdom** is at 3100 Massachusetts Ave. NW, Washington, DC 20008 (✆ 202/588-7800; www.britainusa.com). Other British consulates are in Atlanta, Boston, Chicago, Cleveland, Houston, Los Angeles, New York, San Francisco, and Seattle.

EMERGENCIES Call ✆ **911** for police, fire, and ambulance service. Fires can also be reported in Manhattan by dialing ✆ **212/628-2900** or 212/999-2222. The **Poison Control Center** can be reached at ✆ **800/222-1222** toll-free from any phone. If you encounter serious problems, contact **Traveler's Aid International** (✆ **202/546-1127**; www.travelersaid.org) to help direct you to a local branch. This nationwide, nonprofit, social-service organization geared to helping travelers in difficult straits offers services that might include reuniting families separated while traveling, providing food and/or shelter to people stranded without cash, or even emotional counseling.

GASOLINE (PETROL) At press time, in the U.S., the cost of gasoline (also known as gas, but never petrol) was abnormally high, often topping $4 per gallon. Taxes are already included in the printed price. One U.S. gallon equals 3.8 liters or .85 imperial gallons. Fill-up locations are known as gas or service stations.

HOLIDAYS Banks, government offices, post offices, and many stores, restaurants, and museums are closed on the following legal national holidays: January 1 (New Year's Day), the third Monday in January (Martin Luther King Day), the third Monday in February (Presidents' Day), the last Monday in May (Memorial Day), July 4 (Independence Day), the first Monday in September (Labor Day), the second Monday in October (Columbus Day), November 11 (Veterans Day/Armistice Day), the fourth Thursday in November (Thanksgiving Day), and December 25 (Christmas). The Tuesday after the first Monday in November is Election Day, a federal government holiday in presidential-election years (held every 4 years, and next in 2012).

For more information on holidays, see "Kids' Favorite New York City Events" in chapter 3.

HOSPITALS The following hospitals have full-service emergency rooms: **New York University Medical Center,** 550 First Ave., at 33rd Street (✆ 212/263-7300); **New York Presbyterian Hospital,** 510 E. 70th St. (✆ 212/746-5454); **St. Vincent's Hospital,** 12th Street and Seventh Avenue (✆ 212/604-7000); and **St. Luke's-Roosevelt Hospital,** 59th Street and Tenth Avenue (✆ 212/523-6800).

HOT LINES For information on theater, music, and dance performances, check out **NYC On Stage** online at www.tdf.org. Review current offerings at **Lincoln Center** (✆ 212/LINCOLN; www.lincoln center.org). The **City Parks Special Events Hot Line** (✆ 888/NY-PARKS; www.nyc govparks.org) gives details on outdoor concerts and performances and New York Roadrunner Club events. Listings of commercial films are available through **Moviefone** (✆ 212/777-FILM [777-3456]) and **Fandango** (✆ 800/326-3264), which allows you to prepurchase movie tickets via credit card. **Sports Scores** (✆ 212/976-1717) gives updates on the most recent pro sports events.

INTERNET ACCESS The **Times Square Visitor Information Center,** 1560 Broadway, between 46th and 47th streets (✆ 212/768-1560; open daily 7am–7pm), has computer terminals that you can use to send e-mails courtesy of Yahoo!. In Times Square, **easyInternetCafé,** 234 W. 42nd St., between Seventh and Eighth avenues (✆ 212/398-0775; www.easyeverything. com), is open 24/7. Most hotels have Internet access in their public spaces.

LEGAL AID If you are "pulled over" for a minor infraction (such as speeding), never attempt to pay the fine directly to a police officer; this could be construed as attempted bribery, a much more serious crime. Pay fines by mail, or directly into the hands of the clerk of the court. If accused of a more serious offense, say and do nothing before consulting a lawyer. In the U.S. the burden is on the state to prove a person's guilt beyond a reasonable doubt, and everyone has the right to remain silent, whether he or she is suspected of a crime or actually arrested. Once arrested, a person can make one telephone call to a party of his or her choice. International visitors should call their embassy or consulate.

LIBRARIES At any branch of the **New York Public Library,** you can pick up a monthly brochure listing all the kids' activities planned—films, story hours, puppet shows, and the like—at the system's many branches. These are usually wonderful programs, and they're absolutely free. The magnificent **Humanities & Social Science Library** at Fifth Avenue and 42nd Street, 20 W. 53rd St. (© **212/ 930-0830**), is a good place to start. The **Donnell Library,** 20 W. 53rd St. (© **212/ 621-0636**), has the main children's room for the entire system, with lots of scheduled readings and events. Branches with good children's rooms include **Jefferson Market,** 425 Sixth Ave., at West 10th Street (© **212/243-4334**); **Yorkville,** 222 E. 79th St. (© **212/744-5824**); **Epiphany,** 228 E. 23rd St. (© **212/679-2645**); and **St. Agnes,** 444 Amsterdam Ave., at 82nd Street (© **212/877-4380**).

The **Early Childhood Resources & Information Center** at 66 Leroy St. (© **212/929-0815**) has lots of parenting books, as well as a big indoor play space for kids 6 and under.

LOST & FOUND Be sure to tell all of your credit card companies the minute you discover your wallet has been lost or stolen and file a report at the nearest police precinct. Your credit card company or insurer may require a police report number or record of the loss. Most credit card companies have an emergency toll-free number to call if your card is lost or stolen; they may be able to wire you a cash advance immediately or deliver an emergency credit card in a day or two. Visa's U.S. emergency number is © **800/847- 2911** or 410/581-9994. American Express cardholders and traveler's check holders should call © **800/221-7282.** Master-Card holders should call © **800/307- 7309** or 636/722-7111. For other credit cards, call the toll-free number directory at © **800/555-1212.**

If you need emergency cash over the weekend when all banks and American Express offices are closed, you can have money wired to you via **Western Union** (© **800/325-6000;** www.westernunion. com).

MAIL At press time, domestic postage rates were 27¢ for a postcard and 42¢ for a letter. For international mail, a first-class letter of up to 1 ounce costs 94¢ (72¢ to Canada and Mexico); a first-class postcard costs 94¢ (72¢ to Canada and Mexico). For more information go to **www.usps. com** and click on "Calculate Postage."

If you aren't sure what your address will be in the United States, mail can be sent to you, in your name, c/o General Delivery at the main post office of the city or region where you expect to be. (Call © **800/275- 8777** for information on the nearest post office.) The addressee must pick up mail in person and must produce proof of identity (driver's license, passport, and so on). Most post offices will hold your mail for up to 1 month, and are open Monday to Friday from 8am to 6pm, and Saturday from 9am to 3pm.

Always include zip codes when mailing items in the U.S. If you don't know your zip code, visit www.usps.com/zip4.

NEWSPAPERS & MAGAZINES New York City has three vigorous daily newspapers: the well-known *New York Times* and the tabloids the *New York Daily News* and the *New York Post.* The *Wall Street Journal* is also published here, though its scope is national rather than local. Weekly newspapers include the downtown-oriented *Village Voice* and the uptown-oriented *New York Observer,* printed on distinctive peach-colored paper. Weekly magazines with comprehensive cultural listings include *New York Magazine, Time Out,* and the *New Yorker.*

PASSPORTS For Residents of Australia: You can pick up an application from your local post office or any branch of Passports Australia, but you must schedule an interview at the passport office to present your application materials. Call the **Australian Passport Information Service** at © **131-232,** or visit the government website at www.passports.gov.au.

For Residents of Canada: Passport applications are available at travel agencies throughout Canada or from the central **Passport Office,** Department of Foreign Affairs and International Trade, Ottawa,

ON K1A 0G3 (© **800/567-6868;** www. ppt.gc.ca). *Note:* Canadian children who travel must have their own passport. However, if you hold a valid Canadian passport issued before December 11, 2001, that bears the name of your child, the passport remains valid for you and your child until it expires.

For Residents of Ireland: You can apply for a 10-year passport at the **Passport Office,** Setanta Centre, Molesworth Street, Dublin 2 (© **01/671-1633;** www. irlgov.ie/iveagh). Those under age 18 and over 65 must apply for a 3-year passport. You can also apply at 1A South Mall, Cork (© **021/272-525**), or at most main post offices.

For Residents of New Zealand: You can pick up a passport application at any New Zealand Passports Office or download it from their website. Contact the **Passports Office** at © **0800/225-050** in New Zealand or 04/474-8100, or log on to www.passports.govt.nz.

For Residents of the United Kingdom: To pick up an application for a standard 10-year passport (5-year passport for children 15 and under), visit your nearest passport office, major post office, or travel agency, or contact the **United Kingdom Passport Service** at © **0870/521-0410** or search its website at www. ips.gov.uk.

POLICE Dial **911.**

POST OFFICES The **main post office** at Eighth Avenue between 31st and 33rd streets (© **212/330-3668**) is open daily 24 hours. There are many other branches around town. Call the **Postal Answer Line** at © **800/ASK-USPS** (275-8777) for information.

RESTROOMS See "Finding a Restroom," in chapter 4.

SAFETY Areas to avoid after dark if you're not a local: the deserted after-hours Wall Street area, the Lower East Side, the East Village east of First Avenue, Midtown

west of Ninth Avenue, and uptown north of 96th Street (except for the corridor along Broadway up to 120th St.).

SMOKING New York's laws against smoking in public places are among the country's strictest. There is no smoking allowed inside theaters, museums, stores, buses, or subways; on trains, you must find a designated smoking car; and in restaurants or bars, unless they are large enough to include a designated smoking area, smoking is off-limits. When you book a hotel room, specifically request a smoking room or you may be placed on a no-smoking floor.

TAXES The United States has no value-added tax (VAT) or other indirect tax at the national level. New York City's **sales tax** is 8.375%; this tax will not appear on price tags. You do not have to pay sales tax on groceries, takeout food, or any clothing and shoe purchases. **Hotels** add a 13.375% hotel tax to room rates.

TELEPHONES For directory assistance, dial © **411** or [area code] + **555-1212.** There are public phones on every other street corner in Manhattan, though not all are in what you'd call working order; large hotels generally have a bank of public phones off the lobby, too. A local call costs 50¢. Pay phones do not accept pennies, and few will take anything larger than a quarter.

Generally, hotel surcharges on long-distance and local calls are astronomical, so you're better off using your **cellphone** or a **public pay telephone** (if you can find one). Many convenience groceries and packaging services sell **prepaid calling cards** in denominations up to $50; for international visitors these can be the least expensive way to call home. Many public phones at airports now accept American Express, MasterCard, and Visa credit cards.

Most long-distance and international calls can be dialed directly from any phone. **For calls within the United States**

and to Canada, dial 1 followed by the area code and the seven-digit number. **For other international calls,** dial 011 followed by the country code, the city code, and the number you are calling.

Calls to area codes **800, 888, 877,** and **866** are toll-free. However, calls to area codes **700** and **900** (chat lines, bulletin boards, "dating" services, and so on) can be very expensive—usually a charge of 95¢ to $3 or more per minute, and they sometimes have minimum charges that can run as high as $15 or more.

For **reversed-charge or collect calls,** and for person-to-person calls, dial the number 0 then the area code and number; an operator will come on the line, and you should specify whether you are calling collect, person-to-person, or both. If your operator-assisted call is international, ask for the overseas operator.

Telegraph and telex services are provided primarily by Western Union. You can telegraph money, or have it telegraphed to you, very quickly over the Western Union system, but this service can cost as much as 15% to 20% of the amount sent.

Most hotels have **fax machines** available for guest use (be sure to ask about the charge to use it). Many hotel rooms are even wired for guests' fax machines. A less expensive way to send and receive faxes may be at stores such as **The UPS Store** (formerly Mail Boxes Etc.).

TIME   New York City is in the **Eastern Time Zone.** (The continental United States has four time zones, each 1 hr. apart: Eastern, Central, Mountain, and Pacific, with Alaska and Hawaii having their own zones.) From November to early March, it is on Eastern Standard Time **(EST),** which is 5 hours behind Greenwich Mean Time; **daylight saving time (EDT)** takes effect at 2am the second Sunday in March and holds sway until 2am the first Sunday in November, moving the clock 1 hour ahead of standard time.

TIPPING   Tips are a very important part of certain workers' income, and gratuities are the standard way of compensating them for services provided. In hotels, tip **bellhops** at least $1 per bag ($2–$3 if you have a lot of luggage) and tip the **chamber staff** $1 to $2 per day (more if you've left a disaster area for him or her to clean up). Tip the **doorman** or **concierge** only if he or she has provided you with some specific service (for example, calling a cab for you or obtaining difficult-to-get theater tickets). Tip the **valet-parking attendant** $1 every time you get your car.

In restaurants, bars, and nightclubs, tip **service staff** 15% to 20% of the check (25% in cheaper restaurants—especially if your waiter has provided extra attention to keep your children happy—or for food deliveries). Tip **checkroom attendants** $1 per garment, package, or stroller.

Tip **cab drivers** 10% to 20% of the fare; tip **skycaps** at airports at least $1 per bag ($2–$3 if you have a lot of luggage); and tip **hairdressers** and **barbers** 15% to 20%.

TOILETS   See "Finding a Restroom," in chapter 4.

USEFUL PHONE NUMBERS   U.S. Dept. of State Travel Advisory: ☎ 202/647-5225 (manned 24 hr.).

U.S. Passport Agency: ☎ 202/647-0518.

U.S. Centers for Disease Control International Traveler's Hotline: ☎ 404/332-4559.

For local **time** and **weather,** call ☎ 212/976-2828 or 976-4111 (you'll also get current winning lottery numbers).

VISAS   For information about U.S. visas, go to **http://travel.state.gov** and click on "Visas." Or go to one of the following sites:

Australian citizens can obtain up-to-date visa information from the **U.S. Embassy Canberra,** Moonah Place, Yarralumla, ACT 2600 (☎ **02/6214-5600**), or by checking the U.S. Diplomatic

Mission's website at **http://usembassy-australia.state.gov/consular**.

British subjects can obtain up-to-date visa information by calling the **U.S. Embassy Visa Information Line** (© **0891/200-290**) or by visiting the "Visas to the U.S." section of the American Embassy London's website at **www.usembassy.org.uk**.

Irish citizens can obtain up-to-date visa information through the **Embassy of the USA Dublin**, 42 Elgin Rd., Dublin 4,

Ireland (© **353/1-668-8777,** or by checking the "Consular Services" section of the website at **http://dublin.usembassy.gov**.

Citizens of **New Zealand** can obtain up-to-date visa information by contacting the **U.S. Embassy New Zealand,** 29 Fitzherbert Terrace, Thorndon, Wellington (© **644/472-2068**), or get the information directly from the "For New Zealanders" section of the website at **http://newzealand.usembassy.gov**.

---

2 TOLL-FREE NUMBERS & WEBSITES

AIRLINES

Air Canada
© 888/247-2262
www.aircanada.ca

Air Jamaica
© 800/523-5585 in the U.S.
© 888/359-2475 in Jamaica
www.airjamaica.com

Air New Zealand
© 800/262-1234 or -2468 in the U.S.
© 800/663-5494 in Canada
© 0800/737-767 in New Zealand
www.airnewzealand.com

AirTran Airlines
© 800/247-8726
www.airtran.com

Alaska Airlines
© 800/252-7522
www.alaskaair.com

American Airlines
© 800/433-7300
www.aa.com

America West Airlines
© 800/235-9292
www.americawest.com

British Airways
© 800/247-9297
© 0345/222-111 or 0845/77-333-77
   in Britain
www.british-airways.com

BWIA
© 800/538-2492
www.bwee.com

Continental Airlines
© 800/525-0280
www.continental.com

Delta Air Lines
© 800/221-1212
www.delta.com

Frontier Airlines
© 800/432-1359
www.frontierairlines.com

JetBlue Airlines
© 800/538-2583
www.jetblue.com

Mexicana
© 800/531-7921 in the U.S.
© 01800/502-2000 in Mexico
www.mexicana.com

Midwest Express
© 800/452-2022
www.midwestexpress.com

North American Airlines
© 718/656-2650
www.northamair.com

Northwest Airlines
© 800/225-2525
www.nwa.com

Olympic Airways
☎ 800/223-1226 in the U.S.
☎ 80/111-44444 in Greece
www.olympic-airways.gr

Southwest Airlines
☎ 800/435-9792
www.southwest.com

Spirit Airlines
☎ 800/772-7117
www.spiritair.com

TACA
☎ 800/535-8780 in the U.S.
☎ 503/267-8222 in El Salvador
www.taca.com

United Airlines
☎ 800/241-6522
www.united.com

US Airways
☎ 800/428-4322
www.usairways.com

Virgin Atlantic Airways
☎ 800/862-8621 in Continental U.S.
☎ 0293/747-747 in Britain
www.virgin-atlantic.com

MAJOR HOTEL & MOTEL CHAINS

Best Western International
☎ 800/528-1234
www.bestwestern.com

Clarion Hotels
☎ 800/CLARION (252-7466)
www.clarionhotel.com or
www.hotelchoice.com

Comfort Inns
☎ 800/228-5150
www.hotelchoice.com

Courtyard by Marriott
☎ 800/321-2211
www.courtyard.com or
www.marriott.com

Days Inn
☎ 800/325-2525
www.daysinn.com

Doubletree Hotels
☎ 800/222-TREE (222-8733)
www.doubletree.com

Econo Lodges
☎ 800/55-ECONO (553-2666)
www.hotelchoice.com

Fairfield Inn by Marriott
☎ 800/228-2800
www.marriott.com

Four Seasons
☎ 800/819-5053
www.fourseasons.com

Hampton Inn
☎ 800/HAMPTON (426-7866)
www.hampton-inn.com

Hilton Hotels
☎ 800/HILTONS (445-8667)
www.hilton.com

Holiday Inn
☎ 800/HOLIDAY (465-4329)
www.holiday-inn.com

Howard Johnson
☎ 800/654-2000
www.hojo.com

Hyatt Hotels & Resorts
☎ 800/228-9000
www.hyatt.com

InterContinental
Hotels & Resorts
☎ 888/567-8725
www.interconti.com

ITT Sheraton
☎ 800/325-3535
www.starwood.com

La Quinta Motor Inns
☎ 800/531-5900
www.laquinta.com

Marriott Hotels
☎ 800/228-9290
www.marriott.com

Motel 6
☏ 800/4-MOTEL6 (466-8356)
www.mote16.com

Omni
☏ 800/THE-OMNI (843-6664)
www.omnihotels.com

Quality Inns
☏ 800/228-5151
www.hotelchoice.com

Radisson Hotels International
☏ 800/333-3333
www.radisson.com

Ramada Inns
☏ 800/2-RAMADA (272-6232)
www.ramada.com

Red Lion Hotels & Inns
☏ 800/RED-LION (733-5466)
www.redlion.com

Red Roof Inns
☏ 800/843-7663
www.redroof.com

Renaissance
☏ 800/228-9290
www.renaissancehotels.com

Residence Inn by Marriott
☏ 800/331-3131
www.marriott.com

Ritz-Carlton
☏ 800/241-3333
www.ritzcarlton.com

Sheraton Hotels & Resorts
☏ 800/325-3535
www.sheraton.com

Super 8 Motels
☏ 800/800-8000
www.super8.com

Travelodge
☏ 800/255-3050
www.travelodge.com

Westin Hotels & Resorts
☏ 800/937-8461
www.westin.com

Wyndham Hotels and Resorts
☏ 800/822-4200 in Continental U.S. and Canada
www.wyndham.com

INDEX

See also Accommodations and Restaurants indexes, below.

FROMMER'S® COMPLETE TRAVEL GUIDES

Alaska
Amalfi Coast
American Southwest
Amsterdam
Argentina
Arizona
Atlanta
Australia
Austria
Bahamas
Barcelona
Beijing
Belgium, Holland & Luxembourg
Belize
Bermuda
Boston
Brazil
British Columbia & the Canadian
　Rockies
Brussels & Bruges
Budapest & the Best of Hungary
Buenos Aires
Calgary
California
Canada
Cancún, Cozumel & the Yucatán
Cape Cod, Nantucket & Martha's
　Vineyard
Caribbean
Caribbean Ports of Call
Carolinas & Georgia
Chicago
Chile & Easter Island
China
Colorado
Costa Rica
Croatia
Cuba
Denmark
Denver, Boulder & Colorado Springs
Eastern Europe
Ecuador & the Galapagos Islands
Edinburgh & Glasgow
England
Europe
Europe by Rail

Florence, Tuscany & Umbria
Florida
France
Germany
Greece
Greek Islands
Guatemala
Hawaii
Hong Kong
Honolulu, Waikiki & Oahu
India
Ireland
Israel
Italy
Jamaica
Japan
Kauai
Las Vegas
London
Los Angeles
Los Cabos & Baja
Madrid
Maine Coast
Maryland & Delaware
Maui
Mexico
Montana & Wyoming
Montréal & Québec City
Morocco
Moscow & St. Petersburg
Munich & the Bavarian Alps
Nashville & Memphis
New England
Newfoundland & Labrador
New Mexico
New Orleans
New York City
New York State
New Zealand
Northern Italy
Norway
Nova Scotia, New Brunswick &
　Prince Edward Island
Oregon
Paris
Peru

Philadelphia & the Amish Country
Portugal
Prague & the Best of the Czech
　Republic
Provence & the Riviera
Puerto Rico
Rome
San Antonio & Austin
San Diego
San Francisco
Santa Fe, Taos & Albuquerque
Scandinavia
Scotland
Seattle
Seville, Granada & the Best of
　Andalusia
Shanghai
Sicily
Singapore & Malaysia
South Africa
South America
South Florida
South Korea
South Pacific
Southeast Asia
Spain
Sweden
Switzerland
Tahiti & French Polynesia
Texas
Thailand
Tokyo
Toronto
Turkey
USA
Utah
Vancouver & Victoria
Vermont, New Hampshire & Maine
Vienna & the Danube Valley
Vietnam
Virgin Islands
Virginia
Walt Disney World® & Orlando
Washington, D.C.
Washington State

FROMMER'S® DAY BY DAY GUIDES

Amsterdam
Barcelona
Beijing
Boston
Cancun & the Yucatan
Chicago
Florence & Tuscany

Hong Kong
Honolulu & Oahu
London
Maui
Montréal
Napa & Sonoma
New York City

Paris
Provence & the Riviera
Rome
San Francisco
Venice
Washington D.C.

PAULINE FROMMER'S GUIDES: SEE MORE. SPEND LESS.

Alaska
Hawaii
Italy

Las Vegas
London
New York City

Paris
Walt Disney World®
Washington D.C.

FROMMER'S® PORTABLE GUIDES

Acapulco, Ixtapa & Zihuatanejo
Amsterdam
Aruba, Bonaire & Curacao
Australia's Great Barrier Reef
Bahamas
Big Island of Hawaii
Boston
California Wine Country
Cancún
Cayman Islands
Charleston
Chicago
Dominican Republic

Florence
Las Vegas
Las Vegas for Non-Gamblers
London
Maui
Nantucket & Martha's Vineyard
New Orleans
New York City
Paris
Portland
Puerto Rico
Puerto Vallarta, Manzanillo &
    Guadalajara

Rio de Janeiro
San Diego
San Francisco
Savannah
St. Martin, Sint Maarten, Anguila &
    St. Bart's
Turks & Caicos
Vancouver
Venice
Virgin Islands
Washington, D.C.
Whistler

FROMMER'S® CRUISE GUIDES

Alaska Cruises & Ports of Call

Cruises & Ports of Call

European Cruises & Ports of Call

FROMMER'S® NATIONAL PARK GUIDES

Algonquin Provincial Park
Banff & Jasper
Grand Canyon

National Parks of the American West
Rocky Mountain
Yellowstone & Grand Teton

Yosemite and Sequoia & Kings
    Canyon
Zion & Bryce Canyon

FROMMER'S® WITH KIDS GUIDES

Chicago
Hawaii
Las Vegas
London

National Parks
New York City
San Francisco

Toronto
Walt Disney World® & Orlando
Washington, D.C.

FROMMER'S® PHRASEFINDER DICTIONARY GUIDES

Chinese
French

German
Italian

Japanese
Spanish

SUZY GERSHMAN'S BORN TO SHOP GUIDES

France
Hong Kong, Shanghai & Beijing
Italy

London
New York
Paris

San Francisco
Where to Buy the Best of Everything.

FROMMER'S® BEST-LOVED DRIVING TOURS

Britain
California
France
Germany

Ireland
Italy
New England
Northern Italy

Scotland
Spain
Tuscany & Umbria

THE UNOFFICIAL GUIDES®

Adventure Travel in Alaska
Beyond Disney
California with Kids
Central Italy
Chicago
Cruises
Disneyland®
England
Hawaii

Ireland
Las Vegas
London
Maui
Mexico's Best Beach Resorts
Mini Mickey
New Orleans
New York City
Paris

San Francisco
South Florida including Miami &
    the Keys
Walt Disney World®
Walt Disney World® for
    Grown-ups
Walt Disney World® with Kids
Washington, D.C.

SPECIAL-INTEREST TITLES

Athens Past & Present
Best Places to Raise Your Family
Cities Ranked & Rated
500 Places to Take Your Kids Before They Grow Up
Frommer's Best Day Trips from London
Frommer's Best RV & Tent Campgrounds in the U.S.A.

Frommer's Exploring America by RV
Frommer's NYC Free & Dirt Cheap
Frommer's Road Atlas Europe
Frommer's Road Atlas Ireland
Retirement Places Rated